T0138910

Secure Semantic Service-Oriented Systems

Bhavani Thuraisingham

CRC Press
Taylor & Francis Group
Boca Raton   London   New York

CRC Press is an imprint of the
Taylor & Francis Group, an **informa** business

AN AUERBACH BOOK

Auerbach Publications
Taylor & Francis Group
6000 Broken Sound Parkway NW, Suite 300
Boca Raton, FL 33487-2742

© 2011 by Taylor and Francis Group, LLC
Auerbach Publications is an imprint of Taylor & Francis Group, an Informa business

No claim to original U.S. Government works

Printed in the United States of America on acid-free paper
10 9 8 7 6 5 4 3 2 1

International Standard Book Number: 978-1-4200-7331-7 (Hardback)

Visit the Taylor & Francis Web site at
http://www.taylorandfrancis.com

and the Auerbach Web site at
http://www.auerbach-publications.com

To My Dearest Grandmother
Victoria Ponnamma

For teaching me to laugh, enjoy myself, and live life to its fullest.

Contents

Preface

Background

Recent developments in information systems technologies have resulted in computerizing many applications in various business areas. Data has become a critical resource in many organizations, and therefore, efficient access to data, sharing the data, extracting information from the data, and making use of the information has become an urgent need. As a result, there have been many efforts on not only integrating the various data sources scattered across several sites, but extracting information from these databases in the form of patterns and trends has also become important. These data sources may be databases managed by database management systems, or they could be data warehoused in a repository from multiple data sources.

The advent of the World Wide Web (WWW) in the mid-1990s has resulted in even greater demand for managing data, information, and knowledge effectively. During this period, the consumer service provider concept has been digitized and enforced via the Web. This way we now have Web-supported services where a consumer may request a service via the Web site of a service provider and the service provider provides the requested service. This service could be making an airline reservation or purchasing a book from the service provider. Such Web-supported services have come to be known as Web services. Note that services do not necessarily have to be provided through the Web. A consumer could send an email message to the service provider and request the service. Such services are computer-supported services. However, much of the work on computer-supported services has focused on Web services.

There is now so much data on the Web that managing it with conventional tools is becoming almost impossible. New tools and techniques are needed to effectively manage this data. Therefore, to provide interoperability as well as to ensure machine-understandable Web pages, the concept of semantic Web was conceived by Tim Berners-Lee who heads W3C (the World Wide Web Consortium).

As the demand for data and information management increases, there is also a critical need for maintaining the security of the databases, applications, and information systems. Data and information have to be protected from unauthorized access as well as from malicious corruption. With the advent of the Web it is even more important to protect the data and information as numerous individuals now have access to this data and information. Therefore, we need effective mechanisms to secure the semantic Web technologies.

This book will review the developments in Web services technologies and describe ways of securing these technologies. The focus will be on confidentiality, privacy, trust, and integrity management for Web services. I will also discuss applications of secure Web services and the integration of secure Web services with semantic Web technologies. In particular, secure interoperability, secure knowledge management, secure e-business, and secure information sharing will be discussed.

I have written two series of books for CRC Press on data management/data mining and data security. The first series consists of nine books. Book #1 (*Data Management Systems Evolution and Interoperation*) focused on general aspects of data management and also addressed interoperability and migration. Book #2 (*Data Mining: Technologies, Techniques, Tools, and Trends*) discussed data mining. It essentially elaborated on Chapter 9 of Book #1. Book #3 (*Web Data Management and Electronic Commerce*) was focused on Web database technologies and reviewed e-commerce as an application area. It essentially elaborated on Chapter 10 of Book #1. Book #4 (*Managing and Mining Multimedia Databases*) addressed both multimedia database management and multimedia data mining. It elaborated on both Chapter 6 of Book #1 (for multimedia database management) and Chapter 11 of Book #2 (for multimedia data mining). Book #5 (*XML Databases and the Semantic Web*) described XML technologies related to data management. It elaborated on Chapter 11 of Book #3. Book #6 (*Web Data Mining and Applications in Business Intelligence and Counter-Terrorism*) elaborated on Chapter 9 of Book #3.

Book #7 (*Database and Applications Security*) examines security for technologies discussed in each of the previous books. It focuses on the technological developments in database and applications security. It is essentially the integration of information security and database technologies. Book #8 (*Building Trustworthy Semantic Webs*) applies security to semantic Web technologies. The current book (Book #9) is an elaboration of Chapter 16 of Book #8.

This second series of books at present consists of one book. It is *Design and Implementation of Data Mining Tools*. For this series, I am converting some of the practical aspects of my work with students into books. The relationships between the texts will be illustrated in Appendix A.

Organization of This Book

This book is divided into five parts, each describing some aspect of secure service-oriented information systems. The major focus of this book will be on security and confidentiality. Other features such as trust management, integrity, and data quality will also be given some consideration. Applications that utilize secure Web services such as knowledge management and e-business will also be discussed.

Part I consisting of six chapters discusses concepts in services technologies, information management, semantic Web, and security. Chapter 2 discusses the notion of service-oriented computing. Chapter 3 examines SOA and Web services. Service-oriented analysis and design will be discussed in Chapter 4. Specialized Web services is featured in Chapter 5. Semantic Web services will be the topic of Chapter 6. Secure systems will be discussed in Chapter 7.

Part II consisting of six chapters will discuss the core topics in secure Web services and SOA. Chapter 8 talks about secure services computing. Chapter 9 provides an overview of secure Web services and SOA. Security for service-oriented analysis and design methods is given in Chapter 10. Access control models for Web services will be discussed in Chapter 11. Identity management, which is a key aspect of Web services, is discussed in Chapter 12. Some of our research on secure Web services, including access control and delegation, will be analyzed in Chapter 13.

While much of the discussion in Part II focuses on the confidentiality aspects of Web services, in Part III, consisting of three chapters, will provide an overview of privacy, trust, and integrity for Web services. Chapter 14 covers trust for Web services. Privacy issues will be discussed in Chapter 15. Integrity aspects will be the subject of Chapter 16.

Part IV, which consists of five chapters, describes the relationship between secure semantic Web and Web services. Secure semantic Web will be discussed in Chapter 17. XML security and Web services will be viewed in Chapter 18. RDF security and Web services are the subjects of Chapter 19. Secure ontologies and Web services are covered in Chapter 20. Security, rules, and Web services are examined in Chapter 21.

Part V, which consists of four chapters, discusses specialized Web services and security issues. Secure Web services for data, information management, and knowledge management are the subject of Chapter 22. Secure geospatial Web services will be looked at in Chapter 23. Chapter 24 discusses secure Web services for activity management such as e-business and collaboration. Chapter 25 covers emerging secure Web services, including secure Web services for healthcare and finance.

Each part begins with an introduction and ends with a conclusion. Furthermore, each of Chapters 2 through 25 starts with an overview and ends with a summary and references. Chapter 26 summarizes the book and discusses future directions. We have included four appendices. Appendix A provides an overview of data management and discusses the relationship between the texts we have written. This has been the standard practice with all of our books. Database management, which is important to understand the concepts in this book, is the focus of Appendix B. In Appendix C secure object technologies may be found due to the fact that services technologies have been influenced by object technologies. Appendix D will provide an overview of relevant standards for Web services and semantic Web. This book ends with an index.

Data, Information, and Knowledge

In general, data management includes managing the databases, interoperability, migration, warehousing, and mining. For example, the data on the Web has to be managed and mined to extract information and patterns and trends. Data could be in files, relational databases, or other types of databases such as multimedia databases. Data may be structured or unstructured. I repeatedly use the terms data, data management, and database systems and database management systems in this book. I elaborate on these terms in the appendices. I define data management systems to be systems that manage the data, extract meaningful information from the data, and make use of the information extracted. Therefore, data management systems include database systems, data warehouses, and data mining systems. Data could be structured data such as those found in relational databases, or it could be unstructured such as text, voice, imagery, and video.

There have been numerous discussions in the past to distinguish data, information, and knowledge. In some of the previous books on data management and mining, I did not attempt to clarify these terms. I simply stated that data could be just bits and bytes or it could convey some meaningful information to the user. However, with the Web and also with increasing interest in data, information and knowledge management as separate areas, in this book I take a different approach to data, information, and knowledge by differentiating these terms as much as possible. For me, data is usually given some value like numbers, integers, and strings. Information is obtained when some meaning or semantics is associated with the data such as John's salary is $20K. Knowledge is something that you acquire through reading and learning, and, as a result, understand the data and information and take action. That is, data and information can be transferred into knowledge when uncertainty about the data and information is removed from someone's mind. It should be noted that it is rather difficult to give strict definitions of data, information, and knowledge. Sometimes I will use these terms interchangeably, also. The framework for data management discussed in the appendices helps clarify some of the differences. To be consistent with the terminology in my previous books, I will also distinguish between database systems and database management systems. A database management system is that component that manages the database containing persistent data. A database system consists of both the database and the database management system.

Final Thoughts

The goal of this book is to explore security issues for the Web services and discuss their applications. Another objective is to integrate secure Web services with semantic Web technologies. The goal is also to show the breadth of the applications of secure semantic

Web services in multiple domains. I have used the material in this book together with the numerous papers listed in the references in each chapter for a graduate-level course at the University of Texas at Dallas on building trustworthy semantic Webs.

It should be noted that the field is expanding very rapidly with emerging standards. Therefore, it is important for the reader to keep up with the development of the prototypes, products, tools, and standards for securer Web services. Security cannot be an afterthought. Therefore, while the technologies for Web services are being developed it is important to include security at the onset.

Acknowledgments

I would like to thank the administration at the Erik Jonsson School of Engineering and Computer Science at the University of Texas at Dallas for giving me the opportunity to direct the Cyber Security Research Center and teach courses on data and applications security and secure semantic services. I thank my students for giving me many insights, especially those who took my class on building trustworthy semantic Webs in 2006, 2008, and 2010. I would especially like to thank my Ph.D. student Wei-She for his research on secure Web services, which gave me many insights. I thank Rhonda Walls, my administrative assistant, for proofreading the chapters.

I would also like to thank many people who have supported my work, including the following:

- My husband, Thevendra, for his continued support for my work and my son, Breman, for being such a wonderful person and for motivating me.
- Professor C. V. Ramamoorthy at the University of California–Berkeley for his constant encouragement.
- Henry Bayard at MITRE for his continued mentoring and encouragement.
- Professor Elisa Bertino and Professor Lorenzo Martino, both from Purdue University, for sharing their lecture notes with me on secure Web services.
- Professor Hal Sorenson for inviting me to give a full-day seminar at the University of California–San Diego in January 2008, which started my writing of this book.
- Professors Elena Ferrari and Barbara Carminati for collaborating with me on various aspects of XML and RDF security.
- My colleagues at the University of Texas–Dallas, especially Professors Latifur Khan, Murat Kantarcioglu, Kevin Hamlen, and I-Ling Yen for their collaboration on related topics.
- My colleagues who have collaborated with me, especially during the 6 years since I joined the University of Texas–Dallas.
- To the sponsors of my research from the U.S. federal government, who have enabled me to enhance my knowledge in secure semantic service-oriented information systems.

Chapter 1

Introduction

1.1 Overview

We live in a service-oriented world in which service providers provide a variety of services to consumers. These include healthcare and medical services, financial and baking services, telecommunication and television services, entertainment and video services, and education services. Typically, a consumer may request a service from the service provider. Contracts may be negotiated between the consumer and the service provider. The service provider provides the services for which the consumer may pay in accordance with the contract. The service provider may invoke other service providers to provide certain services to satisfy the consumer. For example, a customer may request a service from an airline. The airline may have a negotiated contract with a hotel service and may invoke the hotel service provider. The airline may then provide both airline and hotel service to the customer.

During the past ten years, with the advent of the World Wide Web, the consumer service provider concept has been digitized and enforced via the Web. In this way, we now have Web-supported services where a consumer may request a service via the Web site of a service provider and the service provider provides the requested service. This service could be making an airline reservation or purchasing a book from the service provider. Such Web-supported services have come to be known as Web services. Note that services do not necessarily have to be provided through the Web. A consumer could send an e-mail message to the service provider and request the service. Such services are computer-supported services. However, much of the work on computer-supported services has focused on Web services.

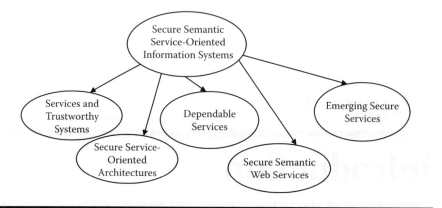

Figure 1.1 Secure semantic service-oriented information systems.

An information system that supports service implementation is a service-oriented information system. An architecture that provides support for the implementation of services has come to be known as a service-oriented architecture (SOA). In supporting the services, it is critical that security be enforced. For example, only authorized entities may request certain services, and only authorized entities may provide certain services. In this book, we will discuss the details involved in designing and implementing secure services. We will essentially review the developments with SOAs as well as Web services and describe the various security issues related to these developments.

This chapter details the organization of this book. The organization of this chapter is as follows. Services and security technologies will be discussed in Section 1.2. In addition, some special services such as semantic Web services will also be discussed in Section 1.2. Security for SOA and Web services will be discussed in Section 1.3. Trustworthy Web services will be discussed in Section 1.4. Secure services related to semantic Webs will be discussed in Section 1.5. Specialized Web services will be discussed in Section 1.6. Note that each of the Sections 1.2 through 1.6 will be elaborated in Parts I through V of this book. Figure 1.1 shows the various topics addressed in this book.

1.2 Services and Security Technologies

1.2.1 Services Technologies

The basic service technologies include multiple thrusts, including service-oriented concepts, SOA and Web services, semantic Web services, and service-oriented analysis and design. We discuss all these areas in this chapter. Service-oriented computing has evolved from object-oriented computing. In object-oriented computing, the world is viewed as a collection of objects, and these objects communicate with

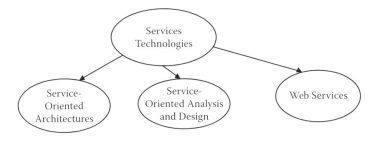

Figure 1.2 Services.

each other through messages. Similarly, in service-oriented computing, the world is viewed as a collection of services. Therefore, services could communicate with each other as well as with consumers through messages. While numerous object-oriented programming languages have been developed, including Smalltalk, Java, and C++, there is no computing language for service-oriented computing. One can, however, implement services through packages and objects.

As we have stated in Section 1.1, SOA is the architecture that is the foundation of service-oriented computing. This architecture specifies the services and the communication between the services. Web services are services that are involved via the Web. At present, Web services is the most popular representation of service-oriented computing, although it should be noted that Web services are only a subset of service-oriented computing.

SOAD (service-oriented analysis and design) follows the OOAD (object-oriented analysis and design paradigm). Note that OOAD, similar to UML, has evolved over several years of research and experimentation. The idea here is to develop a methodology to model applications, data, and activities surrounding the notion of objects. Similarly, in SOAD, the idea is to model, analyze the reasons for the services, and the interactions between them. Often, I see OOAD being taught as prerequisite for SOA. While OOAD is essential for OOP (object-oriented programming), we need SOAD for SOP. In Part I of this book, we will elaborate on all of the basic services (Figure 1.2).

1.2.2 Specialized Web Services

In this section, we will discuss specialized Web services, which we will also refer to as advanced Web services. Advanced services include semantic Web services. Here, the Web services make use of semantic Web technologies. In addition, grids and clouds also take advantage of service-oriented computing. There are also several specialized services such as mobile services, geospatial data services, and multimedia services. Note that whether we are dealing with basic or advanced services, security has to be given the utmost consideration as we are not utilizing service providers outside of our corporation, agency, and even country.

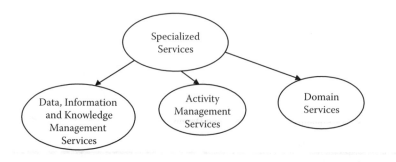

Figure 1.3 Specialized services.

What we call advanced service technologies are those that go beyond basic services. For example, there is now work directed at thinking about data as well as software as services. With respect to data, there are various service providers that offer data to different organizations to conduct various activities, including market research. Furthermore, several agencies, especially in countries such as India and China, now provide software services to large corporations in the United States and Europe. On the other hand, services themselves could be implemented as software, which is what service computing is about. There are several challenges in considering data as well as software as services. For example, data service providers have to ensure the privacy of the individuals referenced in the data. Software service providers have to deliver high-quality software (Figure 1.3). Specialized Web services are discussed in Part I of this book. Secure specialized Web services are the subject of Part V.

1.2.3 Semantic Services

Semantic services are services that integrate services technologies with semantic Web technologies. The semantic Web was invented by Tim Berners-Lee to support the idea of machine-understandable Web pages. Today, the semantic Web is viewed as very large linked graphs with semantics associated with nodes and links. The semantic Web is a collection of technologies including eXtensible Markup Language (XML) and the Resource Description Framework. Web services that utilize these semantic Web technologies are semantic Web services. We will elaborate on semantic Web services in Part I and the secure semantic Web in Part IV. Figure 1.4 depicts semantic Web services.

1.2.4 Security Technologies

Secure service information systems essentially integrate service technologies with security technologies. Security technologies will be lumped into trustworthy

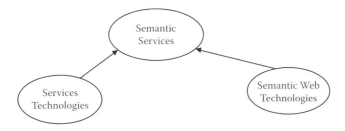

Figure 1.4 Semantic services.

information systems. These systems consist of many elements, including trustworthy systems, secure data and information systems, and concepts of confidentiality, privacy, and trust management that will be addressed throughout this book.

Trustworthy systems are systems that are secure and dependable. By dependable systems, we mean systems that have high integrity, are fault tolerant, and meet real-time constraints. Trustworthy systems may include information systems, including data management systems, information management systems, and trustworthy networks. In other words, for a system to be trustworthy, it must be secure, fault tolerant, meet timing deadlines, and manage high-quality data. However, integrating these features into a system means that the system has to meet conflicting requirements. For example, if a system passes all the access control checks, then it may miss some of its deadlines. The challenge in designing trustworthy systems is to design systems that are flexible. For example, in some situations it may be important to meet all the timing constraints while in some other situations it may be critical to satisfy all the security constraints.

Trustworthy systems have sometimes been refereed to as dependable systems. In some other cases, dependability is considered to be part of trustworthiness. For example, in some papers, dependability includes mainly fault-tolerant systems, and when one integrates fault tolerance with security, then one gets trustworthy systems. Regardless of what the definitions are, for systems to be deployed in operational environments, especially for command and control and other critical applications, we need end-to-end dependability as well as security. For some applications, not only do we need security and confidentiality, we also need to ensure that the privacy of the individuals is maintained. Therefore, privacy is also another feature of trustworthiness.

For a system to be dependable/trustworthy, we need end-to-end dependability/ trustworthiness. Note that the components that make up a system include the network, operating systems, middleware and infrastructure, data manager, and applications. We need all of the components to be dependable/trustworthy. However, more recently, the goal of secure systems is to build trustworthy systems from untrustworthy components. It is assumed that the components may come from multiple vendors and even from multiple countries and, therefore, it is not feasible

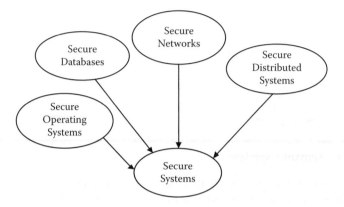

Figure 1.5 Security technologies.

to trust all the components. Therefore, the challenge is to develop trustworthy systems from untrustworthy components.

As stated earlier, other security technologies for secure services are secure data, information, and knowledge management systems. Secure data and information systems include secure database systems such as secure relational database systems and secure information systems such as secure multimedia information systems and digital libraries.

The underlying focus of trustworthy information systems is the notions of confidently, privacy, and trust. Therefore, we will also discuss these notions. Confidentiality is about Web sites or servers only releasing data to authorized individuals. Privacy is about an individual determining what information should be released about him or her. Trust is about how much value one can place on the various individuals (e.g., parties, organizations) and the information they produce. Figure 1.5 shows the security technologies for secure services. These technologies will be discussed in Part I.

1.3 Secure Services

While Section 1.2 addressed services and security technologies, in this section we will discuss secure services technologies, which integrate the contents of Sections 1.2 and 1.4. Details will be given in Part II of this book. As we have stated in Section 1.1, secure services essentially are about incorporating security into services. Furthermore, SOA and Web services are key aspects of services. Therefore, security for SOA and Web services is needed to develop secure SOA and Web services.

Now, SOA-based Web services consist of three concepts: the consumer, service provider, and directory. The directory is called UDDI. The service provider will

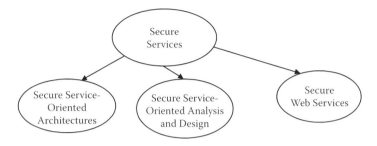

Figure 1.6   Aspects of secure services.

publish its services on the UDDI. The consumer will query the UDDI for the services. The UDDI will give the consumer the address of the service provider. The consumer then invokes the service. Communication is carried out through simple object access protocol (SOAP) messaging, which is based on XML. From a security point of view, we need to incorporate security into this communication. Web Services 1.0 provides support for secure services. More recently, with Web Services 2.0, there are more advanced concepts for SOA.

Before we design secure applications based on services, we need to apply SOAD methodology. However, SOAD as it has been defined is not adequate for secure applications. In this book, we will detail our work on extending SOAD for secure applications. We will base this on the work we carried out in the 1990s on extending object modeling technologies for secure applications. Figure 1.6 shows aspects of secure services.

Various standards have been developed for services and secure services that are mainly based on Web services. For example, the World Wide Web consortium has developed standards for XML and XML security that are an essential part of the Web services framework. In addition, standards such as WSDL have been developed for specifying services and SOAP for message communication. XML security standards include XML encryption and XML key management for confidentiality and integrity.

More advanced standards for specifying security policies include those proposed by OASIS as well as W3C. For example, SAML specifies a language for security assertions. XACML specifies a language for policy specification. In addition, there are standards for federated identify management such as the consortium work of Liberty Alliance and standards for advanced Web services security, including WS and WS* Security.

Federated identity management is another area that is receiving a lot of attention, and is related to services technologies. Consortiums such as Liberty Alliance have come up with standards for identity management. Some of our research on secure Web services includes models for delegation. These topics will also be addressed in Part II of this book.

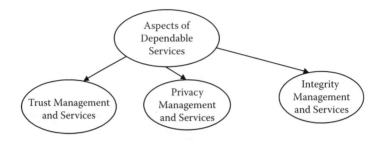

Figure 1.7 Trustworthy services.

1.4 Trustworthy Services

By trustworthy or dependable systems, we mean systems that are not only secure but also have integrity, high assurance, and fault tolerance and can meet real-time constraints. Similarly, a dependable service is a service that has integrity; the information is of high quality, is fault tolerant, and meets timing constraints. We have also added privacy as well as trust management and rights management as part of dependability. Note that this is not a standard definition. That is, some papers and books have used security and trustworthiness interchangeably. Furthermore, some papers have also implied that security includes confidentiality, integrity, and privacy. By security, we mainly consider confidentiality.

Figure 1.7 illustrates aspects of a trustworthy service. The challenge is to ensure that services, including Web services, have all of the features such as privacy, trust, and integrity. Part III will focus on trustworthy services and will address trust, privacy, integrity, as well as multilevel security.

1.5 Secure Semantic Services

In this section, we will discuss secure semantic Web services. Note that secure semantic information systems essentially integrate the semantic Web, services, and security technologies. Semantic Web technologies provide machine-understandable Web services. Web services that utilize semantic Web technologies can handle semantic heterogeneity and other interoperability problems. Secure Web services need to utilize secure semantic Web technologies. That is, the XML and RDF documents that are utilized by Web services have to be secure documents.

Some of the key aspects of secure semantic Web services include the relationship between XML security and Web services, RDF security and Web services, secure ontologies and Web services and, finally, secure rules and Web services. Figure 1.8 shows secure semantic services. Details will be given in Part IV of this book.

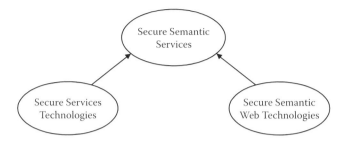

Figure 1.8 Secure semantic services.

1.6 Specialized Secure Services

Specialized services include services for secure data, information, and knowledge and activity management as well as domain-Web services. Data management services include those for secure transactions, secure storage, and secure query processing. Complex data management services include secure multimedia and geospatial Web services. Information management services include secure information retrieval and secure information visualization. Knowledge management services include secure intellectual property management. Activity management services include secure e-business and assured information sharing.

We will elaborate on some of these points. Knowledge management is about reusing the knowledge and expertise of an organization in order to improve profits and other benefits. In this chapter, we will examine in more detail security issues for data, information, and knowledge management and then discuss how semantic Web technologies may be applied for managing data, information, and knowledge. Interoperability of heterogeneous data sources is key for many applications. The challenge is, how do the different secure systems interoperate with each other? How do you integrate the heterogeneous security policies? E-business (also referred to as e-commerce) is about organizations conducting transactions on the Web. Various models, architectures, and technologies are being developed for e-business. Because we are dealing with critical data such as funds and accounts when carrying out e-business, confidentiality and privacy of information is crucial. We also have to ensure that the data is not maliciously corrupted. AIS is about organizations sharing information but at the same time enforcing policies and procedures so that the data is integrated and mined to extract nuggets, and maintaining security. For all of the foregoing applications, Web services play a major role.

Web services are being deployed for many applications, including medical, financial, command and control, and telecommunications. They are also applied to many other technologies such as e-business, knowledge management, and assured information sharing. Other emerging Web services include Web services for grids; recently, corporations such as Oracle have developed grid-based Web services.

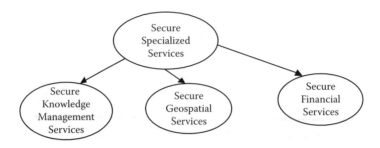

Figure 1.9 Specialized Web services.

Furthermore, Amazon Web Services are also based on the grid paradigm. We will discuss such Web services in this book and explore security.

Two other types of Web services are data as a service and software as a service. For example, data centers manage data for customers. Customers can invoke such data services through Web services. Customers can also invoke various software (such as compilers and operating systems) as Web services. Figure 1.9 illustrates the specialized Web services. They will be discussed in greater detail in Part V.

1.7 Organization of This Book

This book is divided into five parts, each describing some aspect of secure service-oriented information systems. The major focus of this book will be on security and confidentiality. Other features such as trust management, integrity, and data quality will also be considered. Applications that utilize secure Web services such as knowledge management and e-business will also be discussed.

Part I, consisting of six chapters, discusses concepts in services technologies, information management, semantic Web, and security. Chapter 2 discusses the notion of service-oriented computing. Chapter 3 discusses SOA and Web services. Service-oriented analysis and design will be discussed in Chapter 4. Specialized Web services will be discussed in Chapter 5. Semantic Web services will be discussed in Chapter 6. Secure systems will be discussed in Chapter 7.

Part II, consisting of six chapters, will discuss the core topics in secure Web services and SOA. Chapter 8 discusses secure services computing. Chapter 9 provides an overview of secure Web services and SOA. Security for service-oriented analysis and design methods is given in Chapter 10. Access control models for Web services will be discussed in Chapter 11. Identity management, which is a key aspect of Web services, is discussed in Chapter 12. Some of our research on secure Web services, including access control and delegation, will be discussed in Chapter 13.

While much of the discussion in Part II focuses on confidentiality aspects of Web services, Part III, which consists of three chapters, will provide an overview of privacy, trust, and integrity for Web services. Chapter 14 discusses trust for Web services. Privacy issues will be discussed in Chapter 15. Integrity aspects will be discussed in Chapter 16.

Part IV, which consists of five chapters, describes the relationship between secure semantic Web and Web services. The secure semantic Web will be discussed in Chapter 17. XML security and Web services will be discussed in Chapter 18. RDF security and Web services will be discuss in Chapter 19. Secure ontologies and Web services will be discussed in Chapter 20. Security, rules, and Web services are discussed in Chapter 21.

Part V, which consists of four chapters, discusses specialized Web services and security issues. Secure Web services for data, information management, and knowledge management will be discussed in Chapter 22. Secure geospatial Web services will be discussed in Chapter 23. Chapter 24 discusses secure Web services for activity management such as e-business and collaboration. Chapter 25 discusses emerging secure Web services, including secure Web services for healthcare and finance.

Each part begins with an introduction and ends with a conclusion. Furthermore, each chapter (2 through 25) starts with an overview and ends with a summary and references. Chapter 26 summarizes the book and discusses future directions. We have included four appendices. Appendix A provides an overview of data management and discusses the relationship between the texts we have written. This has been the standard practice with all of our books. Database management, which must be understood in order to grasp the concepts in this book, is discussed in Appendix B. Appendix C discusses secure object technologies because services technologies have been influenced by object technologies. Appendix D will provide an overview of relevant standards for Web services and the semantic Web. This book ends with a bibliography and an index.

We have essentially developed a three-layer framework to better explain the concepts in this book. This framework is illustrated in Figure 1.10. Layer 1 is the supporting technologies layer and is covered in Part I of this book. Layer 2 is the core technologies layer that is covered in Parts II and III of this book. Layer 3 is the applications layer and is covered in Parts IV and V of this book. The content of our book is mapped to the framework in Figure 1.10. The relationship between the various parts of these book is given in Figure 1.11.

1.8 Next Steps

This chapter has provided an introduction to the book. We first provided a brief overview of the supporting technologies for secure services technologies that include services technologies and security technologies. Then we discussed secure Web services. This was followed by discussions of trustworthy Web services and secure semantic Web services, as well as secure specialized Web services. Finally, we provided the organization of this book and our framework for explaining the concepts

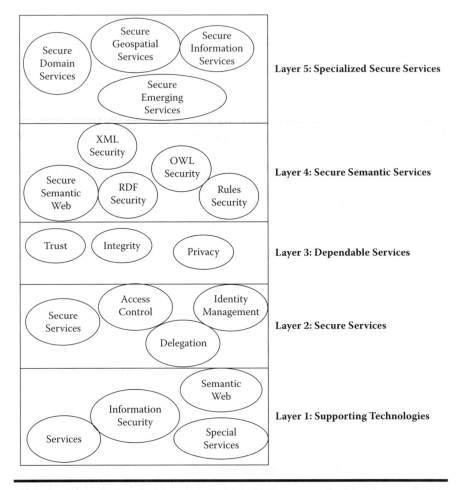

Figure 1.10 Framework for secure semantic service-oriented information systems.

in this book. This book provides the information for a reader to get familiar with secure services and trustworthy systems. We discuss some topics such as the secure semantic Web in more depth as we have carried out much research on this topic. Some other topics are less concrete, such as service-oriented analysis and design. In fact, many of the topics we have discussed are still in the research stages.

Note that one could argue that Web services are the most common realization of services technologies and that the technologies are not yet mature. Furthermore, since the developments are rapid, with so many standards emerging, it is not feasible to write a book that is completely up to date. While this is true to some extent, we discuss mainly principles rather than the standards that are evolving, although we do discuss the popular standards such as SAML and XACML.

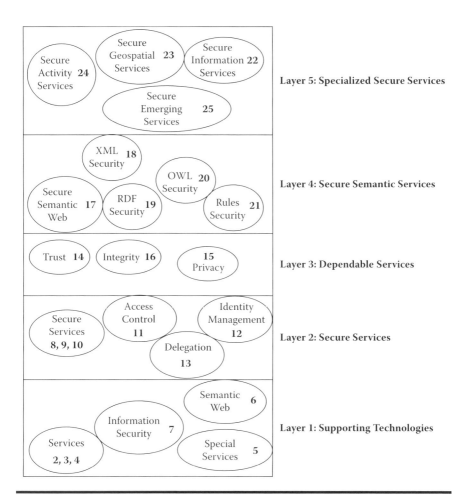

Figure 1.11 Contents of the book with respect to the framework.

Therefore, we feel that such a book is very timely. Furthermore, as we have stated, security cannot be an afterthought. It has to be incorporated while the standards for these semantic Webs are being developed by W3C and others. One of the main contributions of this book is raising the awareness of the importance of security and trustworthiness. We have also given a set of exercises at the end of Chapters 2 through 25 intended for those who wish to pursue research in the area. That is, to be consistent with our previous books, our purpose is to explain, especially to technical managers, what secure services is all about. However because of our fairly extensive research on secure information systems, we have also tried to include technical details that would help technologists and researchers.

We do provide several references that can help the reader in understanding the details of data and applications security. These concepts can be applied to secure services. My advice to the reader is to keep up with the developments in semantic Webs as well as in data and applications security. Various data and applications security as well as information-security-related conferences and workshops are being held. These include the IFIP11.3 Data and Applications security conference series and the newly formed ACM conference series called CODASPY (Conference in Data and Applications Security and Privacy). Other security conferences include the IEEE Symposium on Security and Privacy, the ACM Conference on Computers and Communications Security, ACM SACMAT and IEEE POLICY, and the Computer Security Applications Conference. Journals include the *Journal of Computer Security, Computers and Security Journal, ACM Transactions on Information and Systems Security, IEEE Magazine on Security and Privacy, IEEE Transactions on Dependable and Secure Computing*, and the *Journal of Privacy Technologies*. Several semantic Web and Web services conferences are also being conducted. These include the International Semantic Web Symposium and the WWW Conference as well as the highly popular international conferences on Web services and services computing and, more recently, conferences on semantic computing. Journals include *Web Semantics, IEEE Transactions on Services Computing, Journal of Web Services Research*, and *Semantic Web Journal*. Papers on this topic have also appeared in database and intelligent systems conferences, including the Very Large Database Conference, ACM SIGMOD Conference, and IEEE Data Engineering Conference. We list the references to these conference series and some useful texts in semantic Webs throughout the book.

We believe that as progress is made on trustworthy Web services technologies, conferences and journals devoted entirely to secure Web services will emerge. We encourage the reader to keep up with the developments of this very rapidly growing field. We strongly believe that the future of computing is with services computing. Services and components will be developed by multiple vendors from all over the world. The challenge is to put these services and components together and build secure systems and applications. Furthermore, even if part of the system is corrupted, it is critical that the system stay operational and secure until the mission is accomplished.

SERVICES AND SECURITY TECHNOLOGIES

I

Introduction to Part I

To understand the concepts in secure service-oriented information systems, we need to understand the services and security concepts; that is, secure service-oriented information systems essentially integrate services and security technologies. In Part I, we provide an overview of relevant services and security technologies.

Part I consists of six chapters: 2 through 7. Chapter 2 will provide an overview of the paradigm of services computing. Chapter 3 will discuss the foundations of services computing and includes discussions of service-oriented architecture and Web services. Service-oriented analysis and design for modeling services will be discussed in Chapter 4. Some specialized services such as those for data management and healthcare domains will be discussed in Chapter 5. Chapter 6 will provide an overview of semantic Web services that take advantage of the emerging and popular semantic Web technologies. Finally, Chapter 7 will describe security technologies.

SERVICES
AND SECURITY
TECHNOLOGIES

SERVICES AND SECURITY TECHNOLOGIES

Introduction to Part I

To understand the concepts in a services-oriented information system, we have to understand the basic technology concepts that make a services-oriented information system essentially integrate services and security technologies. In Part I, we provide an overview of the core services and security technologies.

Part I consists of six chapters, Chapters 2 through 7. Chapter 2 will provide an overview of the paradigm of services computing. Chapter 3 will discuss the foundations of services computing and includes discussions of service-oriented architecture and Web services development. Standards and the languages for modeling services will be discussed in Chapter 4. Some specialized services such as those for data management and healthcare domains will be discussed in Chapter 5. Chapter 6 will provide an overview of semantic Web technologies that are at the core of the emerging and popular semantic Web technologies. Finally, Chapter 7 will discuss security technologies.

Chapter 2

Service-Oriented Computing

2.1 Overview

Computing paradigms have evolved over the years. In the beginning, computers were used for numerical processing. Later, they were used to store and manage data in databases, where the world was viewed as a collection of tables. Then came the migration to object-oriented computing, where the world was viewed as a collection of objects. Not only were the databases viewed as a collection of objects, objects were also the main unit of computation. More recently, the world has evolved into a collection of services. Essentially, a consumer requests a service from a service provider. The service provider and the consumer draw up a contract, the service is provided, and the consumer pays for the service. Services could be healthcare services, financial services, or telecommunication services. This has resulted in what has come to be known as service-oriented computing or services computing (see also [ZHAN07] and [ERL05]).

Zhang et al. have differentiated the services model from the manufacturing model [ZHAN07]. They claim that with the manufacturing model, the request is for a product, and the manufacturer returns a product. Now, one could also view this product as a service that is provided. However, once the product is purchased the consumer owns the product, whereas in a service model the service provider owns the product and leases the product to the consumer for use.

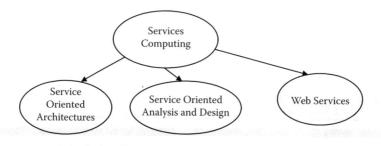

Figure 2.1 Services computing.

In this chapter, we will provide an overview of service-oriented computing. The notion of services is discussed in more detail in Section 2.2. Realizing services through Web services and service-oriented architectures is discussed in Section 2.4 and elaborated on in Chapter 3. Service-oriented analysis and design is discussed in Section 2.5 and elaborated on in Chapter 4. Some specialized services including geospatial services are discussed in Section 2.6 and elaborated on in Chapter 5. Semantic Web–based services are discussed in Section 2.7 and elaborated on in Chapter 6. Figure 2.1 shows the various aspects of services computing.

2.2 Services

To best illustrate the notion of a service, we will use the example of telecommunication. We wish to use a telephone service. We then sign up with a service provider, which could be AT&T or Sprint or some other service provider. We know about them through the yellow pages or some advertisement in the newspaper. We can discuss our requirements with them and negotiate for the best service. After the service provider is decided, a contract is produced by the selected service provider. After the contract is signed, we can use the service provider's telephone lines for telephone communication with our friends, relatives, and business associates. Figure 2.2 shows this example of service.

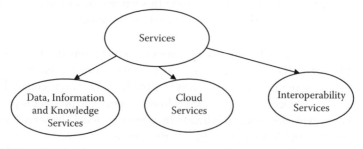

Figure 2.2 Services.

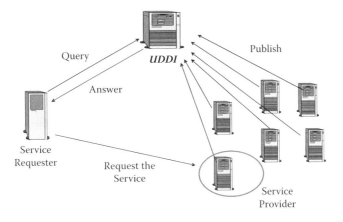

Figure 2.3   SOA and Web services.

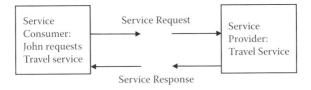

Figure 2.4   Service-oriented computing example.

Similarly, for an e-mail service, the service provider will publish its services in this case either in the yellow pages or on the Web. We contact the service provider, sign a contract, and then use the e-mail service provided by the service provider. In both cases, the service provider will publish its services in some language that we understand. We contact the service provider, draw up a contract and then utilize the service. Figure 2.3 illustrates the service paradigm. Figure 2.4 illustrates a travel service.

We use numerous services in a typical day, which include not only the telephone service and the e-mail service but also healthcare service and financial service. With the healthcare service provider, we get consultation about our health; our financial service provider manages our money for us, and even our pastor provides us with a religious service.

As stated earlier, the manufacturing model is not typically a service model as a manufacturer produced a product that is sold to the consumer. However, one can view this also as a service, because this manufacturer provides a service to the consumer in the form of a product. The manufacturer can use products from other manufacturers in order to assemble another product. This typically is a supply chain model. Ultimately, any activity can be regarded as providing a service.

One can also provide data and software as services. In the case of data, the various data centers store lots of data and allow consumers to use the data for various purposes. In the case of software, some software companies develop software for customer relationship management and healthcare management and allow consumers to use their software as a service. We will discuss these special services in Section 2.6. In the next section, we will discuss how services are integrated with computing. Figure 2.2 illustrates the various types of services.

2.3 Service-Oriented Computing

Service-oriented computing is essential to implementing the services as software. Consider, for example, the process of ordering a book at the brick-and-mortar Barnes & Noble. We go to the bookstore section, look at their catalog, find the book we want, and place our order with their sales representative. The sales representative will possibly call the warehouse manager and request the book. The warehouse manager sends the book to the store, and the store informs the customer. The customer then buys the book.

Now, this service can be implemented in software as follows. The customer checks the Web site of Barnes & Noble, finds the book, and places the order. The order management service implemented by Barnes & Noble as an order management system takes the order, sends a message to the warehouse service, and requests the book. The warehouse service then finds that the book is in its inventory and sends a message to the order management service, which then sends a message to the customer. The warehouse then sends a request to the shipping service, which then ships the book to the customer. So, there is a composition of services starting from the order management service, the warehouse service, and the shipping service. These three services provide the customer with what he or she wants.

Another example is purchasing an airline ticket. The customer calls the airline reservation system, talks to the agent, and the agent books the seat and sends the ticket to the customer. With service-oriented computing, the customer will book the reservation online, the reservation service will then find a seat and assign it to the customer. This service asks the customer if he or she wants a hotel reservation and, if a reservation is required, the service automatically sends a message to the hotel reservation service and books a hotel room for the customer. Then the service sends a message to the car rental service for a booking and finally sends a message to the customer. Here again, the airline reservation service, the hotel reservation service, and the rental car booking services comprise a single service.

Note that while the unit of computation of object-originated computing is an object, one could regard the unit of computing for service-oriented computing to be a service. However, the actual implementation of services could be carried

Figure 2.5 Service-oriented analysis and design.

out using packages or even objects. We believe that service-oriented computing is still in its infancy and at the conceptual stage. As we make more progress in this field, an appropriate programming language for service-oriented computing may be developed. In the next section, we examine service-oriented computing on the Web. Note that at present, most applications in service-oriented computing are Web-based applications, especially to do with e-business. Figure 2.3 illustrates service-oriented computing.

2.4 SOA and Web Services

Service-oriented architecture (SOA) is the architecture of the system that implements services with software technology. In this architecture, there are three major components: the service consumer, the service provider, and the service directory. The service publisher publishes its service in a standard language with the service directory. The service consumer requests the directory to find the service. The directory gives the name and/or address of the service provider to the service consumer. The service consumer then contacts the service provider.

As we have stated earlier, much of the software on services is implemented with Web technology. Therefore, the service technology that implements SOA is called Web services. The service provider published its service (that is, the Web service) on a Web-based directory. The service consumer queries this directory which then guides the consumer to the service provider. The Web-based directory is called UDDI. The language used to publish the service is called WSDL. The messages exchanged between the three components use a protocol called SOAP. These messages are communicated in the XML language. Figure 2.4 illustrates the implementation of SOA with Web services. More details are given in Chapter 3.

2.5 Service-Oriented Analysis and Design

Note that with object-oriented information systems, one needs to first identify the objects, the object classes, the methods, and the relationship between the objects.

In addition, the activities are also analyzed and incorporated into the design of the system. Such an approach has come to be known as object-oriented analysis and design (OOAD), and UML is now the standard OOAD approach. After the system is designed, an appropriate object language may be selected for the implementation. Similarly, before we design a service-oriented information system, we need to determine the services, how they are composed, how they are involved, as well as the relationship between services. Such an approach has come to be known as service-oriented analysis and design (SOAD).

While OOAD is not mature, SOAD is in its infancy. Before we design an information system to implement airline reservations, we need to determine what the services are. The services may include reserve airline seat, reserve hotel room, and reserve rental car. Next, the relationships between the services are analyzed. Here, one could invoke reserve hotel room from reserve airline seat and invoke reserve rental car also from reserve airline seat. The two services may be invoked in parallel or sequentially. After the services and the relationships are designed, the service descriptions are specified. Figure 2.5 illustrates the application of SOAD to service-oriented information systems design. Chapter 6 describes SOAD in more detail.

2.6 Specialized Services

Every industry provides various services. We have discussed some of them in Section 2.2. For example, the telecommunications industry provides services for telephone use, mobile phone user, wireless computing services, as well as e-mail services. Computer companies provide computer support services and e-mail services as well as general order management services. The medical and healthcare industry provides patient management services, billing and accounting services, and physician referral services. The financial industry provides wealth management and investment banking services. The insurance industry provides various insurance-related services, including life insurance and health insurance services. All of the foregoing are essentially domain-specific services.

Therefore, domain-specific services including accounting, billing, customer relationship management, order management, accounting, and enterprise resource management may also be applied to any of the domain-specific industries. There are also technology-oriented services, including geospatial data management services that provide directions, locations, and maps to travelers as well as multimedia services that provide audio and video services as entertainment. Finally, data and software are also provided as services. Data centers provide data services to companies to test various algorithms and techniques, and software services include providing software to develop a system. For example, a company that wants to develop an operating system may contract out the individual components, including memory

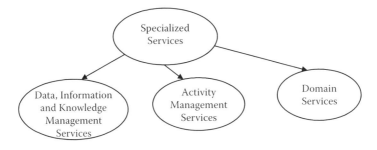

Figure 2.6 Specialized services.

management, and interposes communication services and then assembles the components to develop the system. Note the difference between software for services and service as software. In the former case, a company provides software services to construct a software system. In the latter case, the various services such as order management and accounting are implemented in software. Our focus will mainly be on the latter case for service-oriented computing. The development of Web services for the various industries is discussed in Chapter 5. Figure 2.6 illustrates some of the specialized services.

2.7 Semantic Web and Services

Tim Berners-Lee conceived the idea of the semantic Web. He wanted to develop technologies that would enable machine-readable Web pages. The semantic Web consists of a collection of technologies, including XML, RDF, and OWL. These technologies are essentially markup languages that machines can read and understand. His goal was for the machines to carry out the activities without human intervention.

Now, current Web services do not understand the various activities they have to carry out. They simply invoke the services as specified in the service descriptions. They do not know that if someone wants to book an airline seat, then that person will also want to book a hotel as well as rent a car. Furthermore, if the person pays for a first-class ticket, then that person will likely want to stay in a high-end hotel and rent an expensive car. For the Web services to understand such services, semantic Web technologies have to be utilized. For example, with the Web rules language, one could specify statements such as "if a person purchases a first class airline ticket, then he would want to stay in a five star hotel and rent a Mercedes." These semantic Web technologies will be utilized so that the Web service can be more intelligent. Further details will be given in Chapter 4. Figure 2.7 illustrates the semantic Web and its services.

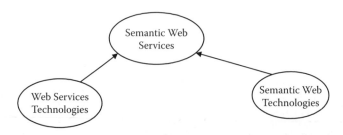

Figure 2.7   Semantic Web and services.

2.8 Summary and Directions

This chapter has provided an overview of service-oriented computing. We first discussed what is meant by services. Next, we discussed high-level concepts in service-oriented computing. Realizing service-oriented information systems through service-oriented architectures and Web services was discussed next. Semantic Web services were introduced next. Some specialized services such as services in healthcare and telecommunication industries were then discussed. Finally, we discussed how service-oriented information systems may be designed.

Details of the various concepts introduced in this chapter will be given in Chapters 3 through 6. The security aspects of the concepts discussed in this chapter will be discussed in Part II of this book, whereas Chapter 7 will discuss security technologies. Note that secure service technologies integrate service and security technologies. While much of the focus in Part II will be on confidentiality, trust, privacy and integrity for Web services will be discussed in Part III. Secure semantic Web services will be discussed in Part IV. Various other aspects, including applications of secure services, will be discussed in Part V of this book. Details of services computing and Web services are given in [ERL05] and [ZHAN07]. While much progress has been made, there are several areas, including more complex aspects of Web services such as choreography, workflow, and composition as well as metadata and security issues that need further work.

Exercises

1. Develop a scenario, and explain the various service computing concepts.
2. What are the advantages and disadvantages of services computing?

References

[ERL05] Erl, T. *Service-Oriented Architecture (SOA): Concepts, Technology, and Design*, Prentice Hall, Upper Saddle River, New Jersey, 2005.
[ZHAN07] Zhang, L.-J., J. Zhang, and H. Cai, *Services Computing*, Springer, Heidelberg, Germany, 2007.

Chapter 3

SOA and Web Services

3.1 Overview

In Chapter 2, we introduced the notion of services computing (also known as service-oriented computing) and discussed its various aspects. In this chapter, we will describe service computing through service-oriented architecture (SOA) and Web services (WS). SOA is the architecture that implements service-oriented computing. WS is one way to realize service-oriented computing through the World Wide Web. The most popular implementation of service-oriented computing is through SOA and WS. WS is defined by the various standards that are emerging from organizations such as W3C and OASIS (formerly Organization for the Advancement of Structured Information Standards).

The organization of this chapter is as follows. Standards organizations that are defining WS are discussed in Section 3.2. The SOA paradigm is discussed in Section 3.3. WS is discussed in Section 3.4. The protocol stack for WS is elaborated on in Section 3.5. An alternative way to implement WS is discussed in Section 3.6. Finally, a popular WS technology by Amazon is discussed in Section 3.7. The chapter is summarized in Section 3.8. Figure 3.1 depicts the various concepts discussed in this chapter.

It should be noted that this chapter does not focus on security. Security and SOA and WS are discussed in Part IV. We give several references at the end of this chapter. These references are essentially various URLs that describe the standards that are evolving. As we stress throughout this book, WS technology is evolving very

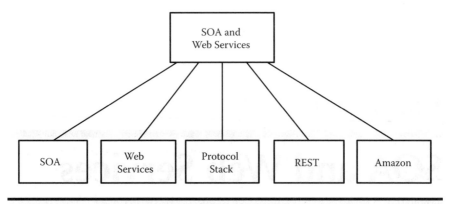

Figure 3.1   Aspects of SOA and Web services.

rapidly. Therefore, the discussions in this book could soon be outdated. We urge the reader to keep up with the developments with standards organization such as OASIS and W3C. This is one of the main reasons we have not delved into the details of the standards. Our goal is to introduce the various concepts at a higher level.

3.2 Standards Organizations

Two major standards organizations for SOA and Web services are W3C (World Wide Web Consortium) and OASIS. W3C developed standards for XML as well as secure XML, including XML encryption and XML signature. In addition, W3C has also developed standards for the semantic Web, RDF, OWL, SWRL, and many others. OASIS has developed standards for authentication and authorization for Web services, including SAML and XACML. In addition, WS-Security as well as WS-* Security Framework are major security standards developed by OASIS [OASIS].

Another key standards organization is WS-I (Web Services Interoperability). Although WS-I does not itself specify standards, it oversees the standards that are being developed. Another consortium relevant to secure Web services is Liberty Alliance. This consortium has proposed standards for identity management. Organizations such as the Object Management Group as well as the Open Geospatial Consortium have also developed Web-service-related standards. We will discuss security-relevant Web services standards in Part II. Much of the discussion in this book is based on the standards development of W3C and OASIS. As we have stated in Section 3.1, it should be noted that standards often become outdated as new standards emerge. We urge the reader to keep up with the developments with these standards organizations. Figure 3.2 shows the various standards relevant to SOA and Web services.

W3C: World Wide Web Consortium

OGC: Open Geospatial Consortium

OASIS: Organization for the Advancement
of Structured Information Standards

Figure 3.2   Standards organizations.

3.3 SOA

As stated in [OASIS], Web services refer to the technologies that allow connections
to be made. Services are what you connect together using Web services. Examples
of Web services are query service and directory service. A service is the endpoint
of a connection. Also, a service has some type of underlying computer system that
supports the connection offered. The combination of services internal and external
to an organization makes up a service-oriented architecture.

A service-oriented architecture (SOA) supports a collection of services [SOA].
These services communicate with each other. The communication can involve either
simple data passing or it could involve two or more services coordinating some activity
such as planning travel. Some means of connecting services to each other is needed.
Service-oriented architectures are not new. The first service-oriented architecture can
be considered to be DCOM (distributed component object model) and object request
brokers (ORBs) based on the CORBA (common object request architecture) specification [OMG]. If a service-oriented architecture is to be effective, we need a clear
understanding of the term *service*. A service is a function that is well defined and self-
contained, and does not depend on the context or state of other services.

As stated in the earlier chapters, SOA has three major components: a service
provider, a service consumer, and a directory. The service provider publishes its
service on the directory. The service consumer requests the directory for a service.
The directory sends back the name and address of the service. The consumer then
sends the request to the service provider and obtains the service. Now, Web services
are the most popular way to date that implement the SOA paradigm. We will discuss the specific technologies and specifications for SOA with Web services in the
next section. Figure 3.3 shows the SOA paradigm.

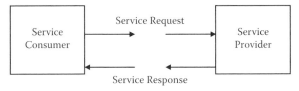

Figure 3.3   The SOA paradigm.

3.4 Web Services

3.4.1 Overview

The early Web models were based on the client-server paradigm, in which the Web client accesses a Web server through the HTTP protocol. The Web server would typically store Web pages that the client would request for retrieval. This model, while sufficient for displaying Web pages, is not sufficient for conducting e-business activities on the Web. With e-business, multiple corporations have to work together to carry out a common goal. In such an environment, there may be asynchronous communication between the multiple organizations, and each organization may provide a service to another organization. We need a more powerful mechanism to conduct e-business activities.

In the late 1990s and early 2000s, we saw both of the second generation of Web technologies that went beyond the display of Web pages and consumers purchasing items on the Web. Around the same time, the notion of service-oriented computing was born, and the technologies for e-business and service-oriented computing merged. This resulted in the invention of Web services.

In this section, we will discuss the various developments associated with Web services. The security aspects of Web services will be discussed in Part IV. The organization of this section is as follows. The Web services architecture, which is the architecture of a simple Web service, will be discussed in Section 3.4.2. Composite Web services, where a Web service calls another Web service, are discussed in Section 3.4.3. More advanced concepts will be discussed in the next section. Figure 3.4 shows Web services.

3.4.2 Web Services Architecture

The technology of Web services is the most likely connection technology of service-oriented architectures. Web services essentially use XML technology to create a robust connection. A service consumer sends a service request message to a service provider. The service provider returns a response message to the service consumer. The request and subsequent response connections are defined in some way that

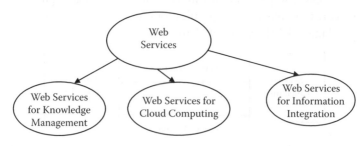

Figure 3.4   Aspects of Web services.

is understandable to both the service consumer and service provider. A service provider can also be a service consumer. The Web Services Description Language (WSDL) forms the basis for Web services. WSDL uses XML to define messages. The steps involved in providing and consuming a service are as follows:

- A service provider describes its service using WSDL. This definition is published to a directory of services. The directory could use Universal Description, Discovery, and Integration (UDDI). Other forms of directories can also be used.
- A service consumer issues one or more queries to the directory to locate a service and determines how to communicate with it.
- Part of the WSDL provided by the service provider is passed to the service consumer. This tells the service consumer what the requests and responses are for the service provider.
- The service consumer uses the WSDL to send a request to the service provider.
- The service provider provides the expected response to the service consumer.

The UDDI registry is intended to eventually serve as a means of "discovering" Web services described using WSDL. The idea is that the UDDI registry can be searched in various ways to obtain contact information and the Web services available for various organizations. The UDDI registry is a way to keep up to date on the Web services your organization currently uses. An alternative to UDDI is ebXML Directory. All the messages are sent using SOAP. (SOAP at one time stood for simple object access protocol; now, the letters in the acronym have no particular meaning.) SOAP essentially provides the envelope for sending the Web services messages. SOAP generally uses HTTP, but other means of connection may be used. Security and authorization are important topics with Web services. The basic Web services architecture is illustrated in Figure 3.5.

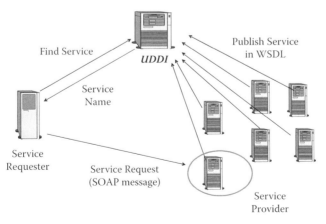

Figure 3.5   Web services architecture.

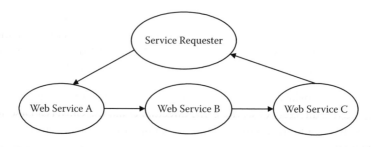

Figure 3.6 Composition of Web services.

3.4.3 Composition of Web Services

In Section 3.4.2, we discussed the basic functions of a Web service. As we have mentioned in Chapter 2, Web services can be composed of multiple Web services. For example, a customer may request a trip from a travel service. The travel service will then invoke three services: flight service, hotel service, and car rental service. WSDL will specify these services and register them with UDDI. However, we need a language to specify the flow of the services. The language that has been developed for this purpose is Business Process Execution Language (BPEL). The specific BPEL that is commonly used is the one proposed by IBM and Microsoft and is called BPEL4WS (BPEL for Web Services).

Now when booking the flight, hotel, and car, the order is not important. Therefore, BPEL statements will be specified in XML and will issues requests to make flight reservations, hotel reservations, and car rental reservations. The WSDL for each of these services will then specify the actions for carrying out the services. Now, if the order of booking the flight is most important, then BPEL has constructs to specify the order of the invocation of the services. For more details of BPEL, we refer the reader to [BPEL]. Figure 3.6 illustrates the composition of Web services.

3.5 Web Services Protocol Stack

In Section 3.3, we discussed SOA, and in Section 3.4, we discussed Web services, both single and composite. In this section, we discuss the Web service protocol stack. This stack includes specifications for metadata, messaging, transactions and business processes, portal and presentation, security, management, and business domains. It should be noted that this stack is continually evolving. Some of the standards have been adopted, while others are in the experimental stages. Yet others are only in the specification stages. Therefore, the stage of a particular protocol could change with time. We have given URLs as references for the various protocols. As stated earlier, it should be noted that these URLs could change and, therefore, we urge the reader to check the W3C and OASIS Web pages as well as

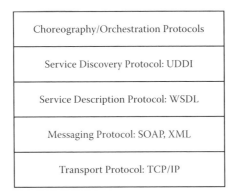

| Choreography/Orchestration Protocols |
| Service Discovery Protocol: UDDI |
| Service Description Protocol: WSDL |
| Messaging Protocol: SOAP, XML |
| Transport Protocol: TCP/IP |

Figure 3.7   Web services protocol stack.

the Web pages of corporations developing standards such as Microsoft and IBM to keep up with the developments.

In this section, we will not be discussing the security protocols. These protocols will be discussed in Part IV of this book. We will focus mainly on the lower layers: metadata, messaging, and transactions and business processes. Figure 3.7 illustrates the protocol stack. The metadata protocols include those for metadata retrieval (WS-Metadata Exchange), data service and message description (WSDL), policy (WS-Policy, WS-Policy Assertions), and publication and discovery (UDDI, WSIL). We discussed WSDL and UDDI in Section 3.4. WS-Metadata Exchange essentially specifies the metadata that other endpoints need to know to access the Web service. As stated in [META], "To bootstrap communication with Web services, this specification defines how metadata can be treated as resources for retrieval purposes, how metadata can be embedded in Web service endpoint references, and how Web service endpoints can optionally support a request-response interaction for the retrieval of metadata." WS-Policy provides a policy framework for specifying various policies and policy alternatives. As stated in [POLICY], "WS-Policy provides a flexible and extensible grammar for expressing the capabilities, requirements, and general characteristics of entities in an XML Web-services-based system. WS-Policy defines a framework and a model for the expression of these properties as policies." WS-Policy Assertions specifies a language by which policies can be stated [PA]. As stated in [WSIL], the WS-Inspection specification provides an XML format for assisting in the inspection of a site for available services and a set of rules for how inspection-related information should be made available for consumption.

The messaging protocols include the following: message packing (SOAP, MTOM), reliable messaging (WS-ReliableMesaging, ES-Reliability), routing/addressing (WS-Addressing, WS-MessageDelivery), multiple message sessions (WS-Enumeration, WS-Transfer), and events and notification (WS-Events, WS-Notification). We discussed SOAP in Section 3.3. MTOM (Message Transmission and Optimization) provides an optimized mechanism for exchanging messaging between Web services and may be used with SOAP. WS-Reliable Messaging is an OASIS specification that allows for messages to be exchanged reliably between nodes [RELIABILITY]. As stated in [RELIABILITY], WS-Reliability is a generic and open model for ensuring reliable message delivery for Web services. Essentially, WS-Reliability and WS-Reliable Messaging are competing specifications with much commonality. It is also stated in [RELIABILITY] that WS-Reliable Messaging will oust WS-Reliability. WS-Addressing is a transport-neutral-mechanism to address Web services and to identify their endpoints [ADDRESS]. Another routing protocol is WS-Message Delivery, which presents a "mechanism to deliver and correlate messages in the context of message exchange patterns (MEPs), found in the service description." An MEP "describes the pattern of messages required by a communications protocol to establish or use a communication channel [MEP]." There are two major message exchange patterns—a *request-response* pattern, and a *one-way* pattern. For example, TCP has a *request-response* pattern protocol, and the UDP has a *one-way* pattern. WS-Enumeration is a specification that "describes how to enable an application to ask for items from a list of data that is held by a Web service. In this way, WS-Enumeration is useful for reading event logs, message queues, or other data collections" [ENUM]. WS-Transfer is a specification defining the transfer of an XML-representation of a WS-addressable resource, as well as creating and deleting such resources [ADDRESS]. WS-Eventing is used for a Web services (subscriber) to register with another Web service (subscriptor) to notify it when certain events occur [EVENT]. WS-Notification is a collection of specifications that enable multiple Web services to be notified of the occurrence of various events [NOTIFY].

Protocols for transactions and business processing include orchestration (BPEL4WS, WS-CDL), transaction (WS-Transaction, WS-Coordination, WS-CAF), and asynchronous services (ASAP). We discussed BPEL4WS in Section 3.4. WS-CDL is the Web Services Choreography Description Language. It is stated in [CHORE] that "While BPEL is a programming language to specify the behavior of a participant in choreography, it is concerned with describing the message interchanges between participants. Participants of choreography are peers, there is no center of control." Essentially, WS-CDL is an XML-based language that describes peer-to-peer collaboration between multiple parties/agents [WSCDL]. WS-Transaction specifications define mechanisms for transactional interoperability between Web services domains [TRANS]. WS-Coordination describes an extensible framework for providing protocols that coordinate the actions of distributed applications [COORD]. WS-CAF, which stands for Web Services Composite Application Framework, is an open framework developed by OASIS so that applications that contain multiple services are used in combination. Such applications are called composite applications [CAF]. ASAP (Asynchronous Service Access Protocol) is an OASIS standard that creates an extension of SOAP that supports generic asynchronous Web services or long-running Web services [ASAP]. Figure 3.7 shows the Web services protocol stack.

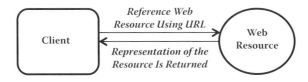

Figure 3.8   RESTful Web services.

3.6 RESTful Web Services

We have discussed the basic components of Web services, which include HTTP, SOAP, and WSDL. However, there is an alternative to designing software systems that is not based on HTTP and WWW. This approach is called REST (representational state transfer interface). REST is described in its wiki entry as follows [REST]: An important concept in REST is the existence of resources (sources of specific information), each of which is referenced with a global identifier (e.g., a URL in HTTP). In order to manipulate these resources, *components* of the network (user agents and origin servers) communicate via a standardized interface (e.g., HTTP) and exchange *representations* of these resources (the actual documents conveying the information).

It is also stated in [REST-SOAP] that any number of *connectors* (e.g., clients, servers, caches, tunnels) can mediate the request, but each does so without "seeing past" its own request (referred to as "layering," another constraint of REST and a common principle in many other parts of information and networking architecture). Thus, an application can interact with a resource by knowing two things: the identifier of the resource, and the action required—it does not need to know whether there are caches, proxies, gateways, firewalls, tunnels, or anything else between it and the server actually holding the information. The application does, however, need to understand the format of the information (*representation*) returned (e.g., HTML, XML document). Figure 3.8 illustrates the use of the REST Interface.

3.7 Amazon Web Services

A discussion of SOA and Web services cannot be complete without a discussion of Amazon Web Services (AWS). As stated in the Web pages of Amazon Web services [AMAZON], since early 2006, AWS has provided companies of all sizes with an infrastructure Web services platform in the cloud. With AWS, you can requisition computing power, storage, and other services, gaining access to a suite of elastic IT infrastructure services as your business demands them. With AWS, you have the flexibility to choose whichever development platform or programming model makes the most sense for the problems you are trying to solve. You pay only for what you use, with no up-front expenses or long-term commitments, making AWS

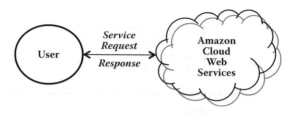

Figure 3.9　Amazon Web services.

the most cost-effective way to deliver your application to your customers and clients. And, with AWS, you can take advantage of Amazon.com's global computing infrastructure that is the backbone of Amazon.com's retail business.

AWS has several components including database (called SimpleDB), storage (Amazon S3), and Cloud (Amazon EC2). These various components are illustrated in Figure 3.9. We will describe one such component as discussed in [AMAZON]. Details of other components are also given in the Amazon Web site. Amazon SimpleDB is a Web service providing the core database functions of data indexing and querying. This service works in close conjunction with Amazon Simple Storage Service (Amazon S3) and Amazon Elastic Compute Cloud (Amazon EC2), collectively providing the ability to store, process, and query data sets in the cloud. It is also stated that Amazon Web services provides both SOAP protocol and REST interfaces. More details are found in [REST-SOAP].

3.8　Summary and Directions

In this chapter, we have discussed various aspects of SOA and Web services. We started with a discussion of the various relevant standards organizations and then provided an overview of both SOA and Web services. This was followed by a discussion of the WS protocol stack; as we have stressed, this protocol stack will continue to evolve. Then we discussed an alternate way to implement service-oriented computing through REST interface. Finally, we discussed a popular WS technology by Amazon.

In the next chapter, we will conclude our discussion of basic services computing with a discussion on service-oriented analysis and design. Part II will introduce secure services technologies. There is still lot of work to be carried out on service-oriented architectures, including building complex services. We also need to extend various object-oriented computing platforms such as object request brokers to build Web services.

Exercises

1. Give a description of each of the standards discussed in this chapter.
2. Explain the XACML protocol with an example.

References

[ADDRESS] http://www.w3.org/Submission/ws-addressing/

[AMAZON] http://aws.amazon.com/

[ASAP] http://www.oasis-open.org/committees/tc_home.php?wg_abbrev=asap

[BPEL] http://www.zurich.ibm.com/pdf/ebizz/icaps-ws.pdf

[CAF] http://en.wikipedia.org/wiki/WS-CAF

[CHORE] http://www.w3.org/TR/2004/WD-ws-cdl-10-20041217/

[COORD] http://www.ibm.com/developerworks/library/specification/ws-tx/#coor

[ENUM] http://www.w3.org/Submission/2006/02/

[EVENT] http://www.w3.org/Submission/WS-Eventing/

[MEP] http://en.wikipedia.org/wiki/Message_Exchange_Pattern

[META]http://download.boulder.ibm.com/ibmdl/pub/software/dw/specs/ws-mex/
    metadataexchange.pdf

[MTOM] http://en.wikipedia.org/wiki/MTOM

[NOTIFY] http://www.ibm.com/developerworks/library/specification/ws-notification/

[OASIS] http://www.oasis-open.org/specs/

[OMG] www.omg.org

[PA] http://xml.coverpages.org/ws-policyassertionsV11.pdf

[POLICY] http://www.w3.org/Submission/2006/SUBM-WS-Policy-20060425/

[RELIABILITY]   http://www.service-architecture.com/web-services/articles/web_services_
    reliability_ws-reliability.html

[REST] http://en.wikipedia/wiki/web-service

[REST-SOAP] http://www.oreillynet.com/pub/wlg/3005

[SOA] http://en.wikipedia/wiki/service-oriented-architecture

[TRANS] http://www.ibm.com/developerworks/library/specification/ws-tx/

[WSCDL] http://www.ebpml.org/ws_-_cdl.htm\

[WSIL] http://www.ibm.com/developerworks/library/specification/ws-wsilspec/

[WSRM] http://docs.oasis-open.org/ws-rx/wsrm/200608/wsrm-1.1-spec-cd-04.html

Chapter 4

Service-Oriented Analysis and Design

4.1 Overview

Design and analysis approaches are crucial for good software development. In the beginning, we had software design and analysis approaches for better software engineering. Then, with the explosion of object-oriented software development, including languages such as Smalltalk, C++, and Java, there came several object-oriented analysis and design approaches, also called OOAD. Eventually, after much debate, UML (unified modeling language) became the unified approach for OOAD. Today, service-oriented computing is exploding. Unlike object-oriented programming, service-oriented programming does not have its own language. Languages such as C, C++, and Java are used for service-oriented computing. However, the main question is, how do we model and analyze these services? Is there a unified service-oriented analysis and design methodology? For now at least, several approaches are being proposed. We believe that eventually it is very likely that there will be a unified approach.

In this chapter, we provide an overview of service-oriented analysis and design (SOAD). Our goal is to introduce the basic concepts so that we can discuss security and SOAD in Part II of this book. The organization of this chapter is as follows. The service-oriented life cycle is discussed in Section 4.2. Service-oriented analysis and design is discussed in Section 4.3. Service modeling is discussed in Section 4.4. SOAD approaches are discussed in Section 4.5. The chapter is summarized in Section 4.6. Aspects of SOAD are shown in Figure 4.1.

Figure 4.1   Aspects of SOAD.

4.2 Service-Oriented Life Cycle

There have been several attempts to define the software life cycle as well as the life cycle of objects. For example, in the case of software, the first step is to gather requirements, determine the inputs/outputs, design the algorithms, develop the software, test the software, integrate the software into the system, conduct system testing and, finally, deploy the software. This is not the end of the process. The software has to be maintained, the bugs fixed, and support provided to the customer. This is also the top-down approach to developing software. In the bottom-up approach, software modules are developed as needed. Similarly, in the case of object software development, in the top-down approach one has to analyze the application, determine the objects, the relationships between them, develop them, test them, and integrate them. The system also has to be maintained. In the bottom-up approach, objects are developed as needed.

Similarly, services also have life cycles. In his book on SOA, Thomas Erl has explained the service life cycle. He has stated three ways to develop services: one is the top-down approach, the second is the bottom-up approach, and the third is what he called the agile approach. In the top-down approach, one has to conduct analysis, design the services, develop them, test them, integrate them, and then maintain them. In the bottom-up approach, services are designed and developed as needed. In the agile approach, an integrated approach is used. That is, the application is analyzed, and the services are identified. However, one does not have to wait until all the services are identified. One develops some of the critical services, then conducts more of the analysis and design, and then develops some other services. The process continues and is adaptable to changes in the applications. Figure 4.2 describes the service life cycle. In the next section, we will discuss some of the key points in service-oriented analysis and design. For more details, the reader is referred to [ERL05].

4.3 Service-Oriented Analysis and Design

As we have stated earlier, object-oriented analysis methods and UML are often taught in SOA classes. While one can learn some of the principles behind object-oriented analysis and design, SOAD is not the same as OOAD. SOAD is about designing services. Note that objects may be used to implement the services.

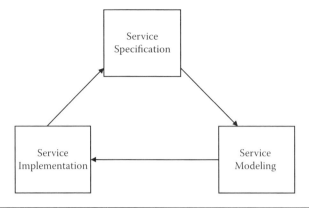

Figure 4.2 Service-oriented life cycle.

However, the concept of service is not the same as the concept of objects. Therefore, it is important to introduce the concept of SOAD if one has to design good service-based systems.

The first step is to analyze the application and determine the services that describe the applications. The logic encapsulated by each service, the reuse of the logic encapsulated by the service, and the interfaces to the service have to be identified. It is also desirable for a service to be autonomous. The next step is identification of the relationship between the services, including the composition of services. In a top-down strategy, one has to identify all the services and the relationships before conducting their detailed design and development. For large application design, this may not be feasible. In the case of bottom-up design, one has to identify services and start developing them. In agile design, both strategies are integrated. In an airline reservation application, the services are reserve airline, reserve hotel, and reserve rental car. They can be implemented as three independent services, or the reserve hotel and reserve rental car services can be invoked by the reserve airline service.

Erl, in his book, makes a strong case for business services. That is, the business logic is modeled as services. He further states that such an approach sets the stage for orchestration-based service-oriented architectures. Orchestration essentially implements workflow logic that enables different applications to interoperate with each other. It should be noted that orchestrations themselves may be implemented as services. Therefore, the orchestration service may be invoked for different applications—also implemented as services—to interoperate with each other. Business services also promote reuse. For example, an accounts payable service may be reused by different applications.

In this section, we have discussed some of the key points in service-oriented analysis and design. In the next section, we will elaborate on service modeling. For more details, refer to [ERL05]. A high-level view of SOAD is shown in Figure 4.3.

Figure 4.3   Service-oriented analysis and design.

4.4 Service Modeling

In this section, we will summarize some of the key points on service modeling. A detailed discussion is given in [ERL05]. The main question is, how do you define a service? At the highest level, an entire application such as order management can be one service. However, this is not desirable. At the other extreme, a business process can be broken into several steps, and each step can be a service. In the case of order management, the steps include (1) search the Web for a bookstore that has the book you want, (2) compare the price of the book at different bookstores, (3) examine the shipping rules and return policies, (4) check whether the bookstores will accept the credit card you have, (5) select a bookstore, (6) search for the book, (7) place the book in the shopping cart, (8) purchase the book by filling out all details, (9) wait for confirmation, and (10) check out. Now each step could be a service. But this would mean that for a medium-sized application there could be hundreds of services. Therefore, the challenge is to group steps that carry out some specific task into a service. As Erl states, there are two major design principles in a good service design: one is reusability, and the other is autonomy. Services can also be defined based on the operations that are performed. Initially, one does not define the explicit service or the operations. The services and operations are called candidate services and candidate operations.

Next, examine the service candidates, and determine the relationships between them. One service may call other services. Two services may be composed to obtain a composite service. This would mean identifying the boundaries, and the interface, which could make the composition and separations as clean as possible. Dependencies may result in complex service designs. The service operations could be simple operations such as performing calculations or complex operations such as invoking multiple services.

Once the candidate services and the service operations are identified, the next step is to refine the candidates and state the design of the services and the service operations. Note that this also depends on whether one follows the top-down, bottom-up, or agile strategies. This decision would determine whether all the services have to be defined before the development or whether one can define some of the services and then start the development while other services are still being defined.

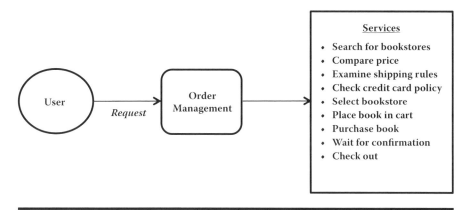

Figure 4.4   Service modeling.

Details of the various methods for SOAD as well as those related to the service-oriented enterprise and enterprise modeling are given in [ERL05]. We discuss some of the approaches being investigated in the next section. Figure 4.4 shows some of the key aspects of service modeling.

4.5 SOAD Approaches

In the late 1980s and early 1990s, several object-oriented edit methodologies were competing. These included Rumbaugh's OMT, Booch's method, and Ivar Jacobson's Use Cases. Then, with unified modeling language (UML), the various approaches were unified, and there is now a standard OOAD. However, with services, standards have not yet been laid down for SOAD. There are multiple approaches, and as we get a better understanding of SOAD, we expect that these various approaches would be unified. Some of the current approaches include IBM's SOAD, called SOMA, as well as Services UML, among others. We discuss some of these approaches in this section, and Figure 4.5 shows them.

SOMA: Service Oriented Modeling Architecture

SOMF: Service Oriented Modeling Framework

UML for Services

Figure 4.5   SOAD approaches.

A good discussion of service-oriented modeling is discussed in [MODEL], [SURVEY], and [SOAD]. We will now discuss some of the well-known SOAD approaches.

IBM Service-Oriented Analysis and Design (SOAD): IBM first coined the term SOAD and then refined it with SOMA. As stated in the survey paper by Ramollari et al. on SOAD approaches, IBM's SOAD proposes elements that could be part of a service-oriented analysis and design methodology; hence, it is an abstract framework rather than a holistic methodology [IBM]. SOAD builds upon existing, proven techniques, such as OOAD. It also introduces SOA-specific techniques, such as service conceptualization, service categorization, and aggregation.

IBM Service-Oriented Modeling Architecture (SOMA): IBM's SOMA can be considered to be an implementation of IBM's SOAD. As stated in [SOMA], SOMA implements Service-Oriented Analysis and Design (SOAD) through the identification, specification, and realization of services, components that realize the service components, and flows that can be used to compose services. IBM's approach extends object-oriented component-based analysis and design approaches for SOA. It is also stated that SOMA identifies services, component boundaries, flows, compositions, and information through complementary techniques that include domain decomposition, goal-service modeling, and existing asset analysis.

Service-Oriented Modeling Framework (SOMF): Another SOAD approach is SOMF. As stated in [SOAD], SOMF is a service-oriented development life cycle methodology and offers a number of modeling practices and disciplines that contribute to a successful service-oriented life cycle management and modeling. Modeling is divided into four sections: practices, environments, disciplines, and artifacts.

UML for Services: Those who have worked with UML are strongly promoting UML for SOAD. IBM's Rational Rose product has the UML-to-SOA Transformation tool. As stated by IBM [IBM], the UML-to-SOA transformation typically accepts the UML model as its source and creates domain-specific SOA output.

In general, the following phases have been identified as the major phases of SOAD, especially with SOMF:

- Service-oriented discovery and analysis modeling: Discover and analyze services for granularity, reusability, interoperability, loose coupling, and identify consolidation opportunities
- Service-oriented business integration modeling: Identify service integration and alignment opportunities with business domain processes (organizations, products, geographical locations)

- Service-oriented logical design modeling: Establish service relationships and message exchange paths, address service visibility, craft service logical compositions, model service transactions
- Service-oriented conceptual architecture modeling: Establish an SOA architectural direction, depict an SOA technological environment, craft an SOA technological stack, identify business ownership
- Service-oriented logical architecture modeling: Integrate SOA software assets, establish SOA logical environment dependencies, foster service reuse, loose coupling, and consolidation

It can be seen that much of the work on SOAD has been influenced by OOAD, which also includes UML-based modeling. SOAD is still in its infancy. Therefore, we believe that just as UML won the battle with OOAD, there will very likely be a uniform SOAD methodology. We examine security aspects of SOAD in Part II of this book. Details of UML can be found in [UML].

4.6 Summary and Directions

In this chapter, we have summarized SOAD. We started with a discussion of modeling services and the top-down and bottom-up approaches to services modeling. We also discussed the service-oriented life cycle. Finally, we discussed SOAD approaches such as SOMA, SOAF, and UML.

As we have stated, SOAD is in its infancy. Once SOA technologies mature, we can expect a uniform SOAD approach. For the time being, we have to examine the various SOAD approaches and select the one that is most appropriate for security modeling. Note that this was the case with object-oriented modeling and design. In the early 1990s, numerous object-oriented analysis and design approaches had been proposed. It was only in the mid-1990s that UML unified the various approaches. We can expect similar progress with SOAD. It should, however, be noted that many SOA courses are teaching UML as the modeling approach. However, this should not be the case. We need to focus on services right from the beginning instead of objects. We discuss SOAD and security in Part II of this book.

Exercises

1. Compare and contrast the various SOAD approaches.
2. Select a SOAD approach, and illustrate how an application may be modeled with this approach.

References

[ERL05] Erl, T., *Service-Oriented Architecture (SOA): Concepts, Technology, and Design*, Prentice Hall, Upper Saddle River, New Jersey, 2005.

[IBM] http://www.ibm.com/developerworks/rational/library/08/0115_gorelik/

[MODEL] http://www.perspectivesonwebservices.de/download/INF05-ServiceModelingv11.pdf

[SURVEY] http://www.dcs.shef.ac.uk/~ajhs/research/papers/soasurvey.pdf

[SOAD] Service Oriented Analysis and Modeling, http://en.wikipedia.org/wiki/Service-oriented_modeling

[UML] Unified Modeling Language, http://en.wikipedia.org/wiki/Unified_Modeling_Language

Chapter 5

Specialized Web Services

5.1 Overview

While Chapters 2, 3, and 4 discussed some of the basic concepts in Web services, in this chapter we discuss specialized Web services. By specialized Web services, we mean services that have been developed for special areas. There are various types of specialized Web services. These include services for data, information as well as knowledge management, Web services for activity management such as information interoperability and e-commerce, and Web services for domain industries such as healthcare and finance. We also discussed another type of special Web services, and these are based on providing data as a service, software as a service, and infrastructure as a service.

There are other specialized Web services, and these are semantic Web services. Semantic Web services utilize semantic Web technologies, which include ontologism and the resource description framework. Since semantic Web technologies are the way of the future, we will devote Chapter 5 to a discussion of semantic Web technologies as well as semantic Web services.

The organization of this chapter is as follows. In Section 5.2, we will discuss Web services for data management, and in Section 5.3, we will discuss Web services for complex data management. Web services for information and knowledge management will be discussed in Sections 5.4 and 5.5, respectively. Web services for activity management will be discussed in Section 5.6. In Section 5.7, we discuss Web services for domain industries. In Section 5.8, we discuss some emerging Web services such as data as a service and safari as a service. The chapter is concluded in Section 5.9. Figure 5.1 illustrates the various types of Web services.

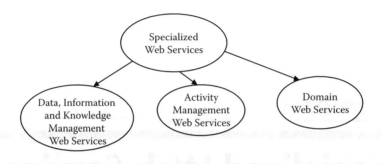

Figure 5.1 Specialized Web services.

5.2 Web Services for Data Management

5.2.1 Data Management

We have divided data management into two parts. In the following sections, we discuss database management, which includes a discussion of both data models and database functions, distributed data management, and Web data management. We first discuss data management, and then discuss how Web services may be utilized for data management. In Section 5.3, we cover complex data management, which includes a discussion of multimedia and geospatial data management. By complex data management, we mean databases that manage complex data such as multimedia and geospatial data.

5.2.1.1 Data Model

The purpose of a data model is to capture the universe that it is representing as accurately, completely, and naturally as possible [TSIC82]. Data models include hierarchical models, network models, relational models, entity relationship models, object models, and logic-based models. The relational data model is the most popular data model for database systems. With the relational model [CODD70], the database is viewed as a collection of relations. Each relation has attributes and rows. Various languages to manipulate the relations have been proposed. Notable among these languages is the ANSI Standard SQL (Structured Query Language). This language is used to access and manipulate data in relational databases [SQL3]. A detailed discussion of the relational data model is given in [DATE90] and [ULLM88].

5.2.1.2 Functions

A database management system (DBMS) essentially manages a database, and provides support to the user by enabling him to query and update it. Therefore, the

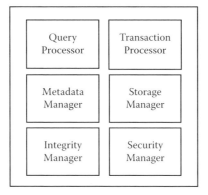

Figure 5.2   Architecture for a DBMS.

basic functions of a DBMS are query processing and update processing. In some applications such as banking, queries and updates are issued as part of transactions. Therefore, transaction management is also another function of a DBMS. To carry out these functions, information about the data in the database has to be maintained. This information is called the metadata. The function that is associated with managing the metadata is metadata management. Special techniques are needed to manage the data stores that actually store the data. The function that is associated with managing these techniques is storage management. To ensure that the foregoing functions are carried out properly and that the user gets accurate data, there are some additional functions. These include security management, integrity management, and fault management (i.e., fault tolerance). The functional architecture of a DBMS is illustrated in Figure 5.2 (see also [ULLM88]).

5.2.1.3 Data Distribution

As stated by [CERI84], a distributed database system includes a distributed database management system (DDBMS), a distributed database, and a network for interconnection. The DDBMS manages the distributed database. A distributed database is data that is distributed across multiple databases. The nodes are connected via a communication subsystem, and local applications are handled by the local DBMS. In addition, each node is also involved in at least one global application, so there is no centralized control in this architecture. The DBMS are connected through a component called the distributed processor (DP). Distributed database system functions include distributed query processing, distributed transaction management, distributed metadata management, and enforcing security and integrity across the multiple nodes. It has been stated that the semantic Web can be considered to be a large distributed database.

5.2.1.4 Web Data Management

A major challenge for Web data management researchers and practitioners is coming up with an appropriate data representation scheme. The question is, is there a need for a standard data model for Web database systems? Is it at all possible to develop such a standard? If so, what are the relationships between the standard model and the individual models used by the databases on the Web?

Database management functions for the Web include query processing, metadata management, security, and integrity. In [THUR00], we have examined various database management system functions and discussed the impact of Web database access on these functions. Some of the issues are discussed here. Figure 5.3 illustrates the functions. Querying and browsing are two of the key functions. First of all, an appropriate query language is needed. Since SQL is a popular language, appropriate extensions to SQL may be desired. XML-QL, which has evolved from XML (eXtensible Markup Language, to be discussed later) and SQL, is moving in this direction. Query processing involves developing a cost model. Are there special cost models for Internet database management? With respect to the browsing operation, the query processing techniques have to be integrated with techniques for following links. That is, hypermedia technology has to be integrated with database management technology.

Updating Web databases could mean different things. One could create a new Web site, place servers at that site, and update the data managed by the servers. The question is, can a user of the library send information to update the data at a Web site? An issue here is with security privileges. If the user has write privileges, then he could update the databases that he is authorized to modify. Agents and mediators could be used to locate the databases as well as to process the update.

Transaction management is essential for many applications. There may be new kinds of transactions on the Web; for example, various items may be sold through the Internet. In this case, the item should not be locked immediately when a potential buyer makes a bid. It has to be left open until several bids are received, and the item is sold. That is, special transaction models are needed. Appropriate concurrency control and recovery techniques have to be developed for the transaction models.

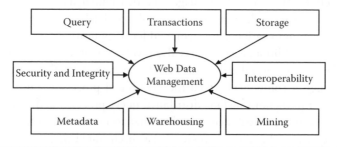

Figure 5.3   Web database functions.

Metadata management is a major concern for Web data management. The question is, what is metadata? Metadata describes all of the information pertaining to the library. This could include the various Web sites, the types of users, access control issues, and policies enforced. Where should the metadata be located? Should each participating site maintain its own metadata? Should the metadata be replicated or should there be a centralized metadata repository? Metadata in such an environment could be very dynamic, especially since the users and the Web sites may be changing continuously.

Storage management for Web database access is a complex function. Appropriate index strategies and access methods for handling multimedia data are needed. In addition, due to the large volumes of data, techniques for integrating database management technology with mass storage technology are also needed. Other data management functions include integrating heterogeneous databases, managing multimedia data, and mining.

5.2.2 Web Services for Data Management

The various data management functions may be invoked as Web services. For example, the query Web services will include the composition of multiple Web services such as query modification services and the query optimization service. The query service will include the storage service to retrieve the data from the storage. The transaction service will execute transactions.

Semantic Web technologies may also be utilized by Web services to produce semantic Web services. First of all, the security policies may be expressed in languages such as XML and RDF. This is one of the significant contributions of the semantic Web. Now, databases may also consist of XML and RDF documents. For example, products such as those by Oracle Corporation now have the capability of managing XML and RDF documents. Therefore, we need to apply data management techniques for managing XML and RDF documents.

Semantic Web technologies have applications in heterogeneous database integration. For example ontologies are needed for handling semantic heterogeneity. XML is now being used as the common data representation language. With respect to data warehousing, XML and RDF may be used to specify the policies. Furthermore, ontologies may be used for data transformation in order to bring the data into the warehouse. Ontologies have applications in data mining as they clarify various concepts to facilitate data mining. On the other hand, the vast quantities of data on the Web will have to be mined to extract information to guide the agents to understand the Web pages. Semantic Web technologies, including the reasoning engines, may be applied to handle the inference and privacy problems. For example, languages such as RDF and OWL may be used to specify the policies, and then inference controllers could be developed based on descriptive logic-based engines such as Pellet to determine whether security violations via inference occur.

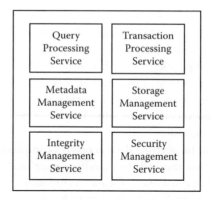

Figure 5.4 Web services for data management.

In summary, every aspect of secure data management, Web services, and semantic Web technologies has applications. Figure 5.4 illustrates the relationships between secure data management and the semantic Web.

5.3 Web Services for Complex Data Management

We first discuss multimedia, then geospatial sensor data management and, finally, how Web services may be utilized for complex data management.

5.3.1 Concepts

5.3.1.1 Multimedia Data Systems

A multimedia data manager (MM-DM) provides support for storing, manipulating, and retrieving multimedia data from a multimedia database. In a sense, a multimedia database system is a type of heterogeneous database system, as it manages heterogeneous data types. Heterogeneity is due to the multiple media of the data such as text, video, and audio. Because multimedia data also conveys information such as speeches, music, and video, we have grouped this under information management. One important aspect of multimedia data management is data representation. Both extended relational models and object models have been proposed.

An MM-DM must provide support for typical database management system functions. These include query processing, update processing, transaction management, storage management, metadata management, security, and integrity. In addition, in many cases, the various types of data such as voice and video have to be synchronized for display and, therefore, real-time processing is also a major issue in an MM-DM.

Various architectures are being examined to design and develop an MM-DM. In one approach, the data manager is used just to manage the metadata, and a multimedia file manager is used to manage the multimedia data. There is a module for integrating the data manager and the multimedia file manager. In this case, the MM-DM consists of the three modules: the data manager managing the metadata, the multimedia file manager, and the module for integrating the two. The second architecture is the tight coupling approach. In this architecture, the data manager manages both the multimedia data as well as the metadata. The tight coupling architecture has an advantage because all of the data management functions could be applied to the multimedia database. This includes query processing, transaction management, metadata management, storage management, and security and integrity management. Note that with the loose coupling approach, unless the file manager performs the DBMS functions, the DBMS only manages the metadata for the multimedia data.

There are also other aspects to architectures as discussed in [THUR97]. For example, a multimedia database system could use a commercial database system such as an object-oriented database system to manage multimedia objects. However, relationships between objects and the representation of temporal relationships may involve extensions to the database management system. That is, a DBMS together with an extension layer provide complete support to manage multimedia data. In the alternative case, both the extensions and the database management functions are integrated so that there is one database management system to manage multimedia objects as well as the relationships between the objects. Further details of these architectures as well as managing multimedia databases are discussed in [THUR01]. Figure 5.5 illustrates a multimedia information management system.

Figure 5.5   Multimedia information management.

5.3.1.2 Geospatial Data Management

A geospatial data manager, also often referred to as geographical information system (GIS), is any system that captures, stores, analyzes, manages, and presents data that is linked to location. As stated in [GIS], a GIS is a system that includes mapping software with applications in remote sensing, land surveying, aerial photography, mathematics, photogrammetry, and geography. GIS can be regarded as the integration of cartography and database technology. Therefore, the challenges include representing spatial data (e.g., maps) as well as storing and querying such data.

Geospatial data management has gained prominence mainly due to the activities of OGC (Open Geospatial Consortium). In addition to developing GML (Geography Markup Language), which is essentially XML for geospatial data, OGC is also involved in specifying standers for representing, storing, and managing geospatial data. Many of the challenges we have described for multimedia data systems (which manage a combination of text, voice, video, and audio data) are applicable to geospatial systems. Other complex data include sensor data. Technologies such as SensorML are being developed for representing sensor data.

5.3.2 Web Services for Complex Data Management

Multimedia and geospatial data management operations such as querying can be invoked as Web services. Furthermore, XML is being extended for multimedia and geospatial data. For example, SMIL is a markup language for video, while Voice is a markup language for audio data. The access control policies specified in, say, XML and RDF or more descriptive language such as REI, can be enforced on video data represented in SMIL. Organizations such as OGC have specified GML. OGC specifies geospatial standards that rely on GML as the data layer encoding. OWL-S provides a semantic-rich application-level platform to encode the Web service metadata using descriptive logic. OGC is monitoring innovative ways to integrate these two methods as part of its Geospatial Semantic Web Interoperability experiment. Sensor data management operations may also be invoked as Web services. These include querying and fusing sensor data. Semantic Web technologies such as Sensor are being developed for sensor data. Figure 5.6 illustrates Web services for complex data management.

We have extended RDF to develop GRDF (geospatial RDF) for geospatial data. We are using ontologies specified in GRDF for handling semantic heterogeneity. This ontologism is then used for semantic interoperability. Our details of GRDF can be found in [ALAM06]. On top of GRDF we have developed geospatial ontologies. Our team (Thuraisingham, Ashraful, Subbiah, and Khan) has developed a system called DAGIS that reasons with the ontologies and answers queries. This system is described in [THUR07]. It is a framework that provides a methodology to realize the semantic interoperability both at the geospatial data encoding level and also for

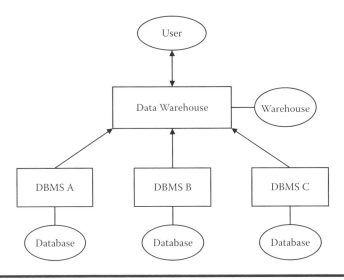

Figure 5.6   Web services for complex data management.

the service framework. DAGIS is an integrated platform that provides the mechanism and architecture for building geospatial data exchange interfaces using the OWL-S Service ontology. Coupled with the geospatial domain-specific ontology for automatic discovery, dynamic composition, and invocation of services, DAGIS is a one-stop platform to fetch and integrate geospatial data. The data encoding is in GRDF and provides the ability to reason about the payload data by the DAGIS or client agents to provide intelligent inferences. DAGIS at the service level and GRDF at the data encoding layer provide a complete unified model for realizing the vision of the geospatial semantic Web. The architecture also enhances the query response to client queries posed to the DAGIS interface.

Another effort on Web services for geospatial data is the GeoRSS effort. As stated in [OGC], GeoRSS is a simple proposal for geoenabling, or tagging, "really simple syndication" (RSS) feeds with location information. GeoRSS proposes a standardized way in which location is encoded with enough simplicity and descriptive power to satisfy most needs to describe the location of Web content. GeoRSS is also intended to be a lightweight way to express geography in other XML-based formats, including XHTML.

5.4 Web Services for Information Management

We include data warehouses data mining, and information management as these systems extract some nuggets from the raw data possibly stored in databases. We also discuss information retrieval and digital libraries under information management.

We discuss these technologies as well as how Web services may be utilized for information management.

5.4.1 Data Mining and Warehousing

Data warehousing is one of the key data management technologies to support data mining and data analysis. As stated by Inman [INMO93], data warehouses are subject oriented. Their design depends to a great extent on the application utilizing them. They integrate diverse and possibly heterogeneous data sources. They are persistent. That is, the warehouses are very much like databases. They vary with time. This is because as the data sources from which the warehouse is built get updated, the changes have to be reflected in the warehouse. Essentially, data warehouses provide support for decision support functions of an enterprise or an organization. For example, while the data sources may have the raw data, the data warehouse may have correlated data, summary reports, and aggregate functions applied to the raw data.

Figure 5.7 illustrates a data warehouse. The data sources are managed by database systems A, B, and C. The information in these databases is merged and put into a warehouse. With a data warehouse, data may often be viewed differently by different applications. That is, the data is multidimensional. For example, the payroll department may want data to be in a certain format, while the project department may want data to be in a different format. The warehouse must provide support for such multidimensional data.

Data mining is the process of posing various queries and extracting useful information, patterns, and trends often previously unknown from large quantities

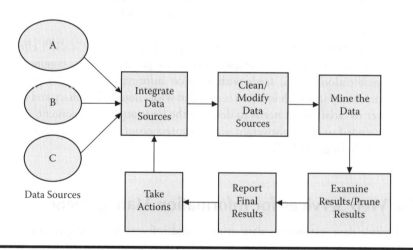

Figure 5.7   Data warehouse.

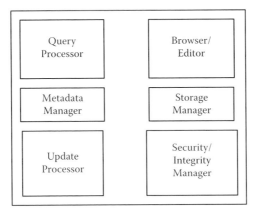

Figure 5.8   Steps to data mining.

of data possibly stored in databases. Essentially, for many organizations, the goals of data mining include improving marketing capabilities, detecting abnormal patterns, and predicting the future based on past experiences and current trends.

Some data mining techniques are based on statistical reasoning techniques, inductive logic programming, machine learning, fuzzy sets, and neural networks, among others. The data mining outcomes include classification (finding rules to partition data into groups), association (finding rules to make associations between data), and sequencing (finding rules to order data). Essentially, one arrives at some hypothesis, which is the information extracted from examples and patterns observed. These patterns are observed from posing a series of queries; each query may depend on the responses obtained to the previous queries posed. There have been several developments in data mining. A discussion of the various tools is given in [KDN]. A good discussion of the outcomes and techniques are given in [BERR97]. Figure 5.8 illustrates the data mining process.

5.4.2 Information Retrieval

Information retrieval systems essentially provide support for managing documents. The functions include document retrieval, document update, and document storage management, among others. These systems are essentially database management systems for managing documents. There are various types of information retrieval systems, and they include text retrieval systems, image retrieval systems, and audio and video retrieval systems. Figure 5.9 illustrates a general-purpose information retrieval system that may be utilized for text retrieval, image retrieval, audio retrieval, and video retrieval. Such an architecture can also be utilized for a multimedia data management system. We will discuss the special features of each type of information retrieval system (see also [THUR01]).

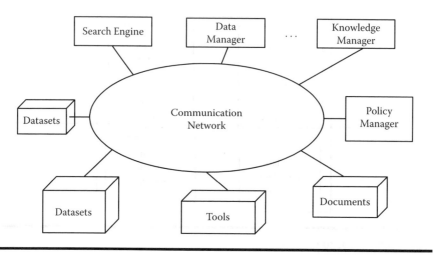

Figure 5.9 Information retrieval system.

5.4.2.1 Text Retrieval

A text retrieval system is essentially a database management system for handling text data. Text data could be documents such as books, journals, magazines, etc. One needs a good data model for document representation. A considerable amount of work has gone into developing semantic data models and object models for document management. For example, a document could have paragraphs, and a paragraph could have sections, etc.

Querying documents could be based on many factors. One could specify keywords and request that documents with the keywords be retrieved. One could also retrieve documents that have some relationships with one another. Recent research on information retrieval focuses on querying documents based on semantics. For example, "retrieve documents that describe scenic views" or "retrieve documents that are useful to children under ten years" are types of such queries.

Much of the information is now in textual form. This could be data on the Web or library data or electronic books, among others. One of the problems with text data is that, unlike relational data, it is not structured. In many cases, it is unstructured, and in some cases, it is semistructured. Semistructured data, for example, is an article that has a title, author, abstract, and paragraphs. The paragraphs are not structured, while the format is structured.

Information retrieval systems and text-processing systems have been developed over the past few decades. Some of these systems are quite sophisticated and can retrieve documents by specifying attributes or keywords. There are also text-processing systems that can retrieve associations between documents.

5.4.2.2 *Image Retrieval*

An image retrieval system is essentially a database management system for handling image data. Image data could be x-rays, pictures, satellite images, and photographs. One needs a good data model for image representation. Some work has gone into developing semantic data models and object models for image management. For example, an image could consist of a right image and a left image (an example is the x-ray of the lungs).

Querying images could be based on many factors. One could extract text from images and then query the text. One could tag images and then query the tags. One could also retrieve images from patterns. For example, an image could contain several squares. With a picture of a square, one could query the image and retrieve all the squares in the image. We can also query images depending on content. For example, "retrieve images with sunsets" or "retrieve images with Victorian buildings" are types of queries.

Image processing has been around for quite a while. We have image processing applications in various domains, including medical imaging for cancer detection, processing satellite images for space and intelligence applications, and also handling hyper-spectral images. Images include maps, geological structures, biological structures, and many other entities. Image processing has dealt with areas such as detecting abnormal patterns that deviate from the norm, retrieving images by content, and pattern matching.

5.4.2.3 *Video Retrieval*

A video retrieval system is essentially a database management system for handling video data. Video data could be documents such as books, journals, magazines, etc. There are various issues that need to be considered. One needs a good data model for video representation. Some work has gone into developing semantic data models and object models for video data management (see [WOEL86]). For example, a video object could have advertisements, main film, and coming attractions.

Querying documents could be based on many factors. One could extract text from the video and query the text. One could also extract images from the video and query the images. One could store short video scripts and carry out pattern matching. That is, "find the video that contains the following script." Examples of queries include "find films where the hero is John Wayne" or "find video scripts that show two presidents shaking hands." Recently, there have been some investigations about mining video data.

5.4.2.4 *Audio Retrieval*

An audio retrieval system is essentially a database management system for handling audio data. Audio data could include books, journals, magazines, etc. One needs a good data model for audio representation. Some work has gone into developing semantic data models and objects models for audio data management (see WOEL86]). For example, an audio object could have introductory remarks, speech, applause, and music.

Querying audio data could be based on many factors. One could extract text from the audio and query the text. One could store short audio scripts and carry out pattern matching, for example, "find the audio that contains the following script." Examples include "find audio tapes containing the speeches of President John" or "find audio tapes of poems recited by female narrators." Recently, there have been some studies on audio mining [IEEE03].

5.4.3 Digital Libraries

Digital libraries gained prominence with the initial effort by the National Science Foundation (NSF), Defense Advanced Research Projects Agency (DARPA), and National Aeronautical and Space Administration (NASA). NSF continued to fund special projects in this area and, as a result, the field has grown very rapidly. The idea behind digital libraries is to digitize all types of documents and provide efficient access to these digitized documents.

Several technologies have to work together to make digital libraries a reality. These include Web data management, markup languages, search engines, and question-answering systems. In addition, multimedia information management as well as information retrieval systems play an important role. This section will review the various developments in some digital library technologies. Figure 5.10 illustrates an example of a digital library system.

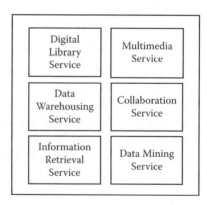

Figure 5.10   Digital libraries.

5.4.3.1 *Search Engines*

Since the early 1990s, numerous search engines have been developed. They have their origin in the information retrieval systems developed in the 1960s and beyond. Typically, when we invoke a browser such as Netscape or Microsoft's Internet Explorer, we have access to several search engines. Some of the early search engines were AltaVista, Yahoo, Infoseek, and Lycos. These systems were around in 1995 and were fairly effective for their times. They are much improved now. Since around 1999, one of the popular search engines has been Google. It started off as a Stanford University research project funded by organizations such as the National Science Foundation and the Central Intelligence Agency as well as the industry, and was later commercialized. Systems such as Google as well as some of the other search engines provide intelligent searches. However, they still have a long way to go before users can get precise answers to their queries.

Search engines are accessed via browsers. When you click on a search engine, you will get a window requesting what you want to search for. Then you list the keywords and, subsequently, the various Web pages are listed. The question is, how does a search engine find Web pages? It essentially uses information retrieval on the Web.

The rating of a search engine is determined by the speed in which it produces results and, more importantly, the accuracy with which it produces results. That is, does the search engine list relevant Web pages for the query? For example, when you type a query called "lung cancer," does it provide the relevant information you are looking for with respect to lung cancer? It can for example list resources on lung cancer or list information about who has had lung cancer. Usually, people want to get resources on lung cancer. If they want to find out who has lung cancer, then they could type in "people with lung cancer."

Searches, although extremely useful, often provide a lot of irrelevant information. To get accurate results, they have to build sophisticated indexing techniques. They also may cache information from Web servers for frequently posed queries. Search engines have a directory about the various Web servers they have to search. This directory is updated as new servers enter. Then the search engines build indices for the various keywords. When a user poses a query, the search engine will consult its knowledge base, which consists of information about Web servers and various indices. It also examines the caches, if it has any, and will then search the Web servers for the information. All this has to be carried out in real time.

Web mining enables one to mine the user log and build profiles for the various users so that search can be made more efficient. Note that there are millions of users, and building profiles is not straightforward. We need to mine the Web logs and find out what the preferences of the users are. Then we list those Web pages for the user. Furthermore, if a user is searching for some information, from time to time, the search engines can list Web pages that could be relevant to the user's request. That is, search engines will have to dynamically carry out searches depending on what the user wants.

5.4.3.2 Question-Answering Systems

Question-answering systems are similar to the early information retrieval systems and were developed in the late 1960s. They would typically give yes/no answers. Since then, there have been many advances in information retrieval systems including text, image, and video systems. However, with the advent of the Web, question-answering systems have received much prominence. They are not just limited to a yes/no answer. They give answers to various complex queries such as, "what is the weather forecast today in Chicago?" or "retrieve the flight schedules from London to Tokyo that make at most one stop."

The various search engines such as Google are capable of performing complex searches. But they are yet to answer complex queries. The research on question-answering systems is just beginning, and we can expect search engines to have this capability. Question-answering systems integrate many technologies, including natural language processing, information retrieval, and search engines and data management.

5.4.4 Web Services for Information Management

Web services may be involved in various information management applications. For example, data mining and data warehousing operations may be implemented as Web services. Similarly, the information retrieval operation as well as the digital library management operations may also be invoked as Web services. As in the case of data management, semantic Web technologies such as XML, RDF, and OWL can be used to reprint security policies, including confidentiality, privacy, and trust policies. Furthermore, the reasoning engines based on, say, descriptive logic such as Pellet, can be used to infer unauthorized conclusions via inference. Semantic Web technologies can also be used to represent the data. Figure 5.11 illustrates Web services for information management.

Semantic Web technologies have also been applied for information management, especially for digital library management. A significant direction in applying the semantic Web to digital libraries has been provided by Sure and Studer in their article "Semantic Web Technologies for Digital Libraries" [SURE05]. They state that "Typical usage scenarios for Semantic Technologies in Digital Libraries include among other user interfaces and human–computer interaction (displaying information, allowing for visualization and navigation of large information collections), user profiling (taking into account the overall information space), personalization (balancing between individual and community-based personalization), user interaction." They describe their SEKT project, which attempts to solve many of the challenges. They further state that while there will be several digital libraries,

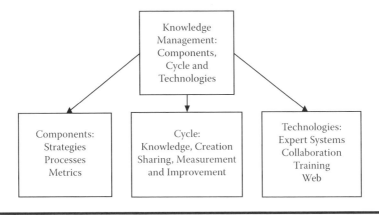

Figure 5.11   Web services for information management.

with the use of ontologies and semantic Web technologies, it will be possible to provide a consistent view of digital libraries. We will summarize some of the prominent semantic Web technologies they have discussed in their paper that are useful for digital libraries. They are ontologies, ontology editors, annotation tools, and inference engines:

- Ontologies: OntoBroker and SHORE. OntoBroker was developed at the University of Karlsruhe, and SHORE was developed at the University of Maryland and are useful for managing digital libraries.
- Ontology Editors: These could be graphical tools to manage the numerous ontologies for digital libraries.
- *OntoEdit* is one such editor (http://www.ontoprise.com) and has a strong inferencing component.
- *Protégé* is an academic ontology (http://protege.stanford.edu/).
- *KAON* (http://kaon.semanticweb.org) is an open-source ontology as well as an ontology editor and used for business applications.
- Annotation Tools: These tools automate the annotation task; that is, information about the content of a document (e.g., metadata) is annotated. (http://annotation.semanticweb.org/).
- *Annotea* (http://www.w3.org/2001/Annotea/) is a LEAD (Live Early Adoption and Demonstration) project and provides support for shared annotations. Note that annotations include comments, notes, and explanations.
- OntoMat-*Annotizer* (http://annotation.semanticweb.org/ontomat) is an example of a prominent annotation tool with an associated framework called CREAM.
- *KIM* (http://www.ontotext.com/kim) provides Knowledge and Information Management (KIM).
- Infrastructure supports the annotation and indexing of semistructured data.

- Inference Engines deduce information and reason about the information. There are logic-based inferencing methods and special algorithms for problem solving.
- *OntoBroker* (http://www.ontoprise.com) is a commercial inference engine based on Frame Logic.
- *FaCT* (http://www.cs.man.ac.uk/~horrocks/FaCT/) is an inference engine based on Description Logics.
- *KAON2* (http://kaon2.semanticweb.org/) is a description-logic-based inference engine for OWLDL and OWL-Lite reasoning.

5.5 Web Services for Knowledge Management

5.5.1 Strategies, Processes, and Models

Knowledge management is the process of using knowledge as a resource to manage an organization. It could mean sharing expertise, developing a learning organization, teaching the staff, learning from experiences, as well as collaboration. Essentially, knowledge management will include data management and information management. However, this is not a view shared by everyone. Various definitions of knowledge management have been proposed. Knowledge management is a discipline invented mainly by business schools. The concepts have been around for a long time. But the term *knowledge management* was coined as a result of information technology and the Web.

In the collection of papers on knowledge management by Morey et al. [MORE01], knowledge management is divided into three areas. These are strategies such as building a knowledge company and making the staff knowledge workers, processes (such as techniques) for knowledge management including developing a method to share documents and tools, and metrics that measure the effectiveness of knowledge management. In the *Harvard Business Review* on knowledge management, there is an excellent collection of articles describing a knowledge-creating company, building a learning organization, and teaching people how to learn [HARV96]. Organizational behavior and team dynamics play major roles in knowledge management.

Knowledge management technologies include several information management technologies, which in turn include knowledge representation and knowledge-based management systems. Other knowledge management technologies include collaboration tools, tools for organizing information on the Web, as well as tools for measuring the effectiveness of the knowledge gained such as collecting various metrics. Knowledge management technologies essentially include data management and information management technologies as well as decision support technologies. Figure 5.12 illustrates some of the knowledge management components and technologies. It also lists the aspects of the knowledge management cycle. Web

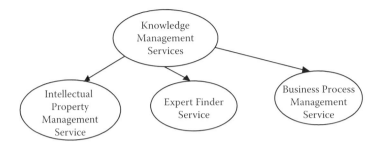

Figure 5.12   Knowledge management components and technologies.

technologies play a major role in knowledge management and therefore are closely related. While knowledge management practices have existed for many years, it is the Web that has promoted knowledge management.

Many corporations now have intranets, and an intranet is the single most powerful knowledge management tool. Thousands of employees are connected through the Web in an organization. Large corporations have sites all over the world, and the employees are becoming well connected with one another. E-mail can be regarded as one of the early knowledge management tools. Now there are many tools such as search engines and e-commerce tools.

With the proliferation of Web data management and e-commerce tools, knowledge management will become an essential part of the Web and e-commerce. A collection of papers on knowledge management experiences, including strategies, processes, and metrics is given in [MORE01]. Collaborative knowledge management is discussed in [THUR02].

5.5.2 Web Services for Knowledge Management

Various knowledge management operations such as creating and managing intellectual property, storing and managing the expertise in a corporation, and maintaining the corporate Web site, may be invoked as Web services. These Web services may involve semantic Web technologies.

Semantic Web technologies have many applications in knowledge management. For example, we need ontologies to capture and represent knowledge and reason about the knowledge. In his article on the semantic Web and knowledge management, Paul Warren gives an example on how "a political scientist, Sally, who wants to research the extent to which British Prime Minister Tony Blair's stance on Zimbabwe has changed over a year and what factors might have caused that change." He further states that "in the world of the Semantic Web, Sally could search for everything written by Blair on this topic over a specific time period. She could also search for transcripts of his speeches. Information markup wouldn't stop at the article or report level but would also exist at the article section level. So, Sally could also locate articles written by political commentators that contain transcripts of Blair's speeches" [WARR06].

Figure 5.13 Web services for secure knowledge management.

Now, knowledge management also has applications for building the semantic Web. For example, prior knowledge captured as a result of knowledge management can be used by agents to better understand Web pages. With respect to security, in the example by Warren, confidentiality, privacy, and trust policies will determine the extent to which Sally trusts the articles and has access to the articles in putting together her report on Tony Blair's speeches. Figure 5.13 illustrates the relationships between secure knowledge management and the semantic Web.

5.6 Web Services for Activity Management

Activities include e-business, information integration, information sharing, and supply chain management. We discuss these activities and also describe how Web services may be utilized.

5.6.1 E-Business and E-Commerce

Various models, architectures, and technologies are being developed. Business-to-business e-commerce is all about two businesses conducting transactions on the Web. We give some examples. Suppose corporation A is an automobile manufacturer and needs microprocessors to be installed in its automobiles. It will then purchase the microprocessors from corporation B, which manufactures the microprocessors. Another example is when an individual purchases some goods such as toys from a toy manufacturer. This manufacturer then contacts a packaging company via the Web to deliver the toys to the individual. The transaction between the manufacturer and the packaging company is a business-to-business transaction. Business-to-business e-commerce also involves one business purchasing a unit of another business or two businesses merging. The main point is that such transactions have to be carried out on the Web. Business-to-consumer e-commerce is when a consumer, such as an individual, makes purchases on the Web. In the toy manufacturer example, the purchase between the individual and the toy manufacturer is a business-to-consumer transaction.

The modules of the e-commerce server may include modules for managing the data and Web pages, mining customer information, security enforcement, as well as transaction management. E-commerce client functions may include presentation

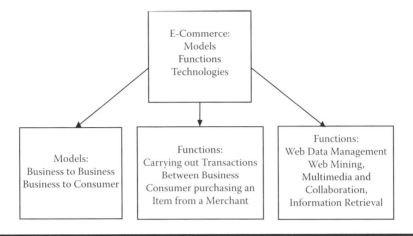

Figure 5.14 Aspects of e-commerce.

management, user interface as well as caching data, and hosting browsers. There could also be a middle tier, which may implement the business objects to carry out the business functions of e-commerce. These business functions may include brokering, mediation, negotiations, purchasing, sales, marketing, and other e-commerce functions. The e-commerce server functions are impacted by information management technologies for the Web. In addition to the data management functions and the business functions, the e-commerce functions also include those for managing distribution, heterogeneity, and federations.

E-commerce also includes nontechnological aspects such as policies, laws, social impacts, and psychological impacts. We are now doing business in an entirely different way and, therefore, we need a paradigm shift. We cannot do successful e-commerce if we still want the traditional way of buying and selling products. We have to be more efficient and rely on technologies a lot more to gain a competitive edge. Some key points for e-commerce are illustrated in Figure 5.14.

5.6.2 Collaboration and Workflow

Although the notion of computer-supported cooperative work (CSCW) was first proposed in the early 1980s, it was only in the 1990s that much interest was shown in this topic. Collaborative computing enables people, groups of individuals, and organizations to work together with one another in order to accomplish a task or a collection of tasks. These tasks could vary from participating in conferences, solving a specific problem, or working on the design of a system (see [ACM91]).

One aspect of collaborative computing of particular interest to the database community is workflow computing. Workflow is defined as the automation of a series of functions that make up a business process, such as data entry, data review, and monitoring performed by one or more persons. An example of a process that is well suited for workflow automation is the purchasing process. Some early commercial workflow system products targeted for office environments were based on a messaging architecture. This architecture supports the distributed nature of current work teams. However, the messaging architecture is usually file based and lacks many of the features supported by database management systems such as data representation, consistency management, tracking, and monitoring. The emerging workflow systems utilize data management capabilities.

Figure 5.15 illustrates an example where teams A and B are working on a geographical problem such as analyzing and predicting the weather in North America. The two teams must have a global picture of the map as well as any notes that go with it. Any changes made by one team should be instantly visible to the other team, and both teams should communicate as if they are in the same room.

To enable such transparent communication, data management support is needed. One could utilize a database management system to manage the data or some type of data manager that provides some of the essential features such as data integrity, concurrent access, and retrieval capabilities. In the above example, the database may consist of information describing the problem the teams are working on, the data that is involved, history data, as well as the metadata information. The data manager must provide appropriate concurrency control features so that when both teams simultaneously access the common picture and make changes, these changes are coordinated.

The Web has increased the need for collaboration even further. Users now share documents on the Web and work on papers and designs on the Web. Corporate information infrastructures promote collaboration and sharing of information and

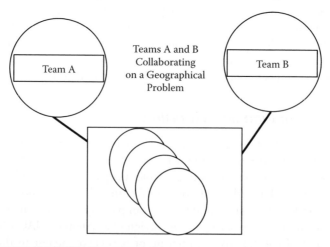

Figure 5.15 Collaborative computing system.

documents. Therefore, the collaborative tools have to work effectively on the Web. More details are given in [IEEE99].

5.6.3 Information Integration

Figure 5.16 illustrates an example of interoperability between heterogeneous database systems or information sources. The goal is to provide transparent access, both for users and application programs, for querying and executing transactions (see, for example [WIED92]). Note that in a heterogeneous environment, the local DBMSs may be heterogeneous. Furthermore, the modules of the DP have both local DBMS-specific processing as well as local DBMS-independent processing. We call such a DP a heterogeneous distributed processor (HDP). There are several technical issues that need to be resolved for the successful interoperation between these diverse database systems. Note that heterogeneity could exist with respect to different data models, schemas, query processing techniques, query languages, transaction management techniques, semantics, integrity, and security.

Some of the nodes in a heterogeneous database environment may form a federation. Such an environment is classified as a federated data mainsheet environment.

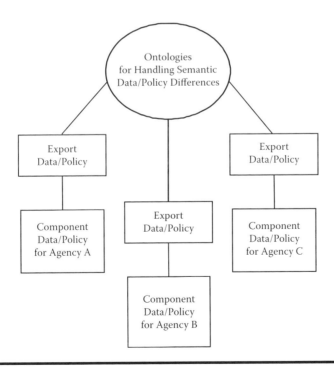

Figure 5.16   Information integration.

As stated by Sheth and Larson [SHET90], a federated database system is a collection of cooperating but autonomous database systems belonging to a federation. That is, the goal is for the database management systems that belong to a federation to cooperate with one another and yet maintain some degree of autonomy.

5.6.4 Information Sharing

The 9/11 Commission Report has encouraged organizations to move from a need-to-know to a need-to-share paradigm. Information sharing is important not only for the defense and intelligence organizations but also for healthcare organizations. For example, in an emergency situation (e.g., accident), patient data may have to be released so that the most appropriate care can be provided to the patient, while during normal operations, patient data may be released only if the patient has authorized the release.

Information sharing adds complexity with respect to security and privacy. Organizations have to enforce appropriate security and privacy policies so that only inappropriate data is shared. Furthermore, organizations should also enforce policies to determine the actions to be taken in emergency situations. Another important aspect of information sharing is managing trust. For example, do organizations in a coalition trust one another? Should an organization share information with another organization that it does not trust? Are there different levels of trust?

Perhaps the most important aspect of information sharing is providing incentives for sharing. Even if there are policies conducive to information sharing, why should organizations share information when they have no incentives to do so? Furthermore, what are the incentives? Should they be monetary or should they be recognition awards, or providing the tools for an organization to effectively carry out its functions?

We are conducting extensive research on information sharing under a MURI project funded by AFOSR. For more details, we refer the reader to [FINI09]. Figure 5.17 illustrates a scenario for information sharing. Our main focus is on applying policies for information sharing as well as determining the incentives for sharing. The requests for information between the coalition's organizations may be implemented as Web service client requests, while the servers that respond to the requests may be implemented as Web services. Furthermore, semantic Web technologies may also be utilized as the data may be represented as XML or RDF, and ontologies may be utilized for understanding the various concepts for information sharing. We will discuss the security issues involved in applying Web services for information sharing in Part V.

5.6.5 Social Networking

An activity that is receiving much attention is social networking. The idea is to study how networks are formed. These networks may be a friend's network, terror

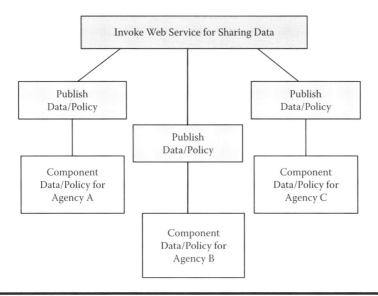

Figure 5.17   Information sharing.

networks, transportation networks, communication networks, and human networks. These networks are often referred to as social networks. The technologies that are utilized to develop and manage the social networks are graph-theory-based techniques, data mining techniques to extract social networks from the behavior of the individuals, as well as to mine existing networks to determine patterns, and visualization techniques to visualize the activities of the members of a network.

Social networks are formed by analyzing/mining the data on the Web or otherwise and determining the links between the data. Essentially, this amounts to forming nodes and links. Once the network is constructed, it continually evolves as new members enter the world. Furthermore, these networks are also analyzed/mined to extract nuggets that will feed into the network. Figure 5.18 illustrates this process.

5.6.6 Supply Chain Management

The final activity that we will consider in our discussion is supply chain management. Organizations cannot function by themselves. They need other organizations from which they can purchase parts or supply parts to. For example, consider a company that makes automobiles. Such a company would need to get supplies from other companies, including electronic devices, engines, and other parts that are needed to manufacture an automobile. Its supplier could get its parts from other suppliers. Suppose a supplier provides a GPS system for the automobile. This supplier will get its parts (e.g., chips, processors) from other companies. The challenge is for the organizations to form partnerships so that the benefits can be maximized. One does not want redundant parts. The parts have to arrive at the right time at the right place.

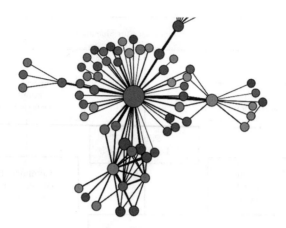

Figure 5.18   Social networking.

Information technologies play a major role in supply chain management. Database systems are used to keep track of all the parts and where they came from. Data mining techniques may be used to analyze the data and determine the suppliers to select. Information-sharing techniques are needed for the partners in a supply chain to share information and maximize their benefits. Information integration techniques are used for disparate databases from multiple suppliers to be integrated so that a common picture is presented to the customer. Figure 5.19 illustrates supply chain management.

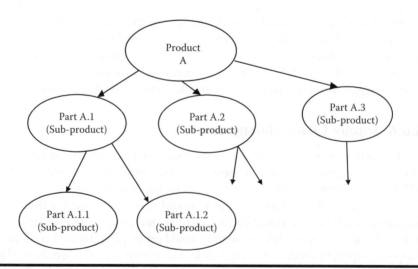

Figure 5.19   Supply chain management.

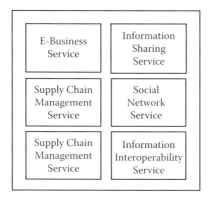

Figure 5.20 Web services for activity management.

5.6.7 Web Services for Activity Management

Figure 5.20 illustrates Web service for the various activity management types. We will discuss the details for each activity.

5.6.7.1 E-Business

Web services and the semantic Web have been applied to e-business in multiple directions.

One is developing specialized markup languages such as ebXML for e-business applications and another is semantic e-business, where e-business processes make use of semantic Web technologies, and the third is applying Web services to invoke e-business applications.

As stated in [WIKI], Electronic Business using eXtensible Markup Language (ebXML) "is a family of XML-based standards sponsored by OASIS and UN/CEFACT (between the United Nations Centre for Trade Facilitation and Electronic Business) whose mission is to provide an open, XML-based infrastructure that enables the global use of electronic business information in an interoperable, secure, and consistent manner by all trading partners." The initial goal of this project was to specify XML standards for business processes. These standards include collaboration protocol agreements, core data components, messaging, registries, and repositories. Some of the ongoing efforts of this project include the following:

- Messaging (ebMS): This is a specialization of Web services for business-to-business applications.
- Business Process and Collaboration (ebBP): This set of specifications enables collaboration among business partners.

- Collaboration Protocol Profile and Agreement (CPPA): This effort provides definitions for the sets of information used in business collaborations.
- Registry and Repository: The goal of this effort is to come up with a specification that enables interoperable registries and repositories.
- Core Components (CCTS): This effort focuses on technologies such as context and content assembly.

Ontologies have also been developed for e-commerce applications specified in languages such as RDF, RDF-S, OWL, and OWL-S (see, for example, [ONTO]). For example, in the Obelix project, a very good description of e-business and ontologies is provided. The authors state that a problem with e-commerce is the vague ideas that lack precise description. They then discuss their approach, which is based on requirements engineering, and then define ontologies for e-commerce.

More details of this project are given in [OBLIE2]. It is stated that "OBELIX is the first ontology-based e-business system of its kind in the world to provide smart, scalable integration and interoperability capabilities." They also state that this project "incorporates ontology management and configuration, an e-business application server and ontology-based e-application tools as well as an e-business library." OBELIX is a European Commission project, and the goal is to automate e-business services in a semantic Web environment, which has come to be called semantic e-business.

Some interesting efforts on semantic e-business are being carried out by the group at the University of North Carolina–Greensboro. They have stated that semantic e-business is about organizations collaboratively designing business processes that utilize knowledge of the corporation [SING06]. It essentially integrates semantic Web technologies with business process management and knowledge management. The business processes utilize knowledge management to improve their efficiency and utility and use semantic Web technologies such as ontologies for better understanding.

Semantic commerce, which is more or less semantic e-business, is also being investigated. For example, researchers at HP Labs in Bristol present a life cycle of a business-to-business e-commerce interaction, and show how the semantic Web can support a service description language that can be used throughout this life cycle. They show that by using DAML+OIL, they were able to develop a service description language that is useful not only to represent advertisements but also implement matchmaking queries, negotiation proposals, and agreements [TRAS].

5.6.7.2 Collaboration and Workflow

Semantic Web technologies can also be applied for workflow and collaborative applications. For example, the Workflow Management Coalition has developed two languages, the first being Wf-XML (Workflow XML). As stated in [WFMC], "Wf-XML extends the ASAP (Asynchronous Service Access Protocol by OASIS) model to include BPM (Business Process Management) and workflow interchange capabilities." This coalition has also developed XPDL (XML Process Definition Language). As stated in [WFMC], "XPDL provides a framework for implementing business process management and workflow engines, and for designing, analyzing, and exchanging business processes."

While the markup languages we have discussed here are comparable to XML for text, these languages have been extended with ontologies to provide semantics for multimedia, workflow, and collaborative computing applications. For example, RDF-based languages have been developed by researchers in Scotland for collaborative and workflow applications [CHEN04].

5.6.7.3 Information Integration

While semantic Web technologies were developed for machine-understandable Web pages, and XML in particular was developed for document exchange on the Web, these technologies have extensive use for information interoperability. Syntactic heterogeneity such as data model heterogeneity was a major issue in the 1990s. Various communities were discussing the development of common object models and extended relational models for common data resonation [THUR97]. However, since the development of XML, it is the choice language for global data representations. Many organizations, including the Department of Defense, are using XML and XML schemas to publish the metadata for the individual databases. This has been a significant development toward the common data model.

While XML is ideal for representing syntax, we have shown in Part II that we need RDF and OWL-like languages for representing semantics. Therefore, RDF-based languages are being used to handle semantic heterogeneity. For example, ontologies are specified to define various terms, as well as to represent common semantics or to distinguish between different semantics. These ontologies are then used for information interoperability and to understand the various terms used by different organizations.

5.6.7.4 Other Activities

Organizations may invoke Web services for information sharing as well as for social networking and supply chain management. For example, organization A may invoke one Web service to place relevant information into a shared space and another Web service to retrieve information placed by another organization. An organization may request parts from a supplier by invoking a Web service. That Web service may invoke other Web services to request additional parts.

Semantic Web technologies may also be used for information sharing, social networking, and supply chain management. For example, the information to be shared may be represented in XML, RDF, or OWL. A framework based on semantic Web technologies may be used as a platform for information sharing. In the case of social networking, first, monologues may be extracted from the data to form social networks. These ontologies may be mined to extract patterns. A good example of a semantic-Web-based social network is FOAF (Friend of a Friend) that is specified in RDF.

5.7 Domain Web Services

In the following sections, we will discuss Web services for the domain industries, including defense, homeland security, and healthcare (Figure 5.21). Figure 5.22 illustrates a data as a service model.

5.7.1 Defense

One of the earliest domains to utilize Web services were defense and intelligence. Under the management of Dr. Jim Handler, the DAML (Darpa Agent Markup Language) program at DARPA developed technologies for the DoD (Department of Defense). While security was not a consideration in that program, the ontology language called DAML was developed. This program worked closely with the W3C to develop technologies for machine-understandable Web pages. DAML was then

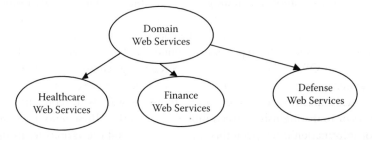

Figure 5.21   Web service domain.

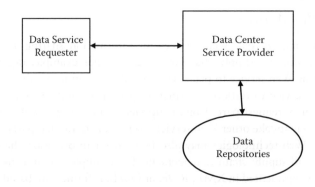

Figure 5.22   Data as a service.

integrated with the European standard called OIL (Ontology Interface Language) to develop DAML+OIL. While the United States and Europe together developed DAML+OIL, the W3C developed OWL for ontologies. As we have mentioned earlier, OWL evolved from RDF, DAML, and OIL. In addition to representation of the data, reasoning about the data was also a focus for the DAML program.

About the time that the DAML program was implemented in the late 1990s and early 2000s, the DoD was involved in the development of the GCCS (Global Command and Control System) program. Under this program, the DII COE (Defense Information Infrastructure Common Operating Environment) was developed. DII COE essentially consists of several working groups, including for distributed computing systems, multimedia, and data management. However, with the emergence of Web services, the DoD began to invest heavily in Network Centric Enterprise Services for Network Centric Operations. This then led to the development of the Global Information Grid, which was essentially the Infrastructure for NCES. This infrastructure is based on service-oriented architecture and Web services. Much of the development is influenced by XML and ontologies. Furthermore, communities of interest (COI) have been formed, and these communities have developed common ontologies for their applications. Web services also play a major role for applications in homeland security. For example, the use of semantic Web technologies and Web services for enforcing RFID tags have been explored in [RFID],

5.7.2 Healthcare and Life Sciences

W3C hosted a workshop in October 2004 to bring together researchers in life sciences to determine how semantic Web technologies can be utilized. Today, several efforts are focusing on developing ontologies, Web services, and markup languages for healthcare and life sciences applications. For example, ontologies are used to specify drugs and various medical terms. For example, Jonathan Borden, who is part of the W3C Web Ontology Working Group, has specified XML for healthcare applications [BORD]. He states that his goal is to use ontologies and markup languages to answer questions such as, "Of all the patients I operated on for brain tumors between 1996 and 2000, matching severity of pathology and matching clinical status and who have the P53 mutation, did PCV chemotherapy improve the cure rate at five years?" He then illustrates how XML, RDF, and OWL could be utilized to effectively answer these questions.

Ontologies have been developed for electronic healthcare records as well as for several terms in the life sciences [SMIT03]. For example, the authors state in [LIFE] that "Contemporary life science research includes components drawn from physics, chemistry, mathematics, medicine, and many other areas, and all of these dimensions, as well as fundamental philosophical issues, must be taken into account in the construction of a domain ontology." They then describe how to go about developing domain ontologies for the life sciences.

5.7.3 Finance

The financial domain includes any domain that has to deal with finance, including banking and trading, insurance, and investment management. Almost all of these activities are now being carried out electronically. We now have electronic trading, electronic banking, and electronic insurance management, among others. In this section, we will examine the applications of trustworthy semantic Webs for the financial domain.

Several groups are developing Web services and semantic Web technologies for financial domains. For example, the group in Madrid has done some very good research on applying the semantic "ontology-based platform that provides (a) the integration of contents and semantics in a knowledge base that provides a conceptual view on low-level contents, (b) an adaptive hypermedia-based knowledge visualization and navigation system, and (c) semantic search facilities" [CAST]. Furthermore, they have developed a topology of economic and financial information. Another group in Belgium is developing ontologies for financial security fraud detection. They have used ontology-based knowledge engineering in projects to detect financial security fraud. In particular, they have developed a fraud forensic ontology from regulation and laws [ZHAO].

In addition to specific projects such as the work in Madrid and Belgium to develop ontologies and semantics for financial data management, XML is being used extensively for financial services. It is now considered the norm for finance. As stated in [XML], "the Financial Services industry is creating a variety of standard XML formats to meet their special needs." The list of standards being developed include the following:

Interactive Financial Exchange (IFX) and Open Financial Exchange (OFX), which address consumer and other forms of retail banking.

Financial Information eXchange (FIX) is emerging as a standard communications protocol for equity trading data.

FIX Markup Language (FIXML) uses XML to express business messages for the FIX protocol.

Financial Products Markup Language (FpML) is an XML-based interchange format for transactions in financial derivative markets.

Market Data Definition Language (MDDL) is a consortium standard for the definition and communication of market data in XML, including data required to analyze, trade, and account for market value in the handling of financial instruments.

eXtensible Business Reporting Language (XBRL) is an "XML-based specification for the preparation and exchange of financial reports and data." It is developed by a global consortium of organizations and institutions.

5.7.4 Telecommunication

Another domain application for Web services is telecommunication. Corporations such as Ericsson, Nokia, and AT&T are developing Web services for this industry. Parlay X is such an effort by the Parlay group. As stated in the wiki article, "The Parlay Group is a technical industry consortium (founded 1998) that specifies APIs for the telephone network. These APIs enable the creation of services by organizations both inside and outside of the traditional carrier environment." In 2003, this group developed a new set of Web services called Parlay X that is a simpler set of APIs to be used by developers. As stated in [TELE], "The Parlay X Web services include Third Party Call Control (3PCC), location and simple payment."

An interesting and useful survey on Web services for the telecommunications industry is presented in [TELE]. The article states that the telecommunication industry has been in a flux over recent years due to regulatory changes, competition, and progress in technology. The authors make a strong case for the use of Web services for this industry and explain event-driven architectures and developments with Parlay X.

5.8 Emerging Web Services

5.8.1 X as a Service

What is becoming increasingly popular is using X as a service. X could be data, a software platform, infrastructure, or anything of interest. With data as a service, an organization can utilize a data provider to obtain data and invoke data as a service. In the case of software, an organization can obtain a compiler or an operating system or an application as a service from a service provider. In this section, we will elaborate on each of these services. In general, X as a Service is denoted by XaaS.

5.8.1.1 Data as a Service

Data as a service has been provided for quite a while. For example, corporations such as Choice Point and Acxiom manage data for various corporations in financial and medical industries. These data services may include data security and privacy services, and data quality and cleansing services. Figure 5.23 illustrates a software as a service model. We will refer to Data as a Service as DaS instead of Daas because Daas has been used for Desktop as a Service.

Integrating data services with Web service technology is a recent conceit. As stated in [DATA], once you move past novelty Web services that echo a string you sent or perform, say, a mathematical computation, services are either facilitating the insertion or retrieval of data. Whether you want to retrieve customer and product

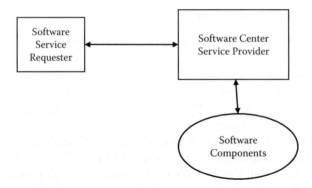

Figure 5.23 Software as a service.

data via a service request or you want to be able to expose supply chain operations to key business partners, folding your data access layer into your SOA architecture is key. WSO2 Data Services provide a convenient and well-engineered mechanism for service-orienting your data.

The WSO2 Enterprise Service Bus enables the loose-coupling of services, connecting systems in a managed virtualized manner that allow administrators to control and direct communication without disrupting existing applications. WSO2 has many components, and the data server component essentially provides data services, including smashups such as integrating various data sources, database management, and related services.

Another concept that is evolving is using database management as a service. Sharad Mehrotra and his team at UCI together with researchers at IBM, Purdue, and the University of Texas at Dallas are working on this concept. The idea is to explore a new paradigm for data management in which a third-party service provider hosts "database as a service," providing its customers seamless mechanisms to create, store, and access their databases at the host site. Such a model alleviates the need for organizations to purchase expensive hardware and software, deal with software upgrades, and hire professionals for administrative and maintenance tasks, which are taken over by the service provider. Mehrotra's team has developed and deployed a database service on the Internet, called NetDB2, which is in constant use. In a sense, data management models supported by NetDB2 provide an effective mechanism for organizations to purchase data management as a service, thereby freeing them to concentrate on their core businesses. An interesting direction is to combine the Web services concept that is present in WSO2 data services with the research being carried out by Mehrotra and his team to incorporate more advanced data management services into the standards.

5.8.1.2 Software as a Service

Another concept that is really exploding is the software as a service model, also referred to as SaSS. As stated in [SOFT], Software as a Service is a model of software deployment whereby a provider licenses an application to customers for use as a service on demand. SaaS software vendors may host the application on their own Web servers or download the application to the consumer device, disabling it after use or after the on-demand contract expires. The on-demand function may be handled internally to share licenses within a firm or by a third-party application service provider (ASP) sharing licenses between firms.

It is also stated that Software as a Service can also take advantage of service-oriented architecture to enable software applications to communicate with each other. Each software service can act as a service provider, exposing its functionality to other applications via public brokers, and can also act as a service requester, incorporating data and functionality from other services. Enterprise Resource Planning (ERP) software providers leverage SOA in building their SaaS offerings; an example is SAP Business ByDesign from SAP AG.

There are also those who are skeptical of SaaS as they state that this could be quite expensive and there is lot of hype. Therefore, the trade-off a corporation has to make is whether to build the software, purchase it, or license it as part of the SaaS model among other choices. There is still a lot to do before SaaS becomes a common trend.

5.8.1.3 Other X as a Service

There are several other types of X as a service. These include Desktop as a service, Network as a service, Platform as a service, and Infrastructure as a service. We discuss two such services. As stated in the wiki definition, "*Platform as a service* (PaaS) is the delivery of a computing platform and solution stack as a service. It often goes further with the provision of a software development platform that is designed for cloud computing at the top of the cloud stack." In this way, an organization can invoke the service and obtain the hardware and software stack and deploy applications. In the case of Infrastructure as a Service (IaaS), the wiki definition states the following: "Infrastructure as a Service (IaaS) is the delivery of computer infrastructure (typically, a platform virtualization environment) as a service. These virtual infrastructure stacks are an example of the Everything as a Service trend and share many common characteristics. Rather than purchasing servers, software, data center space, or network equipment, clients instead buy those resources as a fully outsourced service. The service is typically billed on a utility computing basis and amount of resources consumed (and therefore the cost) will typically reflect the level of activity. It is an evolution of Web hosting and virtual private server offerings."

5.8.2 *Amazon Web Services*

As stated in the Web pages of Amazon Web Services [AMAZON], since early 2006, Amazon Web Services (AWS) has provided companies of all sizes with an infrastructure Web services platform in the cloud. With AWS, you can requisition compute power, storage, and other services, gaining access to a suite of elastic IT infrastructure services as your business demands them. With AWS, you have the flexibility to choose whichever development platform or programming model makes the most sense for the problems you are trying to solve. You pay only for what you use, with no up-front expenses or long-term commitments, making AWS the most cost-effective way to deliver your application to your customers and clients. And, with AWS, you can take advantage of Amazon.com's global computing infrastructure, which is the backbone of Amazon.com's retail business.

AWS has several components, including database (called SimpleDB), storage (Amazon S3), and cloud (Amazon EC2). We will describe one such component as discussed in [AMAZON]. Details of other components are also given in the Amazon Web site. Amazon SimpleDB is a Web service providing the core database functions of data indexing and querying. This service works in close conjunction with Amazon Simple Storage Service (Amazon S3) and Amazon Elastic Compute Cloud (Amazon EC2), collectively providing the ability to store, process, and query data sets in the cloud. It is also stated that Amazon Web Services provides both SOAP protocol and REST interface. More details can be found in [REST-SOAP].

5.8.3 *Web Services for Grids and Clouds*

A grid essentially consists of a collection of computers harnessed to execute various applications. The goal is to optimize resource usage and schedule the machines for various tasks. The grid concept has been extended recently to clouds, where there is a virtual computing space that consists of numerous virtual machines mapped to the physical machines. This concept is known as virtualization. *Information Week* reports that cloud computing represents a new way, in some cases a better and cheaper way, of delivering enterprise IT. Often, grids and clouds are used interchangeably. However, in general, although the grid focuses on scheduling resources, the cloud focuses on delivering an efficient computing platform for an enterprise.

Web services play a major role in grid and cloud computing. The Globus Alliance was formed with the goal of developing the Open Grid Services Architecture (OGSA). As stated in [GLOB], OGSA "represents an evolution towards a Grid system architecture based on Web services concepts and technologies." The Globus Alliance has released a series of toolkits, the most recent of which is the Globus Toolkit 3.0. It consists of an "open source collection of Grid services that follow OGSA architectural principles. The Globus Toolkit also offers a development environment for producing new Grid services that follow OGSA principles."

Web services for cloud computing include Amazon Web Services (discussed in the previous section), Google Apps, and Salesforce.com CRM. These clouds may utilize grid computing paradigms such as resource scheduling. It is expected that service virtualization will play a major role in cloud computing. In a recent article, it is stated that "Service virtualization is the ability to create a virtual service from one or more predefined service files. Service files are usually generated as a Web Service Description Language (WSD) file by service containers running business applications developed in Java, .NET, PHP type programming languages." The author further states that the services may include outsourced services such as Saas, PaaS, or IaaS or in-house services.

5.9 Summary and Directions

In this chapter, we discussed various types of specialized Web services. First, we discussed Web services for data management and complex data management. Then we discussed Web services for information management and knowledge management. Next we discussed Web services for activity management. This was followed by a discussion of domain Web services. Finally, we discussed some emerging Web services, including the paradigm of "X as a Service."

There is still lot of work to be done on specialized Web services. We need standards for specialized Web services, including Web services for data, information, and knowledge management. Emerging Web services need to be precisely defined, especially the notion of X as a Service. Finally, special services such as Amazon.com Web services need to be developed further. In Part V, we will discuss security for emerging Web services.

Exercises

1. Describe the Web services that may be utilized for data, information, and knowledge management.
2. Describe with an example how Software as a Service may be utilized.

References

[AMAZON] http://en.wikipedia.org/wiki/Amazon_Web_Services

[CAST] Castells, P., B. Foncillas, R. Lara, M. Rico, and J. L. Alonso, Semantic Web Technologies for Economic and Financial Information Management, http://nets.ii.uam.es/aniceto/publications/esws04.pdf

[CERI84] Ceri, S. and G. Pelagatti, *Distributed Databases, Principles and Systems*, McGraw-Hill, New York, 1984.

[CODD70] Codd, E. F., A Relational Model of Data for Large Shared Data Banks, *Communications of the ACM*, 13, 6, 1970.

[DATA] http://www.xml.com/pub/a/2007/10/25/data-sources-as-web-services.html

[DATE90] Date, C., *An Introduction to Database Systems*, Addison-Wesley, Reading, MA, 1990.

[FINI09] Finin, T. et al., Assured information sharing lifecycle, *Proceedings Intelligence and Security Informatics Conference*, Dallas, TX, June 2009.

[GLOB] Globus Alliance, http://en.wikipedia.org/wiki/Globus_Alliance

[HARV96] Knowledge management, *Harvard Business Review*, 1996.

[IEEE03] Audio mining, Special Issue, *IEEE Computing*, January 2003.

[MORE01] Morey, D., M. Maybury, and B. Thuraisingham (Editors), *Knowledge Management*, MIT Press, Cambridge, MA, 2001.

[OBLIE2] http://www.e3value.com/projects/ourprojects/obelix

[ONTO] http://www.semantic-web.at/57.219.219.press.ontologies-for-e-business.htm

[REST-SOAP] http://intertwingly.net/stories/2002/07/20/restSoap.html

[RFID] http://dvs.tu-darmstadt.de/staff/bornhoevd/ISWC%2704.pdf

[LIFE] Ontologies for the life sciences. 222.jonathanborden-md.com/HealthcareSemWeb. ppt

[SING06] Singh, R. and A. F. Salam, Semantic information assurance for secure distributed knowledge management: A business process perspective, *IEEE Transactions on Systems, Man and Cybernetics*, May 2006.

[SMIT03] Smith, B., Williams, J., and Schulze-Kremer, S., The ontology of the gene ontology", in *Biomedical and Health Informatics: From Foundations to Applications*, Proceedings of the Annual Symposium of the American Medical Informatics Association, Washington DC, November 2003, 609–613.

[SOFT] Software as a Service, http://en.wikipedia.org/wiki/Software_as_a_service

[SQL3] SQL3, American National Standards Institute, Draft, 1992.

[Sure05] Sure, Y. and Studer, R., Semantic Web technologies for digital libraries, *Library Management*, 26:4/5, 190–195.

[XML] Thinking XML: A glimpse in XML in the financial services industry. http://www-128.ibm.com/developerworks/xml/library/x-think22.html

[THUR97] Thuraisingham, B., *Data Management Systems Evolution and Interoperation*, CRC Press, Boca Raton, FL, 1997.

[THUR98] Thuraisingham, B., *Data Mining: Technologies, Techniques, Tools and Trends*, CRC Press, Boca Raton, FL, 1998.

[THUR00] Thuraisingham, B., *Web Data Management and Electronic Commerce*, CRC Press, Boca Raton, FL, 2000.

[THUR01] Thuraisingham, B., *Managing and Mining Multimedia Databases for the Electronic Enterprise*, CRC Press, Boca Raton, FL, 2001.

[THUR07] Thuraisingham, B. et al., An Integrated Platform for Secure Geospatial Information Exchange through the Semantic Web, Technical Report, UTDCS 01-07, January 2007.

[TELE] Parlay-X, http://en.wikipedia.org/wiki/Parlay_X

[TRAS] Trastour, D. et al., Semantic Web Support for the Business-to-Business E-Commerce Lifecycle, http://www2002.org/CDROM/refereed/211/

[ULLM88] [VLDB] *Proceedings of the Very Large Database Conference Series*, Morgan Kaufman, San Francisco, CA.

[WFMC] Workflow Management Coalition, http://en.wikipedia.org/wiki/Workflow_Management_Coalition

[ZHAO] Zhao, G. et al., Engineering an Ontology for Financial securities fraud, http://www.ffpoirot.org/Publications/eofsf_20-08-final.pdf

Chapter 6

Semantic Web Services

6.1 Overview

In the previous chapters, we discussed service-oriented computing, SOA, and Web services, and service-oriented analysis and design as well as some of the emerging Web services. While services are becoming an essential aspect of computing, at present they are not semantically enabled. Furthermore, while the current Web technologies facilitate the integration of information from a syntactic point of view, there is still a lot to be done to handle the different semantics of various systems and applications. That is, current Web technologies depend a lot on the "human-in-the-loop" for information management integration. In this chapter, we will discuss semantic Web technologies and how Web services could exploit these technologies so that they are semantically enabled.

Tim Berners-Lee, the father of the World Wide Web (WWW), realized the inadequacies of current Web technologies and subsequently strived to make the Web more intelligent. His goal was to have a Web that will essentially free humans from the burden of having to integrate disparate information sources as well as to carry out extensive searches. He then came to the conclusion that one needs machine-understandable Web pages and the use of ontologies for information integration. This resulted in the notion of the semantic Web [LEE01]. The Web services that take advantage of semantic Web technologies are semantic Web services.

A semantic Web can be thought of as a Web that is highly intelligent and sophisticated so that little or no human intervention is necessary to carry out tasks such as scheduling appointments, coordinating activities, searching for complex documents, as well as integrating disparate databases and information systems. While much progress has been made toward developing such an intelligent Web, there is still a lot to be done. For example, technologies such as ontology matching, intelligent agents, and markup languages are contributing a lot toward developing the semantic Web. Nevertheless, one still needs the human to make decisions and take actions.

Recently, there have been many developments on the semantic Web front. The World Wide Web Consortium (W3C) is specifying standards for the semantic Web [W3C]. These standards include specifications for XML, RDF, and interoperability. However, it is also very important that the semantic Web be secure. That is, the components constituting the semantic Web have to be secure. The components include XML, RDF, and ontologies. In addition, we need secure information integration. We also need to examine trust issues for the semantic Web. It is, therefore, important that we need standards for securing the semantic Web, including specifications for secure XML, secure RDF, and secure interoperability (see [THUR05]). In this chapter, we will discuss the various components of the semantic Web and discuss semantic Web services.

While agents are crucial to manage the data and the activities on the semantic Web, agents are not usually treated as part of semantic Web technologies by some, while others consider agents as part of the semantic Web. Because the subject of agents is vast and numerous efforts to develop agents as well as secure agents are under way, we do not discuss agents as part of this book. However, we mention agents throughout the book as it is these agents that use XML and RDF and make sense of the data and understand Web pages. Agents act on behalf of the users. Agents communicate with each other using well-defined protocols. Various types of agents have been developed, depending on the tasks they carry out. These include mobile agents, intelligent agents, search agents, and knowledge management agents. Agents invoke Web services to carry out the operations. For details of agents, we refer to [HEND01].

The organization of this chapter is as follows. In Section 6.2, we will provide an overview of the layered architecture for the semantic Web as specified by Tim Berners-Lee. Components such as XML, RDF, Ontologies, and Web Rules are discussed in Sections 6.3 through 6.6. Semantic Web services are discussed in Section 6.7. The chapter is summarized in Section 6.8. Much of the discussion of the semantic Web is summarized from the book by Antoniou and van Harmelen [ANTO03]. For an up-to-date specification, we refer the reader to [W3C].

6.2 Layered Technology Stack

Figure 6.1 illustrates the layered technology stack for the semantic Web (also illustrated in Chapter 1). This is the architecture that was developed by Tim Berners-Lee. Essentially, the semantic Web consists of layers where each layer takes advantage

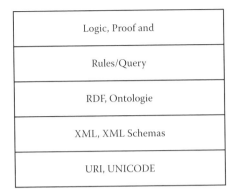

| Logic, Proof and |
| Rules/Query |
| RDF, Ontologie |
| XML, XML Schemas |
| URI, UNICODE |

Figure 6.1   Layered architecture for the semantic Web.

of the technologies of the previous layer. The lowest layer is the protocol layer, and this is usually not included in the discussion of the semantic technologies. The next layer is the XML layer. XML is a document representation language and will be discussed in Section 6.3. While XML is sufficient to specify syntax, semantic such as "the creator of document D is John" is hard to specify in XML. Therefore, the W3C developed RDF, which uses XML syntax. The semantic Web community then went further and came up with a specification of ontologies in languages such as OWL. Note that OWL addresses the inadequacies of RDF. In order to reason about various policies, the semantic Web community has come up with a Web rules language such as SWRL (Semantic Web Rules Language) and Rules ML (Rules Markup Language).

The functional architecture is illustrated in Figure 6.2. It is essentially a service-oriented architecture that hosts Web services. The semantic Web technologies are used by the Web services, as we will see in Part IV.

6.3 XML

XML is needed due to the limitations of HTML and complexities of SGML. It is an extensible markup language specified by the W3C (World Wide Web Consortium) and designed to make the interchange of structured documents over the Internet easier. An important aspect of XML used to be Document Type Definitions (DTDs), which define the role of each element of text in a formal model. XML schemas have now become critical to specify the structure. XML schemas are also XML documents. This section will discuss various components of XML, including statements, elements, attributes, and schemas. The components of XML are illustrated in Figure 6.3.

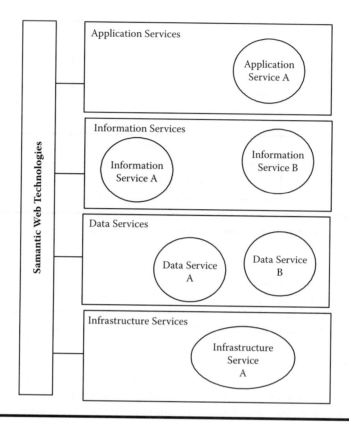

Figure 6.2   Functional architecture for the semantic Web.

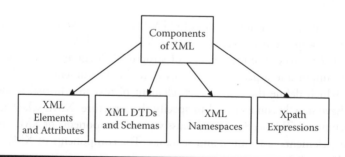

Figure 6.3   Components of XML.

6.3.1 XML Statement and Elements

The following is an example of an XML statement that describes the fact that "John Smith is a Professor in Texas." The elements are name and state. The XML statement is as follows:

```
<Professor>
      <name> John Smith </name>
      <state> Texas </state>
</Professor>
```

6.3.2 XML Attributes

Suppose we want to specify that there is a professor called John Smith who makes $60K, then we can use either elements or attributes to specify this. The following example shows the use of attributes Name and Salary:

```
<Professor
      Name = "John Smith", Access = All, Read
      Salary = "60K"
      </Professor>
```

6.3.3 XML DTDs

DTDs (Document Type Definitions) essentially specify the structure of XML documents.

Consider the following DTD for Professor with elements Name and State. This will be specified as:

```
<!ELEMENT Professor Officer (Name, State)>
<!ELEMENT name (#PCDATA)>
<!ELEMENR state (#PCDATA)>
<!ELEMENT access (#PCDATA).>
```

6.3.4 XML Schemas

While DTDs were the early attempts to specify structure for XML documents, XML schemas are far more elegant to specify structures. Unlike DTDs, XML schemas essentially use the XML syntax for specification.

Consider the following example:

```
<ComplexType = name = "ProfessorType">
      <Sequence>
      <element name = "name" type = "string"/>
      <element name = "state" type = "string"/>
      <Sequence>
</ComplexType>
```

6.3.5 XML Namespaces

Namespaces are used for DISAMBIGUATION. An example follows.

```
<CountryX: Academic-Institution
      Xmlns: CountryX = http://www.CountryX.edu/Instution DTD"
      Xmlns: USA = "http://www.USA.edu/Instution DTD"
      Xmlns: UK = "http://www.UK.edu/Instution DTD"
<USA: Title = College
      USA: Name = "University of Texas at Dallas"
      USA: State = Texas"
<UK: Title = University
      UK: Name = "Cambridge University"
      UK: State = Cambs
</CountryX: Academic-Institution>
```

6.3.6 XML Federations/Distribution

XML data may be distributed and the databases may form federations. This is illustrated in the following segment:

Site 1 document:

```
<Professor-name>
      <ID> 111 </ID>
      <Name> John Smith </name>
      <State> Texas </state>
</Professor-name>
```

Site 2 document:

```
<Professor-salary>
      <ID> 111 </ID>
      <salary> 60K </salary>
<Professor-salary>
```

6.3.7 XML-QL, XQuery, XPath, and XSLT

XML-QL and XQuery are query languages that have been proposed for XML. XPath is used to specify the queries. Essentially, Xpath expressions may be used to reach a particular element in the XML statement. In our research, we have specified policy rules as Xpath expressions (see [BERT04]). XSLT is used to present XML documents. Details are given in www.w3c.org as well as in [ANTO03]. Another useful reference is [LAUR00].

6.4 RDF

While XML is ideal to specify the syntax of various statements, it is difficult to specify the semantics of a statement with XML. For example, with XML it is difficult to specify statements such as

Engineer is a subclass of Employee.
Engineer inherits all properties of Employee.

Note that the foregoing statement specifies the class/subclass and inheritance relationships. RDF was developed by Tim Berners-Lee and his team so that the inadequacies of XML could be handled. RDF uses XML Syntax. Additional constructs are needed for RDF, and we discuss some of them. Details can be found in [ANTO03].

Resource Description Framework (RDF) is the essence of the semantic Web. It provides semantics with the use of ontologies to various statements and uses XML syntax. RDF Concepts include the basic model, which consists of Resources, Properties, and Statements; and the container model, which consists of Bag, Sequence, and Alternative. We discuss some of the essential concepts. The components of RDF are illustrated in Figure 6.4.

6.4.1 RDF Basics

The RDF basic model consists of Resource, Property, and Statement. In RDF, everything is a resource, such as Person, Vehicle, and Animal. Properties describe relationships between resources such as "bought," "invented," and "ate." Statement is a triple of the form: (Object, Property, Value). Examples of statements are

Berners-Lee invented the Semantic Web
Tom ate the Apple
Mary bought a Dress

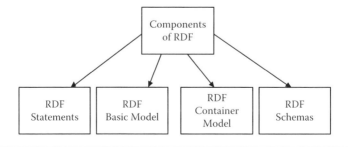

Figure 6.4   Components of RDF.

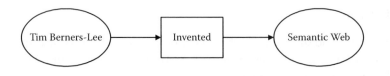

Figure 6.5   RDF statement.

Figure 6.5 illustrates a statement in RDF. Here, Berners-Lee is the Object, Semantic Web is the Value, and "invented" is the property.

6.4.2 RDF Container Model

The RDF container model consists of Bag, Sequence, and Alternative. As described in [ANTO03], these constructs are specified in RDF as follows:

Bag: Unordered container, may contain multiple occurrences
   Rdf: Bag
Seq: Ordered container, may contain multiple occurrences
   Rdf: Seq
Alt: A set of alternatives
   Rdf: Alt

6.4.3 RDF Specification

As stated in [ANTO03], RDF specifications have been given for Attributes, Types, Nesting, Containers, etc. An example is the following:

"Berners-Lee is the author of the book *Semantic Web*"

The above statement is specified as follows (see also [ANTO03]):

```
<rdf: RDF
 xmlns: rdf = "http://w3c.org/1999/02-22-rdf-syntax-ns#"
 xmlns: xsd = "http:// - - -
 xmlns: uni = "http:// - - - - -
<rdf: Description: rdf: about = "949352"
 <uni: name = Berners Lee</uni:name>
 <uni: title> Professor < uni:title>
 </rdf: Description>
<rdf: Description rdf: about: "ZZZ"
       < uni: bookname> semantic web <uni:bookname>
       < uni: authoredby: Berners Lee <uni:authoredby>
 </rdf: Description>
 </rdf: RDF>
```

6.4.4 RDF Schemas

While XML schemas specify the structure of the XML document and can be considered to be metadata, the RDF schema specifies relationships such as the class/subclass relationships. For example, we need the RDF schema to specify statements such as "engineer is a subclass of employee." The following is the RDF specification for this statement.

```
<rdfs: Class rdf: ID = "engineer"
<rdfs: comment>
The class of Engineers
All engineers are employees
<rdfs: comment>
<rdfs: subClassof rdf: resource = "employee"/>
<rdfs: Class>
```

6.4.5 RDF Axiomatic Semantics

First-order logic is used to specify formulas and inferencing. The following constructs are needed:

Built in functions (First) and predicates (Type)
Modus Ponens: From A and If A then B, deduce B

The following example is taken from [ANTI03]:

Example: All Containers are Resources; that is if X is a container, then X is a resource.
Type(?C, Container) $\Rightarrow$ Type(?C, Resource)
If we have Type (A, Container) then we can infer (Type A, Resource)

6.4.6 RDF Inferencing

Unlike XML, RDF has inferencing capabilities. While first-order logic provides a proof system, it will be computationally infeasible to develop such a system using first-order logic. As a result, Horn clause logic was developed for logic programming [LLOY87]; this is still computationally expensive. The semantic Web is based on a restricted logic called descriptive logic, and details can be found in [ANTO03]. RDF uses If–Then rules as follows:

```
IF E contains the triples (?u, rdfs: subClassof, ?v)
and (?v, rdfs: subClassof ?w)
THEN
E also contains the triple (?u, rdfs: subClassOf, ?w)
```

```
That is, if u is a subclass of v, and v is a subclass of w,
then u is a subclass of w.
```

6.4.7 RDF Query

Similar to XML query languages such as X-Query and XML-QL, query languages are also being developed for RDF. One can query RDF using XML, but this will be very difficult as RDF is much richer than XML. Therefore, RQL has been developed. RQL is an SQL-like language has been developed for RDF. It is of the form:

Select from "RDF document" where some "condition"

SPARQL. The RDF Data group at W3C has developed a query language for RDF called SPARQL which is becoming the standard now for querying RDF documents. We are developing SPARQL query processing algorithms for clouds. We have also developed a query optimizer for SPARQL queries.

6.5 Ontologies

Ontologies are common definitions for any entity, person, or thing. Ontologies are needed to clarify various terms and, therefore, they are crucial for machine-understandable Web pages. Several ontologies have been defined and are available for use. Defining a common ontology for an entity is a challenge as different groups may come up with different definitions. Therefore, we need mappings for multiple ontologies. That is, these mappings map one ontology to another. Specific languages have been developed for ontologies. Note that RDF was developed because XML is not sufficient to specify semantics such as the class/subclass relationship. RDF is also limited as one cannot express several other properties such as Union and Intersection. Therefore, we need a richer language. Ontology languages were developed by the semantic Web community for this purpose.

OWL (Web Ontology Language) is a popular ontology specification language. It is a language for ontologies and relies on RDF. DARPA (Defense Advanced Research Projects Agency) developed an early language, DAML (DARPA Agent Markup Language). Europeans developed OIL (Ontology Interface Language). DAML+OIL combine both and were the starting point for OWL. OWL was developed by W3C. OWL is based on a subset of first-order logic, and that is descriptive logic.

OWL features include Subclass relationship, Class membership, Equivalence of classes, Classification, and Consistency (e.g., x is an instance of A, A is a subclass of B, x is not an instance of B, etc.).

There are three types of OWL: OWL-Full, OWL-DL, and OWL-Lite. Ontology engineering comprises automated tools for managing ontologies.

The following is an example of an OWL specification:

Textbooks and Coursebooks are the same
EnglishBook is not a FrenchBook
EnglishBook is not a GermanBook

```
< owl: Class rdf: about = "#EnglishBook">
 <owl: disjointWith rdf: resource "#FrenchBook"/>
 <owl: disjointWith rdf: resource = #GermanBook"/>
</owl:Class>
<owl: Class rdf: ID = "TextBook">
 <owl: equivalentClass rdf: resource = "CourseBook"/>
</owl: Class>
```

The following is an OWL specification for Property:

English books are read by Students

```
< owl: ObjectProperty rdf: about = "#readBy">
 <rdfs domain rdf: resource = "#EnglishBook"/>
 <rdfs: range rdf: resource = "#student"/>
<rdfs: subPropertyOf rdf: resource = #involves"/>
</owl: ObjectProperty>
```

The following is an OWL specification for property restriction:

All French books are read only by Frenchstudents

```
< owl: Class rdf: about = "#"FrenchBook">
<rdfs: subClassOf>
 <owl: Restriction>
<owl: onProperty rdf: resource = "#readBy">
<owl: allValuesFrom rdf: resource = #FrenchStudent"/>
</rdfs: subClassOf>
</owl: Class>
```

6.6 Web Rules and SWRL

6.6.1 Web Rules

RDF is built on XML, and OWL is built on RDF. We can express subclass relationships in RDF, and additional relationships can be expressed in OWL. However, reasoning power is still limited in OWL. Therefore, we need to specify rules and subsequently a markup language for rules so that machines can understand and make inferences.

The following are some examples as given in [ANTO03]:

Studies(X,Y), Lives(X,Z), Loc(Y,U), Loc(Z,U) $\Rightarrow$ DomesticStudent(X)
    i.e., if John Studies at UTDallas and John lives on Campbell Road and the
        location of Campbell Road and UTDallas are Richardson then John is a
        Domestic student

Note that Person (X) $\Rightarrow$ Man(X) or Woman(X) is not a rule in predicate logic.

That is, "if X is a person, then X is either a man of a woman" cannot be expressed in first-order predicate logic. Therefore, in predicate logic, we express the foregoing as "if X is a person and X is not a man then X is a woman" and similarly "if X is a person and X is not a woman then X is a man." That is, in predicate logic, we can have a rule of the form:

Person(X) and Not Man(X) $\Rightarrow$ Woman(X)

However, in OWL we can specify the rule "if X is a person then X is a man or X is a woman."

Rules can be monotonic or nonmonotonic.

The following is an example of a monotonic rule:

$\Rightarrow$ Mother(X,Y)
Mother(X,Y) $\Rightarrow$ Parent(X,Y)
If Mary is the mother of John, then Mary is the parent of John.
The rule is of the form:
    B1, B2, ---- Bn $\Rightarrow$ A
That is, if B1, B2, ---Bn hold, then A holds.

In the case of nonmonotonic reasoning, if we have X and NOT X, we do not treat them as inconsistent as in the case of monotonic reasoning. For example, as discussed in [ANTO03], consider the example of an apartment that is acceptable to John. That is, in general, John is prepared to rent an apartment unless the apartment has fewer than two bedrooms and does not allow pets. This can be expressed as follows:

■ $\Rightarrow$ Acceptable(X)
■ Bedroom(X,Y), Y<2 $\Rightarrow$ NOT Acceptable(X)
■ NOT Pets(X) $\Rightarrow$ NOT Acceptable(X)

The first rule states that an apartment is in general acceptable to John. The second rule states that if the apartment has fewer than two bedrooms it is not acceptable to John. The third rule states that if pets are not allowed, then the apartment is not acceptable to John. Note that there could be a contradiction.

But with nonmonotonic reasoning, this is allowed while it is not allowed in monotonic reasoning.

We need rule markup languages for the machine to understand the rules. The various components of logic are expressed in the Rule Markup Language called RuleML developed for the semantic Web. Both monotonic and nonmonotonic rules can be represented in RuleML.

An example representation of Fact Parent(A), which is "A is a parent," is expressed as follows:

```
<fact>
      <atom>
<predicate>Parent</predicate>
<term>
<const>A</const>
</term>
</atom>
</fact>
```

6.6.2 SWRL

W3C has come up with a new rules language that integrates both OWL and Web Rules, and this is SWRL (Semantic Web Rules Language). The authors of SWRL state that SWRL extends the set of OWL axioms to include Horn-like rules. This way, Horn-like rules can be combined with an OWL knowledge base. Such a language will have the representational power of OWL and the reasoning power of logic programming. We illustrate SWRL components in Figure 6.6.

The authors of SWRL (Horrocks et al.) also state that the proposed rules are in the form of an implication between an antecedent (body) and consequent (head). The intended meaning can be read as: whenever the conditions specified in the antecedent hold, then the conditions specified in the consequent must also hold. An XML syntax is also given for these rules based on RuleML and the OWL XML presentation syntax. Furthermore, an RDF concrete syntax based on the OWL RDF/XML exchange syntax is presented. The rule syntaxes are illustrated with several running examples. Finally, we give usage suggestions and cautions.

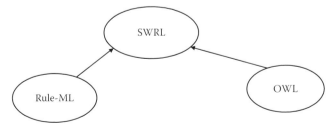

Figure 6.6 SWRL components.

The following is an SWRL example that we have taken from the W3C specification of SWTL [SWRL]. It states that if x1 is the child of x2 and x3 is the brother of x2, then x3 is the uncle of x1. For more details of SWRL, we refer the reader to the W3C specification [SWRL]. The following example uses XML syntax:

```
<ruleml:imp>
 <ruleml:_rlab ruleml:href="#example1"/>
 <ruleml:_body>
 <swrlx:individualPropertyAtom swrlx:property="hasParent">
 <ruleml:var>x1</ruleml:var>
 <ruleml:var>x2</ruleml:var>
 </swrlx:individualPropertyAtom>
 <swrlx:individualPropertyAtom swrlx:property="hasBrother">
 <ruleml:var>x2</ruleml:var>
 <ruleml:var>x3</ruleml:var>
 </swrlx:individualPropertyAtom>
 </ruleml:_body>
 <ruleml:_head>
 <swrlx:individualPropertyAtom swrlx:property="hasUncle">
 <ruleml:var>x1</ruleml:var>
 <ruleml:var>x3</ruleml:var>
 </swrlx:individualPropertyAtom>
 </ruleml:_head>
</ruleml:imp>
```

6.7 Semantic Web Services

Semantic Web services utilize semantic Web technologies. As we have stated in Chapter 3, Web services utilize WSDL and SOAP messages, which are based on XML. With semantic Web technologies, one could utilize RDF to express semantics in the messages as well as with Web services description languages. Ontologies could be utilized for handling heterogeneity. For example, if the words in the messages or service descriptions are ambiguous, then ontologies could resolve these ambiguities. Finally, rule languages such as SWRL could be used for reasoning power for the messages as well as the service descriptions.

As stated in [SWS], the mainstream XML standards for interoperation of Web services specify only syntactic interoperability, not the semantic meaning of messages. For example, WSDL can specify the operations available through a Web service and the structure of data sent and received, but cannot specify the semantic meaning of the data or the semantic constraints on the data. This requires programmers to reach specific agreements on the interaction of Web services and makes automatic Web service composition difficult.

Semantic Web services are built around semantic Web standards for the interchange of semantic data, which makes it easy for programmers to combine data

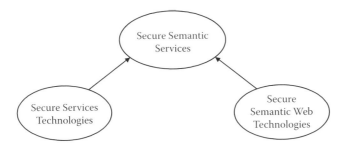

Figure 6.7   Semantic Web services.

from different sources and services without losing meaning. Web services can be activated "behind the scenes" when a Web browser makes a request to a Web server, which then uses various Web services to construct a more sophisticated reply than it would have been able to do on its own. Semantic Web services can also be used by automatic programs that run without any connection to a Web browser.

Later on in this book we will discuss how the semantic Web, security, and Web services could be integrated for semantic Web services. Figure 6.7 illustrates various components of semantic Web services.

6.8 Summary and Directions

This chapter provided an overview of semantic Web technologies and the concept of semantic Web services. In particular, we discussed Tim Berners-Lee's technology stack as well as a functional architecture for the semantic Web. Then we discussed XML, RDF, and ontologies as well as Web rules for the semantic Web. Finally, we discussed semantic Web services and how they can make use of semantic Web technologies.

There is still a lot of work to be carried out on semantic Web services. Much of the development of Web services focuses on XML technologies. We need to develop standards for using RDF for Web services. For example, we need to develop RDF-like languages for Web services descriptions. Research on semantic Web services is just beginning. Secure semantic Web services essentially integrate semantic Web services technologies and security technologies. In Part IV, we will provide details of secure semantic Web services.

Exercises

1. Describe with an example the use of XML for data sharing.
2. Redo Problem 1 with RDF specifications.
3. Describe how ontologies may facilitate interoperability in Problem 1.
4. Show how SWRL may be used to reason across organizations in Problem 1.

References

[ANTO03] Antoniou, G. and F. van Harmelan, *A Semantic Web Primer*, MIT Press, Cambridge, MA, 2003.

[BERT] Bertino, E., Carminati, B., Ferrari, E., and Gupta, A. Selective and authentic third party publication of XML documents, *IEEE Transactions on Knowledge and Data Engineering*, 16:10, 1263–1278, 2004.

[HEND01] Hendler, J., Agents and the Semantic Web, *IEEE Intelligent Systems Journal*, March 2001.

[LAUR00] St. Laurent, S., *XML: A Primer*, M&T Books, NY, NY, 2001.

[LEE01] Berners-Lee, T. and J. Hendler, The Semantic Web, *Scientific American*, May 2001.

[LLOY87] Lloyd, J., *Logic Programming*, Springer, NY, NY, 1987.

[SWRL] http://www.w3.org/Submission/SWRL/#1

[SWS] http://en.wikipedia.org/wiki/Semantic_Web_Services

[THUR05] Thuraisingham, B., *Database and Applications Security: Integrating Data Management and Information Security*, CRC Press, Boca Raton, FL, 2006.

[W3C] www.w3c.org

Chapter 7

Trustworthy Systems

7.1 Overview

As we have stated in Chapter 1, secure Web services integrate trustworthy information systems and Web services. Trustworthy information systems include trustworthy systems, as well as secure data and information systems. Trustworthy systems are systems that are secure and dependable. By dependable systems, we mean systems that have high integrity, are fault-tolerant, and meet real-time constraints. In other words, for a system to be trustworthy, it must be secure, fault-tolerant, meet timing deadlines, and manage high-quality data.

This chapter provides an overview of the various developments in trustworthy systems with special emphasis on secure systems, including secure data systems. The organization of this chapter is as follows. In Section 7.2, we discuss secure systems in some detail. Section 7.3 provides an overview of dependable systems, which include coverage of trust, privacy, integrity, data quality, high-assurance systems, real-time processing, and fault tolerance. In Section 7.4, we discuss Web security in some detail. The chapter is summarized in Section 7.5.

7.2 Secure Systems

7.2.1 Overview

Secure systems include secure operating systems, secure data management systems, secure networks, and other types of systems such as Web-based secure systems, and secure digital libraries, among others. This section provides an overview of the various developments in information security.

In Section 7.2.2, we discuss basic concepts such as access control for information systems. Section 7.2.3 provides an overview of the various types of secure systems. Secure operating systems will be discussed in Section 7.2.4. Secure database systems will be discussed in Section 7.2.5. Network security will be discussed in Section 7.2.6. Emerging trends is the subject of Section 7.2.7. The impact of the Web is given in Section 7.2.8. An overview of the steps to building secure systems will be provided in Section 7.2.9.

7.2.2 Access Control and Other Security Concepts

Access control models include those for discretionary security and mandatory security. In this section, we discuss both aspects of access control and also consider other issues. In discretionary access control models, users or groups of users are granted access to data objects. These data objects could be files, relations, objects, or even data items. Access control policies include rules such as "User U has read access to Relation R1 and write access to Relation R7." Access control could also include negative access control, where user U does not have read access to Relation R.

In mandatory access control, subjects that act on behalf of users are granted access to objects based on some policy. A well-known policy is the Bell and La Padula policy [BELL73], where subjects are granted clearance levels and objects have sensitivity levels. The set of security levels forms a partially ordered lattice where Unclassified < Confidential < Secret < Top Secret. The policy has two properties: A subject has read access to an object if its clearance level dominates that of the object, and a subject has write access to an object if its level is dominated by that of the object.

Other types of access control include role-based access control. Here, access is granted to users depending on their roles and the functions they perform. For example, personnel managers have access to salary data, while project mangers have access to project data. The idea here is generally to give access on a need-to-know basis.

While the early access control policies were formulated for operating systems, these policies have been extended to include other systems such as database systems, networks, and distributed systems. For example, a policy for networks includes policies for not only reading and writing but also for sending and receiving messages.

Other security policies include administration policies. These policies include those for ownership of data as well as how to manage and distribute the data. Database administrators as well as system security officers are involved in formulating the administration policies.

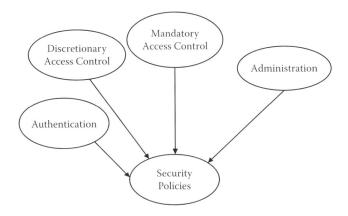

Figure 7.1   Security policies.

Security policies also include policies for identification and authentication. Each user or subject acting on behalf of a user has to be identified and authenticated, possibly using some password mechanisms. Identification and authentication become more complex for distributed systems. For example, how can a user be authenticated at a global level?

The steps to developing secure systems include developing a security policy, developing a model of the system, designing the system, and verifying and validating the system. The methods used for verification depend on the level of assurance that is expected. Testing and risk analysis are also part of the process. These activities will determine the vulnerabilities as well as help assess the risks involved. Figure 7.1 illustrates various types of security policies.

7.2.3 Types of Secure Systems

In the previous section, we discussed various policies for building secure systems. In this section, we elaborate on various types of secure systems. Much of the early research in the 1960s and 1970s was on securing operating systems. Early security policies such as the Bell and LaPadula policy were formulated for operating systems. Subsequently, secure operating systems such as Honeywell's SCOMP and MULTICS were developed (see [IEEE83]). Other policies such as those based on noninterference also emerged in the early 1980s.

While early research on secure database systems was reported in the 1970s, it was not until the early 1980s that active research began in this area. Much of the focus was on multilevel secure database systems. The security policy for operating systems was modified slightly. For example, the write policy for secure database systems was modified to state that a subject has write access to an object if the subject's

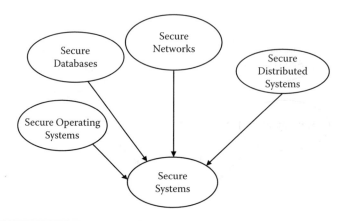

Figure 7.2   Secure systems.

level is that of the object. Since database systems enforced relationships between data and focused on semantics, there were additional security concerns. For example, data could be classified based on content, context, and time. The problem of posing multiple queries and inferring sensitive information from the legitimate responses became a concern. This problem is now known as the inference problem. Also, research was carried out not only on securing relational systems but also on object systems as well as distributed systems, among others.

Research on computer networks began in the late 1970s and continued throughout the 1980s and beyond. The networking protocols were extended to incorporate security features. The result was secure network protocols. The policies include those for reading, writing, sending, and receiving messages. Research on encryption and cryptography has received much prominence due to networks and the Web. Security for stand-alone systems was extended to include distributed systems. These systems included distributed databases and distributed operating systems. Much of the research on distributed systems now focuses on securing the Web, an area known as Web security, as well as securing systems such as distributed object management systems.

As new systems emerge, such as data warehouses, collaborative computing systems, multimedia systems, and agent systems, security for such systems has to be investigated. With the advent of the World Wide Web, security is being given serious consideration by not only government organizations but also commercial organizations. With e-commerce, it is important to protect the company's intellectual property. Figure 7.2 illustrates various types of secure systems.

7.2.4 Secure Operating Systems

Work on security for operating systems was carried out extensively in the 1960s and 1970s. The research still continues as new kinds of operating systems such

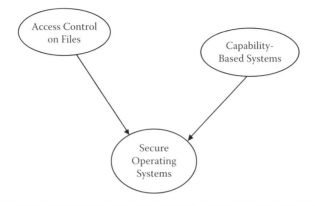

Figure 7.3　Secure operating systems.

as Windows, Linux, and other products emerge. The early ideas included access control lists and capability-based systems. Access control lists specify the types of access that processes, which are called subjects, have on files, which are objects. The access is usually read or write access. Capability lists are capabilities that a process must posses to access certain resources in the system. For example, a process with a particular capability can write into certain parts of the memory.

Work on mandatory security for operating systems started with the Bell and La Padula security model, which has two properties:

- The simple security property states that a subject has read access to an object if the subject's security level dominated the level of the object.
- The *-property (pronounced star property) states that a subject has write access to an object if the subject's security level is dominated by that of the object.

Since then, variations of this model as well as a popular model called the noninterference model (see [GOGU82]) have been proposed. The noninterference model is essentially about higher-level processes not interfering with lower-level processes.

As stated earlier, security is becoming critical for operating systems. Corporations such as Microsoft are putting in many resources to ensure that their products are secure. Often, we hear of vulnerabilities in various operating systems and about hackers trying to break into operating systems. Therefore, this is an area that will continue to receive much attention for the next several years. Figure 7.3 illustrates some key aspects of operating systems security.

7.2.5　Secure Database Systems

Work on discretionary security for databases began in the 1970s when security aspects were investigated for System R at IBM Almaden Research Center. Essentially, the security properties specified the read and write access that a user may have to relations, attributes, and data elements. In the 1980s and 1990s, security issues were investigated for object systems. Here, the security properties specified the access that users had to objects, instance variables, and classes. In addition to read and write access, method execution access was also specified.

Since the early 1980s, much of the focus has been on multilevel secure database management systems. These systems essentially enforce the mandatory policy discussed in Section 7.2.2. Since the 1980s, various designs, prototypes, and commercial products of multilevel database systems have been developed. Ferrari and Thuraisingham give a detailed survey of some of the developments [FERR00]. Examples include the SeaView effort by SRI International and the LOCK Data Views effort by Honeywell. These efforts extended relational models with security properties. One challenge was to design a model where a user sees different values at different security levels. For example, at the Unclassified level, an employee's salary may be $20K and at the secret level it may be $50K. In the standard relational model, such ambiguous values cannot be represented due to integrity properties.

Note that several other significant developments have been made on multilevel security for other types of database systems. These include security for object database systems [THUR89]. In this effort, security properties specify read, write, and method execution policies. Much work was also carried out on secure concurrency control and recovery. The idea here is to enforce security properties and still meet consistency without having covert channels. Research was also carried out on multilevel security for distributed, heterogeneous, and federated database systems. Another area that received a lot of attention was the inference problem. For details on the inference problem, we refer the reader to [THUR93]. For secure concurrency control, we refer the reader to the numerous algorithms by Atluri, Bertino, Jajodia et al. (see, for example, [ATLU97]). For information on secure distributed and heterogeneous databases as well as secure federated databases, we refer to [THUR91] and [THUR94].

As database systems become more sophisticated, securing these systems will become more and more difficult. Some of the current work focuses on securing data warehouses, multimedia databases, and Web databases (see, for example, Proceedings of the IFIP Database Security Conference Series). Figure 7.4 illustrates various types of secure database systems. The functions of a secure data manager are illustrated in Figure 7.5.

7.2.6 Secure Networks

With the advent of the Web and the interconnection of different systems and applications, networks have proliferated over the past decade. There are public networks, private networks, classified networks, and unclassified networks. We continually hear about networks being infected with viruses and worms. Furthermore, networks

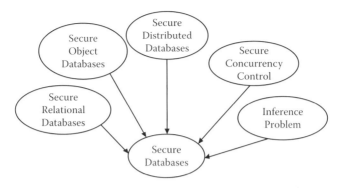

Figure 7.4   Secure database systems.

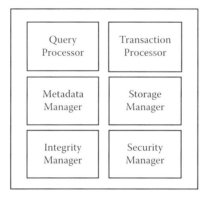

Figure 7.5   Secure data manager.

are being invaded by malicious code and unauthorized individuals. Therefore, network security is emerging as one of the major areas in information security.

Various techniques have been proposed for network security. Encryption and cryptography are still dominating much of the research. For a discussion of various encryption techniques, we refer the reader to [HASS00]. Data mining techniques are being extensively applied for intrusion detection (see [NING04]). There has also been a lot of work on network protocol security, where security is incorporated into the various layers of the protocol stack such as the network layer, transport layer, and session layer (see [TANN90]). Verification and validation techniques are also being investigated for securing networks. Trusted Network Interpretation (also called The Red Book) was developed back in the 1980s to evaluate secure networks. Various books on the topic have also been published (see [KAUF02]). Figure 7.6 illustrates network security techniques.

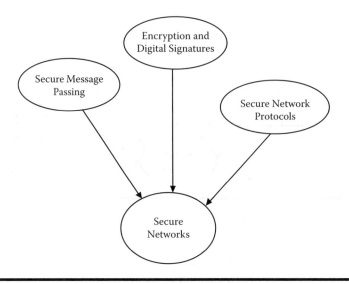

Figure 7.6 Secure networks.

7.2.7 Emerging Trends

In the mid-1990s, research in secure systems expanded to include emerging systems. These included securing collaborative computing systems, multimedia computing, and data warehouses. Data mining has resulted in new security concerns. Since users now have access to various data mining tools and they could make sensitive associations, it could exacerbate the inference problem. On the other hand, data mining could also help with security problems such as intrusion detection and auditing.

The advent of the Web resulted in extensive investigations of security for digital libraries and electronic commerce. In addition to developing sophisticated encryption techniques, security research also focused on securing the Web clients as well as servers. Programming languages such as Java were designed with security in mind. Much research was also carried out on securing agents.

Secure distributed system research focused on security for distributed object management systems. Organizations such as OMG (Object Management Group) formed working groups to investigate security properties [OMG]. As a result, we now have commercially available secure distributed object management systems. Figure 7.7 illustrates the various emerging secure systems and concepts.

7.2.8 Impact of the Web

The advent of the Web has greatly impacted security. Security is now part of mainstream computing. Government organizations as well as commercial organizations are concerned about security. For example, in a financial transaction,

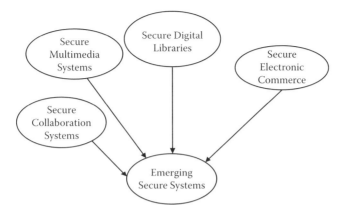

Figure 7.7 Emerging trends.

millions of dollars could be lost if security is not maintained. With the Web, all kinds of information are available about individuals and, therefore, privacy may be compromised.

Various security solutions are being proposed to secure the Web. In addition to encryption, the focus is on securing clients as well as servers. That is, end-to-end security has to be maintained. Web security also has an impact on electronic commerce. That is, when one carries out transactions on the Web, it is critical that security be maintained. Information such as credit card numbers and social security numbers must be protected.

All of the security issues discussed in the previous sections have to be considered for the Web. For example, appropriate security policies have to be formulated. This is a challenge, as no one person owns the Web. The various secure systems, including secure operating systems, secure database systems, secure networks, and secure distributed systems, may be integrated in a Web environment. Therefore, this integrated system has to be secure. Problems such as inference and privacy problems may be exacerbated due to the various data mining tools. The various agents on the Web have to be secure. In certain cases, trade-offs need to be made between security and other features. That is, quality of service is an important consideration. In addition to technological solutions, legal aspects also have to be examined. That is, lawyers and engineers have to work together. While much progress has been made on Web security, there is still a lot to be done as progress is made on Web technologies. Figure 7.8 illustrates aspects of Web security. For a discussion of Web security, we refer the reader to [GHOS98].

7.2.9 Steps to Building Secure Systems

In this section, we outline the steps to building secure systems. Note that our discussion is general and applicable to any secure system. However, we may need to

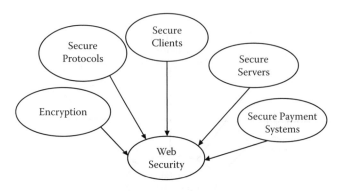

Figure 7.8 Web security.

adapt the steps for individual systems. For example, to build secure distributed database systems, we need secure database systems as well as secure networks. Therefore, multiple systems have to be composed.

The first step to building a secure system is developing a security policy. The policy can be stated in an informal language and then formalized. The policy essentially specifies the rules that the system must satisfy. Then the security architecture has to be developed. The architecture will include the security critical components. These are the components that enforce the security policy and therefore should be trusted. The next step is to design the system. For example, if the system is a database system, the query processor, transaction manager, storage manager, and metadata manager modules are designed. The design of the system has to be analyzed for vulnerabilities. The next phase is the development phase. Once the system is implemented, it has to undergo security testing. This will include designing test cases and making sure that the security policy is not violated. Furthermore, depending on the level of assurance expected of the system, formal verification techniques may be used to verify and validate the system. Finally, the system will be ready for evaluation. Note that initially systems were being evaluated using the Trusted Computer Systems Evaluation Criteria [TCSE85]. There are interpretations of these criteria for networks [TNI87] and for databases [TDI91]. There are also several companion documents for various concepts such as auditing and inference control. Note that more recently some other criteria have been developed, including the Common Criteria and the Federal Criteria.

Note that before the system is installed in an operational environment, one needs to develop a concept of operation of the environment. Risk assessment has to be carried out. Once the system is installed, it has to be monitored so that security violations, including unauthorized intrusions, are detected. Figure 7.9 illustrates the steps. An overview of building secure systems can be found in [GASS88].

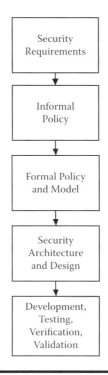

Figure 7.9 Steps to building secure systems.

7.3 Dependable Systems

7.3.1 Overview

As we have discussed earlier, by dependability we mean features such as trust, privacy, integrity, data quality and provenance, and rights management among others. We have separated confidentiality and included it as part of security. Therefore, essentially trustworthy systems include both secure systems and dependable systems. (Note that this is not a standard definition.)

Whether we are discussing security, integrity, privacy, trust, or rights management, there is always a cost involved. That is, at what cost do we enforce security, privacy, and trust? Is it feasible to implement sophisticated privacy policies and trust management policies? In addition to bringing lawyers and policymakers together with the technologists, we also need to bring economists into the picture. We need to carry out economic trade-offs for enforcing security, privacy, trust, and rights management. Essentially, what we need are flexible policies for security, privacy, trust, and rights management.

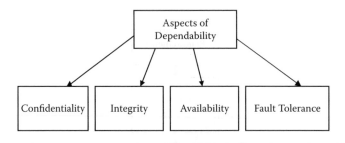

Figure 7.10   Aspects of dependability.

In this section, we will discuss various aspects of dependability. Trust issues will be discussed in Section 7.3.2. Digital rights management is discussed in Section 7.3.3. Privacy is discussed in Section 7.3.4. Integrity issues are discussed in Section 7.3.5. Data quality and data provenance are discussed in Section 7.3.5. Fault tolerance and real-time processing are discussed in Section 7.3.5. Figure 7.10 illustrates the dependability aspects.

7.3.2 Trust Management

Trust management is all about managing the trust that one individual or group has in another. That is, even if a user has access to the data, do I trust the user so that I can release the data? The user may have the clearance or possess the credentials; but he or she may not be trustworthy. Trust depends on the user's behavior. The user may have betrayed one's confidence or carried out some act that is inappropriate in nature. Therefore, I may not trust that user. Now, even if I do not trust say John, Jane may trust John, and she may share her data with John. That is, John may not be trustworthy to Jim, but he may be trustworthy to Jane.

The question is how do we implement trust? Can we trust someone partially? Can we trust John 50% of the time and Jane 70% of the time? If we trust someone partially, then can we share some of the information? How do we trust the data that we have received from Bill? That is, if we do not trust Bill, then can we trust the data he gives us? A lot of work has been done on trusted management systems as well as trust negotiation systems. Winslett et al. have carried out extensive work and developed specification languages for trust as well as designed trust negotiation systems (see [YU03]). The question is, how do two parties negotiate trust? A may share data D with B if B shares data C with A. A may share data D with B only if B does not share this data with F. There are many such rules that one can enforce, and the challenge is to develop a system that consistently enforces the trust rules or policies.

7.3.3 Digital Rights Management

Closely related to trust management is managing digital rights. This whole area has come to be called DRM (Digital Rights Management). This is especially critical for entertainment applications. Who owns the copyright to a video or an audio recording? How can rights be propagated? What happens if the rights are violated? That is, can I distribute copyrighted films and music on the Web?

We have heard a lot about the controversy surrounding Napster and similar organizations. Is DRM a technical issue or is it a legal issue? How can we bring technologists, lawyers, and policymakers together so that rights can be managed properly? There have been numerous articles, discussions, and debates about DRM. A useful source is [DRM].

7.3.4 Privacy

Privacy is about protecting information about individuals. Furthermore, an individual can specify to a Web service provider the information that can be released about him or her. Privacy has been discussed a great deal in the past, especially when it relates to protecting medical information about patients. Social scientists as well as technologists have been working on privacy issues.

Privacy has received enormous attention during recent years. This is mainly because of the advent of the Web, the semantic Web, counterterrorism, and national security. For example, in order to extract information about various individuals and perhaps prevent and/or detect potential terrorist attacks, data mining tools are being examined. We have heard much about national security versus privacy in the media. This is mainly due to the fact that people are now realizing that to handle terrorism, the government may need to collect data about individuals and mine it to extract information. Data may be in relational databases or it may be text, video, and images. This is causing a major concern with various civil liberties unions (see [THUR03]). Therefore, technologists, policymakers, social scientists, and lawyers are working together to provide solutions to handle privacy violations.

7.3.5 Integrity, Data Quality, and High Assurance

Integrity is about maintaining the accuracy of the data as well as the processes. Accuracy of the data is discussed as part of data quality. Process integrity is about ensuring the processes are not corrupted. For example, we need to ensure that the processes are not malicious processes. Malicious processes may corrupt the data due to unauthorized modifications. In order to ensure integrity, the software has to be tested as well as verified in order to develop high-assurance systems.

The database community has ensured integrity by ensuring integrity constraints (e.g., the salary value has to be positive) as well as by ensuring the correctness of the data when multiple processes access the data. In order to achieve correctness, techniques such as concurrency control are enforced. The idea is to enforce appropriate locks so that multiple processes do not access the data at the same time and corrupt the data.

Data quality is about ensuring the accuracy of the data. The accuracy of the data may depend on who touched the data. For example, if the source of the data is not trustworthy, then the data quality value may be low. Essentially, some quality value is assigned to each piece of data. When data is composed, quality values are assigned to the data in such a way that the resulting value is a function of the quality values of the original data.

Data provenance techniques also determine the quality of the data. Note that data provenance is about maintaining the history of the data. This will include information such as who accesses the data for read/write purposes. Then, based on this history, one could assign quality values to the data as well as determine when the data is misused.

Other closely related topics include real-time processing and fault tolerance. Real-time processing is about the processes meeting the timing constraints. For example, if we are to get stock quotes to purchase stocks, we need to get the information in real-time. It does not help if the information arrives after the trading desk is closed for business for the day. Similarly, real-time processing techniques also have to ensure that the data is current. Getting yesterday's stock quotes is not sufficient to make intelligent decisions. Fault tolerance is about ensuring that the processes recover from faults. Faults could be accidental or malicious. In the case of faults, the actions of the processes have to be redone in case the processes aborted.

Note that in order to build high-assurance systems, we need the systems to handle faults, be secure, and also handle real-time constraints. Real-time processing and security are conflicting goals, as we have discussed in [THUR05a]. For example, a malicious process could ensure that critical timing constraints are missed. Furthermore, in order to enforce all the access control checks, some processes may miss the deadlines. Therefore, what we need are flexible policies that will determine which aspects are critical for a particular situation.

7.4 Web Security

7.4.1 Overview

Because the Web is essential for the semantic Web, we will discuss Web security in more detail. In particular, the threats and solutions are discussed. The Web has had a major impact on developments in data management technologies. However, the Web also causes major security concerns. This is because with the Web, users from all over the world can access the data and information on the Web as well as compromise the security of the data, information, systems, and applications. Therefore, protecting the information and applications on the Web is critical.

This section will review the various threats to information systems on the Web with special emphasis on threats to Web databases. Then it will discuss some solutions to managing these threats. The threats include access control violations, integrity violations, unauthorized intrusions, and sabotage. The solutions include data mining techniques, cryptographic techniques, and fault tolerance processing techniques.

In Section 7.4.2, we provide an overview of some of the cyber threats (which are essentially threats to Web security). Much of our focus will be on threats to the public and private databases on the Web. In Section 7.4.3, we discuss potential solutions.

7.4.2 Threats to Web Security

7.4.2.1 Overview

In recent years, we have heard a lot about viruses and Trojan horses that disrupt activities on the Web. These security threats and violations are costing several millions of dollars to businesses. Identity thefts are quite rampant these days. Furthermore, unauthorized intrusions, the inference problem, and privacy violations are also occurring. In this section, we provide an overview of some of these threats. A very good overview of these threats has also been provided in [GHOS98]. We also discuss some additional threats such as threats to Web databases and information systems. Some of the threats and solutions discussed here are also given in [THUR04a].

We have grouped the threats into two. One group consists of some general cyber threats, which may include threats to Web databases. The second group consists of threats to Web databases. Note that we have only provided a subset of all possible threats. There are many more threats such as threats to networks, operating systems, middleware, and electronic payment systems including spoofing, eavesdropping, covert channels, and other malicious techniques. Section 7.4.2.2 focuses on some general cyber threats, while Section 7.4.2.3 discusses threats specific to Web databases. It should be noted that it is difficult to group the threats so that one threat is exclusive for Web databases while another is relevant only for operating systems. Threats such as access control violations are applicable for both databases and operating systems. However, due to complex relationships in databases, access controls are much harder to enforce, while for operating systems access controls are granted or denied at the file level. Another example is natural disasters as well as attacks on infrastructures. These attacks and disasters could damage the networks, databases, and operating systems.

7.4.2.2 General Cyber Threats

We discuss some general cyber threats that are applicable to information systems, including data management systems, operating systems, networks, and middleware. Figure 7.11 illustrates threats to Web security.

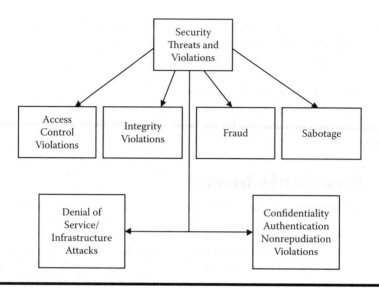

Figure 7.11   Attacks on Web security.

Authentication violations: Passwords could get stolen, and this could result in authentication violations. One may need to have multiple passwords and additional information about the user to solve this problem. Biometrics and other techniques are being examined to handle authentication violations.

Nonrepudiation: The sender of a message could very well deny that he has sent the message. Nonrepudiation techniques will ensure that one can track the message to the sender. Today, it is not difficult to track the owner of the message. However, it is not easy to track the person who has accessed a Web page. That is, while progress has been made in analyzing Web logs, it is still difficult to determine the exact location of a user who has accessed a Web page.

Trojan horses and viruses: Trojan horses and viruses are malicious programs that are responsible for all sorts of attacks. In fact, many of the threats discussed in this section could be caused by Trojan horses and viruses. Viruses can spread from machine to machine and could erase files in various computers. Trojan horses could leak information from a higher level to a lower level. Various virus protection packages have been developed and are now commercially available.

Sabotage: We hear of hackers breaking into systems and posting inappropriate messages. For example, some information on the sabotage of various government Web pages is reported in [GHOS98]. One only needs to corrupt one server, client, or network for the problem to cascade to several machines.

Fraud: With so much of business and commerce being carried out on the Web without proper controls, Internet fraud could cause businesses to lose millions of dollars. Intruders could obtain the identity of legitimate users and may empty bank accounts through masquerading.

Denial-of-service and infrastructure attacks: We hear about infrastructures being brought down by hackers. Infrastructures could be telecommunication systems, power systems, or heating systems. These systems are being controlled by computers, often through the Web. Such attacks would cause denial of service.

Natural disasters: Apart from terrorism, computers and networks are also vulnerable to natural disasters such as hurricanes, earthquakes, fire, and other similar disasters. The data has to be protected, and databases have to be recovered from disasters. In some cases, the solutions to natural disasters are similar to those for threats due to terrorist attacks. For example, fault-tolerant processing techniques are used to recover damaged databases. Risk analysis techniques may contain the damage.

7.4.2.3 Threats to Web Databases

This section discusses some threats to Web databases. Note that while these threats are mainly applicable to data management systems, they are also relevant to general information systems. Figure 7.12 illustrates threats to Web databases.

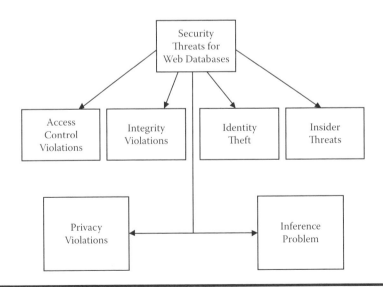

Figure 7.12   Attacks on Web databases.

Access control violations: The traditional access control violations could be extended to the Web. Users may access unauthorized data across the Web. Note that with the Web there is so much of data all over the place that controlling access to this data will be quite a challenge.

Integrity violations: Data on the Web may be subject to unauthorized modifications. Also, data could originate from anywhere, and the producers of the data may not be trustworthy. This makes it easier to corrupt the data. Incorrect data could have serious consequences, such as incorrect bank accounts, which could result in incorrect transactions.

Confidentiality violations: Security includes confidentiality as well as integrity. That is, confidential data has to be protected from those who are not cleared. This book has discussed a great deal on multilevel security, where users access only the information at or below their clearance levels. Statistical database techniques have also been developed to prevent confidentiality violations.

Authenticity violations: This is a form of data integrity violation. For example, consider the case of a publisher, subscriber, and the owner. The subscriber will subscribe to various magazines, the owner creates the magazines (in electronic form), and the publisher (the third party) will publish them. If the publisher is not trusted, he could alter the contents of the magazine. This violates the authenticity of the document. Various solutions have been examined to determine the authenticity of documents. These include cryptography and digital signatures.

Privacy violations: With the Web, one can obtain all kinds of information collected about individuals. Also, with data mining tools and other analysis tools, one can draw all kinds of unauthorized inferences about individuals.

Inference problem: Inference is the process of posing queries and deducing unauthorized information from the legitimate responses. In fact, we consider the privacy problem to be a form of the inference problem. Various solutions have been proposed to handle the inference problem, including constraint processing and the use of conceptual structures. We discuss some of them in the next section.

Identity theft: We are hearing a lot about identity theft these days. The thief gets hold of one's Social Security number and using it can wipe out the bank account of an individual. Here, the thief is posing legitimately as the owner, and he now has much of the critical information about the owner. This is a threat that is very difficult to handle and manage. Viable solutions are yet to be developed. Data mining offers some hope, but may not be sufficient.

Insider threats: Insider threats are considered to be quite common and quite dangerous. In this case, one never knows who the terrorists are. They could be the database administrators or any person who may be considered to be trusted by the corporation. Background checks alone may not be sufficient to detect insider threats. Role-based access controls as well as data mining techniques are being proposed. We will examine these solutions in the next section.

All of the threats/attacks discussed here together with various other cyber security threats/attacks collectively have come to be known as cyberterrorism. Essentially, cyberterrorism is about corrupting the Web and all of its components so that the enemy or adversary's system collapses. Currently, a lot of funds are being invested by the various governments in the United States and Europe to conduct research on protecting the Web and preventing cyberterrorism. Note that terrorism includes cyberterrorism, bioterrroism, and violations to physical security, including bombing buildings and poisoning food and water supplies.

7.4.3 Web Security Solutions

7.4.3.1 Overview

This section will discuss various solutions to the threats mentioned in Section 7.4.2. The goals are to prevent as well as detect security violations and mitigate risks. Furthermore, damage has to be contained and not allowed to spread further. Essentially, we need effective damage control techniques. The solutions discussed include securing components, cryptography, data mining, constraint processing, role-based acccss control, risk analysis, and fault tolerance processing (see also [THUR04a]).

The organization of this section is as follows. In Section 7.4.3.2, we discuss solutions to some general threats. These solutions included firewalls and risk analysis. In Section 7.4.3.5, we will discuss solutions to some threats to Web databases. Note that while the solutions for general threats are applicable for threats to Web databases, solutions for threats to Web databases are also applicable for the general threats. For example, risks analysis has to be carried out for Web databases as well as for general information systems. Furthermore, data mining is a solution for intrusion detection and auditing both for Web databases as well as for networks. We have included them in the section on solutions for Web databases, as data mining is part of data management (see also [THUR04b]). Figure 7.13 illustrates potential solutions.

7.4.3.2 Solutions for General Threats

7.4.3.2.1 Securing Components and Firewalls

Various components have to be made secure for a secure Web. We need end-to-end security and, therefore, the components include secure clients, secure servers, secure databases, secure operating systems, secure infrastructures, secure networks, secure transactions, and secure protocols. One needs good encryption mechanisms to ensure that the sender and receiver communicate securely. Ultimately, whether it be exchanging messages or carrying out transactions, the communication between sender and receiver or the buyer and the seller has to be secure. Secure client solutions include securing the browser, securing the Java virtual machine, securing Java applets, and incorporating various security features

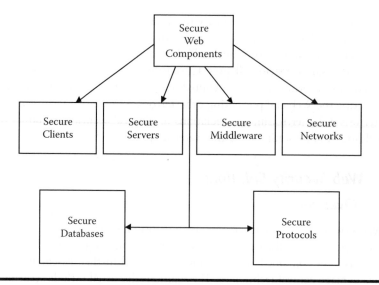

Figure 7.13 Solutions for Web security.

into languages such as Java. Note that Java is not the only component that has to be secure. Microsoft has come up with a collection of products including ActiveX and these products have to be secure also. Securing the protocols includes securing HTTP (Hypertext Transfer Protocol) and the Secure Socket Layer (SSL). Securing the Web server means the server has to be installed securely as well as ensuring that the server cannot be attacked. Various mechanisms that have been used to secure operating systems and databases may be applied here. Notable among them are access control lists, which specify which users have access to which Web pages and data. The Web servers may be connected to databases at the backend, and these databases have to be secure. Finally, various encryption algorithms are being implemented for the networks, and groups such as OMG are investigating security for middleware such as ORBs (object request brokers).

One of the challenges faced by Web managers is implementing security policies. One may have policies for clients, servers, networks, middleware, and databases. The question is, how do you integrate these policies? That is, how do you make these policies work together? Who is responsible for implementing these policies? Is there a global administrator or are there several administrators that have to work together? Security policy integration is an area that is being examined by researchers.

Finally, one of the emerging technologies for ensuring that an organization's assets are protected is firewalls. Various organizations now have Web infrastructures for internal and external use. To access the external infrastructure, one has to go through the firewall. These firewalls examine the information that comes into and out of an organization. This way, the internal assets are protected, and inappropriate information may be prevented from coming into an organization. We can expect sophisticated firewalls to be developed in the future.

7.4.3.2.2 Cryptography

Numerous texts and articles have been published on cryptography (see, for example, [DENN82]). In addition, annual cryptology conferences also take place. Yet cryptography is one of the areas that needs continuous research, as the codes are being broken with powerful machines and sophisticated techniques. There are also many discussions on export/import controls for encryption techniques. This section will briefly provide an overview of some of the technical details of cryptography relevant to the Web and therefore to e-commerce. Cryptography is the solution to various threats, including authenticity verification as well as ensuring data integrity. It is also useful for ensuring privacy.

The main issue with cryptology is ensuring that a message is sent properly. That is, the receiver should get the message the way it was intended for him to receive it. This means that the message should not be intercepted or modified. The issue can be extended to transactions on the Web also. That is, transactions have to be carried out in the way they were intended. Scientists have been working on cryptography for many decades. We hear about codes being broken during World War II. The study of code breaking has come to be known as cryptanalysis. In cryptography, the sender of the message encrypts it with a key. For example, he or she could use the letter B for A, C for B, ..., and A for Z. If the receiver knows the key, then he can decode this message. So a message with the word COMPUTER would be DPNQVUFS. Now, this code is simple and will be easy to break. The challenge in cryptography is to find a code that is difficult to break. Number theorists have been conducting extensive research in this area.

In cryptography, encryption is used by the sender to transform what is called a plaintext message into ciphertext. Decryption is used by the receiver to obtain the plaintext from the ciphertext received. Two types of cryptography are gaining prominence; one is public key cryptography, where there are two keys involved for the sender and the receiver. One is the public key and is visible to everyone, and the other is the private key. The sender encrypts the message with the recipient's public key. Only the recipient can decode this message with his private key. The second method is private key cryptography. Here both users have a private key. There is also a key distribution center involved. This center generates a session key when the sender and receiver want to communicate. This key is sent to both users in an encrypted form using the respective private keys. The sender uses his private key to decrypt the session key. The session key is used to encrypt the message. The receiver can decrypt the session key with his private key and then use this decrypted session key to decrypt the message.

In the preceding paragraphs, we have discussed some of the basic concepts in cryptography. The challenge is how to ensure that an intruder does not modify the message and that the desirable security properties such as confidentiality, integrity, authentication, and nonrepudiation are maintained. The answer is in message digests and digital signatures. Using hash functions on a message, a message digest is created. If appropriate functions are used, each message will have a unique message digest. Therefore, even a small modification to the message will result in a completely different message digest. In this way, integrity is maintained. Message digests together with cryptographic receipts, which are digitally signed ensure that the receiver knows the identity of the sender. That is, the sender may encrypt the message digests with the encryption techniques described in the previous paragraphs. In some techniques, the recipient may need the public key of the sender to decrypt the message. The recipient may obtain this key with what is called a certificate authority. The certificate authority should be a trusted entity and must make sure that the recipient can legitimately get the public key of the sender. Therefore, additional measures are taken by the certificate authority to make sure that this is the case.

7.4.3.3 Risk Analysis

Before developing any computer system for a particular operation, one needs to study the security risks involved. The goal is to mitigate the risks or at least limit and contain them if the threats cannot be eliminated. Several papers have been published on risk analysis, especially at the National Computer Security Conference Proceedings in the 1990s. These risk analysis techniques need to be examined for cyber threats.

The challenges include identifying all the threats that are inherent to a particular situation. For example, consider a banking operation. The bank has to employ security experts and risk analysis experts to conduct a study of all possible threats. Then they have to come up with ways of eliminating the threats. If that is not possible, they have to develop ways of containing the damage so that it does not spread further.

Risk analysis is especially useful for viruses. Once a virus starts spreading, the challenge is, how do you stop it? If you cannot stop it, then how do you contain it and also limit the damage that is caused? Running various virus packages on one's system will perhaps limit the virus from affecting the system or causing serious damage. The adversary will always find ways to develop new viruses. Therefore, we have to be one step or many steps ahead of the enemy. We need to examine the current state of the practice in risk analysis and develop new solutions, especially to handle the new kinds of threats present in the cyber world.

7.4.3.4 Biometrics, Forensics, and Other Solutions

Some of the recent developments in computer security are tools for biometrics and forensic analysis. Biometrics tools include understanding handwriting and signatures as well as recognizing people from their features and eyes, including the pupils. While this is a very challenging area, much progress has been made. Voice recognition tools to authenticate users are also being developed. In the future, we can expect the use of these tools to become more widespread.

Forensic analysis essentially carries out postmortems just as they do in medicine. Once the attacks have occurred, then how do you detect them? Who are the enemies and perpetrators? While progress has been made, there are still challenges. For example, if one accesses the Web pages and uses stolen passwords, then it will be difficult to determine from the Web logs who the culprit is. That is, we still need a lot of research in the area. Digital Forensics also deals with using computer evidence for crime analysis.

Biometrics and forensics are just some of the new developments. Other solutions being developed include smartcards, tools for detecting spoofing and jamming, as well as tools to carry out sniffing.

7.4.3.5 Solutions for Threats to Web Databases

Figure 7.14 illustrates solutions for Web database security. These include data mining, security constraint processing, and role-based access control.

7.4.3.5.1 Data Mining

Data mining is the process of posing queries and extracting patterns, often previously unknown, from large quantities of data using pattern matching or other reasoning techniques (see [THUR98]). In [THUR03], we examine data mining for counterterrorism. We discuss various types of terrorist attacks, including information-related terrorism. As mentioned in [THUR03], by information-related terrorism we essentially mean cyberterrorism. Cyber security is the area that deals with cyberterrorism. We listed various cyber attacks, including access control violations, unauthorized intrusions, and denial of service. We are hearing that cyber

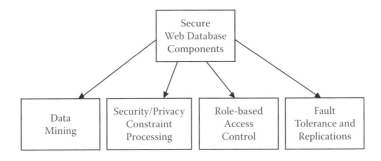

Figure 7.14   Solutions for Web database security.

attacks will cost corporations billions of dollars. For example, one could masquerade as a legitimate user and swindle a bank of billions of dollars.

Data mining may be used to detect and possibly prevent cyber attacks. For example, anomaly detection techniques could be used to detect unusual patterns and behaviors. Link analysis may be used to connect the viruses to the perpetrators. Classification may be used to group various cyber attacks and then use the profiles to detect an attack when it occurs. Prediction may be used to determine potential future attacks depending in a way on information learned about terrorists through e-mail and phone conversations. Also, for some threats, non-real-time data mining may suffice, while for certain other threats such as network intrusions, we may need real-time data mining.

Many researchers are investigating the use of data mining for intrusion detection. While we need some form of real-time data mining, that is, the results have to be generated in real-time, we also need to build models in real-time. For example, credit card fraud detection is a form of real-time processing. However, here models are built ahead of time. Building models in real-time remains a challenge.

Data mining can also be used for analyzing Web logs as well as analyzing the audit trails. Based on the results of the data mining tool, one can then determine whether any unauthorized intrusions have occurred and/or whether any unauthorized queries have been posed. There has been much research on data mining for intrusion detection and reported at the IFIP Database Security Conferences (see also [NING04]). This is an area in which we can expect to see much progress. Some interesting work on data mining for intrusion detection is given in [LAZA03]. More recently, data mining techniques are being examined for insider cyber threat detection. The main question is, do general-purpose data mining techniques work for such applications or do we need special-purpose data mining techniques? We need a research agenda for data mining applications in information security. Note that some directions were given in [THUR05a].

7.4.3.5.2 Constraint Processing

We introduced the idea of security constraint processing for the inference problem. We revisit some of the points. We defined security constraints to assign security levels to the data and then developed a system to process the constraints (see [THUR93]). We have now adapted these techniques for privacy. In a recent paper, we have elaborated on privacy constraint processing [THUR05b]. Privacy constraints are rules that are enforced on the data. These rules determine the level of privacy of the data (called privacy levels or privacy values). Our definition of privacy constraints follows along the lines of our work on security constraints, discussed in [THUR93]. Privacy values of the data could take a range of values, including public, semipublic, semiprivate, and private. Even within a privacy value, we could have different levels of privacy, including low-private, medium-private, and high-private.

We have defined various types of privacy constraints. We give examples using a medical informatics database. The constraints we have identified include simple constraints, content-based constraints, context- or association-based constraints, release constraints, and event constraints. While we use a relational database to illustrate the concepts, constraints can be defined on object as well as on XML databases.

Simple constraints assign privacy values to attributes, relations, or even a database. For example, all medical records are private. Content-based constraints assign privacy values to data depending on content. For example, all financial records are private except for those who are in public office (e.g., the president of the United States). Association-based constraints assign privacy values to collections of attributes taken together. For example, names and medical records are private, but individually they are public. That is, one can release names and medical records separately, but one cannot release them together. Furthermore, one has to be careful that the public user cannot infer medical records for a particular person by posing multiple queries. Event constraints are constraints that change privacy values after an event has occurred. For example, after a patient has been released, some information about him or her could be made public, but while he is in the hospital information about him or her is private. A good example was the sniper shootings that occurred in the Washington, DC, area in the fall of 2007. After the victim died, information about him or her was released. Until then, the identity of the person was not available to the public. Finally, release constraints assign privacy values to the data depending on what has already been released. For example, after the medical records have been released, one cannot release any information about the names or social security numbers that can form a link with the medical information.

One could define many more types of privacy constraints. As we explore various applications, we will start defining various classes of constraints. Our main purpose in [THUR05b] is to show how privacy constraints can be processed in a database management system. We call such a system a privacy-enhanced database system. Our approach is to augment a database management system (DBMS) with a privacy controller. Such a DBMS is called a privacy-enhanced DBMS. The privacy controller will process the privacy constraints. The question is, what are the components of the privacy controller and when do the constraints get processed? We take an approach similar to that proposed in [THUR93] for security constraint processing. In our approach, some privacy constraints are processed during database design, and the database is partitioned according to the privacy levels. Then some constraints are processed during database updates. Here, the data is entered at the appropriate privacy levels. Because the privacy values change dynamically, it is very difficult to change the privacy levels of the data in the database in real-time. Therefore, some constraints are processed during the query operation.

The modules of the privacy controller include the constraint manager, query manager, database design tool, and the update manager. The constraint manager manages the constraints. The database design tool processes constraints during database design and assigns levels to the schema. The query processor processes constraints during the query operation and determines what data is to be released. The update processors process constraints and compute the level of the data [THUR05b].

7.4.3.5.3 Role-Based Access Control

One of the popular access control techniques is role-based access control. The idea here is users, based on their roles, are given access to certain data. For example, the engineer has access to project data, while the accountant has access to financial data. The challenges include handling multiple roles and conflicting roles. For example, if one is an engineer and he or she cannot have access to financial data and if he or she also happens to be an accountant, then how can the conflict be resolved? Maintaining the consistency of the access control rules is also a challenge.

Many papers have been published on role-based access control. There is also now a conference devoted entirely to role-based access control called SACMAT (ACM Symposium on Access Control Models and Technologies). Also, papers relevant to role-based access control on databases have been presented at the IFIP database security conferences. It is also being examined for handling insider threats. That is, using a combination of data mining techniques to find out information about employees and granting them roles depending on their trustworthiness, one could perhaps manage the insider threat analysis problem.

7.4.3.5.4 Fault-Tolerant Processing, Recovery, and Replication

We focus here on handling faults in critical data. The databases could be national databases that contain critical information about individuals or private corporate databases or bank databases that contain financial information. They could also be agency databases that contain highly sensitive information. When such databases are attacked, it is then possible for the enemy to obtain classified information or wipe out bank accounts. Furthermore, even if the enemy does not do anything with the data, just by corrupting the databases, the entire operation could be thwarted. Today, computer systems are controlling the operation of manufacturing plants, process control plants, and many critical infrastructures. Corrupting the data could be disastrous.

The fault tolerance computing community has come up with several algorithms for recovering databases and systems from failures and other problems. These techniques include acceptance testing and check pointing. Sometimes data is replicated so that there are backup copies. These techniques have to be examined for handling malicious attacks on the databases and corrupting the data. We also need to conduct research on dependable computing, that is, security, integrity, fault tolerance, and real-time processing. That is, we need to develop quality of service metrics for dependable computing. We also need flexible security policies as requirements such as security and real-time processing may be conflicting.

7.5 Summary and Directions

This chapter has provided a brief overview of the developments in trustworthy systems. We first discussed secure systems, including basic concepts in access control as well as discretionary and mandatory policies, types of secure systems such as secure operating systems, secure databases, secure networks, and emerging technologies, the impact of the Web, and the steps to building secure systems. Next we discussed dependable systems, including aspects of trust, rights, privacy, integrity, quality, and real-time processing. Then we focused in more detail on aspects of Web security, including threats to Web security and secure Web databases.

While much progress has been made on trustworthy systems, there is still a lot to be done. We need to investigate security for emerging systems such as semantic Web technologies and services technologies. In addition, security for knowledge management systems as well as geospatial systems is critical. In this book, we will focus on one such aspect, secure services. As discussed in Chapter 1, secure Web services integrate services technologies with security technologies. We will describe secure services in Part II with an emphasis on confidentiality. Trust, privacy, and integrity will be discussed in Part III. Secure semantic Web services will be discussed in Part IV. Secure specialized Web services will be discussed in Part V.

Exercises

1. Elaborate on the steps involved in designing a secure system for a secure database system.
2. Conduct a survey of network security technologies.
3. Select three secure operating system products and examine their features.
4. What are the important developments in Database and Applications Security?
5. Conduct a survey of Web security threats and solutions.

References

[ATLU97] Atluri, V., S. Jajodia, and E. Bertino, Transaction processing in multilevel secure databases with Kernelized architectures: Challenges and solutions. *IEEE Transactions on Knowledge and Data Engineering*, 9(5): 697–708, 1997.

[BELL73] Bell, D. and L. LaPadula, *Secure Computer Systems: Mathematical Foundations and Model*, M74-244, The MITRE Corporation, Bedford, MA, 1973.

[DENN82] Denning, D., *Cryptography and Data Security*, Addison Wesley, Reading, MA, 1987.

[DRM] Digital Rights Management Architectures, http://www.dlib.org/dlib/june01/iannella/06iannella.html

[FERR00] Ferrari E. and B. Thuraisingham, Secure database systems, in *Advances in Database Management*, Eds. M. Piatini and O. Diaz, Artech House, London, U.K., 2000.

[GASS88] Gasser, M., *Building a Secure Computer System*, Van Nostrand Reinhold, New York, 1988.

[GHOS98] Ghosh, A., *E-commerce Security, Weak Links and Strong Defenses*, John Wiley & Sons, New York, 1998.

[GOGU82] Goguen, J. and J. Meseguer, Security Policies and Security Models, *Proceedings of the IEEE Symposium on Security and Privacy*, Oakland, CA, April 1987.

[HASS00] Hassler, V., *Security Fundamentals for E-Commerce*, Artech House, London, U.K., 2000.

[IEEE83] *IEEE Computer Magazine*, Special Issue on Computer Security, Volume 16, #7, 1983.

[KAUF02] Kaufmann, C. et al., *Network Security: Private Communication in a Public World*, Pearson Publishers, Upper Saddle River, NJ, 2002.

[LAZA03] Lazarevic, A. et al., Data Mining for Computer Security Applications, Tutorial *Proceedings of the IEEE Data Mining Conference*, 2003.

[NING04] Ning, P. et al., Techniques and tools for analyzing intrusion alerts. *ACM Transactions on Information and Systems Security*, Volume 7, #2, 2004.

[OMG] The Object Management Group, www.omg.org.

[TANN90] Tannenbaum, A., *Computer Networks*, Prentice Hall, Upper Saddle River, NJ, 1990.

[TCSE85] Trusted Computer Systems Evaluation Criteria, National Computer Security Center, Fort Meade, MD, 1985.

[TDI91] Trusted Database Interpretation, National Computer Security Center, Fort Meade, MD, 1991.

[THUR89] Thuraisingham, B., Mandatory Security for Object-Oriented Database Systems, *Proceedings of the ACM OOPOSLA Conference*, New Orleans, LA, October 1989.

[THUR91] Thuraisingham, B., Multilevel security for distributed database systems, *Computers and Security*, 10:8, 727–747, 1991.

[THUR93] Thuraisingham, B., W. Ford, and M. Collins, Design and implementation of a database inference controller, *Data and Knowledge Engineering Journal*, Volume 11, #3, 1993.

[THUR94] Thuraisingham, B., Security issues in federated database management systems, *Computers and Security*, 13:6, 509–525, 1994.

[THUR98] Thuraisingham, B., *Data Mining: Technologies, Techniques, Tools and Trends*, CRC Press, Boca Raton, FL, December 1998.

[THUR03] Thuraisingham, B., *Web Data Mining Technologies and Their Applications in Business Intelligence and Counter-Terrorism*, CRC Press, Boca Raton, FL, 2003.

[THUR04a] Thuraisingham, B., *Managing Threats to Web Databases and Cyber Systems, Issues, Solutions and Challenges*, Eds. V. Kumar et al., Kluwer, Boston, MA, 2004.

[THUR04b] Data Mining for Counter-terrorism, *Next Generation Data Mining*, AAAI Press, Boston, MA, 2004 (Editors: H. Kargupta, A. Joshi, K. Swakumar, and Y. Yesha).

[THUR05a] Thuraisingham, B., *Database and Applications Security: Integrating Data Management and Information Security*, CRC Press, Boca Raton, FL, 2007.

[THUR05b] Thuraisingham, B, Privacy constraint processing in a privacy enhanced database management system, *Data and Knowledge Engineering Journal*, 55:2, 159–188, November 2005.

[TNI87] Trusted Network Interpretation, National Computer Security Center, MD, 1987.

[YU03] Yu, T. and M. Winslett, A Unified Scheme for Resource Protection in Automated Trust Negotiation, *IEEE Symposium on Security and Privacy*, Oakland, CA, May 2003.

Conclusion to Part I

Part I discussed both services technologies and security technologies. We first provided an overview of services computing. Then we discussed service-oriented architecture and standards. This was followed by a discussion of service-oriented analysis and design approaches. Next we discussed some special services, including services for data, information, and knowledge management as well as semantic services. Finally, we provided an overview of security technologies.

Now that we have discussed the supporting technologies, we will describe secure services technologies in Part II. As discussed earlier, secure services integrated services with security. We will provide an overview of secure service-oriented architectures as well as secure Web services and also discuss various aspects such as access control models for services.

SECURE SERVICES TECHNOLOGIES

Introduction to Part II

Now that we have explained the concepts in services and security technologies, we will discuss the key points in secure services. The contents of Part II form the core of secure services. What follows in Parts III, IV and V makes use of the concepts in Part II.

Part II consists of six chapters: 8 through 13. Secure services computing is discussed in Chapter 8. Secure SOA and Web services are discussed in Chapter 9. Secure service-oriented analysis and design is discussed in Chapter 10. Access control for Web services is discussed in Chapter 11. Identity management for Web services is discussed in Chapter 12. Finally in Chapter 13, we discuss our research on delegation models and information flow models for Web services.

Chapter 8

Secure Service-Oriented Computing

8.1 Overview

In Part I, we discussed services technologies, including an overview of specialized services such as services for data, information, and knowledge management. We also discussed security technologies. In this part, we will discuss secure services. Secure services are essentially integrated services and security technologies. Our discussion of secure services will focus mainly on secure Web services.

Secure services essentially incorporate security into services technologies. For example, what credentials should an agent have to invoke a Web service? What credentials should a Web service have to invoke another Web service? Should all Web service descriptions be visible to every agent? How can access control be enforced on Web service descriptions? How can security be incorporated into the service-oriented architectures? What are the security standards being proposed by W3C and OASIS? We will explore answers to these questions in this part. This chapter provides a high-level overview of secure services technologies, and the details will be elaborated on in the remaining chapters in this part.

The organization of this chapter is as follows. Secure services will be discussed in Section 8.2. Secure service-oriented computing will be discussed in Section 8.3. Secure SOA and Web services, which are at the heart of secure Web services technologies, will be discussed in Section 8.4. Security for service-oriented analysis and design (or SSOAD) will be discussed in Section 8.5. Federated identity management,

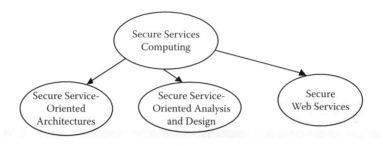

Figure 8.1   Aspects of secure services.

which is a key aspect of Web services, will be discussed in Section 8.6. Security standards for Web services will be discussed in Section 8.7. Some of our research on secure Web services, which is essentially a delegation model for Web services, will be discussed in Section 8.8. The chapter is summarized in Section 8.9. Figure 8.1 illustrates the topics discussed in this chapter. For more details on secure services, we refer to [BERT06]. More recently, an edited book with a collection of papers on secure Web services was published, which gives an excellent overview of the emerging standards and research directions in the field [GUTI10].

8.2 Secure Services

To best illustrate the notion of a secure service, we will use two examples. Suppose we want to get our credit report. We will contact a service provider that gets credit reports. First, we should have the access to read the existence of such a service provider. Once we know about this service provider, we invoke it. The service provider should ensure that we have the access to this particular service. Furthermore, it should ensure that the information about the credit it retrieves can be read by us. In order to do this, we also have to send some identification information to the service provider. If the service is not secure, then anyone can obtain anyone's credit reports. Similarly, to obtain healthcare reports, the secure service provider should ensure that the person requesting the service has the appropriate credentials to read the healthcare records. Furthermore, the owner of the healthcare records may enforce various privacy policies, in which case the service provider should only release appropriate information to the consumer. In some cases, the consumer may use the service provider to purchase information. The service provider can state its privacy policies and if the consumer agrees with the policies, it can release private information about him or her.

These simple examples highlight several aspects. One is that the user of the service has to be verified by the service provider. The service provider has to be trusted in the sense that one does not want to get service from an unreliable provider. The service provider has to ensure that the user/consumer has the proper credentials to

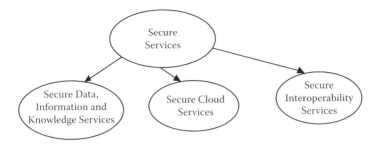

Figure 8.2   Secure services.

obtain the service and that any information released is something the consumer is authorized to read. The service provider also has to ensure that private information about a person is not released to the consumer. Confidentiality, privacy, trust, and integrity features should be enforced by the Web services. Figure 8.2 illustrates secure services.

8.3 Secure Service-Oriented Computing

As we have stated in Chapter 2, service-oriented computing is essentially about implementing services as software. Consider the process of ordering a book from an agency. We go to the catalog published by the agency. The agency has to ensure that we are authorized to read the information about the books (that is, the meta-data). We place the order. The agency will then determine which part of the book we can read, if any. The appropriate parts of the book are then released to us (the consumer). Now, this secure service can be implemented in software as follows. The customer checks the Web site of the agency, finds the book, and places the order. The Web site will only display the books the customer is authorized to see. The secure order management service implemented by the agency takes the order, sends a message to the warehouse service, and requests the book. The warehouse service then finds that the book is in its inventory and sends a message to the order management service. The warehouse would invoke the security service and then send the appropriate parts of the book to the shipping service. The shipping service then ships the book to the customer. If the book has to be displayed elec-tronically, then appropriate parts of the book may be displayed through the order management service. So, there is a composition of secure services starting from the order management service, the warehouse service, and the shipping service. These three services provide the customer with what he wants. All these services have to enforce appropriate security controls. In implementing the secure services, we need to enforce activation, access control, trust management, and privacy control. In addition, the documents that the customer gets must be authentic, which means integrity has to be maintained.

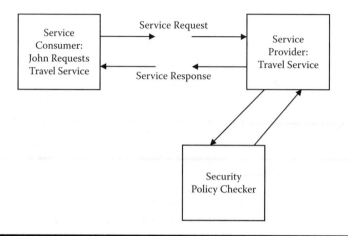

Figure 8.3 Secure services computing.

As we have stated in Chapter 2, the unit of computing for service-oriented computing is a service. The challenges are to represent the services, the relationship between them, and the security levels of the services. For example, if service A is unclassified and service B is secret, then what should be the security level of the service that is imposed on A and B? Furthermore, if a consumer can invoke service A and cannot invoke service B, then should he be able to invoke the composition of A and B? The various security standards that have been developed provide solutions to some of the questions. Note that much of the work on secure services has focused on discretionary security. Multilevel security for Web services has received little attention. Our focus will also be on discretionary security for Web services. We illustrate the notion of secure service-oriented computing in Figure 8.3.

8.4 Secure SOA and Web Services

In Chapter 2, we discussed the SOA paradigm and stated that our focus on SOA implementation will be through Web services. Therefore, our realization of secure SOA will be through secure Web services. The basic SOA is essentially about a consumer requesting a service from the Universal Description, Discovery and Integration (UDDI). The UDDI sends the name/address of the service. The consumer then gets this service from the service provider. With secure SOA, we have to ensure that the communication between the consumer, the UDDI, and the service provider is secure. Furthermore, only authorized consumers can get the required services. Furthermore, the SOAP messages that are encoded in XML have to be secure; the XML encryption standard provides confidentiality, while the XML signature standard provides integrity. Both XML encryption and XML signature are standards provided by W3C.

Security and authorization specifications for Web services are based on XML and can be found in [OASIS], [XACML], and [SAML]. Various types of controls have been proposed, including access control, rights, assertions, and protection. We describe some of them in the next section. The list of specifications includes the following:

eXtensible Access Control Markup Language (XACML)
eXtensible Rights Markup Language (XrML)
Security Assertion Markup Language (SAML)
Service Protection Markup Language (SPML)
Web Services Security (WSS)
XML Common Biometric Format (XCBF)
XML Key Management Specification (XKMS)

OASIS is a key standards organization promoting security standards for Web services. It is a not-for-profit, global consortium that drives the development, convergence, and adoption of e-business standards. Two prominent standards provided by OASIS are XACML and SAML. XACML (eXtensible Access Control Markup Language) provides fine-grained control of authorized activities, the effect of characteristics of the access requestor, the protocol over which the request is made, authorization based on classes of activities, and content introspection. SAML (Security Assertion Markup Language) is an XML framework for exchanging authentication and authorization information. We will discuss details of secure Web services in the ensuing chapters. Figure 8.4 illustrates the notion of secure Web services architecture. More details will be discussed in Chapter 9.

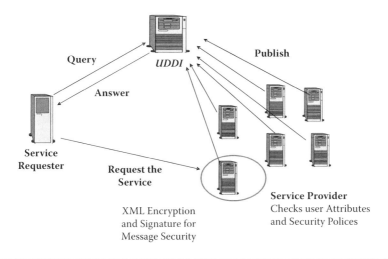

Figure 8.4   Secure SOA and Web services.

Figure 8.5   Secure SOAD.

8.5 Secure Service-Oriented Analysis and Design

We were the first to examine secure object-oriented analysis and design (OOAD) based on the OMT model. We developed a secure object model, secure dynamic model, and secure functional model. Since then, several researchers have developed secure OOAD methodologies based on objects. With the SOAD approach, the goal is to identify the services and the relationships between the services for an application. For example, the services for the book order application will include order management service, warehouse service, and shipping service. These services have associated with them various security policies. The challenge is to capture the services and the policies in an appropriate modeling language.

There is little work on secure service-oriented analysis and design (S-SOAD). In Chapter 13, we will make an attempt based on the developments with secure OOAD. In particular, we will examine the SOAD principles that we discussed in Chapter 4 and examine security for SOAD. It should be noted that as security for Web services as well as SOAD methodologies mature, we will see better approaches, or S-SOAD. Figure 8.5 illustrates the concepts involved in secure SOAD. More details will be discussed in Chapter 10.

8.6 Federated Identity Management

Identity management, usually also referred to as federated identity management, is closely intertwined with Web services. Users as well as Web services have to be authenticated before accessing resources. Single sign-on is the popular solution, where one time sign-on gives a user or a service access to the various resources. Furthermore, SAML currently provides justification facilities for Web services. However, with regulatory requirements for e-business, one needs a stronger mechanism for authentication, and this mechanism has come to be known as identity management.

As discussed in [FED], federated identity "describes the technologies, standards and use-cases which serve to enable the portability of identity information across otherwise autonomous security domains." The goal is to ensure that users of one domain take advantage of all the technologies offered by another domain in a seamless manner. Note that federation is about organizations working together to carry out a task (such as B2B operations) or solve a particular problem. While the ideas

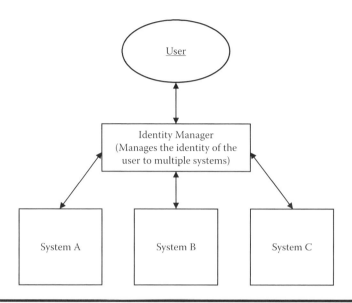

Figure 8.6   Identity management.

have been around for many years, it is only recently with the emerging standards for Web services that we can now develop realistic federations. In such federations, access to the resources by users has to be managed without burdening the user. We will give more details of federated identity management in Chapter 11. Figure 8.6 illustrates identity management.

8.7 Access Control

Security standards for services have essentially been developed by W3C and Security SIS. Standards for Web Services 1.0 essentially consisted of a service consumer requesting a service from the service provider, who then provides the service. The XML messages that are exchanged in the SOAP protocols are encrypted and signed to provide confidentiality and integrity. This goal is to encrypt the message to provide confidentiality and sign the message to ensure that the message is not tampered with. XML Key Management and XML Encryption have played a major role in providing confidentiality and integrity of the messages.

Web Services 2.0 has resulted in several additional standards, including secure messaging, reliability, and identity management. In addition, standards for policy management such as WS-Policy, standards for access control such as XACML, and standards for security assertions such as SAML have also been developed. We will discuss these standards in Chapter 9 as well as in Chapter 13. Figure 8.7 illustrates the XACML access control model for Web services. This model will be elaborated further in Chapter 9.

8.8 Delegation Model

For many applications, the access control models are not sufficient. For example, in the case of composite Web services, one Web service, S1, may invoke another Web service, S2. In such an invocation, S1's privileges will be enforced and not those of the user U who invoked S1. This means that the information that is returned to U may be something the user is not authorized to know. To avoid such security compromises, a user U may have to delegate its privileges to S1 so that U's privileges are used when S1 invokes S2. Such an invocation is governed by the delegation models that are utilized [SHE08].

Another security concern for composite Web services is information flow. That is, when Web services are composed, it is critical that there is no information flow from a high level to a low level. Our research is focusing on various aspects of Web services security, including the delegation models and information flows for Web service composition, and will be described in Chapter 13. Figure 8.8 illustrates the delegation model.

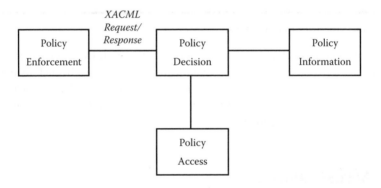

Figure 8.7 Access control.

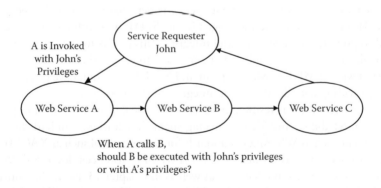

Figure 8.8 Delegation model.

8.9 Summary and Directions

This chapter has provided an overview of secure service-oriented computing. We first discussed what is meant by secure services. Next we discussed high-level concepts in secure service-oriented computing. Realizing service-oriented information systems through secure service-oriented architectures and Web services was discussed next. Then we discussed how secure service-oriented information systems may be designed. Finally, aspects of federated identity management, delegation of Web services, and security standards were discussed. Details of the various concepts introduced in this chapter will be elaborated on in Chapters 9 through 13.

Security for services computing is just beginning. Furthermore, we cannot now back away from services computing. It has been strongly adopted by almost every industry, including the U.S. government. Therefore, there are endless opportunities for investigating security for services computing. We aim to provide the direction. We cannot discuss all of the standards due to the rapid development of these standards. Therefore, we urge the reader to keep up with the developments, especially with W3C and OASIS.

Exercises

1. Describe with an example concepts in secure services computing.
2. Conduct a survey of secure services computing.

References

[BERT06] Bertino, E. and L. Martino, Security in SOA and Web Services, *IEEE SCC 2006*, xli.

[FED] Federated Identity, http://en.wikipedia.org/wiki/Federated_identity

[GUTI10] Gutierrez, C., E. Fernandez-Medina, and M. Piattini (Eds.), *Web Services Security Development and Architecture, Information Science Reference*, Hershey, PA, 2010.

[OASIS] Organization for the Advancement of Structured Information Standards. http://www.oasis-open.org/home/index.php

[SAML] Security Assertion Markup Language. http://en.wikipdebia.org/wiki/Security_Assertion_Markup_Language

[SHE08] She, W., I-L. Yen, and B. M. Thuraisingham, Enhancing security modeling for Web services using delegation and pass-on, *ICWS 2008*: 545–552.

[XACML] XACML. http://en.wikipedia.org/wiki/XACML

Chapter 9

Secure SOA and Web Services

9.1 Overview

Our approach is to implement SOA through Web services; therefore, SOA security essentially is about Web services security. There are specifications to provide security for Web Services 1.0. These specifications are WS-Security, XML-Signature, and XML-Encryption. WS-* Security is the second generation of technologies for SOA security. Single Sign-On (SSO) is a form of centralized security mechanism that complements the WS-Security extensions. Related specifications for SOA security include the following: WS-Security, WS-SecurityPolicy, WS-Trust, WS-SecureConversation, WS-Federation, XACML, eXtensible Rights Markup Language, XML Key Management, XML-Signature, SAML, .NET Passport, Secure Socket Layer, and WS-I Basic Security Profile.

In this chapter, we will provide an overview of both WS and WS-* Security. The organization of this chapter is as follows. In Section 9.2 we will describe the components of WS-Security. Section 9.3 will discuss WS-* Security components. Section 9.4 concludes the chapter. Figure 9.1 illustrates the concepts to be discussed in this chapter. For details on secure SOA, we refer the reader to [BERT06] and [WSS].

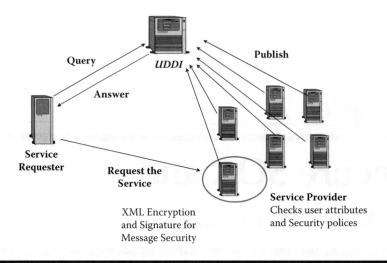

Figure 9.1 SOA Security components.

9.2 WS-Security

Before we get into the details of Web services security, we will discuss some of the security properties that are needed for Web services. They include the following:

Identification: For a service requester to access a secure service provider, it must first provide information that expresses its origin or owner. This is referred to as making a claim.

Authentication: A message being delivered to a recipient must prove that the message is in fact from the sender that it claims.

Authorization: Once authenticated, the recipient of a message may need to determine what the requester is allowed to do.

Single Sign-On: Users sign in once and have access to all the resources. It is supported by SAML, .NET Passport, and XACML.

Confidentiality and Integrity: Confidentiality is concerned with protecting the privacy of the message content; integrity ensures that the message has not been altered.

Transport Level and Message Level Security: Transport-level security is provided by SSL (securing HTTP), and message-level confidentiality and integrity are provided by XML-Encryption and XML-Signature.

Securing Web services mainly requires providing facilities for securing the integrity and confidentiality of the messages and ensuring that the service acts only on requests in messages that express the claims required by policies. Role of Standards includes providing a Web Services Security Framework that is an integral part of

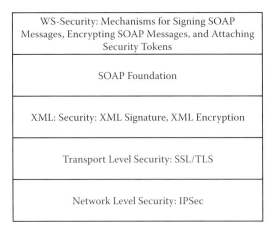

Figure 9.2   WS-Security.

the Web Services Architecture. This framework is a layered and composable set of standard specifications. Next, we will briefly describe the various components of WS-Security. The components are illustrated in Figure 9.2.

XML Encryption: XM Encryption Syntax and Processing is a W3C standard and was recommended in 2002. Its goal is to provide confidentiality for applications that exchange structured data by representing in a standard way digitally encrypted resources, separating encryption information from encrypted data, and supporting reference mechanisms for addressing encryption information from encrypted data sections and vice versa, providing a mechanism for conveying encryption key information to a recipient, and providing for the encryption of an XML document or a part of it.

XML Signature: This is a W3C standard and was recommended in 2002. XML Signature is a building block for many Web services security standards (e.g., XKMS and WS-Security). Its goal is to represent a digital signature as an XML element and process rules for creating it. The signed data items can be of different types and granularity (XML documents, XML Elements, and files containing any type of digital data).

Securing SOAP messages is crucial for WS-Security. SOAP Message Security 1.1 became an approved OASIS Standard Specification in 2006. Its goal is to provide *single* SOAP message integrity and confidentiality by using *existing* digital signature, encryption, and security token mechanisms, provide mechanisms for associating security tokens with message content (header and body blocks), and supporting extensibility (i.e., support multiple security token format). Security Token is a representation of security-related information (e.g., 9.509 certificate, Kerberos tickets and authenticators, mobile device security tokens from SIM cards, username, etc.).

Signed Security Token: A security token that contains a set of related claims (assertions) cryptographically endorsed by an issuer (Examples: 9.509 certificates and Kerberos tickets).

So now we come back to WS-Security. What is it? WS-Security enhances SOAP messaging to provide *quality of protection* through message integrity, message confidentiality, and single message authentication. These mechanisms can be used to accommodate a wide variety of security models and encryption technologies. WS-Security also provides a general-purpose, extensible mechanism for associating security tokens with messages. WS-Security describes how to encode binary security tokens (9.509 certificates and Kerberos tickets).

9.3 WS-* Security

WS-* Security standard specifications address interoperability aspects. Each standard specification provides a specific section describing security threats that are not addressed by that specification. The framework for WS-* Security is illustrated in Figure 9.3. It makes use of WS-Security. The implementation of this framework has been carried out by Microsoft .NET Framework 2.0/WSE3.0, SUN Web Services

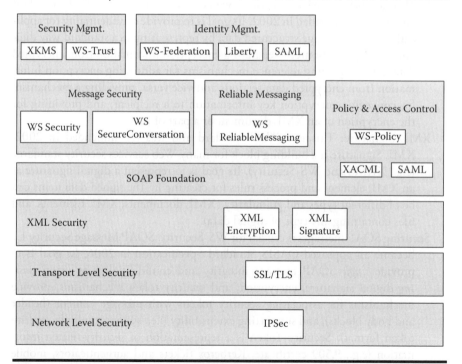

Figure 9.3   WS-* Security.

Interoperability Technology (WSIT)), IBM WebSphere, and Open Software: The Apache Software Foundation Web Services Project (http://ws.apache.org/). In theory, the framework mandates a layered approach in which every upper-layer standard could/should reuse and extend the specification of lower-layer standards. In practice, specifications released by different organizations are not always compatible. However, they adhere to profiles and improve interoperability. It should be noted that the implementations of different vendors are not always interoperable. Three major components that provide security are WS-Policy, WS-Trust, and WS-Addressing. WS-Addressing was discussed in Part I. It is a specification of transport-neutral mechanisms that allow Web services to communicate address information. In the following text, we will discuss WS-Policy and WS-Trust.

WS-Policy: Web Services Policy 1.2 - Framework (WS-Policy) is a W3C submission. A Policy is a potentially empty collection of policy alternatives. Alternatives are not ordered. A Policy Alternative is a potentially empty collection of policy assertions. An alternative with zero assertions indicates no behaviors. Alternatives are mutually exclusive (exclusive OR). A Policy Assertion identifies a requirement (or capability) of a policy subject. Assertions indicate domain-specific (e.g., security, transactions) semantics and are expected to be defined in separate, domain-specific specifications.

WS-Policy can be considered to be an extensible model for expressing all types of domain-specific policy models: transport-level security, resource usage policy, and even end-to-end business-process level policy. It defines a basic policy, policy statement, and policy assertion models. WS-Policy is also able to incorporate other policy models such as SAML and XACML. WS-PolicyAssertions defines a few generic policy assertions. WS-PolicyAttachment defines how to associate a policy with a service, either by directly embedding it in the WSDL definition or by indirectly associating it through UDDI. WS-SecurityPolicy defines security policy assertions corresponding to the security claims defined by WS-Security: message integrity assertion, message confidentiality assertion, and message security token assertion.

The goals of WS-Policy and WS-PolicyAttachment are to offer mechanisms to represent the capabilities and requirements of Web services as Policies. The Policy view in WS-Policy is as follows: A policy is used to convey conditions on an interaction between two Web service endpoints. The provider of a Web service exposes a policy to convey conditions under which it provides the service. A requester might use this policy to decide whether or not to use the service.

WS-Trust: As stated in [WST], WS-Trust is a WS-* specification and OASIS standard that provides extensions to WS-Security. It deals with the issuing, renewing, and validating of security tokens. It also brokers trust relationships between participants in a secure message exchange carried out via Secure Conversation. Security (confidentiality and integrity) is achieved through encryption, digital signatures, and certificates. Ultimately, security depends on the *secure management* of cryptographic keys and security tokens: key/security token issuance, key/security token transmission, key/security token storage, and key/security token exchange. More formally, Web Services Trust Language (WS-Trust) was released in 2005, and its goal is to enable the issuance and dissemination of credentials among different trust domains. WS-Trust defines extensions to WS-Security that provide *methods for issuing, renewing, and validating security tokens and ways to establish, assess the presence of, and broker trust relationships.* The recipient of a WS-Security-protected SOAP message has three potential issues with the security token contained within the Security header—Format: the format or syntax of the token is not known to the recipient; Trust: the recipient may be unable to build a chain of trust from its own trust anchors (e.g., its X.509 Certificate Authority, a local Kerberos KDC, or a SAML Authority) to the issuer or signer of the token; Namespace: the recipient may be unable to directly comprehend the set of claims within the token because of syntactical differences.

Message reliability is provided by WS-ReliableMessaging, which was discussed in Part I. Message security is provided by WS-Security (as discussed in Section 9.2) and SecureConversation. As stated in the wiki article, WS-SecureConversation is a Web Services specification, created by IBM and others, that works in conjunction with WS-Security, WS-Trust, and WS-Policy to allow the creation and sharing of security contexts. The goal of WS-SecureConversation is to establish security contexts for multiple SOAP message exchanges. This in turn reduces the overhead of key establishment. Conversations focus on the public processes in which the participants of a Web service engage. WSCL is the Web Services Conversation Language. More formally, WS-Conversation provides secure communication across one or more messages and extends WS-Security mechanisms. It slows the authentication of a *series* of SOAP messages (conversation) by establishing and sharing between two endpoints of a *security context* for a message conversation using a series of derived keys to increase security. The security context is defined as a new token type that is obtained using a binding of WS-Trust. Security Context is an abstract concept that refers to an established authentication state and negotiated keys that may have additional security-related properties. A *security context token (SCT)* is a representation of that security context abstract concept, which allows a context to be named by a URI and used with WS-Security.

Policy and access control are provided by WS-Policy, XACML, and SAML. SAML was developed by the OASIS XML-Based Security Services Technical Committee (SSTC), and its main goal is to provide *authentication* and *authorization*. It promotes interoperability between disparate authentication and authorization systems. It achieves this by defining an XML-based framework for communicating security and identity information (e.g., authentication, entitlements, and attribute) between computing entities using available different security infrastructures (e.g., PKI, Kerberos, LDAP, etc.). eXtensible Access Control Markup Language 2 (XACML 2.0) is an OASIS Standard. It is a general-purpose access control policy language for managing access to resources. It describes both a policy language and an access control decision request/response language. It also provides fine-grained access control, where access control is based on subject and object attributes. It is consistent with and builds upon SAML. More details of XACML and SAML will be discussed in Chapter 11.

Security Management is essentially provided by SAML and XKMS. As stated by W3C, the XML Key Management Specification (XKMS) comprises two parts: the XML Key Information Service Specification (X-KISS) and the XML Key Registration Service Specification (X-KRSS). As stated in the W3C specification, X-KISS allows a client to delegate part or all of the tasks required to process XML Signature elements to an XKMS service. Essentially, X-KISS minimizes the complexity of applications using XML Signature by becoming a client of the XKMS service. In this way, W3C states that the application is relieved of the complexity and syntax of the underlying PKI used to establish trust relationships. W3C also stated that X-KRSS describes a protocol for registration and subsequent management of public key information.

The final component we will discuss is identity management. The standards for this service are SAML, WS-Federation, and Liberty Alliance. As stated in the wiki article, WS-Federation is an Identity Federation specification, developed by BEA Systems (now Oracle), IBM, Microsoft, and others. It defines mechanisms for allowing disparate security entities to broker information on identities, identity attributes, and authentication. The Liberty Alliance was formed in September 2001 by approximately 30 organizations to establish open standards, guidelines, and best practices for identity management. We will give more details on these identity standards when we discuss Federated Identity Management in Chapter 12.

9.4 Summary and Directions

In this chapter, we provided an overview of secure Web services and secure SOA and discussed security standards for Web services. In particular, we discussed both WS-Security and WS-* Security. While several standards are emerging for secure Web services, we need to ensure that these standards work together and provide security. While end-to-end security is desired, with the emergence of several technologies and products being developed at different locations, what we need is to be able to build secure applications even if the underlying components are compromised.

Web services and service-oriented architectures are at the heart of the next generation Web. We expect them to make use of semantic Web technologies to generate machine understandable Web pages. This was one of the major developments in the late 1990s and early 2000s. While there are numerous developments on Web services, the application of semantic Web technologies and securing Web services are major challenges. Furthermore, major initiatives such as the global information grid and the network-centric enterprise services are based on Web services and service-oriented architectures. Therefore, securing these technologies as well as making Web services more intelligent by using the semantic Web will be critical for the next-generation Web.

Exercises

1. Conduct a survey of secure Web services.
2. Describe the various components of Web services security.

References

[BERT06] Bertino, E. and L. Martino, Security in SOA and Web Services, *IEEE SCC 2006.*
[WSS] WS-Security, http://en.wikipedia.org/wiki/WS-Security
[WST] WS-Trust, http://en.wikipedia.org/wiki/WS-Trust

Chapter 10

Secure Service-Oriented Analysis and Design

10.1 Overview

As services technologies explode in popularity, we need a way to effectively model applications based on services. Services-oriented analysis and design (SOAD) approaches were developed for this purpose, and IBM is one of the leaders in this field. In Chapter 4, we discussed the service-oriented life cycle and approach for SOAD, including SOMA and SOMF. While SOAD works for services modeling, we need secure SOAD for modeling secure services. In this chapter, we discuss some preliminary ideas toward developing secure SOAD.

The organization of this chapter is as follows. Since SOAD has evolved from object-oriented analysis and design (OOAD), we discuss secure OOAD in Section 10.2. The secure service-oriented life cycle is discussed in Section 10.3. Secure SOAD will be discussed in Section 10.4. Some aspects of secure service modeling will be discussed in Section 10.5. Approaches to secure SOAD will be discussed in Section 10.6. Section 10.7 concludes the chapter.

10.2 Secure Object-Oriented Analysis and Design

Secure service modeling has benefited a lot from OOAD. OOAD approaches were developed in the 1980s and 1990s and evolved from entity relationship modeling.

These approaches include Rumbaugh's OMT and Booch's class diagrams. We have incorporated security into OMT in [SELL93]. For example, we developed an approach for modeling the relationships between objects from both dynamic and functional points of view. We also applied the methodology for healthcare applications as well as real-time applications [THUR94a], [THUR94b]. More details of this method will be given in Appendix C.

As we mentioned in Chapter 4, the various OOAD approaches were unified in the mid-1990s. Subsequently, UML (Unified Modeling Language) was developed. UML was applied to secure applications by several researchers, including Indrakshi Ray [RAY04]. Some of the developments were also applied to aspect-oriented modeling and analysis. However, with the emergence of services technologies, UML is now being applied to model services, and we expect that this approach will be applied to secure services. However, as we mentioned earlier, we have to be careful not to artificially model services as objects. Therefore, we need a bottom-up approach to model services and subsequently secure them.

10.3 Secure Service-Oriented Life Cycle

Security has been incorporated into the software engineering life cycle and more recently into the object-oriented life cycle. For example, security engineering deals with defining security policies, incorporating security into the design of the system, security testing, and maintenance. In the case of object-oriented system life cycle, security considerations will include defining the security policies on objects and activities as well as incorporating security into the design of the object system and security testing and maintenance. Similarly, in the case of secure service-oriented life cycle, we need to determine the security policies, the security levels of the services, and the interactions between the services, including the composition of the services, incorporating security into the design and development of the services, and subsequently testing the secure services (Figures 10.1 and 10.2).

As we have discussed in Chapter 4, in his book on SOA, Thomas Erl explained the service life cycle. He stated three ways to develop services: one is the top-down approach, the second is the bottom-up approach, and the third is what he called the agile approach. Security cannot be an afterthought in the design of services. One has to consider security in the top-down, bottom-up, and the agile approaches. In the top-down approach, one has to conduct analysis, then design the services, develop them, test them, integrate them, and then maintain them. Here, security policies act as a guide throughout the process. For example, when two services are composed, what is the resulting policy on the composed service? In the bottom-up approach, services are designed and developed as needed. Therefore, as services are designed, security has to be considered. For example, when a new service is designed, it should not violate the security policies specified for the prior services. In the agile approach, an integrated approach is used. That is, the application

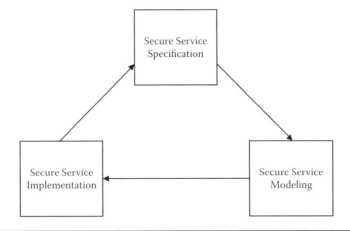

Figure 10.1 Secure service-oriented life cycle.

Figure 10.2 Secure service-oriented analysis and design.

is analyzed and the services are identified. However, one does not have to wait until all the services are identified. The security impact on this agile approach is yet to be investigated.

Another aspect when considering security is dynamic policies. That is, security policies enforced on the services and service compositions may change with time. The challenge is to ensure that there is no security violation when accommodating changing policies and security levels. This is also a major challenge in designing secure service-oriented systems.

10.4 Secure Service-Oriented Analysis and Design

We will consider the SOAD approach that we discussed in Chapter 4 and examine the security impact. The first step is to analyze the application and determine the services that describe the applications. The logic encapsulated by each service, the reuse of the logic encapsulated by the service, and the interfaces to the service have to be identified. From a security policy of view, in defining the services we have to consider the security policies. What is the security level of the service? What are the policies enforced on the service? Who can have access to the service? When we decompose the service into smaller services to see how we can ensure that security is not violated. For example, Service A may not have access to Service B. However, Service B may be decomposed into Services C and D wherein A has access to C and not to D. Now, if A has access to both C and D, then the policy that A does not have access to B may be violated.

The next step is for the relationship between the services, including the composition of services, to be identified. In a top-down strategy, one has to identify all the services and the relationships before conducting the detailed design and development of the services. For large application design, this may not be feasible. In the case of bottom-up design, one has to identify services and start developing them. In agile design, both strategies are integrated. From a security policy point of view, there may be policies that define the relationship between the services. The example we gave earlier regarding services A, B, C, and D shows that while A may have access to C, A may not have access to D if we are to enforce the policy that A does not have access to B. Here, access means invoking a particular service.

In Chapter 4, we discussed that business logic could be modeled as services. Furthermore, such an approach sets the stage for orchestration-based service-oriented architectures. Orchestration essentially implements workflow logic that enables different applications to interoperate with each other. Also, we have stated orchestrations themselves may be implemented as services. Therefore, the orchestration service may be invoked for different applications also implemented as services to interoperate with each other. Business services also promote reuse. From a security point of view we have yet to determine who can involve the business logic and orchestration services. A lot of work has gone into security for workflow systems including the BFA model [BERT99]. Therefore, we needed to examine the principles in this work for business logic and orchestration services. When a service is reused, what happens if there are conflicting policies on reuse? Also, we have to make sure that there is no security violation through reuse.

In this section, we have discussed some of the key points in secure service-oriented analysis and design. In the next section, we will elaborate on secure service modeling.

10.5 Secure Service Modeling

In this section, we will consider the key points in service modeling discussed in Chapter 4 and examine the security impact. The main question is, how do you define a service? At the highest level, an entire application such as order management can be one service. However, this is not desirable. At the other extreme, a business process can be broken into several steps, and each step can be a service. The challenge is to group steps that carry out some specific task into a service. However, when security is given consideration, then not only do we have to group steps that carry out some specific task into a service, we also have to group steps that can be meaningfully executed. If security is based on multilevel security, then we may want to assign a security level for each service. In this way, the service can be executed by someone cleared at an appropriate level. Therefore, the challenge is to group steps in a way that is meaningful not only from a task point of view but also from a security point of view.

Next, we must examine the service candidates and determine the relationships between them. One service may call other services. Two services may be composed to create a composite service. This would mean identifying the boundaries and the interface, and make the composition and separations as clear as possible. Dependencies may result in complex service designs. The service operations could be simple operations such as performing calculations or complex operations such as invoking multiple services. Here again, security may impact the relationships between the services. If two services have some relationships between them, then both services should be accessible to a group of users or users cleared at a particular level. For example, if service A and service B are tightly integrated, it may not make sense for a service C to have access to A and not to B. If A is about making a hotel reservation and B is about making a rental car reservation, then an airline reservation service C should be able to invoke both services A and B.

Once the candidate services and the service operations are indemnified, the next step is to refine the candidates and state the design of the services and the service operations. Therefore, from a security point of view, we have to refine the services and service operations that are not only meaningful but also secure. Mapping of the candidate service to the actual service has to be carried out according to the policies.

10.6 Secure SOAD Approaches

As we have discussed in Chapter 4, there are multiple service-oriented analysis and design methods, and we discussed some of them in that chapter. In this chapter, we will examine the security impact of the various methods. We believe that we make progress toward a uniform service-oriented analysis and design mythology similar to, for instance, UML; we will have a better idea of security for such a methodology. Figure 10.3 illustrates the various secure SOAD approaches. Some details follow:

Secure SOMA: As stated in [SOMA], SOMA implements SOAD through the identification, specification, and realization of services; components that realize the service components; and flows that can be used to compose services. With secure SOMA, we need to identify the policies enforced on the services and the various components. For multilevel secure Web services, we also need to assign security levels of services. In addition, the execution level of services should also be defined.

Secure SOMF: As stated in Chapter 4, SOMF (Service-Oriented Modeling Framework) is a service-oriented development life-cycle methodology and

Secure SOMA: Secure Service Oriented Modeling Architecture
Secure SOMF: Secure Service Oriented Modeling Framework

Figure 10.3 Approaches for secure SOAD.

offers a number of modeling practices and disciplines that contribute to successful service-oriented life cycle management and modeling. The security impact on this framework needs to be examined.

Secure UML for Services: Secure UML for services essentially developed secure UML for service-oriented analysis and modeling. Several approaches to applying UML and other object-oriented analysis and design approaches to secure applications have been proposed. We need to extend these approaches to secure SOAD. We also need to examine the security impact on service-oriented discovery and analysis modeling, service-oriented business integration modeling, service-oriented logical design modeling, service-oriented conceptual architecture modeling, and service-oriented logical architecture modeling.

10.7 Summary and Directions

This chapter has provided a brief overview of secure SOAD. We started with a discussion of secure OOAD. Then we discussed the concept of secure service-oriented life cycles. This was followed by a discussion of secure SOAD and secure services modeling. Finally, approaches to secure SOAD were discussed.

SOAD as well as secure SOAD are in their infancy. While there are currently various approaches for secure SOAD, we believe that eventually these approaches will be combined to develop a unified approach. In the same way, one can also expect secure SOAD approaches to be unified. However, first we need some approaches to securely modeling services, and research is just beginning in this area.

Exercises

1. Examine the various SOAD approaches, and develop an appropriate S-SOAD approach.
2. Describe the S-SOAD approach developed under Problem 1 with an example.

References

[BERT99] Bertino, E., Ferrari, E., and Atluri, V. The specification and enforcement of authorization constraints in workflow management systems, *ACM Trans. Inf. Syst. Secur.* 2(1): 65–104, 1999.

[RAY04] Ray, I., Li, N., France, R.B., Kim, D. Using uml to visualize role-based access control constraints. 115–124, 2004.

[SELL93] Sell, P. J. and B. Thuraisingham, Applying OMT for designing multilevel database applications, *DBSec 1993*: 41–64.

[SOMA] http://en.wikipedia.org/wiki/Service-oriented_modeling

[THUR94a] Thuraisingham, B. and A. Schafer, Applying OMT for real-time applications, *Proceedings of the IEEE Real-time Applications Workshop*, Bethesda, MD, July 1994.

[THUR94b] Thuraisingham, B., Applying OMT for healthcare applications, *Proceedings IEEE Dual Use Technology Conference*, Rome, NY, May 1994.

Chapter 11

Access Control for Web Services

11.1 Overview

Much of our work on Web services is based on access control. As discussed in Part I, access control policies specify rules that must be satisfied for subjects to access objects. Several access control policies have been developed for information systems, including discretionary access control policies, mandatory access control policies and, more recently, role-based access control policies and usage control policies. One type of access control that is being adopted in many applications, including those of the Department of Defense, is attribute-based access control, as such a model is more amenable to open systems such as the Web environment. Furthermore, the models that are being developed by standards organizations such as OASIS are also based on some form of attribute-based access control. In this chapter, we will focus on various standards for access control and then discuss attribute-based access control. In addition, some other features such as establishing trust in a Web environment as well as approaches to inference control based on access control are also discussed. Our current research on Web services security will be discussed in detail in Chapter 13. Details on privacy trust establishment and management as well as integrity aspects will be discussed in Part III.

The organization of this chapter is as follows. In Sections 11.2 and 11.3, we discuss some of the emerging standards for access control for Web services. These are Security Assertion Markup Language (SAML) and eXtensible Access Control Markup Language (XACML), respectively (Figure 11.1). In Section 11.4, we provide

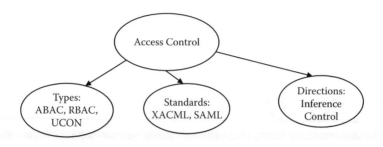

Figure 11.1   Access control concepts.

an overview of attribute-based access control, also called ABAC. In Section 11.5, we discuss some of our ideas on inference control, which extends access control to control inferences in a Web environment. The chapter is summarized in Section 11.6.

11.2 SAML

SAML [SAML] provides a single point of authorization (Figure 11.2). It aims to "solve the Web single sign-on" problem. One identity provider in a group allows access. It has Public/Private Key Foundations. Those who are providing SAML in their products are Microsoft Passport, OpenID (VeriSign), and Global Login System (Open Source). As stated in the SAML specifications, its three main components are

Assertions: SAML has three kinds of assertions. Authentication assertions are those in which the user has proved his identity (example: "John Smith was authenticated with a password at 9:00 am").

Attribute assertions contain specific information about the user, such as his spending limits ("John Smith is an account manager with a $1000 spending limit per one-day travel"). Authorization decision assertions identify what the user can do, for example, whether he can buy an item. (example: "John Smith is permitted to buy a specified item").

SAML Authority: A system entity that makes SAML assertions (also called Identity Provider—IdP—and Asserting Party).

Service Provider: A system entity making use of SAML assertions.

Relying Party: A system entity that uses received assertions (named also SAML requester).

Protocol: This defines the way that SAML asks for and gets assertions, for example, using SOAP over HTTP for now, although using other methods in the future.

Binding: This details exactly how SAML message exchanges are mapped into SOAP exchanges.

SAML addresses one key aspect of identity management, which is how identity information can be communicated from one domain to another. SAML 2.0 will

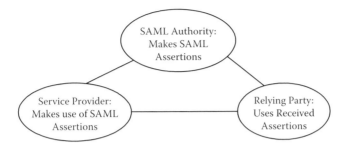

Figure 11.2 Security Assertion Markup Language.

be the basis on which the Liberty Alliance will build additional federated identity applications (such as Web-service-enabled permissions-based attribute sharing).

The SAML profile is another important concept. It defines constraints and/or extensions of the core protocols and assertions in support of the usage of SAML for a particular application. It activates interoperability and stipulates how particular statements are communicated using appropriate protocol messages over specified bindings. (For example, Web Browser SSO Profile specifies how SAML authentication assertions are communicated using the Authentication Query and Response messages over a number of different bindings in order to enable Single Sign-On for a browser user.) By agreeing to support a particular SAML profile (as opposed to the complete specification set), parties who wish to exchange SAML messages have a much simpler job of achieving interoperability.

Outstanding Issues for SAML include performance, federations, and handling legacy applications. With respect to performance, there is no support for caching and, also, it has to be implemented over HTTP protocols using SOAP. Furthermore, it does not specify encryption and, as a result, the policies may be compromised. With respect to federations, SAML does not specify authentication protocols. Furthermore, multiple domains cannot be handled. Therefore, OASIS is examining federated identity management. SAML does not work with legacy applications as it is expensive to retrofit.

11.3 XACML

XACML [XACML] is a general-purpose authorization policy model and XML-based specification language (Figure 11.3). It is independent of the SAML specification and has a triple-based policy syntax: <Object, Subject, Action>. It supports negative authorization. Input/output to the XACML policy processor is clearly defined as XACML context data structure. Input data is referred by XACML-specific attribute designator as well as XPath expression.

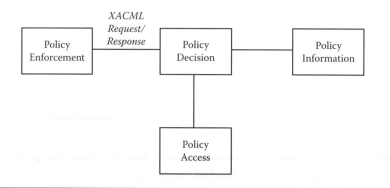

Figure 11.3   eXtensible Access Control Markup Language.

A policy consists of multiple rules, and a set of policies is combined by a higher-level policy (PolicySet element). XACML combines multiple rules into a single policy. It permits multiple users to have different roles. It provides separation between policy writing and application environment. The goal is to standardize access control languages. A Policy has four main components: a target, a rule-combining algorithm identifier, a set of rules, and obligations. The rule is the elementary unit of a policy. The main components of a rule are: a target, an effect (permit or deny), and a condition. A policy target specifies a set of Resources, Subjects, Actions, and the Environment to which it applies.

Some elements of XACML are the following. Users interact with resources. Every resource is protected by an entity known as a Policy Enforcement Point (PEP). This is where the language is actually used and does not actually determine access. PEP sends its request to a Policy Decision Point (PDP). Policies may or may not be actually stored here, but have the final say on access. Decision is relayed to PEP, which then grants or denies access. The architecture for XACML processing is illustrated in Figure 11.3. When a client makes a resource request to a server, the PEP is charged with enforcing the access control polices. However, in order to enforce the policies, the PEP will formalize the attributes describing the requester at the PIP and delegate the authorization decision to the PDP. Applicable policies are located in a policy store, managed by the PAP, and evaluated at the PDP, which then returns the authorization decision. Using this information, the PEP can deliver the appropriate response to the client. As stated earlier, XACML Request is threefold: Subject, Object, and Action. XACML Response is one of the following: Permit, Permit with Obligations, Deny, Not Applicable (the PDP cannot locate a policy whose target matches the required resource), and Indeterminate (an error occurred or some required value was missing).

In summary, the XCML protocol works as follows. The *Policy Administration Point* (PAP) creates security policies and stores them in the appropriate repository. The *Policy Enforcement Point* (PEP) performs access control by making decision requests and enforcing authorization decisions. The *Policy Information Point* (PIP) serves as the source of attribute values, or the data required for policy evaluation. The *Policy Decision Point* (PDP) evaluates the applicable policy and renders an authorization decision. Note that the PEP and PDP might be contained within the same application, or might be distributed across different servers.

Outstanding issues of XACML include distributed responsibility and policy cross-referencing. With respect to distributed responsibility, what happens when the PEP is responsible for multiple objects? What happens when we can compromise the PDP or spoof its communication? How do we guarantee that we reference the right object? While the system is distributed, a policy is still in only one location. With respect to policy cross-referencing, one policy may access another. Typical issues arise as with inheritance and unions/intersections of related work. The challenge is to deal with conflicts.

11.4 Attribute-Based Access Control

XACML essentially implements attribute-based access control. While password-based access control works well in a closed environment, in an open environment such as the Web it is difficult to implement such mechanisms. Therefore, the concept of attribute-based access control was developed in early 2000. With this approach, the user will present his or credentials, credentials are issued by some credential authority. The system (or server) will validate the user's credentials with multiple credential authorities if needed. Once the credentials are verified, the system will then check the policies for the credentials and determine the access that the user has to the resources. Figure 11.4 illustrates attribute-based access control [ABAC].

ABAC has been implemented in many systems, including in DoD's network-centric enterprise services and the global information grid. ABAC can also be utilized to implement RBAC (role-based access control). In this case, a user has credentials depending on his or her roles, and based on the credentials, the user is granted access. The credentials are essentially the user's attributes. More recently, Sandhu has developed a model called UCON (Usage Control) that includes usage of a resource for controlling access to the resource. For example, in the case of a phone card, as one uses the phone card, its value is determined and access is dependent on the value of the phone card, which is essentially the number of minutes

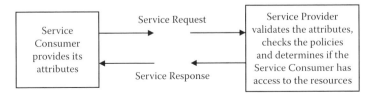

Figure 11.4 Attribute-based access control.

remaining for usage. What would be desirable is to integrate ABAC with UCON so that one has a model that controls access based on attributes of the subject/user and the usage of the resource.

11.5 Inference Control

Our approach to inference control is to reason with the security policies and determine the access that a user has to the objects. We call the security policies security constraints. We have identified several constraints, including those that classify data based on content, context, aggregation, and time. The work reported in [THUR87] and [KEEF89] suggests handling security constraints during query processing in such a way that certain security violations via inference do not occur. The work reported in [MORG87] and HINK88] focuses on handling constraints during database design, where suggestions for database design tools are given. They expect that security constraints during database design will be handled in such a way that security violations cannot occur. We describe the design techniques for processing security constraints. Our approach to handling security constraints has been influenced by the approach taken to process integrity constraints by logic programming researchers [LLOY87], [GALL78].

Before designing a constraint processor, a question that must be answered is whether a constraint should be processed during query processing, during database updates, or during database design. When constraints are handled during query processing, they are treated as a form of derivation rules. That is, they are used to assign security levels to the data already in the database before it is released. In other words, new information (e.g., the security labels) is deduced from information already in the database. When the security constraints are handled during update processing, they are treated as a form of integrity rules. That is, they are constraints that must be satisfied by the data in the multilevel database. When the constraints are handled during database design, then they must be satisfied by the database schema in the same way that functional and multivalued dependency constraints must be satisfied by the schema of a relational database. Our approach is an integrated approach to inference control. Figure 11.5 illustrates the inference controller. Each of the modules, including the data manager, the constraint manager, and the database manager, may be implemented as Web services with one Web service invoking another.

11.6 Summary and Directions

In this chapter, we have discussed access control for services. In particular, we have focused on confidentiality aspects of security. First, we discussed access control in general and provided an overview of the various emerging standards such as

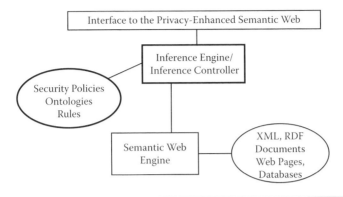

Figure 11.5 Inference controller.

SAML and XACML. Then we discussed ABAC. Finally, we discussed the inference problem for services with respect to access control.

There is a lot of work that needs to be done. We need an appropriate security model for services. ABAC is one such model. We need to examine how ABAC can be integrated with UCON. We also need to examine the inference problem in more details for services. Finally, we need to develop standards similar to SAML and XACML to include more sophisticated forms of fine-grained access control.

Exercises

1. Conduct a survey of various access control models.
2. Give an example illustrating ABAC, XACML, and SAML.

References

[ABAC] Information System Security Operation: Attribute-Based Access Control, http://www.isso.sparta.com/documents/abac.pdf

[GALL78] Gallaire, H. and Minker, J., *Logic and Databases*, Plenum Press, New York, 1978.

[HINK88] Hinke, T.H., Database inference engine design approach, DBSec, 247–262, 1988.

[KEEF89] Keefe, T.F., Thuraisingham, B.M., and Tsai, W., Secure query-processing strategies, *IEEE Computer*, 22(3): 63–70, 1989.

[LLOY87] Lloyd, J., *Foundations of Logic Programming*, Springer, Heidelberg, Germany, 1987.

[MORG87] Morgenstern, M., Security and inference in multilevel database and knowledge-base systems, SIGMOD Conference, 357–373, 1987.

[SAML] Security Assertion Markup Language, http://en.wikipedia.org/wiki/Security_Assertion_Markup_Language

[THUR87] Thuraisingham, B. Security checking in relational database management systems augmented with inference engines, *Computer and Security*, 6(6): 479–492, 1987.

[XACML] XACML, http://en.wiki pedia.org/wiki/XACML

Chapter 12

Digital Identity Management

12.1 Overview

Identity management, also referred to as federated identity management or digital identity management, is closely intertwined with Web services. Users as well as Web services have to be authenticated before they can access resources. Single Sign-On is the popular solution, in which one time sign-on gives a user or a service access to the various resources. Furthermore, SAML currently provides authentication facilities for Web services. However, with regulatory requirements for e-business, one needs a stronger mechanism for authentication, and this mechanism has come to be known as identity management.

As discussed in [FED], federated identity "describes the technologies, standards and use cases which serve to enable the portability of identity information across otherwise autonomous security domains." The goal is to ensure that users of one domain take advantage of all the technologies offered by another domain in a seamless manner. Note that federation is about organizations working together to carry out a task (such as B2B operations) or solving a particular problem. While the idea has been around for many years, it is only recently with the emerging standards of four Web services that we can now have secure federations. In such federations, access to the resources by users has to be managed without burdening the user.

With appropriate federated identity management, users should be able to share data across domains, support single sign-on, and enable cross-domain user attribute management. Cross-domain single sign-on is one of the popular techniques for federated identity management. However, many new techniques are being developed. One of the prominent consortiums for developing standards for federated identity management is the Liberty Alliance. Other projects include the Open ID project as well as Information Card. This chapter will provide an overview of the various developments with identity management.

The organization of this chapter is as follows. In Section 12.2 we will discuss concepts such as single sign-on and federated identity management. The Identity Metasystem and its implementation with Information Card will be discussed in Section 12.3. The OpenID project will be discussed in Section 12.4. A discussion of Shibboleth will be provided in Section 12.5. An overview of the Liberty Alliance will proceed in Section 12.6. Section 12.7 concludes the chapter. Much of the information in this chapter has been obtained from various definitions given in Web pages, including Wikipedia entries.

12.2 Single Sign-On and Federated Identity Management

Two concepts that underlie digital identity management are (1) single sign-on and (2) federated identity management. We discuss these concepts in this section. The following sections discuss the technologies and standards developed for single sign-on and federated identity management. These include the work of Liberty Alliance, the Identity Metasystem and its Information Card implementation, the Open-ID project, and Shibboleth.

As stated in [SSO], single sign-on (SSO) is a property where a user logs in once and gains access to all systems, possibly in a federation. The user only has to log in once to access the resources in the federation or coalition or organization, without being prompted to log in again at each of them. Two types of SSO mechanisms exist: Kerberos based and smart card based. With the Kerberos mechanism, Kerberos ticket granting ticket (TGT) is used to grant credentials. In the smart card based sign-on, the user uses the smart card for sign-on. Enterprise Single Sign-on (ESSO) provides support for minimizing typing passwords and user IDs when accessing multiple applications. Figure 12.1 illustrates single-sign on.

As stated in the wiki article [FED], "federated identity, or the 'federation' of identity, describes the technologies, standards and use-cases which serve to enable the portability of identity information across otherwise autonomous security domains." The use cases include typical use cases, including cross-domain, Web-based single sign-on. Various Web sites are now implementing federated identity management through Open-ID to be explained in a later section.

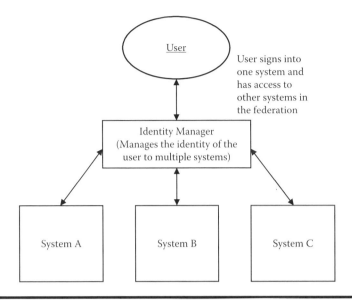

Figure 12.1 Single sign-on.

12.3 Identity Metasystem and Information Card

As stated in [IDEN], Identity Metasystem is an "interoperable architecture for digital identity that enables people to have and employ a collection of digital identities based on multiple underlying technologies, implementations, and providers." With this approach, users can continue to maintain their identities and choose the identity system that will work for them so that the system will manage their identities when migrating to different technologies. The roles of the Identity Metasystem are identity providers, relying parties, and subjects. Identity providers issue digital identities. Relying parties are the ones who require identities such as various services. Subjects include the end users and organizations.

Identities are represented using claims, which are essentially security tokens. With these claims, the identity providers, relying parties, and subjects can carry out the operations such as negotiation. WS-Trust and WS-Federation are used to obtain claims. The negotiation between the parties is carried out with WS-Security Policy (Chapter 9) and WS-MetadataExchange (Chapter 3). The seamless operation experienced by the user is provided by what is called an IdentitySelector client software which may access technologies such as information cards (to be explained in a later section). Figure 12.3 illustrates the entities in the Identity Metasystem.

Information Card is an implementation of the Identity Metasystem. As stated in the wiki article [INFO], information cards are personal digital identities that people can use online. The information cards are card-shaped pictures, and people can use these cards to manage their identities. Since it implements the Identity Metasystems, the parties involved in the Information Card implementation are the identity providers, relying parties, and the subject. Identity selectors such as Windows CardSpace are used to store and manage the user identities. Information cards support single sign-on as users can sign in at one place and have access to the various resources on the Web.

There are two types of information cards. Personal information cards enable a user to issue the claims (e.g., name, phone, etc.) and inform the various sites. The other type is managed information cards, where identity providers make claims about the user.

12.4 Open-ID

As stated in the wiki article [OPEN], OpenID is an open, decentralized user identification standard, allowing users to log onto many services with the same *digital identity*. OpenID is essentially a URL, and the user is authenticated by his or her OpenID provider. Many corporations such as Symantec and Microsoft support OpenID. For example, Microsoft provides interoperability between OpenID and its Windows CardSpace.

OpenID extends the entities of the Identity Metasystem and consists of the following:

End user: The person who wants to assert his or her identity to a site.
Identifier: The URL chosen by the end user as his or her OpenID identifier.
Identity provider or OpenID provider: This entity provides the service of registering OpenID URLs and provides OpenID authentication.
Relying party: The site that wants to verify the end user's identifier (this is essentially the service provider).
Server or server agent: The server that verifies the end user's identifier.
User agent: Users access the identity provider or a relying party through the user agent (e.g., the browser).

OpenID is used as follows. A user visits a relying party's (e.g., service provider) Web site to request a service. This relying party has an OpenID form, which is the login for the user. The user would then give his or her identity, which is provided by an Identity prior to the login process. From this information, the relying party will discover the identity provider Web site. As stated in the wiki article [OPEN], the relying party and the identity provider may have a *shared secret* that is referenced by an association handle and stored by the relying party. The relying party then directs the user's browser to the identity provider so that the user can authenticate with the identity provider, which the relying party then stores. The relying party redirects the user's Web browser to the identity provider so that the user can authenticate with the provider. Usually the identity provider requests a password from the user and then requests of the user whether he or she wants to trust the relying party. If the user rejects this request, then access to the services are denied. If not, the user browser is directed to the relying party with the user's credential. The browser is redirected to the designated return page on the relying party Web site along with the user's credentials. The relying party has to verify that the credential indeed came for the identity provider.

12.5 Shibboleth

As stated earlier, Shibboleth is a distributed Web resource access control system that allows federations to cooperate to share Web-based resources [SHIB]. It defines a protocol for carrying authentication information and user attributes from a home to a resource site. The resource site can then use the attributes to make access control decisions about the user. This Web-based middleware layer uses SAML. Access control is carried out in stages. In stage one, the resource site redirects the user to his or her home site, and obtains a handle for the user that is authenticated by the home site. In stage two, the resource site returns the handle to the attribute authority of the home site, and it returns a set of attributes of the user upon which to make an access control decision.

There are some issues with single sign-on in Shibboleth. How does the resource site know the home site of the user? How does it trust the handle returned? The answer is, it is handled by the system trust model. The authentication procedure is as follows. When the resource site asks for a home site from the user, he or she selects it from the list of trusted sites that are already authenticated by certificates. Handles are validated by the SAML signature along with the message. The user selects the home site from the list. The home site authenticates the user if he or she is already registered. After home server authentication, it returns a message with SAML sign to the Target Resource site. The resource site (if the sign matches) then provides a pseudonym (handle) for the user and sends an assertion message to the home page to find out if the necessary attributes are available with the user. To ensure privacy, the system provides a different pseudonym for the user's identity each time. It needs the release attribute policy from the user attributes each time to provide control over the authority attributes in the target site. The agreement attribute release policy is between the user and the administrator.

Trust is the heart of Shibboleth. It completely trusts the Target Resource site and Origin Home Site registered in the federation. The disadvantage of the existing Trust Model is that there is no differentiation between authentication authorities and attribute authorities. It is possible to allow more sophisticated distribution of trust, such as static or dynamic delegation of authority. Another disadvantage in the existing trust model is that it provides only basic access control capabilities. It lacks the flexibility and sophistication required by many applications that have to provide access control decisions based on role hierarchies or various constraints such as the time of day or separation of duties.

In the basic Shibboleth, the target site trusts the origin site to authenticate its users and manage their attributes correctly, while the original site trusts the target site to provide services to its users. Trust is conveyed using digitally signed SAML messages using target and origin server key pairs. Each site has only one key pair per the Shibboleth system. There is only a single point of trust per Shibboleth system. Thus, there is a need for a finer-grained distributed trust model and the ability to use multiple origin authorities to issue and sign the authentication and attribute assertions. Multiple authorities should be able to issue attributes to users and the target site should be able to verify issuer/user bindings. The target should be able to state, in its policy, which of the attribute authorities it trusts to issue which attributes to which groups of users. The target site should be able to decide independently of the issuing site which attributes and authorities to trust when making its access control decisions. Not all attribute-issuing authorities need be part of the origin site. A target site should be able to allow a user to gain access to its resources if it has attributes issued by multiple authorities. The trust infrastructure should support dynamic delegation of authority, so that a holder of a privilege attribute may delegate (a subset of) this to another person without having to reconfigure anything in the system. The target site should be able to decide if it really does trust the origin's attribute repository, and if not, be able to demand a stronger proof of attribute entitlement than that conferred by a SAML signature from the sending Web server.

Shibboleth defines various trust models. These models have been implemented using X.509. We can look at trust from two different aspects: distribution of trust in attribute issuing authorities, and trustworthiness of an origin site's attribute repository.

The Shibboleth architecture is illustrated in Figure 12.2. Further details of the trust models and their implementations as well as authorization and privacy issues are discussed in [TRUST].

12.6 Liberty Alliance

The Liberty Alliance was formed to promote standards for identity management. It now consists of over a 100 members, including technology developers and vendors as well as consumers. Two major standards released by this consortium are the Liberty Identity Federation (also called identity federation) and the Liberty Identity Web Services (also called identity Web services)

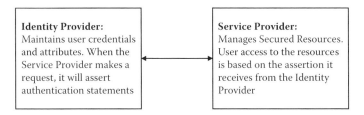

Figure 12.2   Shibboleth architecture.

Liberty Identity Federation enables Web users (e.g., e-commerce users) to authenticate and sign-on a domain and from there access multiple services. This is the basis of SAML 2.0. As stated in the wiki articles [LIB], the identity Web services standard is an open framework for deploying and managing identity-based Web services. These Web services applications include Geo-location, Contact Book, Calendar, Mobile Messaging, and Liberty People Service. With these services, one can manage bookmarks, blogs, photo sharing, and related social services on the Web in a private manner. Privacy and policy management are key aspects of the work of the Liberty Alliance. It is stated in [LIB] that more than a billion Liberty-enabled devices have been tracked globally. More recent efforts include the Identity Governance Framework, and the Identity Assurance Framework. The Identity Governance Framework is a collection of standards that support the storage and management of identity. It uses LDAP, SAML, and WS-Trust standards. The identity assurance framework supports four identity assurance levels. These levels have been determined by the National Institute of Standards and Technology. Figure 12.3 illustrates the contributions of the Liberty Alliance.

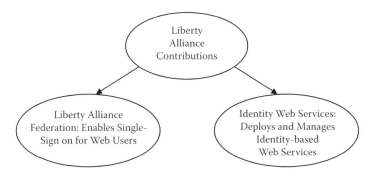

Figure 12.3   Liberty Alliance contributions.

12.7 Summary and Directions

This chapter has provided an overview of identity management systems. First, we discussed the notion of identity management and described single sign-on. Then we discussed the Identity Metasystem and various example systems, including Information Card, Open-ID, and Shibboleth. Finally, we discussed the contributions of the Liberty Alliance.

As Web services explode and we carry out more and more transactions on the Web and get involved in social networks, it is critical that we protect the identity of individuals as well as ensuring authorized access. Furthermore, a user may be involved in multiple social networks and multiple transactions. The user may have different identities in different systems. Therefore, we need an effective mechanism to manage the numerous identities of possibly billions of users. Research on identity management is just beginning. We need a lot more work in this area, including developing appropriate standards.

Exercises

1. Describe identity management technologies.
2. Describe the design of Shibboleth.
3. Describe the standards developed by the Liberty Alliance.

References

[FED] Federated Identity, http://en.wikipedia.org/wiki/Federated_identity
[IDEN] Identity Management, http://en.wikipedia.org/wiki/Identity_management
[INFO] Information Card, http://en.wikipedia.org/wiki/Information_Card
[LIB] Liberty Alliance, http://en.wikipedia.org/wiki/Liberty_Alliance
[OPEN] OpenID, http://en.wikipedia.org/wiki/OpenID
[SHIB] Shibboleth Internet 2, http://en.wikipedia.org/wiki/Shibboleth_%28Internet2%29
[SSO] Single sign-on. Http://en.wikipedia.org/wiki/Single_sign-on
[TRUST] http://en.wikipedia.org/wiki/Trust_negotiation

Chapter 13

Security Models for Web Services

13.1 Overview

Much of the work on secure Web services has focused on access control models. That is, access control policies will determine the access that a user has to the resources provided by Web services. As we have discussed in the previous chapters, several standards such as XACML have been developed based on the access control models. However, for many applications, the access control models are not sufficient. For example, in the case of composite Web services, one Web service, S1, may invoke another Web service, S2. In such an invocation, S1's privileges will be enforced and not those of the user U who invoked S1. This means that the information that is returned to U may be something the user is not authorized to know. To avoid such security compromises, a user U may have to delegate its privileges to S1 so that U's privileges are used when S1 invokes S2. Such an invocation is governed by the delegation models that are utilized.

Another security concern for composite Web services is information flow. That is, when Web services are composed, it is critical that there be no information flow from a high level to a low level. Our research focuses on various aspects of Web services security, including the delegation models and information flows for Web service composition. Therefore, in this chapter, we will provide an overview of our research in Web services security. This research is being carried out by Wei She, I-Ling Yen, Bhavani Thuraisingham, and Elisa Bertino. In particular, we summarize the

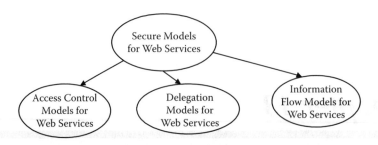

Figure 13.1   Security models for Web services.

work we have reported in our recent papers [SHE07], [SHE08], [SHE09]. The organization of this chapter is as follows. In Section 13.2, we will present our delegation model for Web services. In Section 13.3, we will describe our information flow in service composition. Multilevel security for Web services is discussed in Section 13.4. Section 13.5 concludes the chapter. Figure 13.1 illustrates security models for Web services.

13.2 Delegation Model

Access control models specify the access that subjects have to objects. It does not specify policies for invoking Web services. We need appropriate policies for invoking Web services. For example, suppose service S1 invokes service S2. Further, suppose S1 does not have access to a resource X, while S2 has access to resource X. If S2 has to access X and returns X to S1, then there is a security violation. This means when S2 accesses X on behalf of S1, then S1's privileges must be passed to S2. In the foregoing example, such a policy will work, as S2 has additional credentials that do not belong to S1. The question is, what happens if S2 does not have access to X while S1 has access to X. If S1's credentials are passed to S2, then S2 will have access to X. However, S2 should not have access to X. As a result, we need to pass the credentials that are common to both S1 and S2. In this case, when S1 involves S2, S2 will get the credentials that are common to both S1 and S2. This also means that S2 will be operating with limited credentials. Figure 13.2 illustrates this model.

We have conducted extensive research on delegation models for Web services [SHE07], [SHE08]. We believe that delegation models have to be flexible. In some cases, S2 will operate with a limited set of credentials in which case no access control policies will be violated. That is, if S1 invokes S2, then S2 will not access any resources that are not accessible to S1. However, in some cases, S2 may need to operate using its full credential. Then S2 has to decide what information is to be passed on to S1.

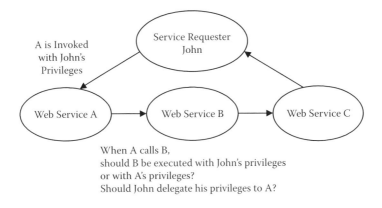

Figure 13.2 Delegation model for Web services.

Delegation models get more complicated if there are no overlapping credentials. That is, if S1 and S2 do not have any credentials in common, then S1 cannot invoke S2. For example, if S1 operates with the credentials of a professor and S2 operates with the credentials of a secretary, and if the professor and secretary do not have any common credentials, then a professor cannot request a secretary to carry out some functions. In such a case, the system has to determine how to delegate. Separation of duty is an important condition in security models. The challenge is how to bring separation of duty concepts into security models for Web services. Combining access control models with delegation models for composition of Web services as well as chain-based Web services needs substantial research. Note that a chain-based Web service is of the form S1 invoking S2, S2 invoking S3, and S3 invoking S4.

13.3 Information Flow Model

To understand information flow models, we need to examine the historical models. Back in 1973, the Bell and La Padula model was developed for access control. While this model prevented a low-level subject from getting high-level data directly, it did not prevent illegal information flow. For example, by manipulating the locks in a file, data could be covertly passed from a high-level subject to a low-level subject. To prevent this type of flow, Goguen and Messeguer developed the noninterference model around 1982. With this model, it was not possible for data to flow from a high-level subject to a low-level subject. Essentially, the actions of a high-level subject did do interfere with those of a low-level subject. Our research applied a similar principle for Web services.

There have been many attempts to prevent illegal information flow for Web services. However, the prior work focused on the following aspects. Each Web service

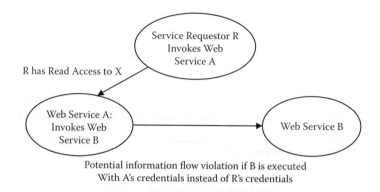

Figure 13.3   Information flow model for Web services.

satisfied security properties. The composition of the Web services also satisfied security properties. However, the information flow between the intermediate services was not considered. For example, if Web service S1 is composed of Web services S2, S3, and S4, while the end result was secure, there could still be illegal information flow from S3 to S1. Figure 13.3 illustrates this illegal information flow.

Our approach prevents such information flows. Another assumption made by previous models is that the composition of Web services was carried out by a trusted process. This is not realistic when in the Web environment, where there are multiple security domains; therefore, we cannot make such an assumption. Our work does not make such an assumption.

Our work on information flow models for Web services is detailed in [SHE09]. In particular, we specify transformation factors that measure how likely it is that the inputs and logical data of a service can be inferred from its outputs. This in turn is used to determine whether information is flowing illegally from a high-level service to a lower-level service. We also develop protocols so that the composition processes are not trusted. We then develop algorithms for collaboratively carrying out security validation in a Web environment.

13.4 Multilevel Secure Web Services

Much of the security research for Web services is based on discretionary severity. In particular, attribute-based access control is enforced in many of the models for Web services. We discussed such models in the previous chapters. Our research focuses on delegation models and information flow models. Our work in information flow models has been influenced by the Goguen and Meseguer model for noninterference.

There is little work reported on multilevel security for Web services. Nevertheless, we believe that it is an important topic. We need to ensure not only the Bell and La Padula model's simple security and star properties, but also Goguen and

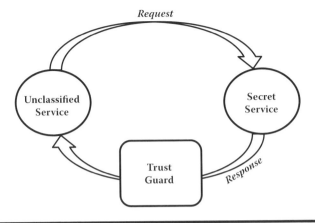

Figure 13.4 Multilevel security for Web services.

Meseguer's noninterference model. In the Bell and La Padula model, a subject can read from an object if the subject's security level dominates that of the object. A subject writes into an object if the subject's security level is dominated by that of the object. In addition, for Web services, we also need policies for invocation. That is, a service S1 invokes another service S2 if the S1 security level of the service description of S1 dominates the security level of the service description of S2. However, when S1 invokes S2, S2 will operate at the operating level of S1. In this way, S2 will have all the credentials of S1. Therefore, if the service description of S2 dominates that of S1, then S1 cannot invoke S2. For example, if the service description of S2 is secret and that of S1 is unclassified and S1 operates at the unclassified level, then S1 cannot invoke S2. If, for example, S1 is allowed to invoke S2, then S2 must operate at the unclassified level, and this is a problem since the description of S2 is secret. Suppose now the service descriptions of S1 and S2 satisfied the policies. If, however, S1 operates at unclassified and S2 is allowed to operate at the secret level, then S2 cannot send any results back to S1 as it will violate the star property.

These are some of our initial ideas on multilevel security for Web services. We have applied some of them in our work on information flow. Figure 13.4 illustrates multilevel security for Web services.

13.5 Summary and Directions

In this chapter, we have discussed our research on secure Web services. While much of the work has focused on access control models for Web services, we have focused on delegation models and information flow models. With delegation models, the idea is for services to delegate their credentials to another service that it invokes for execution. With information flow models, the goal is to ensure that information is not passed from a high level to a low level during service composition.

While access control models for Web services are fairly advanced, research in delegation models and information flow models is still in its infancy. Our work has only explored some initial ideas. We need to formally specify security properties and prove that the services are secure with respect to delegation models and information flow models. We also need to examine the integration of access control, delegation, and information flow models.

Exercises

1. Describe the pros and cons of the delegation model proposed in this chapter.
2. Describe the pros and cons of the information flow control model proposed in this chapter.

References

[SHE07] She, W., B. M. Thuraisingham, and I-L. Yen, Delegation-based security model for Web services, *HASE 2007*: 82–91.

[SHE08] She, W., I-L. Yen, and B. M. Thuraisingham, Enhancing security modeling for Web services using delegation and pass-on, *ICWS 2008*: 545–552.

[SHE09] She, W., I-L. Yen, B. M. Thuraisingham, and E. Bertino: The SCIFC model for information flow control in Web service composition, *ICWS 2009*: 1–8.

Conclusion to Part II

In Part II, we discussed secure services technologies. We first provided an overview of secure services computing, secure service-oriented architectures and Web services, and secure service-oriented analysis and design. This was followed by some emerging topics, including access control, identity management, and delegation and information flow.

Now that we have explained some of the basic concepts, we will focus on some advanced concepts as well as on applications in Parts III, IV, and V. In Part III, we will discuss dependability aspects of services, including trust, privacy, and integrity management. Secure semantic services will be the subject of Part IV, while some of the emerging secure services will be discussed in Part V.

DEPENDABLE WEB SERVICES

Introduction to Part III

Much of the discussions in Part II focused on security for Web services. Note that while security in general encompasses confidentiality, integrity, and trust, our focus on security has mainly been on confidentiality. In Part III, we discuss other aspects of trustworthy services, including trust, privacy, and integrity.

Part III consists of three chapters. Chapter 14 discusses trust management and Web services. Trust is essentially about how much confidence you place on what a person says or whether that person can keep a secret. Trust can also be a measure of whether a person will honor his commitments. In general, before I give out information to a person, I determine whether that person can be trusted, even though he is authorized to get that information from me. Chapter 15 focuses on privacy and Web services. Note that different definitions of privacy have been given. The definition we will use here is that a person must decide what information to release about himself or herself. Therefore, any organization that violates the will of this person violates this person's privacy. Chapter 16 focuses on integrity and Web services. Integrity for us includes accuracy of the data, and quality of the data, as well as provenance of the data.

Chapter 14

Trust Management and Web Services

14.1 Overview

This chapter focuses on trust management for Web services. Trust has been discussed a great deal in developing secure systems. Much of the early focus was on trusting the software to develop high-assurance systems. For example, in designing, say, a multilevel system that has to be evaluated at, say, A1 level according to the TCSEC (Trusted Computer Systems Evaluation Criteria), the software has to go through a formal verification process to ensure that there are no covert channels. Such software is called trusted software. However, during the past ten years or so when data and applications security received prominence, the focus was on trusting the individuals or processes acting on behalf of the individuals. Here, we had to determine the trust that had to be placed on the individuals. Furthermore, the data also had to be assigned trust values. That is, data could have a high trust value if it is emanated from a trustworthy individual or source (e.g., a file or database).

Web services also need to have trust to carry out certain operations. Some Web services that carry out critical functions such as command and control and patient monitoring have to be more trustworthy than, say, other Web services that search for a company that sells shoes. In this chapter, we will discuss issues related to trust management and then discuss trust-based Web services.

The organization of this chapter is as follows. Trust management, including trusting individuals as well as data, will be discussed in Section 14.2. In particular,

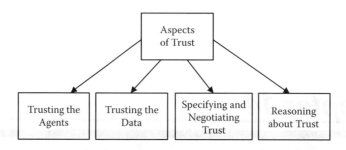

Figure 14.1   Aspects of trust.

trust management and trust negotiation will be discussed in Section 14.2.1. Note that trust and risk are related. That is, if a person is not trustworthy and if you have to give him or her some data, you are taking a risk. Therefore, some of the developments on correlating trust and risk are discussed in Section 14.2.2. Reputation-based trust is discussed in Section 14.2.3. Then, in Section 14.3, we will discuss trust management and Web services. In particular, trust management as a Web service will be discussed in Section 14.3.1. Trust for Web services will be discussed in Section 14.3.2. The chapter is concluded in Section 14.4. Figure 14.1 illustrates the various aspects of trust.

14.2 Trust Management

14.2.1 Trust Management and Negotiation

Before we discuss aspects of trust management and describe its relationship to the semantic Web, we need to determine what is meant by trust. Trust has been defined by philosophers, and it relates to the amount of value that one would place on another. This value will depend on whether the person can keep secrets or carry out safe activities, among others. Based on the trust that is placed on a person, the data that is emanating from that person would also be assigned a trust value. We will address data trust later. First, we will focus on trusting an individual. We can extend the arguments to include not only an individual but also a group of individuals or even a Web site or an organization.

As stated earlier, work on trust initially focused on the amount of verification or testing that has to be carried out to ensure that the software meets the specification. If the software has a Trojan horse, then it is not trusted. If the software is trusted, then depending on the techniques used to trust the software (e.g., formal verification versus testing), one could then determine the assurance that is placed on the software. Later on, with the prominence of data security, trust was assigned to individuals or organizations. In such cases, two approaches were used to define trust; one was based on credentials, and the other was based on reputation. Both schools of thought have received attention in the research community working on trust.

Bertino and her team have conducted extensive research in credential-based trust management. The idea here is to exchange credentials between individuals and, depending on the type of credentials, trust is established between two parties. Credentials are obtained initially through some credential authority. Therefore, if John wants to see Jane's personal data, he has to present Jane with his credentials that were given to him by a credential authority. Other noted research on credential-based trust management is the work of Winslett et al., and Winsborough et al., among others. Numerous papers on credential-based trust management have appeared in the proceedings of conferences such as ACM SACMAT and IEEE POLICY (see also [BERT03], [YU03], [WINS04]).

In reputation-based systems, trust is assigned based on the reputation that one gets based on past behavior. For example, if Jane applies for a position as a teacher, then those who have heard about Jane will discuss her reputation, such as she is not reliable and misses classes a great deal of the time. If this is the case, then Jane's reputation as a teacher is not good, so Jane will not be trusted to be given the job. We use reputation all the time in our daily lives. That is, we trust an individual or an organization based on reputation. It is usually very hard to improve reputation. It, however, does not take much to ruin reputation and, as a result, to decrease the trust value. Reputation-based trust systems are discussed in [SHMA06].The third type of trust is to determine the confidence value that one places on the data. In other words, how much do you trust the data? To give an answer, we need to determine who has produced the data. Who has accessed the data? Has the data gone through an organization that is untrustworthy? We will discuss data trust when we address data quality and data provenance in the chapter on integrity and the semantic Web.

After trust values are assigned, what does it take to manage trust? This involves exchanging data depending on the trust values, as well as increasing and decreasing trust values based on credentials received or revoked or changed reputation. For example, if John is entrusted with some critical data and if it is known that John has misused the data, the trust value will be decreased. Research has been done on formalizing the notion of trust and performing operations on trust. Algebras for trust management are also being developed. One important aspect of trust management is trust negotiation. Here, two parties may negotiate with each other the trust values and the data to be shared among them. Trust negotiation is an active research area in trust management [WINS04]. Figure 14.1 illustrates the various aspects of trust. The trust negotiation process is illustrated in Figure 14.2.

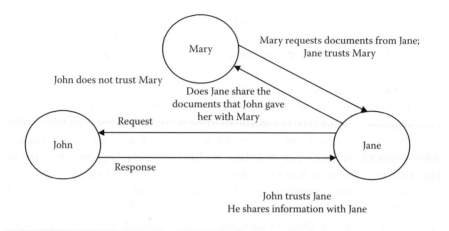

Figure 14.2   Trust negotiation.

14.2.2 Trust And Risk Management

As stated by Murat Kantarcioglu [MURA06], "to manage risks in data sharing, we need to have a thorough understanding of the underlying risk factors." First, although trust and risk are related, they are not one and the same. For example, the more you trust someone, the more you share the data with that person. However, there is also the situation that a hospital A trusts hospital B, but A does not share data with B as B's systems are not secure. One could argue that since B's computers are not secure, B cannot be trusted. In some cases, sharing data with untrustworthy parties may not be risky. For example, a hospital may share its data with a drug company to find a cure, even though the hospital does not trust the company. Again, one could argue that the hospital places some trust that the company will find a cure for the disease even if it may not use the data appropriately. However, if the data is not sensitive, then sharing it may not be an issue. Therefore, one can regard trust and risk to be interrelated but different concepts.

Although different models for the relationship between trust and risk have been proposed, the exact relationship between trust and risk in data-sharing applications is yet to be made clear [BOHN04]. What we need is an appropriate model to specify trust and risk relationships. As stated by Kantarcioglu, "trust is one, but not the only, factor that affects risk." Our research involves understanding trust and risk, and developing a trust-based risk model. Kantarcioglu states that "in order to create a trust based risk model, we need to capture all the risks associated with trust misjudgments." Furthermore, he states that a cost–benefit analysis has to be carried out on whether to share the data even if the risks are high [MURA06]. Trust-based risk management is illustrated in Figure 14.3.

Jane requests document from John
John calculates the risk of sharing the document
Risk is determined on the trust John places on Jane
Depending on the risk John determines whether or not to share the document

Figure 14.3 Trust and risk.

14.2.3 Reputation-Based Systems

Trust may be established using what is called a reputation network. As stated in [GOLB03], a reputation-based network is a distributed Web-based social network. Reputation rating is inferred from one user to another. Individuals are connected to each person they rate, which results in a large interconnected network of users. The only requirement is that the individuals should assert their reputation ratings for one another in the network. Individuals control their own data. Data is maintained in a distributed fashion. Data can be stored anywhere and is integrated through a common foundation.

The FOAF (Friend-Of-A-Friend) [RDF] project illustrates the relationship between the semantic Web and reputation networks. An ontological vocabulary is used for describing people and their relationships. This is extended by providing a mechanism describing the reputation relationships and allowing people to rate the reputation or trustworthiness of another person.

Algorithms are being developed to infer reputations. As stated in [GOLB03], recommendations are made to one person (source) about the reputation of another person (sink). Trust and reputation literature contain many different metrics. These metrics are categorized according to the perspective used for making calculations. For example, global metrics calculate a single value for each entity in the network. Local metrics calculate a reputation rating for an individual in the network. In the global system, an entity will always have the same inferred rating. In the local system, an entity could be rated differently depending on the node for which the inference is made.

An example of a reputation system is TrustMail. It is a message scoring system and adds reputation ratings to the folder views of a message. It helps sort messages accordingly by the user after he sees the reputation ratings. It highlights the important and relevant messages. Figure 14.4 illustrates a reputation network.

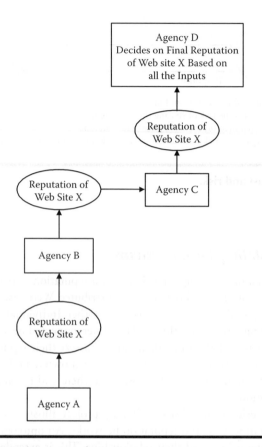

Figure 14.4   Reputation network.

14.3 Trust and Web Services

14.3.1 *Trust Management as a Web Service*

There are two aspects here. One is to implement trust management as a Web service or collection of Web services. The other is to explore trust management for Web services. We illustrate trust management implemented as a Web service in Figure 14.5. A user issues a request to a server to obtain a resource. The query service will issue a request to the trust management service to determine the trust level of the user. Based on this trust level, appropriate resources are then given to the user.

There is also interest in the use of semantic Web technologies for trust management and negotiation. While several trust policy languages have been developed, a notable system that takes advantage of XML for policy representation is the system developed at the University of Milan and Purdue by Bertino and her group. The system developed is called Trust-X and is based on XML. A trust policy language based on XML is used by Trust-X. It is a credential-based system [BERT04].

Figure 14.5   Web services for trust management.

While XML is a suitable policy language, it suffers from the drawback that it cannot adequately represent semantics. For example, statements such as "A trusts B only if B does not trust C" or "A trusts B and B trusts C" do not mean that A trusts C. It is difficult to express such statements in XML. Note that unlike XML, RDF can express class–subclass relationships, and languages such as OWL can represent relationships such as Union and Intersection. Therefore, we need rich policy languages to represent Trust. Furthermore, since the 9/11 Commission Report, the environment is migrating from a need-to-know to a need-to-share environment. Therefore, it is important to represent trust relationships in such an environment. We need policy languages to represent statements of the form "in emergency situations, one needs to share all the data and then determine the consequences of data sharing with respect to trust." Finin et al. are investigating the use of languages such as REI for need-to-share environments [KAGA03].

The advantage of using semantic-Web-based policy languages is that one could use reasoning capabilities based on descriptive logic to reason about trust statements and make inferences about trust that are not explicitly specified. Reasoning engines such as JENA and PELLET are also being explored for representing and reasoning about semantic-Web-based policy specifications. The Policy aware Web project being carried out at MIT is also developing specification languages and reasoning engines for trust policies.

Note that one of the layers of the semantic Web is Logic, Proof, and Trust. This type of trust is different from trust as we have discussed it in this chapter. The Trust layer for the semantic Web is essentially about reasoning about the trustworthiness of statements. For example, how much trust do you place on statements such as "John and James are best friends." Your degree of trust in this statement depends on the source of the statement. We will discuss this type of trust when we discuss data quality and provenance in a later chapter.

While there is lot of research now on specification of policy languages, the advantage of semantic Web languages is that we can utilize the reasoning tools being developed to reason about the policies so that we can check for the consistency of the policies. We also want to ensure that trust policies do not divulge sensitive information that is classified or private. Research along these lines has been carried out by Bertino and her group [SQUI06]. Figure 14.5 illustrates Web services for trust management, while Figure 14.6 illustrates the semantic Web for trust management.

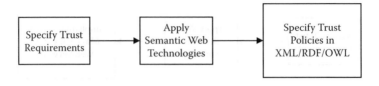

Figure 14.6   Semantic Web for trust management.

14.3.2 Trust Management for Web Services

In Section 14.3.1, we discussed the application of Web services and semantic Web technologies for trust management. Essentially, the idea here is to implement trust management as a Web service as well as use languages such as XML, RDF, and OWL to specify policies and reason about policies based on descriptive logic as well as invoke Web services for managing trust. In this section, we discuss how trust management techniques may be applied to Web services as well as to the semantic Web. Note that the semantic Web is a collection of technologies that give us machine-understandable Web pages. Therefore, the challenge here is, how do we trust the reasoning that is carried out to obtain machine understandable Web pages? Furthermore, do we trust the Web pages that are produced? With respect to trust management for Web services, the idea is to determine how much trust we place on the Web services. Has the Web service been authenticated? If so, what is the level of authentication? How much trust do we place on the Web service? Figure 14.7 illustrates trust for Web services, while Figure 14.8 illustrates trust for the semantic Web.

As we have stated in the previous section, one of the layers of the semantic Web is the Logic, Proof, and Trust layer. Here, we need technologies to reason about the accuracy of the Web pages. Do we trust the data that is produced? Do we trust the decisions that are made by the agents that carry out the activities on behalf of the user? Trusting the Web pages will also determine who produced the Web pages. If the agents who produced the Web pages are highly trustworthy, then we may place higher trust on the results. We will discuss this aspect under data quality and data provenance in a later chapter.

The other aspect trusts the agents that make use of semantic Web technologies such as XML and RDF-based data and carries out the activities. Do we trust the answers produced by the agents? Do these agents carry out trust negotiations

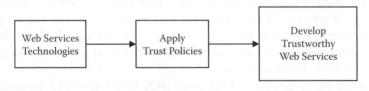

Figure 14.7   Trust management for Web services.

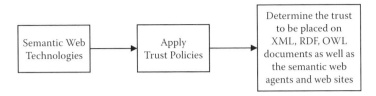

Figure 14.8 Trust management for the semantic Web.

between them? The problem is then reduced to the problem we discussed in Section 14.3.1. That is, trust established between agents is essentially the trust that is established between the people. This trust may depend on credentials or based on reputation. For example, in providing a travel service, the agent has to make reservations and book hotels, as well as making arrangements for the client to participate in tours. The agent who acts on behalf of the client will read the Web pages in XML or RDF and then contact the agent that is acting on behalf of the airlines and hotels. The trust that the first agent places on the other may depend on the credential or the reputation that the travel agent has.

Therefore, when we discuss trust, there are two major aspects. One is the trust placed on the data, and the other is trust placed on the agents. The trust placed on the data will depend on the trust placed on the agent. Similarly, an agent that consistently produces trustworthy data can be regarded to have a higher trust value (see also [MATH03]).

14.4 Summary and Directions

In this chapter, we have discussed trust management and its connection to Web services and the semantic Web. We first discussed aspects of trust management, including defining trust and also describing trust negotiations. Then we discussed enforcing trust within the context of the semantic Web. Furthermore, we also discussed the use of semantic Web technologies for specifying trust policies. Next, we discussed related concepts, including risk-based trust management and reputation networks.

Our goal is to provide a high-level overview of what the challenges are and what is going on in trust related to Web services. Trust management is a fledging research area, and several researchers, including Bertino at Purdue, Berners-Lee at MIT, Finin at UMBC, and Winslett at UIUC, among others, are conducting extensive research on this topic. For example, Finin et al. at UMBC have pioneered techniques for specifying and reasoning about trust using a language called REI. We are collaborating with UMBC on trust management in a need-to-share environment. While numerous trust negotiation approaches have been proposed, we need research on evaluating these approaches and determining which approaches are appropriate and under what context. Therefore, while much has been done on trust management during the past decade, much still remains to be done for specific applications and domains, including for Web services.

Exercises

1. Conduct a survey of trust management and trust negotiation techniques.
2. Design an appropriate trust management approach for Web services.
3. Investigate the use of semantic Web technologies for trust management.

References

[BERT03] Bertino, E., E. Ferrari, and A. C. Squicciarini, *Trust-Chi: An XML framework for trust negotiations, Communications and Multimedia Security*, 2003: 146–157.

[BERT04] Bertino, E., E. Ferrari, and A. C. Squicciarini, Trust-X: A peer-to-peer framework for trust establishment, *IEEE Transactions on Knowledge and Data Engineering*, 16(7): 827–842 (2004).

[BOHN04] Bohnet, I. and R. Zeckhauser, Trust, risk and betrayal, *Journal of Economic Behavior & Organization*, 55, 467–484, 2004.

[DRM] http://en.wikipedia.org/wiki/Digital_Rights_Management

[GARC06] García, R. and R. Gil, An OWL Copyright Ontology for Semantic Digital Rights Management, Workshop on Ontology Content and Evaluation in Enterprise, *Lecture Notes in Computer Science*, Vol. 4278, Berlin, Germany, 2006.

[GOLB03] Golbeck, J., B. Parsia, and J. Hendler, Trust networks on the semantic Web, *Proceedings of Cooperative Information Agents 2003*, August 27–29, 2003, Helsinki, Finland.

[KAGA03] Kagal, L., T. W. Finin, and A. Joshi, A policy based approach to security for the semantic Web. *International Semantic Web Conference*, 2003: 402–418.

[MATH03] Richardson, M., R. Agrawal, and P. Domingos, Trust management for the semantic Web, Proceeding of the Second International Semantic Web Conference, Sanibel Island, FL, 2003.

[MURA06] Kantarcioglu, M., E. Celikel, and B. Thuraisingham, Risk-Based Access Control, Technical Report, The University of Texas at Dallas, 2006.

[RDF] RDFWeb: FOAF: "The Friend of a Friend Vocabulary," http://xmlns.com/foaf/0.1/.

[RICH03] Richardson, M., R. Agrawal, and P. Domingos, Trust Management for the Semantic Web, *Proceedings of the Second International Semantic Web Conference*, Sanibel Island, Florida, 2003.

[SHMA06] Shmatikov, V. and C. Talcott, Reputation-Based Trust Management, http://www.cs.utexas.edu/~shmat/shmat_rtm.pdf

[SQUI06] Squicciarini, A. C., E. Bertino, E. Ferrari, and I. Ray, Achieving privacy in trust negotiations with an ontology-based approach, *IEEE Transactions on Dependable and Secure Computing*, 3(1): 13–30 (2006).

[WINS04] Winsborough, W. H. and N. Li, Safety in automated trust negotiation, *IEEE Symposium on Security and Privacy*, Oakland, CA, 2004.

[YU03] Yu, T. and M. Winslett, A unified scheme for resource protection in automated trust negotiation, *IEEE Symposium on Security and Privacy*, Oakland, CA, 114–122, 2003.

Chapter 15

Privacy and Web Services

15.1 Overview

As we have stated, while confidentiality is about the Web site or system releasing data/information only to those who are authorized according to the policies, privacy is about a person determining what information should be released about him. Therefore, if the Web site's privacy policies are not acceptable to this user, then he or she can decide whether to give the information to the Web site.

Note, however, that while privacy has been discussed a great deal even at the Congressional levels, not everyone agrees with this definition. For example, I teach data mining, national security, and privacy at the unclassified level at the Armed Forces Communication and Electronics Association in Washington, DC. The students who take my courses mainly work for the Department of Defense and Intelligence agencies. For them, privacy is not the same as one feels about releasing, say, one's medical records. It is my understanding that the FBI's (Federal Bureau of Investigation) idea of privacy is to ensure that the personal information of U.S. citizens does not get into the wrong hands. Even to other agencies, the FBI will release private information only if the agency is authorized to get it. In a way, privacy becomes more or less like confidentiality for such organizations.

Much work has been carried out on privacy, including specification and enforcement of privacy policies, developing techniques for privacy-preserving data mining, and specifying standards for privacy. In this book, our interest in privacy is with respect to the semantic Web. One of the significant developments with W3C is the specification of standards that a Web site can use to specify its privacy polices, which is called P3P (Platform for Privacy Preferences). Another challenge is to ensure that private information is not released as a result of semantic Web mining. Finally, Web services have to ensure that private information is not leaked. Likewise, Web services that carry out semantic Web mining have to ensure that the privacy of individuals is protected.

The organization of this chapter is as follows. In Section 15.2, we discuss privacy management in general. In particular, privacy issues are discussed in Section 15.2.1. The privacy problem via inference, including privacy constraint processing and data mining, will be discussed in Section 15.2.2. Platform for privacy preferences will be discussed in Section 15.2.3. The relationship between privacy and Web services is discussed in Section 15.3. In particular, privacy as a Web service will be discussed in Section 15.3.1. Privacy for Web services will be discussed in Section 15.3.2. Section 15.4 concludes the chapter.

15.2 Privacy Management

15.2.1 Privacy Issues

Social scientists have studied privacy for several years, and policy specialists have developed privacy policies for agencies and corporations. However, it is only recently that security specialists have started focusing on privacy. Furthermore, the Terrorism Information Awareness program at DARPA together with the focus on data mining has resulted in work on privacy-preserving data mining and privacy-preserving data management. Today, privacy is an important area of information security. However, it has been difficult to give a precise definition of privacy as each organization and agency has a different view.

So, the question is, what is privacy? The general notion is that a person should decide what personal information should be released about him or her. Such a definition was fine before we had tools for data analysis and data mining and the World Wide Web. Through such tools, it may now be possible for someone to infer private information about another person. Therefore, we need to perhaps redefine the notion of privacy. On the other hand, some organizations want to control personal information about the community and decide to whom they should release the personal information. As stated earlier, my understanding is that when the FBI has information about various individuals, it will determine whether to release the information to, say, the CIA (Central Intelligence Agency). Initially, I argued that this is essentially ensuring confidentiality and not privacy. However, after working more on privacy issues and reading about the subject, I now believe that there can be no universal definition of privacy. Privacy has to be defined by an organization. That is, one organization may define privacy policies as policies protecting its sensitive information. Another organization may define privacy policies to be those that are specified by those who work for the organization as to what information can be released by them. Therefore, whether privacy policies are a subset of

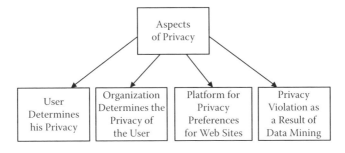

Figure 15.1   Aspects of privacy management.

confidentiality policies or whether they are separate policies is left to an organization to determine.

Our interest also lies in the relationship between privacy, confidentiality, and trust. As we have discussed in the earlier chapters, in our work, we have made the following assumption. Trust is established between, say, a Web site and a user based on credentials or reputations. When a user logs into a Web site to make a purchase, the Web site will specify what its privacy policies are. The user will then determine whether he wants to enter personal information. That is, if the Web site will give out, say, the user's address to a third party, then the user can decide whether to enter this information. However, before the user enters the information, the user has to decide whether he trusts the Web site. This can be based on the credential and reputation. If the user trusts the Web site, then the user can enter his private information if he is satisfied with the policies. If not, he can choose not to enter the information.

We have given a similar reasoning for confidentiality. Here, the user is requesting information from the Web site; the Web site checks its confidentiality policies and decides what information to release to the user. The Web site can also check the level of trust it has with the user and decide whether to part with the information. As stated in Chapter 14, one can also determine the quality of the data based on the trust reposed on the user or on the Web site.

More details on specific aspects of privacy and the semantic Web will be discussed in the next several sections. In particular, applying semantic Web technologies for privacy management, privacy issues for the semantic Web, platform for privacy preferences, privacy problem that occurs via inference, and privacy-preserving semantic Web mining will be discussed. Figure 15.1 illustrates aspects of privacy management.

15.2.2 *Privacy Problem through Inference*

We have conducted extensive research on the inference problem for secure databases. Much of our work has focused on security constraint processing, which has now come to be known as policy management. Policies include those for content- and context-dependent constraints as well as dynamic and event-based constraints. For example, a ship's mission becomes classified after a war begins [THUR05]. We have since adapted this approach for privacy constraint processing where security levels would now become privacy levels (public, private, semipublic, etc.), and the security constraint becomes a privacy constraint; for example, names and healthcare records taken together becomes private. It should be noted that with this approach we are assuming that privacy and confidentiality are one and the same. Now, this agrees with, say, the FBI's notion of privacy, where it has to protect the private information of U.S. citizens. But this is not consistent with medical privacy, where, in this context, privacy is specified by an individual, That is, an individual determines the information he has to keep private. In this case, the privacy controller is managed by the individual. That is, the client will determine that if he or she gives out, say, genetic information, then an insurance company can figure out the illnesses he or she may be prone to. Therefore, the privacy controller will guide the client in what information to release about itself.

Figure 15.2 illustrates the privacy controller. Here, data represented using semantic Web technologies such as XML, RDF, and Ontologies are augmented with inference engines. These engines may carry out rule processing or utilize ontology-based reasoning to deduce new data from existing data. If the new data is private, then it can give advice to the client as to what information should be kept private. Note that under the FBI scenario, the privacy controller is essentially the confidentiality controller (which we have called the inference controller) and, therefore, it acts on the server side and determines what information it has to release to the client (such as the CIA).

Note that we have proved that the inference problem is unsolvable [THUR90]. We have applied similar techniques to prove that the privacy problem is unsolvable [THUR06].

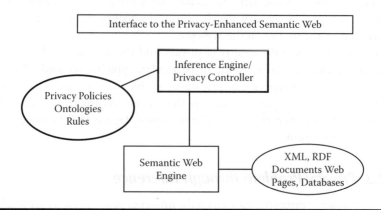

Figure 15.2 Architecture of a privacy controller.

15.2.3 Platform for Privacy Preferences

P3P is an emerging industry standard that enables Web sites to express their privacy practices in a standard format. The format of the policies can be automatically retrieved and understood by user agents. It is a product of W3C (World Wide Web Consortium; www.w3c.org). As we have stated, the main difference between privacy and security as considered in many domains is the following: The user is informed of the privacy policies enforced by the Web site. The user is not informed of the security (or confidentiality) policies in general. When a user enters a Web site, the privacy policies of the Web site are conveyed to the user. If the privacy policies are different from user preferences, the user is notified. The user can then decide how to proceed.

Several major corporations are working on P3P standards, including Microsoft, IBM, HP, NEC Nokia, and NCR. Several Web sites have also implemented P3P. Semantic Web groups have adopted P3P. The initial version of P3P used RDF to specify policies; the recent version has migrated to XML. P3P Policies use XML with namespaces for encoding policies.

Example: Catalog shopping. Your name will not be given to a third party, but your purchases will be given to a third party.

```
<POLICIES xmlns = http://www.w3.org/2002/01/P3Pv1>
                <POLICY name = - - - -
                </POLICY>
        </POLICIES>
```

P3P has its own statements and data types expressed in XML. P3P schemas utilize XML schemas. XML is a prerequisite to understanding P3P. The P3P specification released in January 2005 uses the catalog shopping example to explain concepts. P3P is an international standard and is an ongoing project.

Note that P3P does not replace laws. P3P works together with the law. What happens if the Web sites do not honor their P3P policies? Then appropriate legal actions will have to be taken. Today, XML is the technology to specify P3P policies. Policy experts will have to specify the policies. Technologies will have to develop the specifications. Legal experts will have to take actions if the policies are violated.

15.2.4 Privacy-Preserving Semantic Web Mining

In our previous book [THUR05], we discussed privacy-preserving data mining. The idea is as follows. Using the data mining tools, even naïve users can make unauthorized inferences that could be highly sensitive or private. Furthermore, the goal is to hide private data such as the disease of a particular person while giving out general trends and associations. That is, we could give out the information that "people living in California are more prone to asthma" without giving out the fact

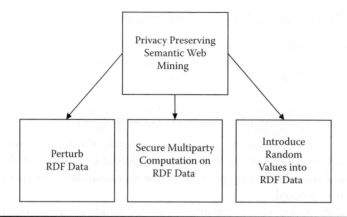

Figure 15.3   Privacy-preserving semantic Web mining.

that John has asthma. Privacy-preserving data mining techniques work with per-turbed or randomized data without revealing the actual data (Figure 15.3).

Recently, there have been reports on semantic Web mining. There are two aspects here. One is to mine the data on the Web represented using semantic Web technologies such as XML, RDF, and OWL. Note that much of the work has focused on mining relational data. More recently, there has been work on min-ing unstructured data such as text, audio, images, and video. The challenge is to mine the databases that store and manage XML and RDF documents. The other aspect is to mine the XML and RDF documents without revealing the actual data but giving out correlations and trends. The former is an aspect of data mining, while the latter is an aspect of privacy-preserving data mining. There is yet a third aspect, and that is to use ontologies to help the mining process. For example, the data mining tool may need clarifications about the meaning of a Web page. Here, ontologies expressed in OWL may be used to clarify the concepts to facilitate the mining process.

15.3 Privacy Management and Web Services

15.3.1 Web Services for Privacy Management

Privacy management can be implemented as a collection of Web services. For example, when a user requests a resource from a Web site, the Web service for pri-vacy management is invoked. This service will present the privacy policies of the Web site to the user, and the user can subsequently determine whether to request the resource or not. Figure 15.4 illustrates Web services for privacy management. Figure 15.5 illustrates the semantic Web for privacy management.

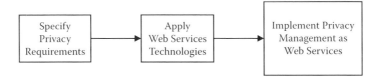

Figure 15.4   Web services for privacy.

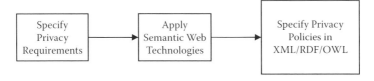

Figure 15.5   The semantic Web for privacy.

The major contributions of semantic Web technologies for privacy management are in specifying policies in semantic Web technologies. These policies could be specified in XML, RDF, OWL, or related semantic Web languages. Another contribution is the platform for privacy preferences. The W3C community has come up with a framework for Web sites to specify privacy policies. This framework is called the Platform for Privacy Preferences [P3P]. We discussed P3P in Section 15.2.3.

As in the case of trust management, one needs to decide the appropriate language to specify privacy polices. XML is becoming a popular language for this purpose. Even the P3P standards that initially focused on using RDF for privacy policy specification switched to XML. However, if one needs to represent the semantics of the privacy policies and reason about privacy, then RDF or OWL would be more appropriate.

In specifying privacy policies, one also needs to determine whether sensitive or private information could be leaked. Therefore, appropriate confidentiality or privacy policies may be enforced on the original privacy policies themselves. Therefore, we may want to control access to various parts of the privacy policy specifications that describe the policies.

15.3.2 Privacy for Web Services and Semantic Web

Privacy for Web services is about ensuring the privacy of Web services. For example, a Web service may be processing highly sensitive information or carrying out surveillance. Private and sensitive information such as Social Security numbers and/or the location of individuals may have to be protected via appropriate policy enforcement. Figure 15.6 illustrates privacy for Web services.

Privacy for the semantic Web is essentially about ensuring that private information is not divulged via the usage of the semantic Web. Note that the semantic Web

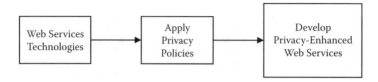

Figure 15.6 Privacy for Web services.

is a collection of representation and reasoning technologies. Therefore, the goal is not to reveal private information. For this, we need to ensure that privacy policies are enforced properly on XML and RDF documents as well as OWL ontologies. Furthermore, the goal of the reasoning engines that are developed based on descriptive logics is such that private information cannot be inferred by deduction.

Privacy for semantic Web technologies has received little attention. Bertino et al. have investigated privacy for XML and also examined aspects of privacy violations that result from trust management based on their Trust-X system [SQUI07]. Finin et al. are examining privacy for their research on the semantic Web, although their research focuses mainly on trust management. In our investigation of CPT (confidentiality, privacy, and trust) for the semantic Web, we have privacy enforcement based on both what we call the basic system and the advanced system [THUR06]. Note that the advanced system consists of a privacy engine that will focus on privacy violations via inference. In Section 11.2, we discussed CPT for a general Web environment. With the semantic Web, the idea is for the machine to examine the Web pages and determine whether any private information is revealed. Furthermore, in an ordinary Web the Web site will display its privacy policies to the user and the user determines whether to enter his or her private information. However, with semantic Web technologies, the Web site will examine the privacy policies and the user preferences and give advice to the user as to whether he or she should enter private information. As we have stated earlier, one of the significant developments of privacy and the semantic Web lies in the platform for privacy preferences. Figure 15.7 illustrates privacy management for the semantic Web.

Since semantic Web services make use of semantic Web technologies (e.g., XML, RDF, OWL), privacy has to be ensured for semantic Web services. That is, private information should not be divulged via the usage of the semantic Web. Note that the

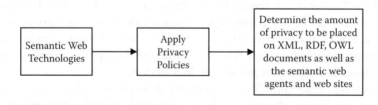

Figure 15.7 Privacy for the semantic Web.

semantic Web is a collection of representation and reasoning technologies. Therefore, the goal is not to reveal private information. For this, we need to ensure that privacy policies are enforced properly on XML and RDF documents as well as OWL ontologies. Furthermore, the goal of the reasoning engines that are developed based on descriptive logics is such that private information cannot be inferred by deduction.

15.4 Summary and Directions

In this chapter, we have discussed the various notions of privacy and provided an overview of privacy management. Then we discussed privacy management and Web services. For example, Web services have to maintain privacy. Privacy controllers may be implemented as Web services. We also discussed privacy for the semantic Web and semantic Web for specifying privacy policies.

Much of the discussion in this chapter is in the early stages of research. We have not attempted to discuss the correct definition of privacy. Our goal is to illustrate the connection between privacy management and the semantic Web. As we have mentioned, the semantic Web technologies are useful in the specification of privacy policies. Furthermore, data represented by XML and RDF could be mined and privacy violated as a result.

We have stressed in our work that technology alone is not sufficient to protect the privacy of the individuals. We need social scientists, technologists, and policy makers to work together. It is also important to bring in the legal specialists. Some have said that it will be impossible to prevent privacy violations, and legal measures are the only viable solution. However, our view is "some privacy is better than nothing," but we have to be careful not to foster a false sense of privacy or security.

Exercises

1. Design a healthcare application, and describe the privacy requirements.
2. Investigate the applications of semantic Web technologies for privacy management.
3. Design and develop a privacy controller for XML and RDF documents.

References

[AGRA00] Agrawal, R. and R. Srikant, Privacy-preserving data mining, *Proceedings of the ACM SIGMOD Conference*, Dallas, TX, May 2000.
[BAIN03] Bainbridge, W., Privacy, *Encyclopedia of Community*, Sage Reference, Thousand Oaks, CA, 2003.

[CLIF02] Clifton, C., M. Kantarcioglu, and J. Vaidya, Defining Privacy for Data Mining, Purdue University, 2002 (see also Next Generation Data Mining Workshop, Baltimore, MD, November 2002).

[P3P] Platform for Privacy Preferences, www.w3c.org

[SQUI07] Squicciarini, A. C., E. Bertino, E. Ferrari, F. Paci, and B. Thuraisingham, PP-Trust-X A system for Privacy Preserving Trust Negotiations, to appear in *ACM TISSEC—Transactions on Systems and Information Security*, 10:3, Article 12, July 2007.

[SWEE04] Sweeney, L., Navigating Computer Science Research through Waves of Privacy Concerns: Discussions among Computer Scientists at Carnegie Mellon University, *ACM Computers and Society*, 2004.

[THUR03a] Thuraisingham, B., *Web Data Mining: Technologies and Their Applications to Business Intelligence and Counter-Terrorism*, CRC Press, Boca Raton, FL, 2003.

[THUR03b] Thuraisingham, B., Data Mining, National Security, Privacy and Civil Liberties, SIGKDD Explorations, January 2003.

[THUR05] Thuraisingham, B., *Database and Applications Security: Integrating Data Management and Information Security*, CRC Press, Boca Raton, FL, 2005.

[THUR05a] Thuraisingham, B., Privacy preserving data mining: Developments and directions, *Journal of Database Management*, January 2005.

[THUR05b] Thuraisingham, B., Privacy constraint processing in a privacy enhanced database system, *Data and Knowledge Engineering Journal*, December 2005.

[THUR06] Thuraisingham, B., N. Isybulnik, and A. Ashraful, Administering the semantic Web, confidentiality, privacy and trust, *Journal of Information Security and Privacy*, 2006.

[THUR90] Thuraisingham, B., Recursion Theoretic Complexity of the Inference Problem, Computer Security Foundations Workshop, 1990 (also, Technical Report, The MITRE Corporation MTP-291).

[W3C] www.w3c.org

Chapter 16

Integrity Management, Data Provenance, and Web Services

16.1 Overview

In this chapter we will discuss integrity management for Web services. Integrity includes several aspects. In the database world, integrity includes concurrency control and recovery as well as enforcing integrity constraints. For example, when multiple transactions execute at the same time, the consistency of the data has to be ensured. When a transaction aborts, it has to be ensured that the database is recovered from the failure into a consistent state. Integrity constraints are rules that have to be satisfied by the data. Rules include "salary value has to be positive" and "age of an employee cannot decrease over time." More recently, integrity has included data quality, data provenance, data currency, real-time processing, and fault tolerance.

In this chapter we discuss aspects of integrity for Web services as well as implementing integrity management as Web services. For example, how do we ensure the integrity of the data and the processes? How do we ensure that data quality is maintained? Some aspects of integrity are already being investigated by the researchers and some other aspects are yet to be investigated. The organization of this chapter is as follows: In Section 16.2, we discuss aspects of integrity, data quality and

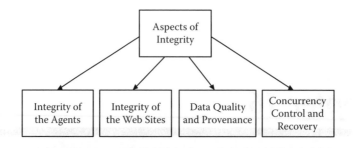

Figure 16.1 Aspects of integrity.

provenance. In particular, integrity aspects will be discussed in Section 16.2.1. Data quality and provenance are covered in Section 16.2.2, as well as detecting security threats and misuse with data provenance. Web services and integrity management are reviewed in Section 16.3. In particular, data integrity and provenance as a Web services will be examined in Section 16.3.1. Data integrity for Web services will be discussed in Section 16.3.2. The chapter is concluded in Section 16.4. Aspects of integrity are illustrated in Figure 16.1.

16.2 Integrity, Data Quality, and Provenance

16.2.1 Aspects of Integrity

As stated in Section 16.1, there are many aspects to integrity. For example, concurrency control, recovery, data accuracy, meeting real-time constraints, data accuracy, data quality, data provenance, fault tolerance, and integrity constraint enforcement are all aspects of integrity management. This is illustrated in Figure 16.1. In this section we will examine each aspect of integrity.

> *Concurrency Control*: In data management, concurrent control is about transactions executing at the same time and ensuring consistency of the data. Therefore, transactions have to obtain locks or utilize time stamps to ensure that the data is left in a consistent state when multiple transactions attempt to access the data at the same time. Extensive research has been carried out on concurrency control techniques for transaction management both in centralized as well as in distributed environments [BERN87].
>
> *Data Recovery:* When transactions abort before they complete execution, the database should be recovered to a consistent state such as its state before the transaction started execution. Several recovery techniques have been proposed to ensure the consistency of the data.
>
> *Data Authenticity:* When the data is delivered to the user its authenticity has to be ensured. That is, the user should get accurate data and the data should not

be tampered with. We have conducted research on ensuring authenticity of XML data during third party publishing [BERT04].

Data Completeness: Data that a user receives should not only be authentic but also be complete. That is, everything that the user is authorized to see has to be delivered to the user.

Data Currency: Data has to be current. That is, data that is outdated has to be deleted or archived and the data that the user sees has to be current data. Data currency is an aspect of real-time processing. If a user wants to retrieve the temperature, he has to be given the current temperature, not a temperature reading that is 24 hours old.

Data Accuracy: The question is how accurate is the data? This is also closely related to data quality and data currency. That is, accuracy depends on whether the data has been maliciously corrupted or whether it has come from an untrusted source.

Data Quality: Is the data of high quality? This includes data authenticity, data accuracy, and whether the data is complete or certain. If the data is uncertain then can we reason with this uncertainty to ensure that the operations that use the data are not affected? Data quality also depends on the data source.

Data Provenance: This has to do with the history of the data, that is, from the time the data originated from the sensors until the present time when it is given to the general. The question is who has accessed the data? Who has modified the data? How has the data traveled? This will determine whether the data has been misused.

Integrity Constraints: These are rules that the data has to satisfy such as the age of a person cannot be a negative number. This type of integrity has been studied extensively by the database and the artificial intelligence communities.

Fault Tolerance: As in the case of data recovery, the processes that fail have to be recovered. Therefore, fault tolerance deals with data recovery as well as process recovery. Techniques for fault tolerance include check pointing and acceptance testing.

Real-time Processing: Data currency is one aspect of real-time processing where the data has to be current. Real-time processing also has to deal with transactions meeting timing constraints. For example, stock quotes have to be given within say 5 minutes. If not, it will be too late. Missing timing constraints could cause integrity violations.

16.2.2 Inferencing, Data Quality, and Data Provenance

Some researchers feel that data quality is an application of data provenance. Furthermore, they have developed theories for inferring data quality. In this section we will examine some of the developments keeping in mind the relationship between data quality, data provenance, and the semantic Web.

Data quality is about accuracy, timeliness, and dependability (i.e., trustworthiness) of the data. It is, however, subjective and depends on the users and the domains. Some of the issues that have to be answered include the creation of the data—that is, where did it come from and why and how was the data obtained? Data quality information is stored as annotations to the data and should be part of data provenance. One could ask the question as to how we can ascertain the trustworthiness of the data. This could depend on how the source is ranked and the reputation of the source. Note that we discussed reputation in Chapter 14.

As we have stated, researchers have developed theories for inferring data quality [PON]. The motivation is due to the fact that data could come from multiple sources; it is shared and prone to errors. Furthermore, data could be uncertain. Therefore, theories of uncertainty such as statistical reasoning, Bayesian theories, and the Dempster–Shafer theory of evidence are being used to infer the quality of the data. With respect to security, we need to ensure that the quality of the inferred data does not violate the policies. For example, at the unclassified level we may say that the source is trustworthy but at the secret level we know that the source is not trustworthy. The inference controllers that we have developed could be integrated with the theories of interceding developed for data quality to ensure security.

Next, let us examine data provenance. For many of the domains including medical and healthcare, as well as defense where the accuracy of the data is critical, we need to have a good understanding as to where the data came from and who may have tampered with the data. As stated in [YOG], data provenance, a kind of metadata sometimes called "lineage" or "pedigree," is the description of the origin of a piece of data and the process by which it arrived in a database. Data provenance is information that helps determine the derivation history of a data product, starting from its original source.

Provenance information can be applied to data quality, auditing, and ownership, among others. By having records of who accessed the data, data misuse can be determined. Usually annotations are used to describe the information related to the data (e.g., Who can access the data? Where did the data come from?) The challenge is to determine whether one needs to maintain coarse-grained provenance data or fine-grained provenance data. For example, in a course-grained situation, the tables of a relation may be annotated, whereas in a fine-grained situation, every element may be annotated. There is, of course, the storage overhead to consider for managing provenance. XML, RDF, and OWL have been used to represent provenance data, and in this way the tools developed for the semantic Web technologies may be used to manage the provenance data.

There is much interest in using data provenance for misuse detection. For example, by maintaining the complete history of data—such as who accessed the data, and when and where the data was accessed—one can answer queries such as "Who accessed the date between January and May 2010?" Therefore, if the data is corrupted one can determine who corrupted the data or when the data was corrupted. Figure 16.2 illustrates the various aspects of data provenance.

> **Data Provenance**
>
> Who created the data?
>
> Where has the data come from?
>
> Who accessed the data?
>
> What is the complete history of the data?
>
> Has the data been misused?

Figure 16.2   Data provenance.

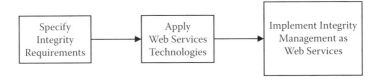

Figure 16.3   Web service for integrity management.

16.3 Integrity Management and Web Services

16.3.1 Web Services for Integrity Management

There are two aspects here. One is that integrity management may be implemented with Web services and the other is ensuring that the Web services have high integrity. For implementing integrity management as Web services, the idea is to invoke Web services to ensure data quality as well as the integrity of the data and the system. Figure 16.3 illustrates implementing integrity management as a Web service.

Like confidentiality, privacy, and trust, semantic Web technologies such as XML may be used to specify integrity policies. Integrity policies may include policies for specifying integrity constraint as well as policies for specifying timing constraints, data currency, and data quality. Here are some examples of the policies:

Integrity Constraints: Age of an employee has to be positive. In a relational representation, one could specify this policy as

```
EMP.AGE>0.
```

In XML, this could be represented as the following:

```
<Condition Object="//Employe/Age">
  <Apply FunctionId="greater-than">
```

```
   <AttributeValue DataType="http://www.w3.org/2001/
XMLSchema#integer">0
     </AttributeValue>
   </Apply>
</Condition>
```

Data Quality Policy: The quality of the data in the employee table is LOW. In the relational model, this could be represented as

```
EMP.Quality = LOW.
```

In XML, this policy could be represented as

```
<Condition Object="//Employe/Quality">
  <Apply FunctionId="equal">
    <AttributeValue DataType="http://www.w3.org/2001/
XMLSchema#string">LOW
    </AttributeValue>
  </Apply>
</Condition>
```

Data Currency: An example: The salary value of EMP cannot be more than 365 days old. In a relational representation this could be represented as

```
AGE(EMP.SAL) <= 365 days.
```

In XML this is represented as

```
<Condition Object="//Employe/Salary">
  <Apply FunctionId="AGE">
    <Apply FunctionId="less-than-or-equal">
      <AttributeValue DataType="http://www.w3.org/2001/
XMLSchema#integer">365
      </AttributeValue>
    </Apply>
  </Apply>
</Condition>
```

The above examples have shown how certain integrity policies may be specified. Note that there are many other applications of semantic Web technologies to ensure integrity. For example, in order to ensure data provenance, the history of the data has to be documented. Semantic Web technologies such as XML are being used to represent say the data annotations that are used to determine the quality of the data or whether the data has been misused. That is, the data captured is annotated with metadata information such as what the data is about, when it was captured, and who captured it. Then as the data moves from place to place or from person to person, the annotations are updated

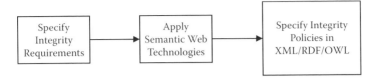

Figure 16.4 Semantic Web for integrity management.

so that at a later time the data may be analyzed for misuse. These annotations are typically represented in semantic Web technologies such as XML, RDF, and OWL.

Another application of semantic Web technologies for integrity management is the use of ontologies to resolve semantic heterogeneity. That is, semantic heterogeneity causes integrity violations. This happens when the same entity is considered to be different at different sites and therefore compromises integrity and accuracy. Through the use of ontologies specified in, say, OWL, it can be expressed that "ship" in one site and "submarine" in another site are one and the same.

Semantic Web technologies also have applications in making inferences and reasoning under uncertainty or mining. For example, the reasoning engines based on RDF, OWL, or, say, Rules may be used to determine whether the integrity policies are violated. We have discussed inference and privacy problems and building inference engines in earlier chapters. These techniques have to be investigated for violation integrity policies. Figure 16.4 illustrates the use of semantic Web technologies for integrity management.

16.3.2 Integrity for Web Services and Semantic Web

In the second aspect, we ensure that the Web services have high integrity. The idea here is to ensure that the Web service is not malicious and does not corrupt the data or other services. Figure 16.5 illustrates integrity management for Web services.

We also need to ensure that integrity is maintained for semantic Web technologies. Annotations that are used for data quality and provenance are typically represented in XML or RDF documents. These documents have to be accurate, complete, and current. Therefore, integrity has to be enforced for such documents. Another aspect of integrity is managing databases that consist of XML or RDF documents. These databases have all of the issues and challenges that are present for

Figure 16.5 Integrity for Web services.

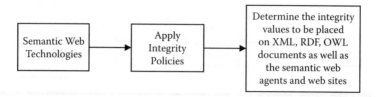

Figure 16.6 Integrity for the semantic Web.

say relational databases. That is, the queries have to be optimized, and transactions should execute concurrently. Therefore, concurrency control and recovery for XML and RDF documents become a challenge for managing XML and RDF databases. This is yet another aspect of integrity for semantic Web documents.

The actions of the agents that make use of the semantic Web to carry out operations such as searching, querying, and integrating heterogeneous databases have to ensure that the integrity of the data is maintained. These agents cannot maliciously corrupt the data. They have to ensure that the data is accurate, complete, and consistent. Finally, when integrating heterogeneous databases, semantic Web technologies such as OWL ontologies are being used to handle semantic heterogeneity. These ontologies have to be accurate and complete and cannot be tampered with.

In summary, in order for the semantic Web technologies to be useful they have to enforce integrity. Furthermore, semantic Web technologies themselves are being used to specify integrity policies. Figure 16.6 illustrates integrity management for the semantic Web.

16.4 Summary and Directions

In this chapter we have provided an overview of data integrity which includes data quality and data provenance. We discussed the applications of semantic Web technologies for data integrity, as well as discussed integrity for semantic Web technologies. Finally, we provided an overview of the relationship between data quality and data provenance.

Data provenance and data quality, while important, are only recently receiving attention. This is due to the fact there are vast quantities of information on the Web, and it is important to know the accuracy of the data and whether the data is copied or plagiarized. We also need to have answers to questions such as who owns the data. Has the data been misused? Therefore, data provenance is important to determine the security of the data.

Web services should have high integrity. Furthermore, integrity techniques can be implemented as Web services. Semantic Web technologies provide a way to represent and store data quality and provenance data. As we make progress with these technologies, we will have improved solutions for data quality and data provenance management. Essentially, data quality and data provenance are part of data security and semantic Web technologies are very useful to manage data quality and data provenance information.

Exercises

1. Conduct a survey of data provenance.
2. Design an appropriate data integrity management approach for an application of your choice.
3. Describe how data provenance may be used to detect security threats.
4. Investigate the use of Web services for integrity management and data provenance.
5. Describe the use of semantic Web technologies for specifying integrity policies.

References

[BERN87] Bernstein, P., U. Hadzilacos, and N. Goodman, *Concurrency Control and Recovery in Database Systems*, Addison-Wesley, Reading, MA, 1987.

[BERT04] Bertino, E., B. Carminati, E. Ferrari, and A. Gupta, Selective and authentic third party publication of XML documents, *IEEE Transactions on Knowledge and Data Engineering*, 16(10), 1263–1278, 2004.

[PON] Pon, R. K. and A. F. Cárdenas, Data Quality Inference, UCLA Report.

[YOG] Simmhan, Y. L., B. Plale, and D. Gannon, A Survey of Data Provenance in e-Science; Indiana University Technical Report.

Conclusion to Part III

While Part II focused mainly on access control models for Web services, in Part III we discussed trust, privacy, and dependability issues for Web services. Privacy control and data quality as well as managing trust, were also reviewed.

Now that we have covered various aspects of secure Web services, we will explore some of the emerging trends in Parts IV and V. In Part IV we will provide an overview of secure semantic Web services. These Web services integrate semantic Web technologies with security and Web services technologies. Some of the emerging trends, including secure domain Web services, will be the subject of Part V.

SECURE SEMANTIC WEB SERVICES

Introduction to Part IV

While Parts II and III focused on some of the core issues in secure Web services, in Parts IV and V we will provide an overview of specialized Web services. Part IV focuses on secure semantic Web services that utilize semantic Web technologies. We devote an entire part to secure semantic Web services due to their importance and popularity for several applications in multiple domains. Part IV consists of five chapters, each discussing some aspect of secure semantic Web services. Chapter 17 provides an overview of secure semantic Web services. Chapter 18 discusses XML security and its relationship to Web services. Chapter 19 reviews RDF security and its relationship to Web services. Chapter 20 focuses on OWL security and its relationship to Web services and finally Chapter 21 examines rules security and its relationship to Web services. These five chapters will essentially provide an overview of secure semantic Web technologies and how Web services may utilize these technologies to provide secure semantic Web services.

SECURE SEMANTIC WEB SERVICES

Introduction to Part IV

Chapter 17

Secure Semantic Web and Web Services

17.1 Overview

As we have stated earlier, as the demand for data and information management increases, there is also a critical need for maintaining the security of the databases, applications, and information systems. Data and information have to be protected from unauthorized access, as well as from malicious corruption. With the advent of the Web, it is even more important to protect data and information as numerous individuals now have access to this data and information. Therefore, we need effective mechanisms to secure the semantic Web technologies.

In Part I, we provided an overview of the semantic Web [Lee01]. In this chapter we focus on securing the semantic Web with emphasis on confidentiality, and then discuss the relationship between secure semantic Web and Web services. In particular, XML security, RDF security, and securing other components such as secure ontologies, and secure Web rules will be discussed. Each of the components of the semantic Web will be elaborated on in Chapters 18, 19, 20, and 21. Other aspects of securing the semantic Web such as privacy and trust will also be discussed.

The organization of this chapter is as follows. Security for the semantic Web is discussed in Section 17.2. Privacy and trust for the semantic Web is addressed in Section 17.3. The relationship between secure semantic Web and Web services will be discussed in Section 17.4. The chapter is summarized in Section 17.5.

215

17.2 Security for the Semantic Web

17.2.1 Overview

We first provide an overview of security issues for the semantic Web and then review some details on XML security, RDF security, and secure information integration, which are components of the secure semantic Web. As more progress is made on investigating these various issues, we hope that appropriate standards would be developed for securing the semantic Web. Security cannot be considered in isolation. That is, there is no one layer that should focus on security. Security cuts across all layers, and this is a challenge. That is, we need security for each of the layers as illustrated in Figure 17.1.

For example, consider the lowest layer. One needs secure TCP/IP, secure sockets, and secure HTTP. There are now security protocols for these various lower layer protocols. One needs end-to-end security. That is, one cannot just have secure TCP/IP built on untrusted communication layers; we need network security. The next layer is XML and XML schemas. One needs secure XML. That is, access must be controlled to various portions of the document for reading, browsing, and modifications. There is research on securing XML and XML schemas. The next step is securing RDF. Now with RDF not only do we need secure XML, we also need security for the interpretations and semantics. For example, under certain contexts, portions of the document may be unclassified while under certain other contexts the document may be classified.

Once XML and RDF have been secured, the next step is to examine security for ontologies and interoperation. That is, ontologies may have security levels attached to them. Certain parts of the ontologies could be secret while certain other parts may be unclassified. The challenge is how does one use these ontologies for secure

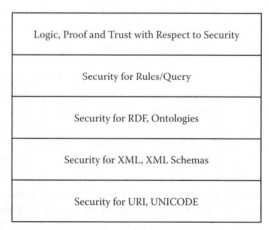

Logic, Proof and Trust with Respect to Security
Security for Rules/Query
Security for RDF, Ontologies
Security for XML, XML Schemas
Security for URI, UNICODE

Figure 17.1 Layers for the secure semantic Web.

information integration? Researchers have done some work on the secure interoperability of databases. We need to revisit this research and then determine what else needs to be done so that the information on the Web can be managed, integrated, and exchanged securely. Logic, proof, and trust are at the highest layers of the semantic Web (see Figure 17.1). That is, how can we trust the information that the Web gives us?

We also need to examine the inference problem for the semantic Web. Inference is the process of posing queries and deducing new information. It becomes a problem when the deduced information is something the user is unauthorized to know. With the semantic Web, and especially with data mining tools, one can make all kinds of inferences. Recently there has been some research on controlling unauthorized inferences on the semantic Web. We need to continue with such research (see for example, [FARK03], [THUR05a], [THUR06]).

Security should not be an afterthought. We have often heard that one needs to insert security into the system right from the beginning. Similarly, security cannot be an afterthought for the semantic Web. However, we cannot also make the system inefficient if we must guarantee 100% security at all times. What is needed is a flexible security policy. During some situations we may need 100% security, while during some other situations, say, 30% security (whatever that means) may be sufficient.

17.2.2 XML Security

Various research efforts have been reported on XML security (see, for example, [BERT02]). We briefly discuss some of the key points. The main challenge is whether to give access to the entire XML documents or parts of the documents. Bertino et al. have developed authorization models for XML. They have focused on access control policies as well as on dissemination policies. They also considered push-and-pull architectures. They specified the policies in XML. The policy specification contains information about which users can access which portions of the documents. In [BERT02], algorithms for access control, as well as computing views of the results, are presented. In addition, architectures for securing XML documents are also discussed. In [BERT04], the authors go further and describe how XML documents may be published on the Web. The idea is for owners to publish documents, subjects to request access to the documents, and untrusted publishers to give the subjects the views of the documents they are authorized to see. We discussed XML security in more detail in Chapter 6.

W3C (World Wide Web Consortium) is specifying standards for XML security. The XML security project (see [XML1]) is focusing on providing the implementation of security standards for XML. The focus is on XML-Signature Syntax and Processing, XML-Encryption Syntax and Processing, and XML Key Management. W3C also has a number of working groups including XML Signature working group (see [XML2]) and XML encryption working group (see [XML3]). Although the standards are focusing on what can be implemented in the near-term, much research is needed on securing XML documents.

17.2.3 RDF Security

RDF is the foundation of the semantic Web. XML is limited in providing machine-understandable documents; RDF handles this limitation. As a result, RDF provides better support for interoperability, as well as searching and cataloging. It also describes contents of documents as well as relationships between various entities in the document. While XML provides syntax and notations, RDF supplements this by providing semantic information in a standardized way.

The basic RDF model has three components: resources, properties, and statements. Resource is anything described by RDF expressions. It could be a Web page or a collection of pages. Property is a specific attribute used to describe a resource. RDF statements are resources together with a named property plus the value of the property. Statement components are subject, predicate, and object. So, for example, if we have a sentence of the form "John is the creator of xxx," then xxx is the subject or resource, property or predicate is "creator," and object or literal is "John." There are RDF diagrams very much like, say, ER diagrams or object diagrams to represent statements. It is important that the intended interpretation be used for RDF sentences. This is accomplished by RDF schemas. Schema is sort of a dictionary and has interpretations of various terms used in sentences.

More advanced concepts in RDF include the container model and statements about statements. The container model has three types of container objects: bag, sequence, and alternative. A bag is an unordered list of resources or literals. It is used to mean that a property has multiple values but the order is not important. A sequence is a list of ordered resources. Here the order is important. Alternative is a list of resources that represent alternatives for the value of a property. Various tutorials in RDF describe the syntax of containers in more detail.

RDF also provides support for making statements about other statements. For example, with this facility one can make statements of the form "The statement A is false" where A is the statement "John is the creator of X." Again, one can use object-like diagrams to represent containers and statements about statements. RDF also has a formal model associated with it. This formal model has a formal grammar. For further information on RDF we refer to the excellent discussion in the book by Antoniou and van Harmelen [ANTO08].

Now to make the semantic Web secure, we need to ensure that RDF documents are secure. This would involve securing XML from a syntactic point of view. However, with RDF, we also need to ensure that security is preserved at the semantic level. The issues include the security implications of the concepts resource, properties, and statements. That is, how is access control ensured? How can statements and properties about statements be protected? How can one provide access control at a finer grain of granularity? What are the security properties of the container model? How can bags, lists, and alternatives be protected? Can we specify security policies in RDF? How can we resolve semantic inconsistencies for the policies? How can we express security constraints in RDF? What are the security implications of statements about statements? How can we protect RDF schemas? These are difficult questions and we need to start research to provide answers. XML security is just the beginning. Securing RDF is much more challenging (see also [CARM04]).

17.2.4 Security and Ontologies

Ontologies are essentially representations of various concepts in order to avoid ambiguity. Numerous ontologies have been developed. These ontologies have been used by agents to understand the Web pages and conduct operations such as the integration of databases. Furthermore ontologies can be represented in languages such as RDF or special languages such as Web ontology language (OWL).

Now, ontologies have to be secure. That is, access to the ontologies have to be controlled. This means that different users may have access to different parts of the ontology. On the other hand, ontologies may be used to specify security policies, just as XML and RDF have been used to specify the policies. Chapter 20 will discuss ontologies and security. That is, we will describe how ontologies may be secured as well as how ontologies may be used to specify the various policies.

17.2.5 Secure Query and Rules Processing for the Semantic Web

The layer above the secure RDF layer is the secure query and rules processing layer. While RDF can be used to specify security policies (see, for example, [CARM04]), the Web rules language being developed by W3C is more powerful to specify complex policies. Furthermore, inference engines are being developed to process and reason about the rules (e.g., the Pellet engine developed at the University of Maryland). One could integrate ideas from the database inference controller that we have developed (see [THUR93]) with Web rules processing to develop an inference or privacy controller for the semantic Web.

The query-processing module is responsible for accessing the heterogeneous data and information sources on the semantic Web. Researchers are examining ways to integrate techniques from Web query processing with semantic Web technologies to locate, query, and integrate the heterogeneous data and information sources. We need to examine the security impact of query processing.

17.3 Privacy and Trust for the Semantic Web

17.3.1 Overview

Privacy is about protecting information about individuals. Furthermore, an individual can specify say to a Web service provider the information that can be released about him or her. Privacy has been discussed a great deal in the past, especially when it relates to protecting medical information about patients. Social scientists as well as technologists have been working on privacy issues. However, privacy has received enormous attention during the past year. This is mainly because of the advent of the Web, the semantic Web, counter-terrorism and national security. For example, in order to extract information about various individuals and perhaps prevent and/or detect potential terrorist attacks, data mining tools are being examined. We have heard much about national security versus privacy in the media. This is mainly due to the fact that people are now realizing that to handle terrorism, the government may need to collect data about individuals and mine the data to extract information. Data may be in relational databases or it may be text, video, and images. This is causing a major concern with various civil liberties unions (see [THUR02c]). Closely related to privacy is anonymity. Some argue that it is more important to maintain anonymity.

In this section we discuss privacy threats that arise due to data mining and the semantic Web. We also discuss some solutions and provide directions for standards. Section 17.3.2 will discuss issues on data mining, national security, and privacy. Some potential solutions are discussed in Section 17.3.3. Trust management will be discussed in Section 17.3.4.

17.3.2 Data Mining, National Security, Privacy, and the Semantic Web

With the Web and the semantic Web, there is now an abundance of data about individuals that one can obtain within seconds. The data could be structured data or could be multimedia data such as text, images, video, and audio. Information could be obtained through mining or just from information retrieval. Data mining is an important tool in making the Web more intelligent. That is, data mining may be used to mine the data on the Web so that the Web can evolve into the semantic Web. However, this also means that there may be threats to privacy. Therefore, one needs to enforce privacy controls on databases and data mining tools on the semantic Web. This is a very difficult problem. In summary, one needs to develop techniques to prevent users from mining and extracting information from data whether they are on the Web or on networked servers. Note that data mining is a technology that is critical for, say, analysts so that they can extract patterns previously unknown. However, we do not want the information to be used in an incorrect manner. For example, based on information about a person, an insurance company could deny insurance or a loan agency could deny loans. In many cases, these denials may not be legitimate. Therefore, information providers have to be very careful in what they release. Also, data mining researchers have to ensure that privacy aspects are addressed.

While little work has been reported on privacy issues for the semantic Web, we are moving in the right direction. As research initiatives are started in this area, we can expect some progress to be made. Note that there are also social and political aspects to consider. That is, technologists, sociologists, policy experts, counter-terrorism experts, and legal experts have to work together to develop appropriate data mining techniques, as well as ensure privacy. Privacy policies and standards are also urgently needed. That is, while the technologists develop privacy solutions, we need the policy makers to work with standards organizations so that appropriate privacy standards are developed. W3C has made a good start with P3P (the platform for privacy preferences).

17.3.3 Solutions to the Privacy Problem

The challenge is to provide solutions to enhance national security but at the same time ensure privacy. There is now research at various laboratories on privacy enhanced/sensitive/preserving data mining (e.g., Agrawal at IBM Almaden, Gehrke at Cornell University, and Clifton at Purdue University; see for example [AGRA00], [CLIF02], [GEHR02]). The idea here is to continue with mining but at the same time ensure privacy as much as possible. For example, Clifton has proposed the use of the multiparty security policy approach for carrying out privacy sensitive data mining. While there is some progress we still have a long way to go. Some useful references are provided in [CLIF02] (see also [EVFI02]).

We give some more details on an approach we are proposing. Note that one mines the data and extracts patterns and trends. The privacy constraints determine which patterns are private and to what extent. For example, suppose one could extract the names and health care records. If we have a privacy constraint that states that names and health care records are private, then this information is not released to the general public. If the information is semiprivate, then it is released to those who have a need to know. Essentially the inference controller approach we have discussed is one solution to achieving some level of privacy. It could be regarded to be a type of privacy sensitive data mining. In our research we have found many challenges to the inference controller approach we have proposed (see [THUR93]). These challenges will have to be addressed when handling privacy constraints (see also [THUR05b]). Figure 17.2 illustrates privacy controllers for the semantic Web. As illustrated, there are data mining tools on the Web that mine the Web databases. The privacy controller should ensure privacy preserving data mining. Ontologies may be used by the privacy controllers. For example, there may be ontology specification for privacy constructs. Furthermore, XML may be extended to include

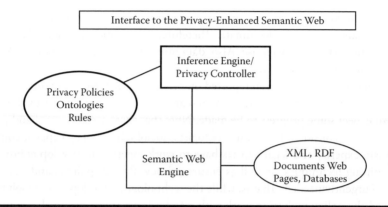

Figure 17.2 Privacy controller for the semantic Web.

privacy constraints. RDF may incorporate privacy semantics. We need to carry out more research on the role of ontologies for privacy control.

Much of the work on privacy preserving data mining focuses on relational data. We need to carry out research on privacy preserving semantic Web data mining. We need to combine techniques for privacy preserving data mining with techniques for semantic Web data mining to obtain solutions for privacy preserving semantic Web data mining.

17.3.4 Trust for the Semantic Web

Recently there has been much work on trust and the semantic Web (see the research by Finin et al. [DENK03], [KAGA03]). The challenges include how do you trust the information on the Web? How do you trust the sources? How do you negotiate between different parties and develop contracts? How do you incorporate constructs for trust management and negotiation into XML and RDF? What are the semantics for trust management?

Researchers are working on protocols for trust management. Languages for specifying trust management constructs are also being developed. Also there is research on the foundations of trust management. For example, if A trusts B and B trusts C, then can A trust C? How do you share the data and information on the semantic Web and still maintain autonomy. How do you propagate trust? For example, if A trusts B at say 50% of the time and B trusts C 30% of the time, then what value do you assign for A trusting C? How do you incorporate trust into semantic interoperability? What is the quality of service primitives for trust and negotiation? That is, for certain situations one may need 100% trust while for certain other situations 50% trust may suffice (see also [YU03]).

Another topic that is being investigated is trust propagation and propagating privileges. For example, if you grant privileges to A, what privileges can A transfer to B? How can you compose privileges? Is there an algebra and calculus for the composition of privileges? Much research still needs to be done here. One of the layers of the semantic Web is Logic, Proof, and Trust. Essentially this layer deals with trust management and negotiation between different agents and examining the foundations and developing logics for trust management.

17.4 Secure Semantic Web and Web Services

As we have mentioned in Chapter 6, integration of the Web services and the semantic Web results in semantic Web services. That is, Web services to the WWW are semantic Web services to the semantic Web. Tim Finin and his team have discussed an architecture for semantic Web services [BURS05]. They have described the inadequacies of Web services and discussed the need for semantic Web services. They state that current technologies allow usage of Web services. In particular, current Web services support syntactic information descriptions as well as syntactic support for service discovery, composition, and execution. They argue that we need semantically marked up content and services and therefore we need to develop semantic Web services. They then define an architecture called the semantic Web service architecture, which consists of a set of architectural and protocol abstractions that serve as a foundation for semantic Web service technologies. These technologies support dynamic service discovery, service engagement, service process enactment, community support services, and quality of service.

Service discovery is the process of identifying candidate services by clients. Matchmakers connect the service requesters to the providers. Ontologies may be needed to specify the services. Service engagement specified the agreements between the requester and the provider. Therefore, contract negotiation is carried out during this phase. Once the service is ready to be initiated, the service enactment phase begins. During this phase the requester determines the information necessary to request performance of service and appropriate reaction to service success or failure. This will also include interpreting the responses and carrying out transitions, Community management services support authentication and security management. Quality of service provides support for negotiation as well as trade-offs say between security and timely delivery of the data.

Security cuts across all these services. Note that while the community management service especially calls for authentication and security management, security services are needed for service discovery, engine segment, and enactment. For example, not all services can be discovered. This will depend on the sensitivity of the service and the security credentials possessed by the requester. Therefore, security specifications for XML, RDF, and OWL have to be examined for semantic Web service descriptions. In the next four chapters, we will discuss in more detail the relationship between secure semantic Web technologies and Web services. In particular, the relationship between security, XML, RDF, OWL, rules, and Web services will be discussed. Figure 17.3 illustrates secure semantic Web services.

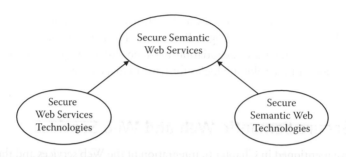

Figure 17.3   Secure semantic Web services.

17.5 Summary and Directions

This chapter has provided an overview of the semantic Web and discussed security standards. We first discussed security issues for the semantic Web. We argued that security must cut across all the layers. Next, we provided some more details on XML security, RDF security, secure information integration, and trust. If the semantic Web is to be secure, we need all of its components to be secure. We also described some of our research on access control and dissemination of XML documents. Next, we discussed privacy for the semantic Web. This was followed by a brief discussion of security for the grid and the semantic grid.

Much research needs to be done. We need to continue with the research on XML security. We must start examining security for RDF. This is more difficult as RDF incorporates semantics. We need to examine the work on security constraint processing and context dependent security constraints and see if we can apply some of the ideas for RDF security. Finally, we need to examine the role of ontologies for secure information integration. We have to address some hard questions such as how do we integrate security policies on the semantic Web? How can we incorporate policies into ontologies? We also cannot forget about privacy and trust for the semantic Web. That is, we need to protect the privacy of individuals and at the same time ensure that the individuals have the information they need to carry out their functions. Finally, we need to formalize the notions of trust and examine ways to negotiate trust on the semantic Web. We have a good start and are well on our way to building the semantic Web. Security must be considered at the beginning and not as an afterthought.

Standards play an important role in the development of the semantic Web. W3C has been very effective in specifying standards for XML and RDF. We need to continue with the developments and try as much as possible to transfer the research to the standards efforts. We also need to transfer the research and standards to commercial products. The next step for the semantic Web standards efforts is to examine security, privacy, quality of service, integrity, and other features such as secure query services. As we have stressed, security and privacy are critical and must be investigated while the standards are being developed.

Exercises

1. Describe with examples the need for security for the semantic Web (include confidentiality, privacy, and trust).
2. Conduct a survey of the various efforts on security for the semantic Web.
3. Describe how semantic Web technologies may be utilized by secure Web services.

References

[AGRA00] Agrawal, R. and R. Srikant, Privacy-preserving data mining, *Proceedings of the ACM SIGMOD Conference*, Dallas, TX, May 2000.

[ANTO08] Antoniou, G. and F. van Harmelen, *A Semantic Web Primer*, MIT Press, Cambridge, MA, 2008.

[ATKI03] Atkins, D., Chair, Blue Ribbon Advisory Panel, Cyber Infrastructure, NSF Report, http://www.communitytechnology.org/nsf_ci_report/

[BERT02] Bertino, E., S. Castano, E. Ferrari, and M. Mesiti, Protection and administration of XML data source, *Data and Knowledge Engineering*, Volume 43, #3, 237–260, 2002.

[BERT04] Bertino, E., B. Carminati, E. Ferrari, and A. Gupta, Selective and authentic Third Party Publication of XML Documents, *IEEE Transactions on Knowledge and Data Engineering*, 16(10), 1263–1278, 2004.

[BHAT04] Bhatty, R., E. Bertino, and A. Ghafoor, Trust-based context aware access control models in Web services, *Proceedings of the Web Services Conference*, San Diego, July 2004.

[BURS05] Burstein, M. H., C. Bussler, M. Zaremba, T. W. Fiin, M. N. Huhns, M. Paolucci, A. P. Sheth, and S. K. Williams, A semantic Web services architechture, *IEEE Internet Computing*, 9(5): 72–81, 2005.

[CARM04] Carminati, B. et al., Using RDF for Policy specification and enforcement, *Proceedings of the DEXA Conference Workshop on Web Semantics*, Zaragoza, Spain, 2004.

[CLIF02] Clifton, C., M. Kantarcioglu, and J. Vaidya, Defining Privacy for Data Mining, Purdue University, 2002 (see also Next Generation Data Mining Workshop, Baltimore, MD, November 2002).

[DENK03] Denker, G., L. Kagal, T. Finin, M. Paslucci, and K. Sycara, Security for DAML Web Services: Annotation and Matchmaking, International Semantic Web Conference 2003.

[EVFI02] Evfimievski, A., R. Srikant, R. Agrawal, and J. Gehrke, Privacy preserving mining of association rules, In *Proceedings of the Eighth ACM SIGKDD International Conference on Knowledge Discovery and Data Mining*, Edmonton, Alberta, Canada, July 2002.

[FARK03] Farkas, C. and A. Stoica, Inference Problem for the Semantic Web, *Proceedings of the IFIP Conference on Data and Applications Security*, Colorado, August 2003 (formal proceedings published by Kluwer, 2004).

[GEHR02] Gehrke, J., Research Problems in Data Stream Processing and Privacy-Preserving Data Mining, *Proceedings of the Next Generation Data Mining Workshop*, Baltimore, MD, November 2002.

[HACI02] Hacigumus, H., B. Iyer, and S. Mehrotsa, Providing database as a service, *Proceedings of IEEE Data Engineering Conference*, San Jose, CA, March 2002.

[HACI04] Hacigumus, H. and S. Mehrotra, Performance-conscious key management in encrypted databases, *Proceedings of the IFIP Database Security Conference*, Sitges, Spain, Kluwer, July 2004 (Editor: C. Farkas and P. Samarati).

[KAGA03] Kagal, L., T. W. Finin, and A. Joshi, iA Policy based approach to security for the semantic Web. *International Semantic Web Conference*, 2003: 402–418.

[LEE01] Berners-Lee, T., J. Hendler, and O. Lassila, The Semantic Web, *Scientific American*, May 2001.

[OASIS] OASIS, http://www.oasis-open.org/home/index.php

[ROUR04] Roure, D. and Hendler, J., E-Science, *IEEE Intelligent Systems*, January/February 2004.

[RDF] RDF Primer, http://www.w3.org/TR/rdf-primer/

[SHET90] Sheth, A. and J. Larson, Federated database systems, *ACM Computing Surveys*, Volume 22, #3, 1990.

[THUR93] Thuraisingham, B. et al., Design and implementation of a database inference controller, *Data and Knowledge Engineering Journal*, Volume 11, #3, 1993.

[THUR97] Thuraisingham, B., *Data Management Systems Evolution and Interoperation*, CRC Press, Boca Raton, FL, 1997.

[THUR02a] Thuraisingham, B., Data and applications security: Developments and directions, *Proceedings IEEE COMPSAC*, 2002.

[THUR02b] Thuraisingham, B., *XML, Databases and the Semantic Web*, CRC Press, Boca Raton, FL, 2002.

[Thur02c] Thuraisingham, B. M., Data mining, national security, privacy and civil liberties, *SIGKDD Explorations*, 4(2), 1–5, 2002.

[THUR05a] Thuraisingham, B., Security standards for the semantic Web, *Computer Standards and Interface Journal*, 27, 257–268, 2005.

[THUR05b] Thuraisingham, B., Privacy constraint processing in a privacy enhanced database system, *Data and Knowledge Engineering Journal*, 155(2), 159–188, 2005.

[THUR06] Thuraisingham, B., N. Tsybulnik, and A. Alam, Administering the semantic Web, confidentiality, privacy and trust, *Journal of Information Security and Privacy*, 2006.

[YU03] Yu, T. and M. Winslett, A unified scheme for resource protection in automated trust negotiation, *IEEE Symposium on Security and Privacy*, Oakland, CA, May 2003.

[WWW] www.w3c.org

[XML1] http://xml.apache.org/security/

[XML2] http://www.w3.org/Signature/

[XML3] http://www.w3.org/Encryption/2001/

Chapter 18

Security, XML, and Web Services

18.1 Overview

In Chapter 6 we provided an overview of the semantic Web and Web services, and in Chapter 17 we discussed secure semantic Web and Web services. In this chapter, we will discuss security aspects of XML and their relationship to Web services. XML has become the standard language for document exchange and more recently data and information interoperability. The components of XML include elements, attributes, document type definitions (DTD), schemas, and namespaces. We have discussed these concepts in our previous book [THUR02]. For an excellent exposition of XML and the semantic Web we refer to the book by Antoniou and van Hamlen [ANTO08].

In this chapter we discuss further security issues for XML. Note that there are two aspects: one is securing XML documents and the other is using XML to specify policies. We discuss both aspects. We give examples and show how access control rules can be enforced on XML documents. We also discuss security for XML schemas and security for name spaces. Then we discuss how policies can be expressed in XML. One of the advantages with a specification language such as XML is that one can specify rules in this language. However, since XML represents data, policies specified in XML can be enforced on data represented in XML.

The organization of this chapter is as follows. In Section 18.2, we will give an example document that we will use in this chapter to discuss the security issues.

We discussed issues in XML security such as securing XML data, DTDs, schemas, and namespaces in Section 18.3. In Section 18.4, we discuss the specification of security policies in XML. Access control for XML including query modification is covered in Section 18.5. Third-party publication of XML documents as discussed in the research by Bertino et al [BERT04] is the focus of Section 18.6. Secure management of XML databases is the subject of Section 18.7. Distribution of XML documents is the subject of Section 18.8. Finally, in Section 18.9 we cover the relationship between secure XML and Web services. The chapter is summarized in Section 18.10.

18.2 Example XML Document

In this section we give an example XML document both in graphical format and XML format (Figure 18.1). Then we discuss the XML DTD and the XML schema for this document. Our discussion of XML security has been influenced a great deal by the work of Bertino, Carminati, and Ferrari at the University of Milan [BERT02], [BERT04].

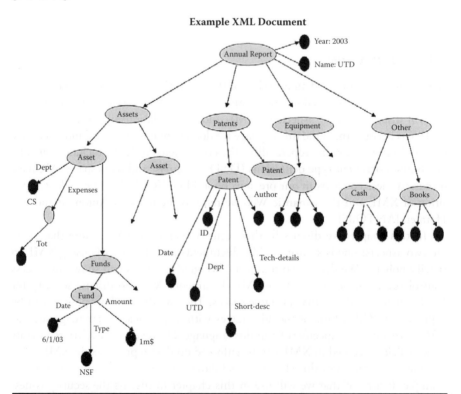

Figure 18.1   Example XML document.

XML Specification for the preceding graph:

```
<? xml version="1.0" encoding="UTF-16"?>
<Annual-Report Year="2003" Name="UTD">
       <Assets>
               <Asset Dept="CS">
                       <Expenses Total="400" />
                       <Funds>
                               <Fund Date="060103" Type="NSF"
                               Amount="1" />
                               .
                               .
                               .
                       </Funds>
               </Asset>
                  .
                  .
                  .
       </Assets>

       <Patents>
       <Patent PID="12345" Date="030704" Dept="UTD" Short-
       desc="This patent deals with Semantic Web Technologies"
       Tech-details="Deals with XML, RDF and OWL technologies"
       Author="Prof XXX" />
       .
       .
       </Patents>
       <Equipment>
       .
       .
       </Equipment>
       <Other>
       <Cash />
       <Books />
       </Other>
</Annual-Report>
```

XML DTD for the preceding XML specification:

```
<! ELEMENT Annual-Report (Assets, Patents, Equipment, Others)>
<! ATTLIST Annual-Report
     Year     ID     #REQUIRED
     Name     CDATA #REQUIRED >

<! ELEMENT Assets (Asset *)>
<! ELEMENT Asset (Expenses, Funds)
<! ATTLIST Asset
     Dept     ID     #REQUIRED>
```

```
<! ELEMENT Expenses>
<! ATTLIST Expenses
      Total    CDATA   #REQUIRED>
<! ELEMENT Funds (Fund*)>
<! ELEMENT Fund>
<! ATTLIST Fund
      Date     CDATA   #REQUIRED
      Type     CDATA   #REQUIRED
      Amount   CDATA   #REQUIRED>

<! ELEMENT Patents (Patent*)>
<! ELEMENT Patent>
<! ATTLIST Patent
      PID      ID
      Date         CDATA   #REQUIRED
      Dept         CDATA   #REQUIRED
      Short-desc   CDATA   #REQUIRED
      Tech-details CDATA   #REQUIRED
      Author       CDATA   #REQUIRED>

<! ELEMENT Equipment>
<! ELEMENT Other (Cash, Books)>
<! ELEMENT Cash>
<! ELEMENT Books>
```

XML Schema for the preceding XML specification:

```
<? xml version="1.0" encoding="UTF-16"?>
<element name="Annual-Report" type="reportType"/>
<complexType name="reportType">
   <sequence>
      <element name="Assets" type="assetsType" minOccurs=1
      maxOccurs=1 />
      <element name="Patents" type="patentsType" minOccurs=1
      maxOccurs=1 />
      <element name="Equipment" type="equipmentType"
      minOccurs=1 maxOccurs=1 />
      <element name="Other" type="otherType" minOccurs=1
      maxOccurs=1 />
   </sequence>
</complexType>

<complexType name="assetsType">
   <sequence>
      <element name="Asset" type="assetType" minOccurs=0
      maxOccurs="unbounded" />
   </sequence>
</complexType>
```

```
<complexType name="assetType">
    <sequence>
        <attribute name="Dept" type="string" use="required" />
        <element name="Expenses" type="expensesType"
        minOccurs=1 maxOccurs=1 />
        <element name="Funds" type="FundsType" minOccurs=1
        maxOccurs=1/>
    </sequence>
</complexType>

<complexType name="expensesType">
        <attribute name="Total" type="string" use="required" />
</complexType>

<complexType name="FundsType">
    <sequence
        <element name="Fund" type="fundType" minOccurs=0
        maxOccurs="unbounded" />
    </sequence>
</complexType>

<complexType name="fundType">
        <attribute name="Date" type="string" use="required" />
        <attribute name="Type" type="string" use="required" />
        <attribute name="Amount" type="integer" use="required"
        />
</complexType>

<complexType name="patentsType">
    <sequence>
        <element name="Patent" type="patentType" minOccurs=0
        maxOccurs="unbounded" />
    </sequence>
</complexType>

<complexType name="patentType">
        <attribute name="Date" type="string" use="required" />
        <attribute name="ID" type="integer" use="required" />
        <attribute name="Dept" type="string" use="required" />
        <attribute name="Short-desc" type="string"
        use="required" />
        <attribute name="Tech-details" type="string"
        use="required" />
        <attribute name="Author" type="string" use="required"
        />
</complexType>
```

```
<complexType name="equipmentType">
    <sequence>
    </sequence>
</complexType>

<complexType name="otherType">
    <sequence>
        <element name="Cash" type="cashType" minOccurs=1
        maxOccurs="1" />
        <element name="Books="booksType" minOccurs=1
        maxOccurs="1" />
    /sequence>
</complexType>
```

18.3 XML Security Standards

In this section we discuss some of the major standards for XML security. In particular, we will discuss the developments with W3C (World Wide Web Consortium) and OASIS (Organization for the Advancement of Structured Information Standards). A list of some of the developments of these organizations is given in Appendix D (see also [W3C] and [OASIS]).

W3C has developed three major standards related to security. They are the following: XML Encryption, XML Key Management, and XML Signature. The XML Encryption working group has developed a process to encrypting/decrypting digital content, which includes XML documents. This group does not address XML security issues. XML Key Management working group has developed a protocol for a client to obtain key information (e.g., value, certificates, etc.) from a Web service. This group also does not address the security issues. As stated in [W3C], the XML Signature working group has developed "an XML compliant syntax used for representing the signature of Web resources and portions of protocol messages (anything referenceable by a URI) and procedures for computing and verifying such signatures." Like the first two groups, this group also does not address XML security issues.

OASIS is the standards organization promoting security standards for Web services. It is a not-for-profit, global consortium that drives the development, convergence, and adoption of e-business standards. Two standards provided by OASIS are XACML and SAML. XACML (eXtensible Access Control Markup Language) provides fine-grained control of authorized activities, the effect of characteristics of the access requestor, the protocol over which the request is made, authorization based on classes of activities, and content introspection. SAML is an XML framework for exchanging authentication and authorization information. The next section gives details of both XACML and SAML.

18.4 Issues in XML Security

In this section, we will discuss the various components of XML and examine the security impact. Note that we discuss only discretionary security. Multilevel security is the subject of Chapter 13.

XML Elements: First let us consider the following XML statement that states that John Smith is a professor in Texas. This can be expressed as follows:

```
<Professor>
    <name> John Smith </name>
    <state> Texas </state>
</Professor>
```

Now suppose this data can be read by anyone then we can augment the XML statement by an additional element called *access,* as follows.

```
<Professor>
    <name> John Smith </name>
    <state> Texas </state>
    <access> All, Read </access>
</Professor>
```

If only HR can update this XML statement, then we have the following:

```
<Professor>
    <name> John Smith </name>
    <state> Texas </state>
    <access> HR department, Write </access>
</Professor>
```

Note that there are issues with negative authorizations. That is, when an authorization is not specified, then one can assume that the authorization is negative. Furthermore, we have given access to both elements of professor, and they are name and state. We could have more specialized statements that give access to elements such as name or state. For example, we may not wish for everyone to know that John Smith is a professor, but we can give out the information that this professor is in Texas. This can be expressed as

```
<Professor>
    <name> John Smith, Govt-official, Read </name>
    <state> Texas, All, Read </state>
    <access> HR department, Write </access>
</Professor>
```

Note that in discussing access control policies we are giving our own opinions and not the standards. Standards will be discussed later on in this chapter. Also some alternative ways to specifying policies in XML will be discussed in Section 18.5.

XML Attributes: Next, let us examine the concept of attributes in XML. Suppose we want to specify access based on attribute values. One way to specify such access is given below.

```
<Professor
   Name = "John Smith", Access = All, Read
   Salary = "60K", Access = Administrator, Read, Write
   Department = "Security" Access = All, Read
</Professor
```

Here, we assume that everyone can read the name John Smith and Department Security. But only the administrator can read and write the salary attribute.

XML DTDs: Next, let us examine the notion of DTDs. DTDs essentially specify the structure of XML documents. Consider the following DTD for Professor with elements Name and State. This will be specified as:

```
<!ELEMENT Professor Officer (Name, State)>
<!ELEMENT name (#PCDATA)>
<!ELEMENR state (#PCDATA)>
<!ELEMENT access (#PCDATA).>
```

For a discussion of #PCDATA we refer to [ANTO08]. We can give DTDs for the other examples we have given in this section such as assigning access to each element. In this case we may need an element within an element to specify access say to name and access to state.

XML Schemas: While DTDs were the early attempts to specify structure for XML documents, XML schemas are far more elegant to specify structures. Unlike DTDs, XML schemas essentially use the XML syntax for specification. Consider the following example:

```
<ComplexType = name = "ProfessorType">
   <Sequence>
   <element name = "name" type = "string"/>
   <element name = "state" type = "string"/>
   <element name = "access" type = "strong/>
   <Sequence>
</ComplexType>
```

Namespaces: Finally let us examine namespaces. Note that namespaces are used for disambiguation. Since different groups may come up with different XML specifications for the same concept, namespaces are used to resolve conflicts. Consider the concept of academic institutions. In the United Kingdom they may be called *universities* and in the United States they may be called *colleges*. This can be specified using the concept of namespaces as follows:

```
<CountryX: Academic-Institution
    Xmlns: CountryX = "http://www.CountryX.edu/InstiutionDTD"
    Xmlns: USA = http://www.USA.edu/InstutionDTD"
    Xmlns: UK = http://www.UK.edy/InstitutionDTD
    <USA: Title = College
        USA: Name = "University of Texas at Dallas"
        USA: State = Texas"
    <UK: Title = University
        UK: Name = "Cambridge University"
        UK: State = Cambs
</CountryX: Academicx-Institution>
```

One could assign access to the components of the namespaces discussed above as follows:

```
<Country: Academic-Institution
<Access = Government-official, Read </Access>
    Xmlns: CountryX = "http://www.CountryX.edu/InstiutionDTD"
    Xmlns: USA = http://www.USA.edu/InstutionDTD"
    Xmlns: UK = "http://www.UK.edy/InstitutionDTD"
    <USA: Title = College
        USA: Name = "University of Texas at Dallas"
        USA: State = Texas"
    <UK: Title = University
        UK: Name = "Cambridge University"
        UK: State = Cambs
</CountryX: Academic-Institution>
```

This means only government officials have read access to the information in the above XML statement. We will revisit this again when we discuss ontologies and interoperability in the ensuing chapters.

18.5 Policy Specification in XML

While XML documents have to be secure, XML can be used to specify the policies. In this section we will discuss some example policies using XML. In particular, we discuss credential specification as well as policy specification.

18.5.1 Credentials

Credentials are certificates that a user may posses to carry out his/her job. For example, if Alice has the credentials of a professor, then she may grade exams, teach courses, and also advise students. We give examples as follows:

```
<Professor credID="9" subID = "16: CIssuer = "2">
    <name> Alice Brown </name>
    <university> University of X <university/>
    <department> CS </department>
    <research-group> Security </research-group>
</Professor>

<Secretary credID="12" subID = "4: CIssuer = "2">
    <name> John James </name>
    <university> University of X <university/>
    <department> CS </department>
    <level> Senior </level>
</Secretary>
```

18.5.2 Policies

```
<? Xml VERSION = "1.0" ENCODING = "utf-8"?>
  <Policy-base>

    <policy-spec cred-expr = "//Professor[department = 'CS']"
    target =
    "annual_ report.xml" path = "//Patent[@Dept = 'CS']//
    Node()" priv = "VIEW"/>

    <policy-spec cred-expr = "//Professor[department = 'CS']"
    target =
    "annual_ report.xml" path = "//Patent[@Dept = 'EE'] /
    Short-descr/Node() and
    //Patent [@Dept = 'EE']/authors" priv = "VIEW"/>

  <policy-spec cred-expr = - - - -

  <policy-spec cred-expr = - - --

</Policy-base>
```

Explanation: CS professors are entitled to access all the patents of their department. They are entitled to see only the short descriptions and authors of patents of the EE department.

A more complete specification of six policies P1–P6 as discussed in [BERT04] is described below.

```
<?xml version="1.0" encoding="UTF-8"?>
<policy_base>
...
```

```
<policy_spec ID='P1' cred_expr="//
Professor[department='CS']" target="annual_report.xml"
path="//Patent[@Dept='CS']//node()" priv="VIEW"/>
<policy_spec ID='P2' cred_expr="//
Professor[department='CS']" target="annual_report.xml"
path="//Patent[@Dept='IST']/Short-descr/node() and //
Patent[@Dept='IST']/authors" priv="VIEW"/>
<policy_spec ID='P3' cred_expr="//
Professor[department='IST'] " target="annual_report.xml"
path="//Patent[@Dept='IST']//node()" priv="VIEW"/>
<policy_spec ID='P4' cred_expr="//
Professor[department='IST']" target="annual_report.xml"
path="//Patent[@Dept='CS']/Short-descr/node() and //Patent[@
Dept='CS']/authors" priv="VIEW"/>
<policy_spec ID='P5' cred_expr="//secretary[department='CS'
and level='junior']" target="annual_report.xml" path="//
Asset[@Dept='CS']/node()" priv="VIEW "/>
<policy_spec ID='P6' cred_expr="//secretary[department='CS'
and level='senior']" target="annual_report.xml" path="//
Asset[@Dept='IST']/Funds/@Type and //Asset[@Dept='IST']/
Funds/@Funding-Date" priv="VIEW "/>
<policy_spec ID='P7' cred_expr="//secretary[department='IST'
and level='junior']" target="annual_report.xml" path="//
Asset[@Dept='IST']/node()" priv="VIEW "/>
...
</policy_base>
```

18.6 Access Control for XML Documents

Bertino et al. were some of the first to examine security for XML (see [BERT02] and [BERT04]). They first proposed a framework for access control for XML documents and then discussed a technique for ensuring authenticity and completeness of a document for third-party publishing. We briefly discuss some of the key issues.

In the access control framework proposed in [BERT02], security policy is specified depending on user roles and credentials (see Figure 18.2). Users must possess the credentials to access XML documents. The credentials depend on their roles. For example, a professor has access to all of the details of students, while a secretary only has access to administrative information. XML specifications are used to specify the security policies. Access is granted for an entire XML document or portions of the document. Under certain conditions, access control may be propagated down the XML tree. For example, if access is granted to the root, it does not necessarily mean access is granted to all the children. One may grant access to the DTDs and not to the document instances. One may grant access to certain portions of

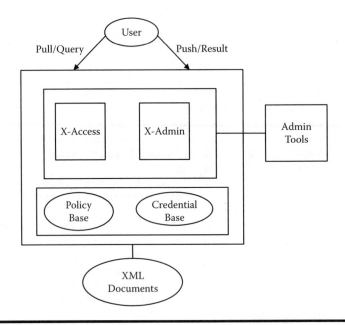

Figure 18.2 Access control for XML documents.

the document. For example, a professor does not have access to the medical information of students while he has access to student grade and academic information. Design of a system for enforcing access control policies is also described in [BERT02]. Essentially the goal is to use a form of view modification so that the user is authorized to see the XML views as specified by the policies. More research needs to be done on role-based access control for XML and the semantic Web.

As discussed in [BERT02], the algorithm for Access Control is as follows:

- Subjects request access to XML documents under two modes: browsing and authoring.
  - With browsing access, subject can read/navigate documents.
  - Authoring access is needed to modify, delete, append documents.
- Access control module checks the policy base and applies policy specs.
- Views of the document are created based on credentials and policy specifications
- In case of conflict, least access privilege rule is enforced

18.7 Secure Publication of XML Documents

In [BERT04] we discussed the secure publication of XML documents (see Figure 18.3). The idea is to have untrusted third-party publishers. The owner of a document specifies access control policies for the subjects. Subjects get the policies

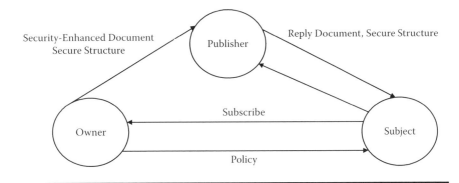

Figure 18.3   Secure XML publishing.

from the owner when they subscribe to a document. The owner sends the documents to the publisher. When the subject requests a document, the publisher will apply the policies relevant to the subject and give portions of the documents to the subject. Now, since the publisher is untrusted, it may give false information to the subject. Therefore, the owner will encrypt various combinations of documents and policies with his/her private key. Using Merkle signature and the encryption techniques, the subject can verify the authenticity and completeness of the document (see Figure 18.3 for secure publishing of XML documents).

In the work by Bertino et al., we defined the notion of a security-enhanced XML document to ensure the authenticity of a document. That is, the owner of an XML document will develop the security enhanced version of the document and send it to the publisher with some additional information. When a user queries for a document, the publisher will give the user the document he is authorized to see together with some other information based on the security enhanced version of the document. The user then verifies the authenticity of the document. To check for completeness—that is, whether the user has received everything he should received—the owner sends to the publisher the secure structure of an XML document, together with the security-enhanced XML document. The publisher sends this secure structure together with the response to the user for a query. The user uses this information and verifies the completeness of the response [BERT04].

18.8 Secure XML Databases

Various commercial data management system vendors such as Oracle are now developing capabilities to manage XML databases. In particular, query, transaction, metadata management, access methods, and indexing algorithms are being developed for XML databases. Data is presented as XML documents. Query languages are being developed including XML-QL and XQuery.

Security has to be incorporated into these XML databases. For example, access control policies that we have discussed in the previous sections have to be enforced on XML databases. In addition, query modification has to be examined for XML data management. Note that query modification is essentially for modifying the queries according to security policies. For example, if professors in the computer science department cannot access the trade secrets in the electrical engineering department and if a professor in the computer science department requests the assets in the electrical engineering department, the query is modified to retrieve all the assets, provided these assets are not trade secrets in the electrical engineering department. This example is illustrated below.

Dr. Thuraisingham is a professor of computer sciences and requests the following query.

```
select Asset
from {EE} depOnt:hasAssets {Asset}
using namespace
    deptOnt = http://www.example.com/departmentOntology#
```

New modified query:

```
select Asset
from {EE} depOnt:hasAsset {Asset}
Where (not {Asset} rdf:type deptOnt:TradeSec)
using namespace
    deptOnt = http://www.example.com/departmentOntology#
```

Security for XML databases has not received much attention. We need to integrate the research carried out by Bertino and her team into data management systems such as Oracle.

18.9 XML, Security, and Web Services

Much of the development of Web services has utilized XML. Therefore, XML security is crucial for current Web services. For example, SOAP messages are specified in XML. Furthermore, WSDL is also based on XML. XACML and SAML are also based on XML. Finally, many other standards, including P3P, are based on XML.

Therefore, we need to make progress in XML security to secure current Web services. XML Key management and XML Encryption are good examples of security standards. XACML is an access control language and used to specify policies. We also need additional standards for third-party publication of XML documents, as well as standards for delegation- and information-flow-based models. Figure 18.4 illustrates the application of XML for secure Web services.

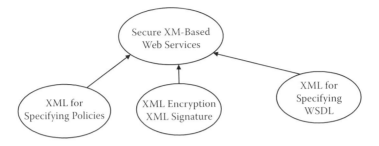

Figure 18.4   XML for secure Web services.

18.10 Summary and Directions

This chapter has provided an overview of XML security and its relationship to Web services. We first discussed issues on securing XML documents including security issues for XML elements attributes and schemas. Then we discussed the use of XML for specifying security policies. We also discussed the secure publications of XML documents. Much of our research on XML security is the result of collaboration with Bertino and her team at the University of Milan.

As we have discussed, XML is widely used, as it has become not only the desired document representation language for exchange on the Web, but also the schema specification language for integrating heterogeneous databases. XML has been extended to numerous applications in multiple domains.

XML security has also received some attention both in the standards community as well as in the research community. However, the progression of standards for security specifications is lagging behind the research. We need a more effective approach to transferring the research to the standards and products. Another issue is the numerous versions of XML floating around. We need to develop some consensus. While organizations such as W3C and OASIS are moving in the right direction, we need better coordination between the diverse groups. Nevertheless, we believe that one of the significant developments in computing during the past decade is the semantic Web in general and XML in particular. Therefore, we need to continue to make enhancements to XML and XML security to realize the ultimate goal of Tim Berners-Lee and that is to have machine-readable Web pages.

With respect to Web services, XML plays a major role. As we have discussed in Part I, Web Services 1.0 and 2.0 use XML for message representation as well as XACML, which is based on XML, for access control. XML security will continue to play a major role for Web services security.

Exercises

1. Investigate security issues for XML documents.
2. Specify complex policies in XML.
3. Design an application and show how secure XML can be used.
4. Investigate the use of XML security for Web services.

References

[ANTO08] Antoniou, G. and F. van Harmelen, *A Semantic Web Primer*, MIT Press, Cambridge, MA, 2008.

[BERT02] Bertino, E., S. Castano, E. Ferrari, and M. Meriti, Protection and administration of XML data sources, *Data and Knowledge Engineering*, 43, 3, 237–260, 2002.

[BERT04] Bertino, E., B. Carminati, E. Ferrari, and A. Gupta, Selective and authentic third party publication of XML documents, *IEEE Transactions on Knowledge and Data Engineering*, October 2004.

[OASIS] Organization for the Advancement of Structured Information Standards. http://www.oasis-open.org/home/index.php

[THUR02] Thuraisingham, B., *XML, Databases and the Semantic Web*, CRC Press, Boca Raton, FL, 2001.

[W3C] World Wide Web Consortium, www.w3c.org

Chapter 19

Security, RDF, and Web Services

19.1 Overview

In this chapter we continue with a discussion of the security issues for the semantic Web technologies and their relationship to Web services. In particular, we will discuss security issues for RDF and their relationship to Web services. As we have stated in Chapter 6, RDF uses the syntax of XML. Furthermore, while XML is not sufficient to express semantics, RDF attempts to address the inadequacies of XML.

Little work has been carried out for securing RDF documents. An early effort is the work of Carminati et al. They discussed a security architecture for RDF [CARM04]. Some further security issues for RDF and the inference problem are discussed in [FARK06]. While standards are being developed for secure XML including the work of OASIS and W3C, little work is reported on standards for securing RDF. In this chapter we attempt to provide a fairly broad overview of what needs to be carried out for securing RDF documents. For a detailed discussion of RDF concepts we refer to [ANTO08].

The organization of this chapter is as follows. We give an example of an RDF document in Section 19.2. In Section 19.3 we discuss security issues for RDF. In particular, we examine each concept in RDF and discuss the security impact. Specification of policies in RDF will be discussed in Section 19.4, and access control for RDF documents in Section 19.5. Managing secure RDF databases is covered in

Section 19.6. The relationship between secure RDF and Web services is the focus of Section 19.7. The chapter is summarized in Section 19.8.

19.2 Example of an RDF Document

In this section we will give part of an RDF document describing two books: *Building_Trustworthy_Semantic_Webs* and *Managing_and_Mining_Multimedia_Databases*. They belong to the class "book" and have properties: author, publisher, year, and ISBN.

```
<?xml version="1.0"?>
<rdf:RDF
xmlns:book="http://www.example.com/book#"
xmlns:owl="http://www.w3.org/2002/07/owl#"
xmlns:rdf="http://www.w3.org/1999/02/22-rdf-syntax-ns#"
xmlns:rdfs="http://www.w3.org/2000/01/rdf-schema#">
<book:Book rdf:ID="Building_Trustworthy_Semantic_Webs">
    <book:author>Bhavani Thuraisingham</book:author>
    <book:publisher>Auerbach Publications</book:publisher>
    <book:year>2007</book:year>
    <book:ISBN>0849350808</book:ISBN>
</book:Book>

<book:Book rdf:ID="Managing_and_Mining_Multimedia_Databases">
    <book:author>Bhavani Thuraisingham</book:author>
    <book:publisher>CRC Press</book:publisher>
    <book:year>2001</book:year>
    <book:ISBN>0849300371</book:ISBN>
</book:Book>
</rdf:RDF>
```

RDF Schema with Policy Specification. (For a larger set of RDF properties, refer to http://www.w3.org/TR/rdf-schema/)

The RDF schema for the above RDF document is as follows:

```
<?xml version="1.0"?>
<rdf:RDF
    xmlns:owl="http://www.w3.org/2002/07/owl#"
    xmlns:rdf="http://www.w3.org/1999/02/22-rdf-syntax-ns#"
    xmlns:rdfs="http://www.w3.org/2000/01/rdf-schema#"
    xmlns:wsp="http://www.w3.org/2004/08/20-ws-pol-pos/ns#">

    <rdfs:Class rdf:ID="Book">
      <rdfs:comment>Book Class</rdfs:comment>
      <rdfs:subClassOf rdf:resource="http://www.
      w3.org/1999/02/22-rdf-syntax-ns#Resource"/>
```

```
    </rdfs:Class>
    <rdf:Property rdf:ID="author">
      <rdfs:Comment>Author of the book</rdfs:Comment>
      <rdfs:domain rdf:resource="#Book"/>
      <rdfs:range rdf:resource="http://www.w3.org/1999/02/22-
      rdf-syntax-ns#Literal"/>
    </rdf:Property>

    <rdf:Property rdf:ID="publisher">
      <rdfs:Comment>Publisher of the book</rdfs:Comment>
      <rdfs:domain rdf:resource="#Book"/>
      <rdfs:range rdf:resource="http://www.w3.org/1999/02/22-
      rdf-syntax-ns#Literal"/>
    </rdf:Property>

    <rdf:Property rdf:ID="year">
      <rdfs:Comment>Year of first publication of the book</
      rdfs:Comment>
      <rdfs:domain rdf:resource="#Book"/>
      <rdfs:range rdf:resource="http://www.w3.org/1999/02/22-
      rdf-syntax-ns#Literal"/>
    </rdf:Property>

    <rdf:Property rdf:ID="ISBN">
      <rdfs:Comment>ISBN of the book</rdfs:Comment>
      <rdfs:domain rdf:resource="#Book"/>
      <rdfs:range rdf:resource="http://www.w3.org/1999/02/22-
      rdf-syntax-ns#Literal"/>
    </rdf:Property>

</rdf:RDF>
```

19.3 Issues in RDF Security

19.3.1 Basic Concepts

The basic concepts of RDF are resources, properties, and statements [ANTO08]. In this section we will discuss these concepts from a security point of view.

Resources: Resources are objects such as airplanes, tables, and people. A resource has an identifier called a URI (Universal Resource Identifier). The question is, what are the access control policies for resources? For example, if the book *Semantic Web* is a resource, then who can access the book? Can a person have read access to certain parts of the book? Can a multilevel security policy be enforced for a book? That is, can different parts of the book have different security levels? Should we control access to the existence of the book? These are the policy questions that need to be answered for a specific application.

Properties: Properties are a special kind of resource and describe relationships between the resources. Example of a property is "written by." Essentially, it is a relationship between the resources Semantic Web and Berners-Lee, and is about the statement "Semantic Web book is written by Berners-Lee." With respect to security, the question is, can we allow access to the resources and not to the relationship between the resources? For example, John could have access to the resource Semantic Web book and also to the resource Berners-Lee. But John does not have access to the property "written by."

Statements: As discussed in the previous paragraph, statement asserts the properties of resources. It is a triple (object, attribute, value). Here object could be the Semantic Web book, attribute is written by, and value is Berners-Lee. As stated in [ANTO08], value could be resources or literals. One would also have a statement "Berners-Lee writes the Semantic Web book." The security considerations here are granting access to say the attribute and not to the object or value. Alternatively, one could grant access to the object and value but not to the attribute. Graphical representations such as semantic models can be used to represent statements as described in Chapter 4. However, the goal of the semantic Web is to develop machine readable technologies. Therefore, we can use RDF to specify resources, attributes, and statements. This will be discussed in Section 19.3.2 when we give examples of RDF documents. Figure 19.1 illustrates the use of a semantic model that show the classification levels assigned to an RDF statement.

Reification: This is essentially "statement/properties about statements" such as Bhavani believes that Berners-Lee is the inventor of the semantic Web. So the security questions are, do we classify what Bhavani believes or do we classify that she believes in something. If we classify "Bhavani believes" then essentially what we are saying is that someone believes that Berners-Lee is the inventor of the semantic Web. If we classify what she believes, then what we are saying is that Bhavani believes in something but we don't know what it is. That is, we don't know that she believes in the fact that Tim Berners-Lee is the inventor of the semantic Web.

Data Types: This is the same notion as data types in languages and systems. How should we say a literal be considered? Is it an integer or a string? Typed literals are provided through XML schemas. The security considerations for XML schemas apply here also.

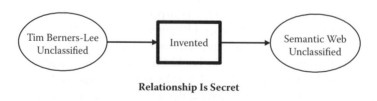

Relationship Is Secret

Figure 19.1 Classifying an RDF statement.

19.3.2 Advanced Concepts

In this section we discuss some of the advanced concepts in RDF along with security properties. Below we describe a complex RDF statement and show how it may be classified.

```
<rdf: RDF
    xmlns: rdf = "http://w3c.org/1999/02-22-rdf-syntax-ns#"
    xmlns: uni = "http://www.example.com/universityonto#">

<rdf: Description  rdf:about = "949352"
    <uni: name> Berners Lee</uni:name>
    <uni: title> Professor </uni:title>
Level = L1
</rdf: Description>

<rdf: Description rdf: about: "ZZZ">
    <uni: bookname> semantic web </uni:bookname>
    <uni: authoredby> Berners Lee </uni:authoredby>
Level = L2
</rdf: Description>
</rdf: RDF>
```

RDF Schema. Unlike XML schema that describe an XMNL document, RDF schema is used to specify some relationships such as the subclass relationship. Below we give an example. The following example classifies the relationship that all engineers are a subclass of employees.

```
<rdfs: Class rdf: ID = "engineer"
<rdfs: comment>
The class of Engineers
All engineers are employees.
<rdfs: comment>
<rdfs: subClassof rdf: resource = "Employee"/>
Level = L
<rdfs: Class>
```

19.4 Policy Specification in RDF

The examples we have discussed in Section 19.2 show how certain policies may be specified for RDF documents. A more detailed example is given below.

```
<?xml version="1.0"?>
<rdf:RDF
xmlns:book="http://www.example.com/book#"
xmlns:owl="http://www.w3.org/2002/07/owl#"
```

```
xmlns:rdf="http://www.w3.org/1999/02/22-rdf-syntax-ns#"
xmlns:rdfs="http://www.w3.org/2000/01/rdf-schema#">
<book:Book rdf:ID="Building_Trustworthy_Semantic_Webs">
    <book:author>Bhavani Thuraisingham</book:author>
    Level = Secret
    <book:publisher>Auerbach Publications</book:publisher>
    Level = Confidential
    <book:year>2007</book:year>
    Level = Unclassified
    <book:ISBN>0849350808</book:ISBN>
    Level = Confidential
</book:Book>

<book:Book rdf:ID="Managing_and_Mining_Multimedia_Databases">
    Level = Confidential
    <book:author>Bhavani Thuraisingham</book:author>
    Level = Secret
    <book:publisher>CRC Press</book:publisher>
    Level = Unclassified
    <book:year>2001</book:year>
    Level = Unclassified
    <book:ISBN>0849300371</book:ISBN>
    Level = Unclassified
</book:Book>
</rdf:RDF>
```

Now, in this example, we have specified policies for RDF documents. Can we use RDF to specify policies? That is, how can RDF be used to specify the following policy?

"Only those attending a class from a professor have read access to the lecture notes of the professor."

Following, we specify this policy in RDF.

```
</rdf:RDF>
    xmlns:uni=http://www.w3.org/2002/07/universityonto#
    xmlns:policy="http://www.example.com/policyonto#"
    xmlns:rdf="http://www.w3.org/1999/02/22-rdf-syntax-ns#">
<uni:LectureNotes rdf:ID="Data_Quality.doc">
  <uni:Author>Bhavani Thuraisingham</uni:author>
  <policy:AccessBy rdf:resource=http://localhost/bhavani/
cs609/>
</rdf:RDF>

<rdf:RDF
    xmlns:uni=http://www.w3.org/2002/07/universityonto#
    xmlns:policy="http://www.example.com/policyonto#"
    xmlns:rdf=http://www.w3.org/1999/02/22-rdf-syntax-ns#>
```

```
<uni:Class rdf:ID="cs609">
    <uni:taughtyBy>Bhavani Thuraisingham</book:author>
</rdf:RDF>
```

Now, in XML we used Xpath expressions to specify policies such as

```
policy_spec ID='P1' cred_expr="//Professor[department='CS']"
target="annual_report.xml" path="//Patent[@Dept='CS']//node()"
priv="VIEW"/>
```

Can we use RDF syntax to specify similar policies? Note that RQL is a language that has been developed to query RDF documents. Therefore, can one access an RDF data element by using policies specified in RQL? Note that Finin et al. at UMBC have developed the RDF-based language REI to specify policies [KAGA03]. We give an example of querying RDF documents in a later section.

19.5 Access Control

Carminati et al. were some of the first to discuss access control for RDF documents [CARM04]. They developed security architecture for RDF and designed ways to enforce access control policies. Subsequently, Farkas has developed access control enforcement techniques and ways to handle the inference problem for RDF documents [FARK06].

The challenge in access control is to determine the granularity of classification. Should access be given to an RDF document as a whole or should access be given to parts of the document? Should access be given to the RDF schemas? That is, should we classify the relationships that are specified using RDF schemas? Again, note that there are two aspects here: one is to control access to RDF documents and the other is to use RDF to specify policies. While Carminati et al.'s work is to specify access to RDF documents, the work of Finin et al. focuses on using the RDF-based language REI to specify policies. Access control for an RDF document is illustrated in Figure 19.2.

The algorithms for access control are similar to the one we proposed for XML.

■ Subjects request access to RDF documents under two modes: browsing and authoring.
  – With browsing access, subject can read/navigate documents.
  – Authoring access is needed to modify, delete, and append documents.
■ Access control module checks the policy base and applies policy specs.
■ Views of the document are created based on credentials and policy specifications.
■ In case of conflict, least access privilege rule is enforced.

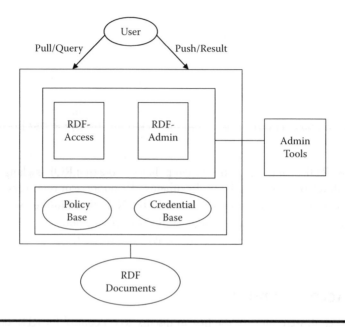

Figure 19.2 Access control for RDF documents.

19.6 Secure RDF Databases

Some commercial data management vendors such as Oracle are now developing approaches to manage RDF databases. While managing RDF documents is not as widespread as managing XML documents, the recent developments are showing a lot of promise. Oracle supports query, transaction, metadata management, access methods, and indexing techniques for managing RDF documents. Furthermore, languages such as RQL are gaining prominence in querying RDF documents.

As in the case of XML, security has to be incorporated into these RDF databases. For example, access control policies that we have discussed in the previous sections need to be enforced on RDF databases. Note that the policies themselves should be specified in RDF or in XML. In addition, query modification has to be examined for RDF data. As we have discussed in [THUR04], query modification is essentially about modifying the queries according to the security policies. In the following text, we give an example of query modification in RQL.

```
Requested Query:

select Book, NumInStock
from  {Book} book:authoredBy {Author}
        . book:Stock  {NumInStock}
```

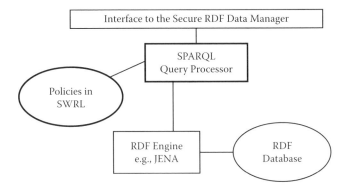

Figure 19.3   Secure RDF databases.

```
Where Author Like "Bhavani*"
using namespace
    book = http://www.example.com/book#
```

The requester does not have access to the number of book copies in the stock. Therefore, the new modified query follows:

```
select Book
from {Book} book:authoredBy {Author}
Where Author Like "Bhavani*"
using namespace
    book = http://www.example.com/book#
```

We need to integrate the research on RDF security with the commercial developments of RDF databases, such as the products being developed by Oracle Corporation. As discussed in Part I, W3C's RFD Data Access Working Group developed a language called SPARQL for querying RDF documents. SPARQL is now widely used for querying RDF documents. We are conducting research on applying query rewriting rules for SPARQL for securing RDF documents. We need to examine the expression of security policies in SPARQL. Figure 19.3 illustrates securing RDF databases.

19.7 Security, RDF, and Web Services

As discussed in Chapter 18, XML is used extensively by Web services. Therefore XML security is crucial for secure Web services. Unlike XML, RDF is only recently being explored for Web services. Note that RDF specifies semantics. Therefore, semantic descriptions of Web services can be specified in Web services descriptions using RDF. Securing RDF is then important for securing Web services.

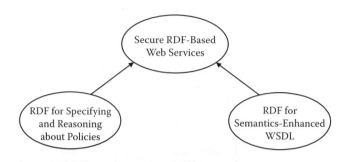

Figure 19.4 Applications of RDF for secure Web services.

RDF can be used to specify more expressive policies. Policies for composite Web services may be improved by using RDF. Another application of RDF is in the use of machine-understandable Web services. Therefore by securing RDF, we can incorporate security into the machine-understandable Web pages. Much needs to be done not only in applying secure RDF for secure Web services, but also applying RDF for Web services. Figure 19.4 illustrates the application of RDF for secure Web services.

19.8 Summary and Directions

This chapter has provided an overview of RDF Security. We first discussed the issues on securing the components of RDF including RDF statements and schemas. Next, we discussed the use of RDF for specifying policies. We also discussed secure RDF databases. Finally, we discussed the application of RDF for secure Web services.

Although just a few years ago RDF was not widely heard of, today RDF is gaining popularity mainly because of the representation of syntax and the semantics. Note that XML is still the most widely used language for document interchange on the Web. Because XML has become so popular, it will be more difficult for RDF to replace it. Note that when XML was introduced, the community was struggling to exchange documents on the Web, as well as to integrate heterogeneous databases. Therefore, XML, together with ontologies became the solution to these problems. As a result, some believe that RDF's use will be limited. Nevertheless, RDF's use is increasing compared to say just 2 years ago.

As RDF is being used, we have to ensure the security of RDF documents. Furthermore, due to the expressiveness of RDF, it can be used to specify more complex policies. Consequently, the semantics of RDF makes it less difficult to build reasoning engines. It is important to examine security for RDF as well as use RDF to specify policies. The works of Finin, Carminati, and Farkas are moving in the right direction. However, we need to express more complex security models such as

RBAC and UCON, and examine RDF-like languages for this purpose [SAND96], [PARK04]. We are beginning collaboration with Finin's group at UMBC and Sanhdu's team at GMU. Together, we believe that we can develop better solutions for RDF security, as well as use RDF to specify complex policies based on RBAC and UCON.

Exercises

1. Investigate security issues for RDF documents.
2. Specify complex policies in RDF.
3. Design an application and show how secure RDF can be used.
4. Describe the relationship between Web services and secure RDF with an example.

References

[ANTO08] Antoniou, G. and F. van Harmelen, *A Semantic Web Premer*, MIT Press, Cambridge, MA, 2003.

[CARM04] Carminati, B., E. Ferrari, and B. Thuraisingham, Security for RDF, *Proceedings of the DEXA Conference Workshop on Web Semantics*, Zaragoza, Spain, 2004.

[FARK06] Farkas, C., Inference problem in RDF, *Proceedings ACM SACMAT*, 2006.

[KAGA03] Kagal, L., T. W. Finin, and A. Joshi, A policy based approach to security for the semantic Web, *International Semantic Web Conference 2003*: 402–418.

[PARK04] Park, J. and R. S. Sandhu, The UCON$_{ABC}$ usage control model, *ACM Transactions on Information and System Security*, 7(1): 128–174, 2004.

[SAND96] Sandhu, R., E. Coyne, H. Feinstein, and C. Youman, Role-based access control models, *IEEE Computer*, 29, 2, 38–47, February 1996.

[THUR04] Thuraisingham, B., *Database and Applications Security: Integrating Information Security and Database Management*, CRC Press, Boca Raton, FL, 2004.

Chapter 20

Security, Ontologies, and Web Services

20.1 Overview

In this chapter we continue with the discussion of the security issues for the semantic Web technologies and their relationship to Web services. In particular, we will discuss security issues for ontologies in general and OWL (Web ontology language). As we have stated in Chapter 19, RDF uses the syntax of XML. Furthermore, while XML is not sufficient to express semantics, RDF attempts to address the inadequacies of XML. OWL is an ontology language that has more expressive power and reasoning capabilities than RDF.

Little work has been carried out on securing OWL documents. Furthermore, OWL can be used to specify policies just like XML and RDF. Access control techniques can be applied to OWL documents. OWL databases need to be secure. This chapter discusses the various security issues for OWL.

The organization of this chapter is as follows. An OWL ontology is described in Section 20.2. We cover security issues for ontologies in Section 20.3. Specification of policies in OWL will be discussed in Section 20.4. Access control is the subject of Section 20.5. Managing secure OWL databases is discussed in Section 20.6. Ontologies for secure interoperability are discussed in Section 20.7. Security, ontologies, and Web services will be discussed in Section 20.8. The chapter is summarized in Section 20.9. For details of OWL and ontologies we refer to [ANTO08].

255

20.2 OWL Example

Before we discuss security for OWL and specify policies in OWL, we need to provide an example of an OWL ontology. The following example describes the University Ontology. The different properties shown are DatatypeProperty (hasCredits) and ObjectProperty (hasTaught, isTaughtBy, etc.). Subproperties are also shown ("has-Completed" is a sub property of "hasRegistered"). The "disjointWith" property ensures that two classes do not have any individuals in common. For example, an individual from the "Faculty" class cannot be an individual of the "Student" class. Using subproperties, policies can be specified. In the following example, a faculty member can access the "AnnualReports" only if she/he is the "Dean."

Note that OWL uses RDF and hence XML syntax. Furthermore, OWL has more powerful reasoning capabilities. The following example and subsequent security examples will make this clear.

```
<?xml version="1.0"?>

<!DOCTYPE rdf:RDF [
  <!ENTITY owl "http://www.w3.org/2002/07/owl#" >
  <!ENTITY xsd "http://www.w3.org/2001/XMLSchema#" >
  <!ENTITY rdfs "http://www.w3.org/2000/01/rdf-schema#" >
  <!ENTITY rdf "http://www.w3.org/1999/02/22-rdf-syntax-ns#" >
] >

<rdf:RDF xmlns="http://www.owl-ontologies.com/
Ontology1178660130.owl#"
  xml:base="http://www.owl-ontologies.com/Ontology1178660130.
owl"
    xmlns:xsd="http://www.w3.org/2001/XMLSchema#"
    xmlns:rdfs="http://www.w3.org/2000/01/rdf-schema#"
    xmlns:rdf="http://www.w3.org/1999/02/22-rdf-syntax-ns#"
    xmlns:owl="http://www.w3.org/2002/07/owl#">
  <owl:Ontology rdf:about=""/>
  <owl:Class rdf:ID="AnnualReports">
    <rdfs:subClassOf rdf:resource="#Department"/>
  </owl:Class>
  <owl:ObjectProperty rdf:ID="canAccess">
    <rdfs:domain rdf:resource="#Faculty"/>
    <rdfs:range rdf:resource="#AnnualReports"/>
    <rdfs:subPropertyOf rdf:resource="#isDean"/>
  </owl:ObjectProperty>
  <owl:Class rdf:ID="Course">
    <rdfs:subClassOf rdf:resource="#Department"/>
  </owl:Class>
  <owl:Class rdf:ID="Department"/>
  <owl:Class rdf:ID="Faculty">
    <rdfs:subClassOf rdf:resource="#Department"/>
    <owl:disjointWith rdf:resource="#Student"/>
```

```
        <owl:disjointWith rdf:resource="#Staff"/>
</owl:Class>
<owl:ObjectProperty rdf:ID="hasCompleted">
    <rdfs:subPropertyOf rdf:resource="#hasRegistered"/>
</owl:ObjectProperty>
<owl:DatatypeProperty rdf:ID="hasCredits">
    <rdfs:domain rdf:resource="#Course"/>
    <rdfs:range rdf:resource="&xsd;int"/>
</owl:DatatypeProperty>
<owl:ObjectProperty rdf:ID="hasDean">
    <rdfs:domain>
        <owl:Class>
            <owl:unionOf rdf:parseType="Collection">
                <owl:Class rdf:about="#Course"/>
                <owl:Class rdf:about="#Department"/>
                <owl:Class rdf:about="#Faculty"/>
                <owl:Class rdf:about="#Staff"/>
                <owl:Class rdf:about="#Student"/>
            </owl:unionOf>
        </owl:Class>
    </rdfs:domain>
    <rdfs:range rdf:resource="#Faculty"/>
</owl:ObjectProperty>
<owl:DatatypeProperty rdf:ID="hasName">
    <rdfs:domain>
        <owl:Class>
            <owl:unionOf rdf:parseType="Collection">
                <owl:Class rdf:about="#Department"/>
                <owl:Class rdf:about="#Faculty"/>
                <owl:Class rdf:about="#Staff"/>
                <owl:Class rdf:about="#Student"/>
            </owl:unionOf>
        </owl:Class>
    </rdfs:domain>
    <rdfs:range rdf:resource="&xsd;string"/>
</owl:DatatypeProperty>
<owl:ObjectProperty rdf:ID="hasPrerequisite">
    <rdf:type rdf:resource="&owl;TransitiveProperty"/>
    <owl:inverseOf rdf:resource="#isPrerequisiteOf"/>
</owl:ObjectProperty>
<owl:ObjectProperty rdf:ID="hasRegistered">
    <rdfs:domain rdf:resource="#Student"/>
    <rdfs:range rdf:resource="#Course"/>
</owl:ObjectProperty>
<owl:ObjectProperty rdf:ID="isDean">
    <rdfs:domain rdf:resource="#Faculty"/>
    <rdfs:range rdf:resource="&xsd;boolean"/>
</owl:ObjectProperty>
```

```
<owl:ObjectProperty rdf:ID="isPrerequisiteOf">
  <rdf:type rdf:resource="&owl;TransitiveProperty"/>
  <owl:inverseOf rdf:resource="#hasPrerequisite"/>
</owl:ObjectProperty>
<owl:Class rdf:ID="Staff">
  <rdfs:subClassOf rdf:resource="#Department"/>
  <owl:disjointWith rdf:resource="#Student"/>
  <owl:disjointWith rdf:resource="#Faculty"/>
  <rdfs:comment rdf:datatype="&xsd;string"
    >This class represents the non-teaching, non-student
    members of the
 department</rdfs:comment>
</owl:Class>
<owl:Class rdf:ID="Student">
  <rdfs:subClassOf rdf:resource="#Department"/>
  <owl:disjointWith rdf:resource="#Staff"/>
  <owl:disjointWith rdf:resource="#Faculty"/>
</owl:Class>
<owl:ObjectProperty rdf:ID="taughtBy">
  <rdfs:domain rdf:resource="#Course"/>
  <rdfs:range rdf:resource="#Faculty"/>
  <owl:inverseOf rdf:resource="#teachesCourse"/>
</owl:ObjectProperty>
<owl:ObjectProperty rdf:ID="teachesCourse">
  <rdf:type rdf:resource="&owl;InverseFunctionalProperty"/>
  <rdfs:domain rdf:resource="#Faculty"/>
  <rdfs:range rdf:resource="#Course"/>
  <owl:inverseOf rdf:resource="#taughtBy"/>
</owl:ObjectProperty>
</rdf:RDF>
```

20.3 Securing Ontologies

Ontologies have to be secure. That is, access to ontologies has to be controlled. Access could be based on content, context, and time. As the ontologies evolve, the access to the ontologies may vary. In the following, we discuss two examples. In the first example, we classify the fact that English books are different from French books and German books at level L1. In the second example we classify the fact that textbooks and coursebooks are the same at level L2.

```
< owl: Class rdf: about = "#EnglishBooks">
 <owl: disjointWith rdf: resource "#FrenchBooks"/>
 <owl: disjointWith rdf: resource = #FrenchBooks"/>
Level = L1
</owl:Class>
```

```
<owl: Class rdf: ID = "TextBooks">
 <owl: equivalentClass rdf: resource = "CourseBooks"/>
Level = L2
</owl: Class>
```

20.4 Policy Specification in OWL

Now, let us consider the example in Section 20.2. In the following text, we have specified policies for segments of this example.

```
<owl:Ontology rdf:about=""/>
<owl:Class rdf:ID="AnnualReports">
  <rdfs:subClassOf rdf:resource="#Department"/>
  Level = L1
</owl:Class>

<owl:ObjectProperty rdf:ID="canAccess">
  <rdfs:domain rdf:resource="#Faculty"/>
  <rdfs:range rdf:resource="#AnnualReports"/>
  <rdfs:subPropertyOf rdf:resource="#isDean"/>
 Level = L2
</owl:ObjectProperty>
```

In this example, we have specified policies for OWL documents. Now, can we use OWL to specify policies? That is, how can OWL be used to specify the following policy?

"Only those attending a class from a professor have read access to the lecture notes of the professor"

Next, we specify this policy in OWL.

```
<owl:Class rdf:ID="BhavaniLectureNotesCS609">
  <rdfs:subClassOf rdf:resource="http://localhost/
unionto#LectureNotes"/>
</owl:Class>

<owl:Class rdf:ID="CS609Students">
  <rdfs:subClassOf rdf:resource="http://localhost/
unionto#Students"/>
</owl:Class>

<owl:ObjectProperty rdf:ID="canAccess">
  <rdfs:domain rdf:resource="#CS609Students"/>
  <rdfs:range rdf:resource=" http://localhost/unionto#
BhavaniLectu-reNotesCS609"/>
</owl:ObjectProperty>
```

20.5 Access Control

While access control for XML has received a lot of attention, and there has been some work on securing RDF documents, access control for OWL and ontologies has received little attention. As in the case of XML and RDF, the challenge in access control is to determine the granularity of classification. Should access be given to OWL documents as a whole or should access be given to parts of the document? Should access be given to the OWL schemas? That is, should we classify the relationships that are specified using OWL schemas? Here, again, note that there are two aspects here: one is to control access to OWL documents and the other is to use OWL to specify policies. (See Figure 20.1.)

The algorithms for access control are similar to the one we proposed for XML.

- Subjects request access to OWL documents under two modes: browsing and authoring.
  - With browsing access, subject can read/navigate documents.
  - Authoring access is needed to modify, delete, append documents.
- Access control module checks the policy base and applies policy specs.
- Views of the document are created based on credentials and policy specifications.
- In case of conflict, least access privilege rule is enforced.

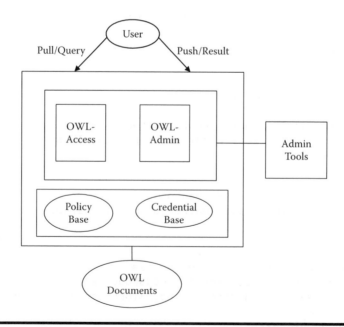

Figure 20.1   Access control for OWL documents.

What makes OWL useful for policy specification is the inherent reasoning capabilities in OWL. Note that OWL is based on descriptive logics. Reasoning engines based on such logics are being developed [MCGU03]. These reasoning engines could be used to reasoning about the security policies.

20.6 Secure OWL Databases

Some commercial data management vendors such as Oracle are now developing approaches to manage XML and RDF databases. While managing RDF documents is not as widespread as managing XML documents, the recent developments are showing a lot of promise. However, to our knowledge there is no work on managing OWL databases. We need techniques for query processing, transaction management, and storage management for OWL documents.

As in the case of XML, security has to be incorporated into the OWL databases. For example, access control policies that we have discussed in the previous sections have to be enforced on OWL databases. Note that the policies themselves may be specified in OWL. In addition, query modification has to be examined for OWL data. As we have discussed in [THUR05a], query modification is essentially about modifying the queries according to the security policies.

20.7 Ontology for Policy and Data Integration

Ontologies have become common practice for information interoperability including handling data heterogeneity [CAST]. They can also be used to handle policy heterogeneity. We will elaborate on this aspect in Part V when we discus applications. We briefly view some of these aspects in this section.

Ontologies are specified to define various terms, as well as to represent common semantics or to distinguish between different semantics. These ontologies are then used for information interoperability. For example, in our research on the geospatial semantic Web we are using ontologies specified in RDF-like languages (which we have called GRDF—Geospatial RDF) for handling semantic heterogeneity. These ontologies are then used for semantic interoperability.

With respect to policy integration, each data management system could use XML or RDF to specify policies and then we integrate the policies using ontologies to handle semantic differences. Figure 20.2 illustrates the use of ontologies for policy integration.

20.8 Security, Ontologies, and Web Services

In Chapters 18 and 19 we discussed the applications of XML and RDF for secure Web services. In this section we will discuss how ontologies may be applied to

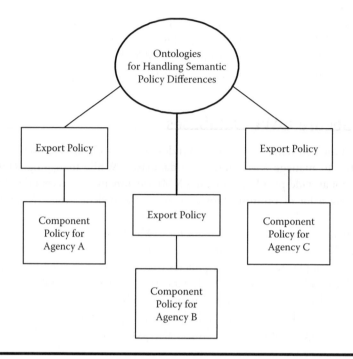

Figure 20.2   Ontologies for policy interoperability.

secure Web services. As in the case of XML and RDF, ontologies may be used to specify security policies for Web services. Ontologies may also be used to enhance the semantic for Web services descriptions; therefore, secure ontologies are needed to secure Web services descriptions.

Ontologies also have applications in several activities such as integrating heterogeneous databases and e-business. Therefore, secure information integration, as well as secure e-business need the ontologies to be secure. More details of Web services for secure activities such as secure information interoperability and secure e-business will be discussed in Part V. Figure 20.3 illustrates the use of ontologies for secure Web services (see also [THUR05a,b]).

20.9 Summary and Directions

In this chapter we discussed ontologies and security for Web services. We argued that portions of the ontologies may need to be classified for different applications. We also showed how ontologies may be used to specify security policies.

Ontologies are critical for many applications including information interoperability, Web services, and knowledge management. OWL and DAML+OIL are excellent starting points for specifying ontologies. We need ontologies to be secure.

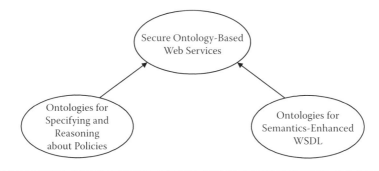

Figure 20.3   Ontologies for secure Web service.

In addition, ontologies may be used to specify policies. Due to the expressiveness of OWL, it can be used to specify more complex policies than say XML and RDF. Furthermore, the semantics of OWL make it a powerful reasoning language. Therefore, it is important to examine security for OWL as well as use OWL to specify policies. Only recently we have examined security for ontologies and the use of ontologies for policy specification. More research needs to be done on the use of ontologies for policy interoperability.

Exercises

1. Investigate security issues for OWL documents.
2. Specify complex policies in OWL.
3. Design an application and show how ontologies may be used for policy integration.
4. Describe the use of ontologies for secure Web services.

References

[ANTO08] Antoniou, G. and F. van Harmelen, *A Semantic Web Primer*, MIT Press, Cambridge, MA, 2008.

[CAST] Castano, S., A. Ferrara, and S. Montanelli, Ontology-Based Interoperability Services for Semantic Collaboration in Open Networked Systems, University of Milan Report, http://interop-esa05.unige.ch/INTEROP/Proceedings/Interop-ESAScientific/PerPaper/I020-1%20400.pdf

[MCGU03] McGuiness, D. and F. van Harmelen (Eds.), Web Ontology Language Overview, <http://www.w3c.org/TR/owl-features/>, 2003.

[THUR05a] Thuraisingham, B., *Database and Applications Security: Integrating Data Management and Information Security*, CRC Press, Boca Raton, FL, 2005.

[THUR05b] Thuraisingham, B., Security standards for the semantic Web, *Computer Standards and Interface Journal*, 27, 257–268, 2005.

Chapter 21

Security, Rules, and Web Services

21.1 Overview

The previous three chapters described security for the three major components of the semantic Web and their relationship to Web services. These components were XML, RDF, and OWL. The fourth component is rules. Languages such as SWRL and RuleML which are semantic Web rule markup languages are being developed [W3C], [ANTO08]. This is because rules have more reasoning power than data represented in, say, RDF or OWL. Recently the work of Finin and his team has shown that we can use RDF-based language to specify policies. We can also use rule-based languages to specify the policies. Note that in the end, machines can only understand markup languages. Therefore, representation of rules in first order logic is not appropriate for agents to understand. We need to convert these rules into markup rules.

In this chapter, we discuss some of our ideas on reasoning with rules. The organization of this chapter is as follows. In Section 21.2, we discuss our prior research on NTML (nonmonotonic-typed multilevel logic) for secure data and knowledge base systems [THUR91], [THUR92]. Our work on rules and security is influenced by NTML. Security issues for rules will be discussed in Section 21.3. Specification of policies in languages such as RuleML will be reviewed in Section 21.4. The Inference Problem and its relationship to rules is covered in Section 21.5. Security, rules, and Web services will be discussed in Section 21.6. The chapter is summarized in Section 21.7.

21.2 Nonmonotonic-Typed Multilevel Logic for Secure Data and Knowledge Management

NTML was developed back in the 1990s for representing and reasoning in multilevel secure databases. As we saw in Chapter 13, in multilevel data management systems a user is cleared at different clearance levels, and the data is assigned different sensitivity levels. Users read data at or below the level and write data at their level. It is assumed that these levels form a particularly ordered lattice with Unclassified < Confidential < Secret < Top Secret. We examined the model and proof theoretic approaches to deductive database management (see [FROS86]) in the 1980s and subsequently developed both model and proof theoretic approaches for secure database using NTML. We also designed a theorem prover for NTML based on a language called NTML prolog.

In the proof theoretic approach, the data and policies are expressed in NTML, and query processing amounts to theorem proving. In the model theoretic approach, the multilevel database is a model for the policies. We also discussed reasoning using both the closed world and open world assumptions.

NTML also focused on having different facts at different security levels. That is, at the unclassified level we could have the fact that the ship is sailing to England and at the secret level we could have the fact that the ship is sailing to India. We also showed how reasoning with NTML could handle problems such as the inference problem.

Note that NTML was developed at a time before the semantic Web, and it was influenced by the developments in logic programming [LLOY87]. Today we have the semantic Web, OWL based on descriptive logic and languages such as RuleML. We also need the capability to carry out nonmonotonic reasoning. Therefore, in order to successfully integrate semantic Web rule processing with policy reasoning and the inference problem, we need to integrate concepts in NTML with RuleML, as well as reasoners such as NTML-Prolog with systems such as Pellet. Research on policy reasoning with semantic Web technologies is just beginning. In the next three sections we will discuss some of our ideas on this problem based on our work and also the presentation on RuleML given in [ANTO08].

21.3 Securing Rules

As we have stated, reasoning power is still limited in OWL. Therefore, the semantic Web community has developed rule-based languages such as SWRL and reasoning. In this section, we will examine the rules we have discussed in Chapter 6 as given in [ANTO08] and also examine security issues. Our work is motivated by NTML.

Consider the following rule R1:

Studies(X,Y), Lives(X,Z), Loc(Y,U), Loc(Z,U) $\Rightarrow$ DomesticStudent(X)
  i.e., if John Studies at UTDallas and John lives on Campbell Road and the
    location of Campbell Road and UTDallas are Richardson then John is a
    Domestic student

Now we can give a user read access to this rule only if he is an administrator
at UTDallas.
  This can be specified as

Administrator(X, UTDallas) $\Rightarrow$ Read-access(X, R1)

We can also assign security levels to the rules. If we wish to classify this rule at the
Confidential level then we can state this as

$\Rightarrow$ Level(R1, Confidential)

We can also assign a level next to the rule as follows:

Level(Studies(X,Y), Lives(X,Z), Loc(Y,U), Loc(Z,U) $\Rightarrow$ DomesticStudent(X),
  Confidential)

As in the case of NTML, we can have different facts at different levels. For example,
at the unclassified level we can have a rule that states that John lives in England
but at the Secret level he is living in Russia. These rules can be specified as follows:

Level($\Rightarrow$ Lives(John, England), Unclassified)
Level($\Rightarrow$ Lives(John, Russia), Secret)

Now in first order logic, this is a contradiction, but in NTML, it is not a contradiction. That is, as discussed in Chapter 6, Person (X) $\Rightarrow$ Man(X) or Woman(X) is not
a rule in predicate logic.
  That is, if X is a person, then that X is either a man or a woman cannot be
expressed in first order predicate logic. Therefore, in predicate logic we express
the above as if X is a person and X is not a man then X is a woman and similarly if
X is a person and X is not a woman then X is a man. That is, in predicate logic, we
can have a rule of the form

Person(X) and Not Man(X) $\Rightarrow$ Woman(X)

However, in OWL we can specify the rule if X is a person then X is a man or X is
a woman.

In NTML, rules can be monotonic or nonmonotonic. In the semantic Web worlds, a similar assumption is made as we have seen in Chapter 4.

That is, in the case of nonmonotonic reasoning, if we have X and NOT X, we do not treat them as inconsistent as in the case of monotonic reasoning. For example, as discussed in [ANTO08], consider the example of an apartment that is acceptable to John. That is, in general John is prepared to rent an apartment unless the apartment has less than two bedrooms and does not allow pets. This can be expressed as follows:

- $\Rightarrow$ Acceptable(X)
- Bedroom(X,Y), Y<2 $\Rightarrow$ NOT Acceptable(X)
- NOT Pets(X) $\Rightarrow$ NOT Acceptable(X)

The first rule states that an apartment is, in general, acceptable to John. The second rule states that if the apartment has less than two bedrooms it is not acceptable to John. The third rule states that if pets are not allowed then the apartment is not acceptable to John. Note that there could be a contradiction. But with nonmonotonic reasoning this is allowed, while it is not allowed in monotonic reasoning.

In the same way regarding access control, we can have a general rule that we do not grant access to any piece of data and then specify exceptions.

Administrator(X, UTDallas) $\Rightarrow$ NOT (Read-access(X, Y))
Salary(Y) $\Rightarrow$ Read-access(X, Y)

That is, we initially deny the administrator access to all data. Then we state that if Y is a salary value, then the administrator is granted access to that value. In first order logic, such rules are not permitted.

We can also have different data values at different levels even for nonmonotonic rules. This is given in the following example:

- Level ($\Rightarrow$ Acceptable(X), Unclassified))
- Level (Bedroom(X,Y), Y<2 $\Rightarrow$ NOT Acceptable(X), Secret)
- Level (NOT Pets(X) $\Rightarrow$ NOT Acceptable(X), TopSecret)

This means that every apartment is acceptable and may be assigned at the unclassified level. At the secret level only those apartments that have more than two bedrooms are acceptable. At the top secret level only those apartments that allow pets are acceptable. Below is another example.

- Level (Country(X) $\Rightarrow$ NOT War (X), Unclassified)
- Level ($\Rightarrow$ Country(USA), Unclassified)
- Level ($\Rightarrow$ Country(Nigeria), Unclassified)
- Level ($\Rightarrow$ War (England), Secret)
- Level ($\Rightarrow$ War (Nigeria), TopSecret)

The first rule states that no country is at war at the unclassified level. The next two rules state that the United States and Nigeria are both countries at the unclassified level. The fourth rule states that England is at war at the secret level. The fifth rule states that Nigeria is at war at the top secret level.

As we have stated in Chapter 6, we need rule markup languages for the machine to understand the rules. The various components of logic are expressed in the Rule Markup Language called RuleML developed for the semantic Web as well as languages such as SWRL (semantic Web rules language). Both monotonic and nonmonotonic rules can be represented in RuleML. Below we state the rule that Nigeria is at war at the top secret level.

Example representation of Fact "War(Nigeria)" which is Nigeria is at war at the top secret level.

```
<fact>
  <atom>
   <predicate>War</predicate>
     <term>
       <const>Nigeria</const>
     </term>
    </atom>
      Level = TopSecret
  </fact>
```

21.4 Policy Specification Using Rules

The agents understand markup languages such as XML, RDF, OWL, and RuleML. Therefore, ultimately the policies have to be expressed in a markup language. In the previous section we showed how the policy

"Nigeria is at war is Secret"

could be represented in a RuleML-like language. We can express many of the policies below in such a language. For example, consider the following policies that we have taken from our previous research [THUR93]:

EMP(X, Y, Z) and Y>50 $\Rightarrow$ Level(EMP) = Secret
EMP(X, Y, Z) $\Rightarrow$ Level(TOGETHER(X,Y) = Secret

The first rule is a content-based policy that classified the employee instance if the salary is greater than $50K at the secret level.

The second rule states that names and salaries taken together is Secret. Note that we mean EMP is an employee predicate with attribute Name, Salary, and Department.

To explain the representation of policies in a RuleML-like language, we will consider the following rule.

R1: HEALTH-RECORD(X) ⇒ Private(X)

The above rule states that all healthcare records are private. This policy may be represented in a markup language as follows:

```
<rule id = R1>
<head>
<atom>
   <predicate>HEATH-RECORD</predicate>
     <term>
       <var> X</var>
     <term>
     </atom>
</head>
<body>
<atom>
   <predicate>Private</predicate>
     <term>
       <var> X</var>
     </term>
     </atom>
</body>
</rule>
```

Note that here we have considered Private to be a predicate. Instead, we could have assumed that Level is a predicate, and the body would have been Level(X, Private); here X is a variable and private would be a constant. The above representation has to be modified to represent this modified body of the rule.

More recently, the SWRL semantic Web rules language is becoming increasingly popular for specifying policies. SWRL is integrated RuleML with OWL and has the advantages of both OWL and RuleML. Essentially, it has the representation power of OWL and the reasoning power of RuleML. We are currently examining the use of SWRL to specify various types of security policies.

21.5 Inference Problem and Policy Reasoning

One of the advantages of representing policies as rules is that we can use the reasoning engines (e.g., theorem provers) to reason about the policies. We have designed a reasoning engine for policies expressed in NTML. Reasoning engines such as Pellet are being used for reasoning about policies by Finin and his team as well as the

Policy Management

Specify policies as rules

Rule processing to enforce the access control

Theorem proving techniques to determine if policies are violated

Consistency and completeness checking of policies

Figure 21.1   Policy management.

Policy aware Web team at MIT. What we need is a combination of NTML theorem provers and reasoning engines such as Pellet to be integrated to develop policy reasoners. These policy reasoners will reason about the policies, check for consistency, and also detect security violations via inference (see Figure 21.1). We will give some examples. Note that to make it simple we reason with the rule format instead of the RuleML format. Note that research on integrating engines such as Pellet with policies is only just beginning.

The reasoning system that we designed is based on a language we developed called NTML-Prolog. We also developed an algorithm for the resolution principle. If there is a security violation via inference, then the system will arrive at a contradiction. Take the following simple example.

Prescription (John, X) and X = Imitrex $\Rightarrow$ Disease(John, Migraine)
$\Rightarrow$ Level (Disease(John, Migraine), Private)
$\Rightarrow$ Level (Prescription (John, Imitrex), Public)

From the first and third rules we can infer $\Rightarrow$ Disease(John, Migraine) at the unclassified level. But this contradicts with the rule that John has migraines at the private level. We arrive at a contradiction and therefore the administrator will then modify the policies. This means that the fact that John is taking Imitrex has to be at least at the public level.

Now, note that with nonmonotonic reasoning one could have contradictions. That is, we could classify an entity both at the secret and unclassified levels. Therefore, to be on the safe side, initially we make everything private or top secret and then make exceptions. However, this could also make the reasoning engines more complex. We need to conduct research in this area to understand the problem and develop appropriate solutions. Figure 21.2 illustrates an inference controller for the semantic Web.

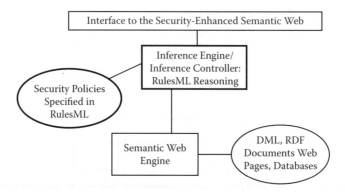

Figure 21.2 Inference controller for the semantic Web.

21.6 Security, Rules, and Web Services

Rules can be used to specify policies including confidentiality policies, delegation policies, trust policies, information flow policies, privacy policies, and integrity policies. Therefore, rules may be used to specify various types of policies for Web services as well as for Web services composition. Rules can also be used for integrating heterogeneous database and e-business applications. The rule-based approach also has applications in inference and privacy control and can therefore be used to control unauthorized inferences for Web services.

Numerous efforts on applying rule-based languages for specifying policies for Web services have been reported. However, there is little investigation in applying languages like RuleML and SWRL for securing Web services. This is an area that needs more research. Figure 21.3 illustrates the use of rules for secure Web services.

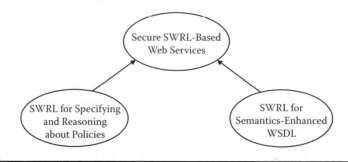

Figure 21.3 Rules for secure Web services.

21.7 Summary and Directions

This chapter has provided an overview of Web rules and security. First, we discussed our system based on a logic we developed for secure databases called NTML, and then discussed security issues for rules. Next, we showed how rules may be used to specify policies. We also discussed the use of rules for handling the inference and privacy problems. Finally, we discussed the application of rules for secure Web services.

As we have stated, rules have more reasoning power than languages such as RDF and OWL. Furthermore, rules for the semantic Web are nonmonotonic in nature. Therefore, we need to develop descriptive logic-based theorem provers for reasoning about policies. These theorem provers will utilize many of the ideas developed in logic programming systems. We believe that integrating NTML-Prolog-based systems with Pellet-like systems will be the solution.

Exercises

1. Investigate security issues for SWRL.
2. Specify complex policies in SWRL.
3. Design a policy reasoning engine based on SWRL.
4. Investigate the application of SWRL for secure Web services.

References

[ANTO08] Antoniou, G. and F. van Harmelen, *A Semantic Web Primer*, MIT Press, Cambridge, MA, 2003.

[FROS86] Frost, R., *On Knowledge Base Management Systems*, Collins Publishers, Berlin, Germany, 1986.

[LLOY87] Lloyd, J., *Logic Programming*, Springer, Berlin, Germany. 1987.

[THUR91] Thuraisingham, B., A nonmonotonic typed multilevel logic for secure data and knowledge base management systems, *Proceedings of the Computer Security Foundations Workshop*, 1991.

[THUR92] Thuraisingham, B., A nonmonotonic typed multilevel logic for secure data and knowledge base management systems—II, *Proceedings of the Computer Security Foundations Workshop*, 1992.

[THUR93] Thuraisingham, B., W. Ford, and M. Collins, Design and implementation of a database inference controller, *Data and Knowledge Engineering Journal*, 11, 3, 271–297, 1993.

[W3C] www.w3c.org

Conclusion to Part IV

We devote an entire part to secure semantic Web services due to their importance and popularity for several applications in multiple domains. Semantic Web technologies are becoming critical for not only representing the data but also reasoning about the data. They were initially developed for machine-understandable Web pages. However, they are now being applied for many applications including information interoperability and e-business. We discussed how Web services may utilize these semantic technologies to be more intelligent.

In Part V we will discuss how secure Web services may be applied to areas such as data management, information interoperability, and assured information sharing. These applications are critical for many domains including healthcare, finance, telecommunications, and defense.

EMERGING SECURE WEB SERVICES

Introduction to Part V

While Part IV provided an overview of secure semantic Web services, in Part V we will continue with discussions of some other specialized secure Web services. In particular, we will further examine the technologies discussed in Part I and how secure Web services may be applied for these technologies.

Part V consists of four chapters: 22, 23, 24, and 25. Chapter 22 discusses Web services for secure data, information, and knowledge management. Chapter 23 discusses Web services for complex data management. Note that we give special attention to geospatial Web services as there is much interest on this topic and standards such as OGC (Open Geospatial Consortium) are focusing on this area. Chapter 24 discusses Web services for secure activity management. Finally in Chapter 25 we cover secure emerging Web services. These include areas such as secure data and secure software as services.

V EMERGING SECURE
WEB SERVICES

Introduction to Part V

Chapter 22

Web Services for Secure Data, Information, and Knowledge Management

22.1 Overview

In the previous chapter, we discussed the application of semantic Web technologies for secure Web services. In this chapter, we will continue with the applications of semantic Web technologies. In particular, we will discuss the applications of semantic Web technologies for secure data, information, and knowledge management. Note that in Part I we discussed briefly data, information, and knowledge management. Data is managed by a data manager. Information is about extracting nuggets from the data and making sense out of the nuggets. Knowledge is about understanding the information and taking actions. Data management technologies include database management and data administration. Information management technologies include multimedia information management and collaborative information management. Knowledge management is about reusing the knowledge and expertise of an organization in order to improve profits and other benefits. In this chapter we will examine in more detail security issues for data, information, and knowledge management, and then discuss how Web services and semantic Web technologies may be applied for managing data, information, and knowledge.

The organization of this chapter is as follows. In Section 22.2 we discuss Web services for secure data management. In Section 22.3, we review Web service for secure information management. In Section 22.4, we cover Web services secure knowledge management. The chapter is summarized in Section 22.5. Note that much of our work is focusing on Web services for secure geospatial data management, and therefore we will devote an entire chapter to this topic (e.g., Chapter 23).

22.2 Web Services for Secure Data Management

The various secure database system functions may be invoked as Web services. For example, the query manager, transaction management, and metadata manager may be executing as Web services. Therefore, to query a database, the query service has to be invoked. This service may invoke the query translation service and the query optimization service. It may also invoke the metadata service to extract appropriate metadata. Security service may be invoked to check for access control policies.

Next semantic Web technologies may be utilized to develop semantic Web service for secure data management. First of all the security policies may be expressed in languages such as XML and RDF. This is one of the significant contributions of the semantic Web. Now, databases may also consist of XML and RDF documents. For example, products such as those by Oracle Corporation now have the capability of managing XML as RDF documents. Therefore, we need to apply data management techniques to managing XML and RDF documents.

Semantic Web technologies have applications in heterogeneous database integration. For example, ontologies are needed for handling semantic heterogeneity. XML is now being used as the common data representation language. With respect to data warehousing, XML and RDF may be used to specify the policies. Furthermore, ontologies may be used for data transformation in order to bring the data into the warehouse. Ontologies have applications in data mining as they clarify various concepts to facilitate data mining. On the other hand, the vast quantities of data on the Web will have to be mined to extract information to guide the agents to understand the Web pages. Semantic Web technologies, including the reasoning engines, may be applied to handle the inference and privacy problems. For example, languages such as RDF and OWL may be used to specify the policies and then inference controllers could be developed based on descriptive logic-based engines such as Pellet to determine whether security violations via inference occur.

In summary, in every aspect of secure data management, Web services as well as semantic Web technologies, have applications. However, data management techniques and data mining techniques can also be applied to manage and mine the data on the Web in order to facilitate agents to understand the Web pages. Figure 22.1 illustrates the relationships between secure data management and Web services.

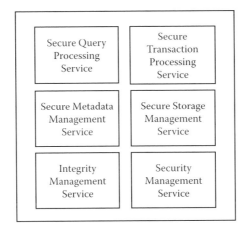

Figure 22.1   Web services for secure data management.

22.3 Secure Information Management

Web services for information management include implementing the various aspects of information management including data warehousing and data mining, information retrieval, and digital library management as Web services. As in the case of data management, semantic Web technologies such as XML, RDF, and OWL can be used to represent security policies including confidentiality, privacy, and trust policies for data warehouses, information retrieval streams, and digital libraries. Furthermore, the reasoning engines based on, say, descriptive logic such as Pellet can be used to infer unauthorized conclusions via inference for data warehouse as well as information retrieval systems. Semantic Web technologies can also be used to represent the nontextual data. For example, SMIL is a markup language for video, while VoiceML is a markup language for audio data. The access control policies specified in, say, XML, RDF, or a more descriptive language such as REI, can be enforced on video data represented in SMIL. Data mining techniques may be applied not only to relational databases but also to text, voice, video, and audio databases, as well as to digital libraries. With data mining, there are privacy and security concerns. For example, data mining makes it possible to inference sensitive associations. Therefore, privacy-preserving data mining not only on relational databases but also on XML, RDF, and OWL data remains a challenge.

Web services have applications in secure information management including in secure data warehousing, secure data mining, secure information retrieval, and secure digital library management. For example, secure data warehouse management may be invoked as a Web service. The secure warehouse management service provider will register its services with the directory. The user who requests warehouse services will invoke the appropriate services. Figure 22.2 illustrates Web services for secure information management.

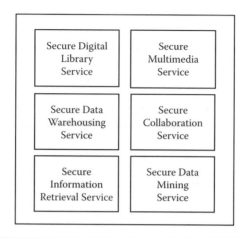

Figure 22.2   Web services for secure information management.

22.4 Secure Knowledge Management

Semantic Web technologies have many applications in knowledge management. For example, we need ontologies to capture the represented knowledge and reason about the knowledge. In his article on the semantic Web and knowledge management, Paul Warren gives an example of "a political scientist, Sally, who wants to research the extent to which British Prime Minister Tony Blair's stance on Zimbabwe has changed over a year and what factors might have caused that change." He further states that "in the world of the Semantic Web, Sally could search for everything written by Blair on this topic over a specific time period. She could also search for transcripts of his speeches. Information markup wouldn't stop at the article or report level but would also exist at the article section level. So, Sally could also locate articles written by political commentators that contain transcripts of Blair's speeches" [WARR06].

Now knowledge management also has applications for building the semantic Web [MORE01]. For example, prior knowledge captured as a result of knowledge management can be used by agents to better understand the Web pages. With respect to security, in the example by Warren, confidentiality, privacy, and trust policies will determine the extent to which Sally trusts the articles and has access to the articles in putting together her report on Tony Blair's speeches. Figure 22.3 illustrates the relationships between secure knowledge management and Web services.

22.5 Summary and Directions

This chapter has discussed secure data, information, and knowledge management, and has then shown how Web services may be applied. We also discussed how data,

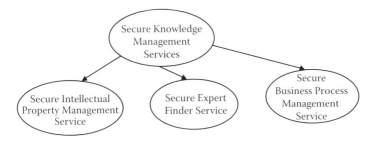

Figure 22.3   Web services for secure knowledge management.

information, and knowledge management could be used to develop the vision of the semantic Web.

While there are efforts such as the work of W3C and OASIS to develop security standards such as XACML and SAML specifications, much needs to be done to address numerous security issues including complex confidentiality policies in addition to trust and privacy policies. Furthermore, we cannot forget about data integrity and quality. Therefore we believe that there are numerous opportunities for research, development, and system-building activities for Web services-based secure data, information, and knowledge management.

Exercises

1. Describe security issues for data, information, and knowledge management.
2. Describe the use of semantic Web technologies for secure data, information, and knowledge management.
3. Describe Web services for secure data, information, and knowledge management.

References

[BERT06] Bertino, E., L. Khan, R. Sandhu, and B. Thuraisingham, Secure Knowledge Management, *IEEE Transactions on Systems, Man and Cybernetics*, May 2006.

[BERT99] Bertino, E., E. Ferrari, and V. Atluri, The specification and enforcement of authorization constraints in workflow management systems, *ACM Transactions on Information and Systems Security*, Volume 2, #1, 1999.

[CHEN] Chen-Burger, Y.-H., K.-Y. Hui, A. D. Preece, P. M. D. Gray, and A. Tate, Supporting Collaboration through Semantic-based Workflow and Constraint Solving, http://www.csd.abdn.ac.uk/~apreece/research/download/ekaw2004.pdf

[DEMU93] Demurjian, S., T. Ting, and B. Thuraisingham, Security for collaborative computer systems, *Multimedia Review: The Journal of Multimedia Computing* (Penton Media publishers), Summer 1993.

[HUAN98] Huang, W. and V. Atluri, Analyzing the safety of workflow authorization models, *Proceedings of the IFIP Database Security Conference*, Chalidiki, Greece, July 1998 (Kluwer, 1999).

[MARI02] Marinescu, D. C., *Internet Based Workflow Management: Towards a Semantic Web*, Wiley Interscience, New York, 2002.

[MORE01] Morey, D., M. Maybury, and B. Thuraisingham (Eds.), *Knowledge Management*, MIT Press, Cambridge, MA, 2001.

[THUR90] Thuraisingham, B., Security for multimedia database systems, *Proceedings IFIP Data Security Conference*, Halifax, U.K., 1990.

[THUR05] Thuraisingham, B., *Database and Applications Security*, CRC Press, Boca Raton, FL, 2005.

[WARR06] Warren, P., Knowledge management and the semantic Web: From scenario to technology, *IEEE Intelligent Systems*, 21, 1, 53–59, 2006.

Chapter 23

Secure Geospatial, Multimedia, and Sensor Web Services

23.1 Overview

In this chapter, we focus on Web services for secure complex data management. By complex data we mean geospatial data, multimedia data, and sensor data. In the case of geospatial data management, our main focus is on geospatial semantic Web and the associated Web services. Secure geospatial semantic Web essentially integrates semantic Web technologies with geospatial technologies and security technologies. Geospatial data emanates from numerous devices at multiple sites. Such data is complex and heterogeneous in nature. Geospatial data has to be compressed, fused, and visualized to support the tasks of the analyst for homeland security applications. Furthermore, geospatial information systems have to enforce flexible security policies to address dynamic environments and changing needs of various applications. While several developments have occurred on geospatial data compression, fusion, and visualization, many of the approaches do not take into consideration the complexity and heterogeneity of the data. Furthermore, we need efficient tools to support the analysis. Finally, little work has been reported on developing flexible security policies.

Our research is focusing on many aspects of geospatial data management for homeland security. These include developing decision-centric fusion algorithms for geospatial data where we are making classifiers for each data source and subsequently fusing the outcomes of the local classifiers [LI07]. We are also developing a flexible security policy, model, and architecture that addresses confidentiality and data quality. Recently we have integrated geospatial data management with security and the semantic Web to develop a secure geospatial semantic Web. This chapter describes our work in this area as well as the security issues and the application of Web services. In addition, we also include discussions of secure multimedia data management and secure sensor Web information management as part of complex data management with the applications of Web services and semantic Web technologies in mind.

The organization of this chapter is as follows: We discuss geospatial semantic Web in Section 23.2 including our research on geospatial semantic Web, as well as the DAGIS (Discovering Annotated Geospatial Information Services) system we have developed. The initial version of DAGIS was developed at the University of Texas–Dallas by Alam Ashraful, Ganesh Subbiah, Latifur Khan, and Bhavani Thuraisingham. Secure multimedia data management and Web services will be reviewed in Section 23.3. Secure sensor and pervasive data management and Web services are the subjects of Section 23.4. The chapter is concluded in Section 23.5.

23.2 Secure Geospatial Semantic Web

23.2.1 Geospatial Semantic Web Concepts

Secure geospatial semantic Web is an integration of secure semantic Web and geospatial semantic Web. We are conducting extensive research on geospatial semantic Web. Our layered architecture is shown in Figure 23.1. At the bottom layer are the protocols for communication. These would include HTTP and related protocols. XML and XML schemas are replaced by GML (Geography Markup Language) and GML schemas. OGC has made tremendous development with GML. We have developed GRDF (Geospatial RDF) to specify the semantics. Our details of GRDF can be found in [ALAM06]. On top of GRDF we have developed geospatial ontologies. These ontologies are described in [THUR07a]. An example of a GRDF ontology is given below. This ontology describes a building.

```
<campusonto:Building rdf:about="#CompScience">
 <grdf:hasSpatialExtent>
  <ogc-gml:Polygon>
   <ogc-gml:exterior_Ring>
     <grdf:LinearRing>
       <grdf:coordinates
         rdf:datatype="&xsd;string">
          0,1 1,0 13,
          0 13,8.5
          0,8.5 0,1
```

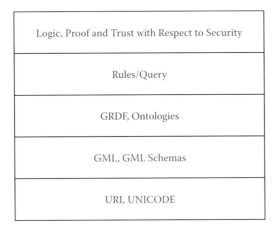

Figure 23.1   Layered architecture for geospatial semantic Web.

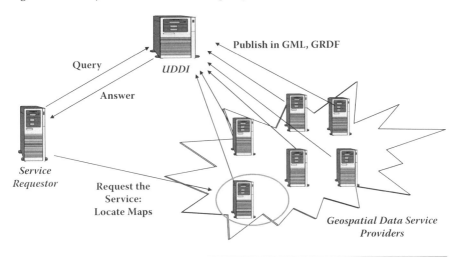

Figure 23.2   Web service architecture for geospatial data.

Web services and the standards provided by OGC define our approach for a geospatial semantic Web. Web services technologies support interoperable machine interactions over a network, and will be developed for the operations to be performed on the different geospatial data sources. Our architecture is as described in Figure 23.2. Each Web service has a high-level service description that is written using GML or OWL-S. OGC specifies geospatial standards that rely on GML as the data layer encoding. OWL-S provides a semantic-rich application level platform to encode Web service metadata using descriptive logic. W3C is monitoring innovative ways to integrate these two methods as part of their Geospatial Semantic Web Interoperability experiment. Regardless of the methods, the description generated by them is used for publishing and for discovery of a Web service. Two Web services then bind through the underlying WSDL layer. Web Services Description Language is a specification defining how to describe Web services in a common XML grammar. SOAP is a standard for exchanging XML-based messages over a computer network, normally using HTTP. SOAP forms the foundation layer of the Web services stack, providing a basic messaging framework on which more abstract layers can build.

Client queries the Service Requestor Web Service, which handles the GIS (Geospatial/Geographic Information Systems) Application. The Service Requestor then discovers the required Service Provider through the Service Registry or the Match Maker. The Service Registry selects the Service Provider that has already registered with this registry. Service Provider can now bind with the Service Requestor to fulfill the service requestor. The underlying protocol stack is shown in the figure. In this way, two different GIS applications with different heterogeneities can interoperate with each other using Web Services.

The ultimate goal is to integrate the work of OGC and WWW to develop a semantic Web for geospatial data. While there are efforts to develop languages such as GRDF (e.g., the work at the University of Texas–Dallas), a comprehensive approach to developing a semantic Web, such as integration of the various ontologies, GRDF, and GML, are yet to be carried out.

Our team (Thuraisingham, Ashraful, Subbiah, and Khan) has developed a system called DAGIS that reasons with the ontologies and answers queries. This system is described in [THUR07a]. It is a framework that provides a methodology to realize the semantic interoperability both at the geospatial data encoding level and also for the service framework. DAGIS is an integrated platform that provides the mechanism and architecture for building geospatial data exchange interfaces using the OWL-S Service ontology. Coupled with the geospatial domain specific ontology for automatic discovery, dynamic composition and invocation of services, DAGIS is a one-stop platform to fetch and integrate geospatial data. The data encoding is in GRDF and provides the ability to reason about the payload data by the DAGIS or client agents to provide intelligent inferences. DAGIS at the service level and GRDF at the data encoding layer provide a complete unified model for realizing the vision of geospatial semantic Web. The architecture also enhances the query response for the client queries posed to DAGIS interface. The system architecture for DAGIS is illustrated in Figure 23.3.

23.2.2 Secure Geospatial Data Management

Before we discuss security for the geospatial semantic Web, we will provide an overview of some of the challenges in securing geospatial data. Much of our discussion has been influenced by our collaborative research with Bertino at Purdue University and Gertz at the University of California–Davis [BERT08]. This research is also influenced by some of our earlier research on security constraint processing and securing

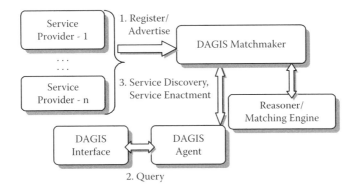

Figure 23.3   DAGIS architecture.

multimedia data ([THUR95], [THUR90]). Atluri has also done some interesting research on geospatial data management and security ([ATLU04], [DAMI07]).

Geospatial data are more complex than relational data. For example, we can classify the pixels as well as classify the points and lines that make up the geospatial data. We can define policies based on content, context, and time. For example, the location and the image taken together could be classified, while individually they could be unclassified. Furthermore, the location and image could be classified at or until a particular time and after that it could be declassified. For example, satellite imagery taken over, say, Iraq could be classified for 6 months from the day the image was captured and unclassified after that. Bertino and her team have developed policy languages for geospatial data and a security model that they call Geo-RBAC, which integrates RBAC with geospatial data.

While there is a clear need for enforcing confidentiality policies for geospatial data, privacy remains a challenge. What does it mean to preserve privacy for geospatial data? Today we have the capability to carry out surveillance, as well as capture the images in, say, Google Maps. Therefore, we cannot expect the image of our house to remain private as the image is out there. However, the fact that it is my house could be private. We need to study the issues on privacy management for geospatial data. For our semantic Web research, our goal is to develop geospatial Web services that can utilize representation technologies such as GML and GRDF so that we get machine-understandable Web pages. However, to secure a geospatial semantic Web, we need to integrate geospatial semantic Web technologies with secure geospatial data management technologies. This will be the subject of the next section. Figure 23.4 illustrates security for geospatial data management.

Geospatial data may be in the form of streams. What are the security policies for stream data? Closely related to geospatial information systems are motion databases where the data is not residing in one place. The data changes continually, and this data must be captured and managed. Geospatial data may emanate from a variety of sources and therefore the data have to be integrated possibly through the

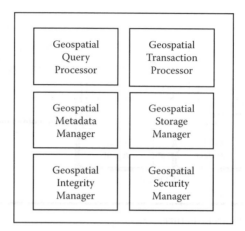

Figure 23.4   Secure geospatial data management.

Web and by other means. Information integration has many security challenges. Some work in this area has been reported in [ATLU04].

Note that we have only raised the security concerns for geospatial information systems. These systems are a special kind of multimedia systems. We need to integrate technologies for secure multimedia databases, secure semantic Web, secure information integration, and secure sensor/stream data management to provide solutions to secure geospatial information systems.

23.2.3 Secure Geospatial Semantic Web

We are developing a set of policies for geospatial information systems. Data representation will be based on GML developed by OGC. The policy will include access control such as role-based and usage control, as well as trust, integrity, temporal constraints, data currency, data quality, and data provenance. Subsequently, we will design and develop secure geospatial Web services that demonstrate interoperability with respect to security. We will also examine security violations via inference for geospatial information systems. For example, inferencing techniques for intelligent data fusion have been developed. By fusing the data, security constraints may be violated. We are adapting the various techniques proposed to handle security for relational databases to the handling of security for fused images. Data ownership and the need for profitability require an organization to safeguard its information bank from others. The technical complexity increases several-fold when the organizational domain consists of data that is more than text or numbers. One such instance is geospatial Web services that cater to queries that need information security beyond the level of traditional role-based access control (RBAC) mechanism. Safeguarding geospatial data requires fine granularity of access privileges, which

Figure 23.5 Secure geospatial semantic Web.

makes RBAC a nonoptimal solution. Our goal is to harness the axiomatic framework provided through OWL in order to define policy assertions for potential clients and let the inference engine do the housekeeping. The layered framework for secure geospatial semantic Web is illustrated in Figure 23.5.

Not all data housed by the geospatial agencies are considered public in nature. For instance, the data might contain critical information about people, exposure of which would jeopardize their privacy. The problem is exacerbated in a data integration environment because of a lack of coherent security framework. If the trend towards on-the-fly data integration continues, Web services providers would very soon perform complicated services that require embedding or combining geospatial data with other kinds of data. However, without appropriate security architecture in place, there will be reluctance by clearinghouses to serve data liberally. In turn, the quality and effectiveness of the data is affected as the clients procure only partial information.

We have distinguished between two kinds of security most prevalent in Web services and that form the foundations of semantic Web services architecture as well. The first kind deals with the general authorization procedures of Web services users and any subsequent execution of over-the-wire security criteria. The current set of standardized protocols for this kind of data security includes encryption methods, digital signature verification, certification generation and exchange, Web services secure exchange and so on. The second kind involves organizational protection of data from intruders or bona fide clients without proper access privileges. The most widely used defensive mechanism employed in this regard is various forms of access control languages. We are developing a semantic-rich, ontology-based access control solution for geospatial data that can have a beneficial bearing on the surge in geospatial data integration across the world.

Security for geospatial data can be compartmentalized into different logical segments based on the layer of application. Our work concentrates on secure access of geospatial resources by clients or other Web services in the context of dynamic composition. In line with the vision of the semantic Web, we are developing a modular access control in a language that makes development of reasoning-enabled enforcement engines feasible. In contrast to the XML-based standards and first-order logic-based access controls, we define the axioms in OWL-DL and the emphasis on policy reuse. In our previous experience with policy-centric access control languages, it was observed that defining policies for resources on an individual basis is not well-suited for integrated GIS applications. If fine-grained resource access is

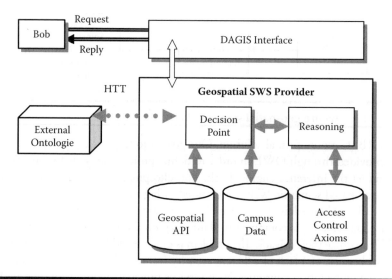

Figure 23.6   Secure DAGIS.

allowed, it amasses policies in policy files that must be navigated by the decision or enforcement module, thus degenerating overall query processing time. Our architecture is illustrated in Figure 23.6.

To improve policy decision time, our access control language keeps the collection of asserted rules as a separate unit. Then client identities can link to appropriate rules to be applied to the client. The modular use of policies by referencing them minimizes rule duplications. Another important characteristic is the shifting of rule navigation from policies to client identities. The geospatial semantic Web service agent in our framework accepts users with established identities or anonymous users.

In order to develop a secure geospatial semantic Web, we need to incorporate security across the entire semantic Web technology framework. We illustrate this in Figure 23.7. Organizations such as OGC are examining security assertions to be specified in GML. In addition, organizations such as OASIS are developing GEO-XACML. We are developing security assertions to be specified in GRDF, which we call Secure GRDF. We are focusing on extending the secure DAGIS framework into a secure geospatial semantic Web. DAGIS also has a responding component that is based on GRDF and can reason about the security policies.

23.2.4 Secure Interoperability with GRDF

While organizational resources can be protected with a semantic access control system, geospatial data protection in a distributed environment can present a lot of difficulties beyond providing or denying access. Geospatial data is unique in that

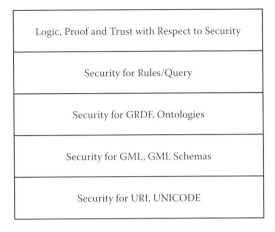

Figure 23.7 Technology stack for secure geospatial semantic Web.

the same piece of data has varying levels of granularity depending on the context. For instance, raster images could be processed in different resolutions, scales, and accuracy. Even vector data is available at differing scales, depending on the particular data collection agency. For this reason, when data from multiple agencies are integrated, access control of the aggregated geospatial data becomes a potential security trap. For instance, if a multilayered view is presented to users with each layer belonging to a different source provider, it is not clear how a user from one particular agency will see the aggregated view. The special traits make it infeasible for generic semantic access control such as SAC to govern over geospatial data.

So far, we have defined two types of constructs. The first type provides alternative abstract elements for vector data and the second type constitutes ontology for subject and action roles. Subjects are classified based on their functional criteria. Currently defined top level classes for various categories of subjects are "Administrator," "Manager," "Regular Professional," "Facility Personnel," and "Guest." The actions defined so far are "Read," "Write," "Save," and "Execute." In an ideal circumstance, all parties in a distributed system have an agreed-on set of measures to combine their policies or resolve them in case of a failure. However, the prearrangement is not always possible, and in such cases, our security constructs would allow a semantic access control processor to interpret the role and action definitions, and to combine the corresponding policies. Our research is focusing on policy integration algorithms, and our policy integration framework is illustrated in Figure 23.8.

23.2.5 GeoRSS

In this section we will discuss an application of geospatial semantic Web technologies—GeoRSS. As stated in [OGC], GeoRSS is a simple proposal for geo-enabling,

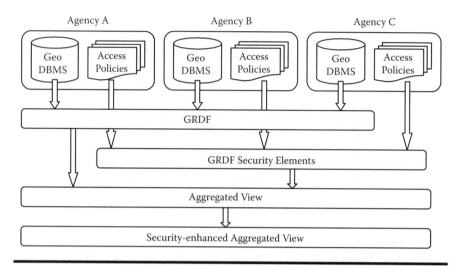

Figure 23.8   Security policy integration framework for geospatial data.

or tagging, "really simple syndication" (RSS) feeds with location information. GeoRSS proposes a standardized way in which location is encoded with enough simplicity and descriptive power to satisfy most needs to describe the location of Web content. GeoRSS is also intended to be a lightweight way to express geography in other XML-based formats—including XHTML.

RSS is a family of XML formats for exchanging news, especially news about Web pages or other Web content. Many dynamic Web sites, especially blogs now provide RSS feeds of their new or changed content. RSS is a simple, brief, and structured XML format. It includes key descriptive elements like author, date, title, narrative description, and hypertext link, elements which help the reader decide what source materials are worth examining in more detail. This concise, structured format has also proven useful for publishing all kinds of small, time-sensitive nuggets of information, including Flickr's photo journals, Craigslist classifieds, and local events. GeoRSS essentially combines RSS with geospatial data. Location needs to be described in an interoperable manner so that applications can Request, Aggregate, Share, and Map geographically tagged feeds. GeoRSS has two encodings: GeoRSS GML and GeoRSS Simple. GeoRSS GML is a formal GML Application Profile, and supports a greater range of features than the coordinate reference system. GeoRSS Simple, the simple serialization of GeoRSS, is designed to be concise but is limited in expressive power.

The Geo RSS model must be expressed in a concrete form such as XML or RDF. The core concepts of GeoRSS are CRS, geometry, tags, and elevation. The geometric shapes that can be used to represent location in GeoRSS are the following: Point contains a single coordinate pair. The coordinate pair contains a latitude value and a longitude value *in that order*. Line contains two or more coordinate pairs. Each pair contains a latitude value and a longitude value *in that order*. Pairs are separated from each other by a *space*. Box contains exactly two coordinate pairs. Each pair contains a latitude value and a longitude value *in that order*. Pairs are separated from each other by a *space*. The first coordinate pair (lower corner) must be a point further west and south of the second coordinate pair (upper corner), and the box is always interpreted as not containing the 180 (or -180) degree longitude line other than on its boundary and not containing the North or South pole other than on its boundary. In the RDF framework, the content and meaning of Simple GeoRSS can be stated in a few words:

georss:point, georss:line, georss:polygon, georss:box.

The resulting language that integrates geospatial concepts with RDF is Geo-RDF, and it competes with GRDF.

GeoRSS is limited in security. Therefore, the work that we have carried out incorporating security into semantic Web can be integrated with the GeoRSS work. Essentially, while there has been work on geospatial data management and building geospatial semantic Webs, security has received little attention. We believe that our research, as well as the work of Bertino, Gertz, and Atluri, sets the stage for research on secure geospatial semantic Web.

23.3 Secure Multimedia Data Management

Security has an impact on all of the functions of a multimedia data manager. Consider the query operation. The query processor has to examine the access control rules and security constraints and modify the query accordingly. For example, if the fact that the existence of Operation X is classified, then this query cannot be sent to an unclassified multimedia data collector such as a video camera to film the event. Similarly, the update processor also examines the access control rules and computes the level of the multimedia data to be inserted or modified. Security also has an impact on multimedia editing and browsing. When one is browsing multimedia data, the system must ensure that the user has the proper access to browse the link or access the data associated with the link. In the case of multimedia editing, when objects at different levels are combined to form a film, then the film object has to be classified accordingly. One may need to classify the various frames or assign the high water mark associated with the levels of the individual objects that compose the film. Furthermore, when films are edited (such as deleting certain portions of the film) then one needs to recompute the level of the edited object.

Secure multimedia transaction processing is another issue. First, what does transaction-processing mean? One could imagine data being gathered from two different locations (e.g., video streams) and make simultaneous updates to the multimedia database. Both updates have to be carried out as a transaction. This is conceivable if, say, an analyst needs both films to carry out the analysis. So assuming that the notion of a transaction is valid, what does it mean to process transactions securely?

Next consider the storage manager function. The storage manager has to ensure that access is controlled to the multimedia database. The storage manager may also be responsible for partitioning the data according to the security levels. The security impact of access methods and indexing strategy for multimedia data are yet to be determined. Numerous index strategies have been developed for multimedia data including for text, images, audio, and video. We need to examine the strategies and determine the security impact. Another issue is the synchronization between storage and presentation of multimedia data. For example, we need to ensure that the video is displayed smoothly and that there are no bursts in traffic. There could be malicious programs manipulating the storage and presentation managers so that information is covertly passed from a higher level to lower level processes.

23.4 Secure Sensor Web Services

23.4.1 Concepts

The sensor nodes in a network have to interoperate with each other, enforce various security policies and carry out activities in real-time. Therefore, there is now much interest to integrate sensor networks with semantic Web technologies. In this section we will discuss some of the directions and in the next section we will go beyond sensor Webs and discuss how semantic Web is integrated with pervasive computing infrastructures.

In the recent workshop on semantic sensor networks in Athens, Georgia [SSN06], there were discussions on the use of semantic Webs to address sensor networking applications using RFID technologies as well as complex, cross-jurisdictional, heterogeneous, dynamic information systems. As stated in the workshop objective, the goal was "to develop an understanding of the ways semantic Web technologies, including ontologies, agent architectures and semantic Web services, can contribute to the growth, application, and deployment of large-scale sensor networks."

Hendler and his team at the University of Maryland have developed techniques for the interactive composition of Web services that can be used in a sensor network environment. They state that "as Web services become more prevalent, tools will be needed to help users find, filter, and integrate these services." Therefore, they have developed ways to compose existing Web services that include "presenting matching services to the user at each step of composition, filtering the possibilities by using semantic descriptions and directly executing the services through WSDL."

A significant development connecting semantic Web with senior technologies is OGC's SensorML standard. As stated in [WIKI], "SensorML is an Open Geospatial Consortium standard markup language (using XML schema) for providing descriptions of sensor systems. By design it supports a wide range of sensors, including both dynamic and stationary platforms and both in situ and remote sensors." It supports many features including sensor discovery, sensor geolocation, processing of sensor observations, a sensor programming mechanism, and subscription to sensor alerts.

While there is much progress, we need to develop ontologies, Web services as well as sensor RDF, so that we have the capability for automated machine understandable sensor data and Web pages. Furthermore, very little research on incorporating security into sensor Webs has been reported. The policies that we have discussed in earlier sections can be expressed in languages like SensorML. Furthermore, we need to build reasoning systems to reason about the policies as well as make deductions and learn. University of Maryland–Baltimore County is leading the way for such research. We discuss some of their work in connecting semantic Webs with pervasive computing in the next section. Figure 23.9 illustrates the integration of sensor Web with semantic Web and security.

Metadata management is also another issue. For example, we need to first determine the types of metadata for multimedia data. Metadata may include descriptions about the data and the source of the data, as well as the quality of the data. Metadata may also include information such as that Frames 100 to 2000 are about the president's speech. Metadata may also be classified. In some cases the metadata may be classified at a higher level than the data itself. For example, the location of the data may be highly sensitive while the data could be unclassified. We should, also ensure that one cannot obtain unauthorized information from the metadata.

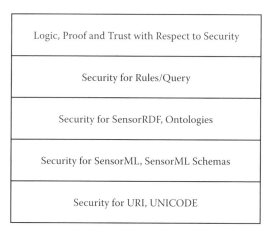

Figure 23.9   Secure sensor semantic Web.

23.4.2 Pervasive Computing and Web Services

Pervasive computing is essentially about a collection of sensors, wireless devices, and embedded processes, all interacting with each other to carry out various activities such as video surveillance, detecting supplies in the registers, automatic washing machine operation, and monitoring the heartbeats of patients. Semantic Web technologies are being integrated with pervasive computing to understand the data and carry out various pervasive computing operations.

Lalana Kagal and others at the University of Maryland–Baltimore County have examined semantic framework for the semantic Web [KAGA]. Their solution is based on Web services and distributed trust management. Key to their architecture is the "The Service Manager" that acts as a mediator between the services and the users. All clients of the system, whether they are services or users, have to register with a Service Manager in what they call the "Smart Space." The Service Manager (SM) is responsible for processing Client Registration/De-Registration requests, responding to registered client requests for a listing of available services, for brokering Subscribe/Un-Subscribe and Command requests from users to services, and for sending service updates to all subscribed users whenever the state of a particular service is modified. They state that the Service Manager is arranged in a tree-like hierarchy, and messages are routed through to other service managers through this tree. The essential points of their trust management approach is as follows: Each client establishes trust with its service manager, and SMs across the hierarchy establish trust among them, hence trust now is a concept that is transparent between all clients in the system. They have also defined a security agent that carries out the security activities. Semantic Web technologies are utilized for policy specification as well as reasoning by the security agent.

Some of the early work on integrating pervasive computing with semantic Web was carried out at Nokia research labs by Lassila et al. [LASS02]. In his presentation on "Pervasive Computing Meets the Semantic Web," Lassila introduced the notion of "semantic gadgets," which combine semantic Web with ubiquitous computing. He states that device capabilities and service functionality explicitly represent everything that is addressable (using URIs), and semantic Web is the basis for "semantic interoperability." In his approach, agents will discover services and carry out reasoning, as well as learn and plan. Lassila also introduced the notion of device coalitions where all devices advertise their services, and a device extends its functionality by discovering missing functionality offered by another device and contracting the use of the service. He further states that everything can be discovered including reasoning services and planning services. One needs to integrate the work by Lassila with the work by Kigali to further trustworthy semantic Web and ubiquitous computing.

In some other work at Fujitsu's Labs, the researchers introduce the notion of task computing as the technology to integrate semantic Web with pervasive computing.

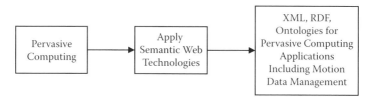

Figure 23.10   Pervasive semantic Web.

They state that task computing shifts the focus to what users want to do as opposed to the specific means of users doing the task. They then state that task computing offers device manufacturers an incentive to incorporate semantic Web technologies into their devices. They have implemented a task computing environment using the semantic Web technologies such as RDF and OWL [MASU03].

There is also now research on integrating sensor Webs with RFID technologies and semantic Webs. For example, the research of Nabil Adam and his team at Rutgers has developed techniques for the composition of Web services for RFID data management and interoperability for border patrol [PALI04]. As we have discussed in Chapter 22, this is an area that is critical for homeland security. In summary, while there is now research on integrating semantic Web with pervasive computing and RFID data management, we also need to focus on security issues. As we have stated, policies could be expressed in semantic Web languages. Furthermore, we need to develop reasoning engines that can reason about the policies and handle problems like the inference and privacy problems. Figure 23.10 illustrates the integration of pervasive computing with semantic Web and security.

23.5 Summary and Directions

This chapter has provided an overview of geospatial data management and geospatial semantic Web and then discussed the security impact as well as the application of Web services. In particular, we have focused on our research in building secure geospatial semantic Webs. We also discuss the work on GeoRSS. In addition, we also provided a brief overview of the application of Web services in secure multimedia data management and secure sensor and pervasive data management.

Our work has examined mainly the confidentiality aspect of security for geospatial data. We also need to examine privacy trust and data quality issues for geospatial data. As we have stated, much of the research on geospatial data management has focused on the data issues and not on policy issues. Our research sets the direction for policy research in geospatial data. We believe that secure geospatial semantic Webs will be critical for integrating heterogeneous geospatial data sources as well as for geospatial Web services and knowledge management. This will also provide the directions for managing complex data such as voice and video data in this semantic Web environment. For many of the applications that deal with geospatial data, security is critical. Therefore, we need to start a program in secure geospatial semantic Web and data management.

Exercises

1. Describe Web services for secure geospatial data management.
2. Design semantic Web technologies for geospatial data.
3. Discuss Web services for secure sensor data management.
4. Develop a suite of trustworthy semantic Web technologies such as SensorML, SensorRDF, and ontologies for sensor information management.
5. Describe Web services for multimedia data management.

References

[ALAM06] Alam, A. and B. Thuraisingham, GRDF and Security Constructs, Technical Report, The University of Texas at Dallas, 2006 (also to appear in *Computer Standards and Interfaces Journal*).

[ATLU04] Atluri, V. and S. A. Chun, An authorization model for geospatial data, *IEEE Transactions on Dependable and Secure Computing*, December 2004.

[BERT08] Bertino, E. et al., Security & privacy for geospatial data, *Proceedings of the SIGSPATIAL ACM GIS International Workshop on Security and Privacy in GIS and LBS*, Irvine CA, Ocober 2008.

[CARN03] Carney, D., U. Cetintemel, A. Rasin, S. Zdonik, M. Cherniack, and M. Stonebraker, Operator Scheduling in a Data Stream Manager, *Proceedings of the 29th International Conference on Very Large Data Bases*, Berlin, Germany, 2003.

[CHAI06] Chaitanya, S. and B. Thuraisingham, Automatic Face Detection for Privacy Preserving Surveillance, Technical Report, The University of Texas at Dallas, 2006.

[DAMI07] Damiani, M. L., E. Bertino, B. Catania, and P. Perlasca, GEO-RBAC: A spatially aware RBAC. *ACM Transactions on Information and System Security*, 10(1), 2007.

[HART06] Hart, Q. and M. Gertz, Optimization of multiple continuous queries over streaming satellite data, *GIS 2006*: 243–250.

[IEEE04] *IEEE Spectrum*, July 2004.

[KAGA] Kagal, L. et al., A Security Architecture Based on Trust Management for Pervasive Computing Systems, http://ebiquity.umbc.edu/_file_directory_/papers/15.pdf

[LASS02] Lassila, O., Semantic Gadgets: Pervasive Computing Meets the Semantic Web, http://www.lassila.org/publications/2002/lassila-nist-pervasive-2002.pdf

[LI07] Li, C., L. Khan, B. Thuraisingham, M. Husain, S. Chen, and F. Qiu, Geospatial data mining, *Proceedings ISI Conference*, New Jersey, 2007.

[LUBI98] Lubinski, A., Security Issues in Mobile Database Access, *Proceedings of the IFIP Database Security Conference*, Chalkidiki, Greece, July 1998 (formal proceedings published by Kluwer 1999).

[MASU03] Masuoka, R., B. Parsi, and Y. Labrou, Task Computing—the Semantic Web meets Pervasive Computing, http://www.flacp.fujitsulabs.com/~rmasuoka/papers/Task-Computing-ISWC2003-202-color-final.pdf

[MEHR04] Mehrotra, S., B. Hore, J. Wickramasuriye, N. Venkata, and D. Massaguer, Privacy Preserving Surveillance, Demonstration, University of California, Irvine, 2004.

[OGC] OGC White Paper, An Introduction to GeoRSS: A Standards Based Approach for Geo-enabling RSS feeds, http://www.opengeospatial.org/

[PALI04] Paliwal, A. V., N. Adam, C. Bornhövd, and J. Schaper, Semantic Discovery and Composition of Web Services for RFID Applications in Border Control, http://www.dvs1.informatik.tu-darmstadt.de/staff/bornhoevd/ISWC"04.pdf

[PERR04] Perrig, A., J. Stankovic, and D. Wagner, Security in wireless sensor networks, *Communications of the ACM*, 2004.

[SIRI03] Sirin, E., J. Hendler, and B. Parisa, Interactive Composition of Semantic Web Services, http://www2003.org/cdrom/papers/poster/p232/p232-sirin/p232-sirin.html

[SSN06] *Proceedings of the Semantic Sensor Network Workshop*, Athens, GA, November 2006.

[THUR95] Thuraisingham, B. and W. Ford, Security constraint processing in a multi-level distributed database management, *IEEE Transactions on Knowledge and Data Engineering*, April 1995.

[THUR90] Thuraisingham, B., Security for Multimedia Database Systems, *IFIP Data Security Conference*, 1990.

[THUR04a] Thuraisingham, B., Secure sensor information management, *IEEE Signal Processing*, May 2004.

[THUR04b] Thuraisingham, B., Security and privacy for sensor databases, sensor letters, Inaugural Issue, *American Scientific*, March 2004.

[THUR06] Thuraisingham, B., G. Lavee, and E. Bertino, Access Control for Video Surveillance, *Proceedings ACM SACMAT*, 2006.

[THUR07] Thuraisingham, B., A. Ashraful, G. Subbiah, and L. Khan, An Integrated Platform for Secure Geospatial Information Exchange through the Semantic Web, University of Texas Dallas Technical Report UTDCS-01-07, January, 2007.

[WIKI] SensorML http://en.wikipedia.org/wiki/SensorML

[Mic03] Microsoft, R. B. Patel, and A. Tolani. T&L Corporation: the square-PKI-aware Pervasive Computing, Demonstration, University of California, Irvine, 2004.

[OGC] OGC, White Paper, An Introduction to GeoRSS: A Standards Based Approach for (en-enabling RSS feeds, http://www.opengeospatial.org/.

[RAI] Römer, A. v., M. Adam, C. Bornhövd, and J. Schaper, Semantic Discovery and Composition of Web Service for RFID Applications in Border control, http://www.dsd-informatik.tu-darmstadt.de/staff/bornhoevd/ISWC04.pdf.

[PSR04] Perrig, A., J. Stankovic, and D. Wagner, Security in wireless sensor networks, Communications of the ACM, 2004.

[SRI04] Srivastava, U., K. Munagala, and J. Widom, Operator Composition of Semantic Web Services, http://ilpubs.stanford.edu:8090/690/1/2004-32.html.

[STA06] Proceedings, 32nd very large Data bases, Seoul, Athens, GA, November 2006.

[TRS] Thuraisingham, B. and W. Ford, Security constraint processing in a multilevel distributed database management, IEEE Transactions on Knowledge and Data Engineering, April 1993.

[THUR90] Thuraisingham, B., Security for Multimedia Database Systems, IFIP Data Security Conference, 1990.

[THUR04] Thuraisingham, B., Secure sensor information management, IEEE Signal Processing, May 2004.

[THUR05] Thuraisingham, B., Security and privacy for sensor database management, Inaugural Issue, Aberdeen Systems, March 2004.

[THUR06] Thuraisingham, B., C. Lyvas, and L. Warner, Access Control for XML Securability, Proceedings, ACM SACMAT, 2006.

[THUR07] Thuraisingham, B., A. Ashraful, C. Subbiah, and L. Khan, An Integrated Platform for Secure Geospatial Information Exchange through the Semantic Web, University of Texas Dallas Technical Report UTDCS-02-07, January 2007.

[WIKI] SensorML, http://en.wikipedia.org/wiki/SensorML.

Chapter 24

Web Services for Secure Activity Management

24.1 Overview

In Chapter 22 we discussed Web services for secure data, information and knowledge management. In this chapter we will discuss Web services for secure activity management. These include Web services for secure information integration, information sharing, and e-business, as well as collaboration and workflow.

Consider for example the integration of two information sources. Each information source may utilize a database system to manage the data. Metadata may include information about the types of data in the database as well as ontologies to handle semantic heterogeneity. When integrating the information, the various security policies as well as the schema have to be integrated to provide a uniform view. With respect to collaborating, we need policies for different users to collaborate with one another. How can the participants trust each other? How can trust be established? What sort of access control is appropriate? There is research in developing security models for workflow and collaboration systems [BERT2424]. Secure e-business is receiving a lot of attention. How can the models, processes and functions be secured? What are these security models? Closely related to e-business is supply chain management. The challenge here is ensuring security as well as timely communication between the suppliers and the customers. In this chapter, we will discuss the various security issues for activity management and then discuss the application of Web services and semantic Web technologies.

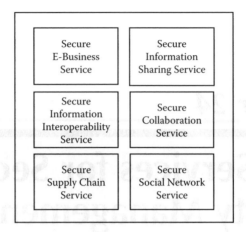

Figure 24.1   Aspects of Web services for secure activity management.

The organization of this chapter is as follows. Secure e-commerce will be discussed in Section 24.2. Secure workflow and collaboration are covered in Section 24.3, and secure information interoperability in Section 24.4. Assured information sharing is the focus of Section 24.5. Secure social networking will be discussed in Section 24.6, and secure supply chain management in Section 24.7. The chapter concludes with Section 24.8. Figure 24.1 illustrates secure activity management and Web services.

24.2 Secure E-Commerce

As stated earlier, e-commerce is about organizations carrying out business transactions such as sales of goods and business agreements, as well as consumers purchasing items from merchants electronically. There have been numerous developments on e-commerce and some discussions on the initial progress that were reported in [THUR00]. Due to the fact that e-commerce may involve millions of dollars in transactions between businesses or credit card purchases between consumers and businesses, it is important that e-commerce systems be secure. Examples of such systems include e-payment systems and supply chain management systems.

There has been some work on secure e-commerce as well as secure supply chain management (see, for example, [GHOS98]). In the case of e-payment systems, the challenges include identification and authentication of both consumers and businesses, as well as tracing the purchases made by consumers. For example, it would be entirely possible for someone to masquerade as a consumer, use the consumer's credit card, and make purchases electronically. Therefore, one solution proposed is for a consumer to have some credentials when he or she makes some purchases.

These credentials, which may be some random numbers, could vary with each purchase. This way the malicious process that masquerades as the consumer may not have the credential and therefore may not be able to make the purchases. There will be a problem if the credentials are also stolen. Various encryption techniques are being proposed for secure e-commerce (see [HASS00]). That is, in addition to possessing credentials, the information may be encrypted say with the public key of the business and only the business could get the actual data. Similarly the communication between the business and the consumer is also encrypted. When transactions are carried out between businesses, the parties involved will have to possess certain credentials so that the transactions are carried out securely. Note that while much progress has been made on e-commerce transactions as well as secure e-commerce transactions, incorporating techniques for secure database transaction management with e-commerce is still not mature. Some work has been reported in [RAY00].

As we have stated, secure supply chain management is also a key aspect of secure e-commerce. Here, the idea is for organizations to provide parts to other corporations for, say, manufacturing or other purposes. Suppose a hospital wants to order surgical equipment from a corporation, then there must be some negotiations and agreements between the hospital and the corporation. Corporation X may request some of its parts from another corporation, Y, and may not want to divulge the information that it is manufacturing the parts for say Hospital A. Such sensitive information has to be protected. Supply chain management is useful in several areas of manufacturing for many domains including medical, defense, and intelligence. Some of the information exchanged between the organizations may be highly sensitive, especially for military and intelligence applications. There needs to be a way to protect such sensitive information. Since the transactions are carried out on the Web, a combination of access control rules and encryption techniques are being proposed as solutions for protecting sensitive information for supply chain management.

We have been hearing of e-commerce only since about the mid 1990s and this has been due to the explosion of the Web. While much progress has been made on developing information technologies such as databases, data mining, and multimedia information management for e-commerce, there is still a lot to do on security. In addition, the information about various individuals will also have to be kept private. Many of the security technologies we have discussed in this book, including secure Web data management and secure semantic Web, will be applicable for secure e-commerce. For example, the semantic Web can be used as a vehicle to carry out e-commerce functions. By having machine-understandable Web pages, e-commerce can be automated without having a human in the loop. This means that it is critical that the semantic Web be secure. As we make progress for secure Web information management technologies, we can vastly improve the security of e-commerce transactions. E-commerce applications may be invoked as Web services. Figure 24.2 illustrates aspects of secure e-commerce and Web services.

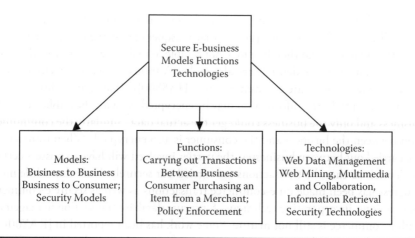

Figure 24.2   Aspects of secure e-business.

24.3 Secure Workflow and Collaboration

As stated earlier, collaboration technologies are important for e-commerce as organizations carry out transactions between each other. Workflow and collaboration are about organizations or groups working together toward a common goal such as designing a system or solving a problem. Collaboration technologies are important for e-commerce as organizations carry out transactions between each other. Workflow is about a process that must be followed from start to finish in carrying out an operation such as making a purchase. The steps include initiating the agreement, transferring funds, and sending the goods to the consumer. Because collaboration and workflow are part of many operations, such as e-commerce and knowledge management, we need secure workflow and secure collaboration. There has been a lot of work by Bertino et al. on this topic. Most notable among the developments is the BFA model (see [BERT99]) for secure workflow management systems. Some work on secure collaborative systems was initially proposed in [DEMU93]. Since then several ideas have been developed (see IFIP Conference Series on Database Security). In this section we will provide an overview of secure workflow and collaboration.

In the case of secure workflow management systems, the idea is for users to have the proper credentials to carry out the particular task. For example, in the case of making a purchase for a project, only a project leader could initiate the request. A secretary then types the request. Then the administrator has to use his/her credit card and make the purchase. The mailroom has the authority to make the delivery. Essentially, what we have proposed is a role-based access control model for secure workflow. There have been several developments on this topic (see SACMAT Conference Proceedings). Various technologies such as Petri nets have been investigated for secure workflow system (see [HUAN98]).

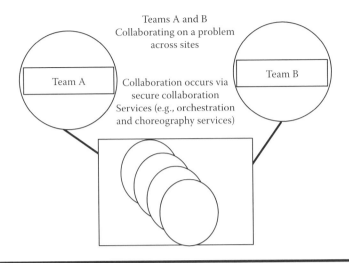

Figure 24.3 Secure collaboration.

Closely related to secure workflow is secure collaboration. Collaboration is much broader than workflow. While workflow is about a series of operations that have to be executed serially or in parallel to carry out a task, collaboration is about individuals working together to solve a problem. Object technologies in general and distributed object management technologies in particular are being used to develop collaboration systems. Here, the individual and the resources in the environment are modeled as objects. Communications between the individuals and resources are modeled as communication between the objects. This communication is carried out via object request brokers. Therefore, security issues discussed for object request brokers apply for secure collaboration. For example, should all parties involved be given the same access to the resources? If the access to resources is different then how can the individuals work together and share data? Figure 24.3 illustrates secure collaboration.

Trust and negotiation systems also play an important role in workflow and collaboration systems. For example, how can the parties trust each other in solving a problem? If A gives some information to B, can B share the information with C even if A and C do not communicate with each other? Similar questions were asked when we discussed secure federations. Also secure data management technologies are necessary to manage the data for workflow and collaboration applications. While much progress has been made, there is still a lot to do, especially with the developments on the semantic Web and emerging technologies such as peer-to-peer data management.

In Part I we discussed Web services for complex activities such as workflow, choreography, and orchestration. Security for such activities is in its infancy. For example, what are the security issues in invoking the Web services that comprise a workflow application? What are the security issues for orchestration and choreography? What are the security issues for Web services composition? We discussed some of the issues in Part II. We need a thorough investigation of the security issues for such complex activities.

24.4 Secure Information Interoperability

There are several challenges for integrating information especially in a heterogeneous environment. One is schema heterogeneity where system A is based on a relational system, and system B is based on object systems. That is, when the two systems are based on different models, we need to resolve the conflicts. One option is to have a common data model. This means that the constructs of both systems have to be transformed into the constructs of the common data model. When you consider security properties, we have to ensure that the policies enforced by the individual systems are maintained. Figure 24.4 illustrates the use of a common secure data model to handle data model heterogeneity. In some cases we may need bi-directional transformation where the constructs of one data model have to be translated into those of another.

Figure 24.5 illustrates the situation in which multiple schemas are integrated to form, say, a federated schema for a secure federated database system. Essentially, we have adopted Sheth and Larson's schema architecture for a secure federated environment. Some of the challenges in integrating heterogeneous schemas are discussed in [THUR94]. We assume that each component exports certain schema to the federation. Then these schemas are integrated to form a federated policy. In a secure environment, we need to ensure that the security properties of the individual systems are maintained throughout the federation.

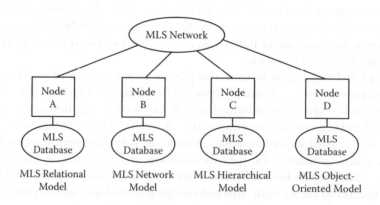

Figure 24.4 Secure data model heterogeneity.

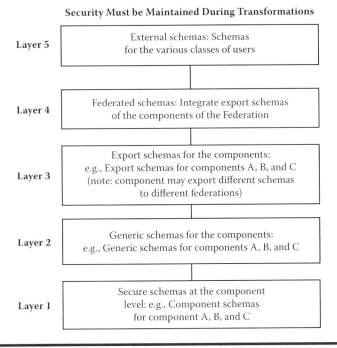

Figure 24.5   Secure schema integration.

Next, we will focus on policy integration. Initial investigation of security policy integration for federated databases was reported in [THUR94]. Here we assumed that heterogeneous MLS/DBMSs had to be integrated to form an MLS/FDBMS (multilevel Secure Federated Database Management System). We illustrate the policy architecture in Figure 24.8. Our approach is very similar to the approach taken by Sheth and Larson for schema integration [SHET90]). In the case of policy integration, each system exports security policies to the federation. We assume that the component systems have more stringent access control requirements for foreign users. That is, export policies may have access control rules in addition to the rules enforced by the local system. The challenge is to ensure that there is no security violation at the federation level. A view of agencies sharing data and enforcing policies is illustrated in Figure 24.6.

Semantic heterogeneity occurs when an entity is interpreted differently at different sites or different entities are interpreted to be the same object. For example, the term speed could be in miles/hr in node 1 and in node 2 it could be km/day. Another example: John Smith could be Smith John at node 1 and John K Smith at node 2. In both cases the same entity is interpreted differently. On the other hand, John Smith at node 1 could really be John J. Smith and at node 2 he is

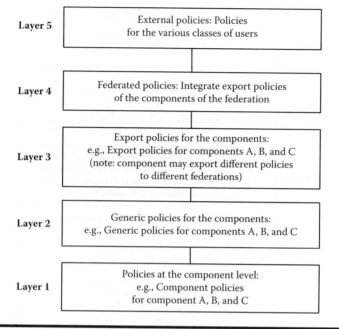

Figure 24.6 Secure policy integration.

John K. Smith. They are different people but mistakenly they are considered to be one in the same.

Semantic heterogeneity is one of the major challenges for data integration as well as information interoperability. They occur not only in relational databases but also in object databases, multimedia databases, and even geospatial databases. For example, when integrating heterogeneous geospatial databases, each database could have different ways of representing the same coordinate system. Various solutions for handling heterogeneity have been proposed since the 1990s; although it is only recently with the use of semantic Web technologies that we have a good handle on the problem. The application of semantic Web technologies and Web services for secure information interoperability will be discussed in Section 24.5. Figure 24.7 illustrates semantic heterogeneity.

Web services may be invoked for integrating heterogeneous databases. That is, the agent acting on behalf of the user may invoke a Web service for integration. This Web service may utilize ontologies for handling semantic heterogeneity to carry out its operation. Therefore, in order for secure information interoperability, we need to secure Web services. Research on Web services for secure information interoperability is just beginning. Some of the challenges include privacy preserving ontology alignment and security policy integration for Web services. Figure 24.8 illustrates aspects of Web services for secure information interoperability.

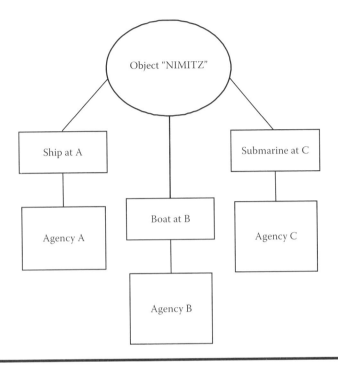

Figure 24.7   Semantic heterogeneity.

24.5 Secure Information Sharing

AIS (Assured Information Sharing) is about organizations sharing information but at the same time enforcing policies and procedures so that the data is integrated and mined to extract nuggets. For example, data from the various data sources at multiple security levels, as well as from different services and agencies including the Air Force, Navy, Army, local, state, and federal agencies, have to be integrated so that the data can be mined, patterns and information extracted, relationships identified, and decisions made. The databases would include, for example, military databases that contain information about military strategies, intelligence databases that contain information about potential terrorists and their patterns of attack, and medical databases that contain information about infectious diseases and stock piles. Data could be structured or unstructured including geospatial/multimedia data. Data also needs to be shared between healthcare organizations such as doctors' offices, hospitals, and pharmacies. Unless the data is integrated and the big picture is formed, it will be difficult to inform all the parties concerned about the incidences that have occurred. While the different agencies have to share data and information, they also need to enforce appropriate security and integrity policies so that the data does not get into the hands of unauthorized individuals. Essentially the agencies have to share information but at the same time maintain the security

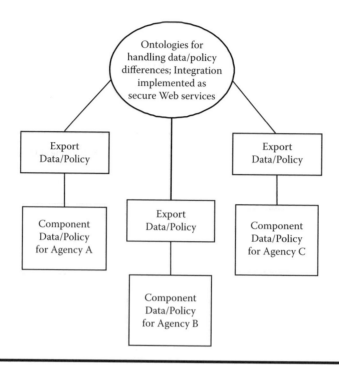

Figure 24.8   Secure information interoperability and Web services.

and integrity requirements. A coalition consists of a set of organizations, which may be agencies, universities, and corporations that work together in a peer-to-peer environment to solve problems such as intelligence and military operations as well as health care operations. Figure 24.9 illustrates an architecture for a coalition where three agencies have to share data and information. Coalitions are usually dynamic in nature. That is, members may join and leave the coalition in accordance with the policies and procedures. A challenge is to ensure the secure operation of a coalition. We assume that the members of a coalition, which are also called its partners, may be trustworthy, untrustworthy, or partially (semi) trustworthy. Various aspects of coalition data sharing are discussed in the Markle report [MARK03].

Figure 24.10 illustrates security policy integration in a coalition environment. In this example, A and B form a coalition while B and C form a second coalition. A could be California, B could be Texas, and C could be Oklahoma. California and Texas could form a coalition as part of the larger states in the United States, and Texas and Oklahoma could form a coalition as part of the neighboring states in the South of the United States for emergency management. There is also an urgent need for multiple organizations to share data and at the same time enforce security policies. These policies include policies for confidentiality, privacy, and trust. For example, patient data may be shared by multiple organizations including hospitals, levels of government, and agencies.

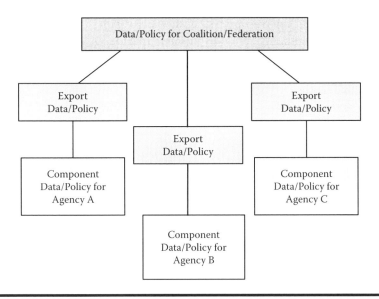

Figure 24.9   Architecture for organizational data sharing.

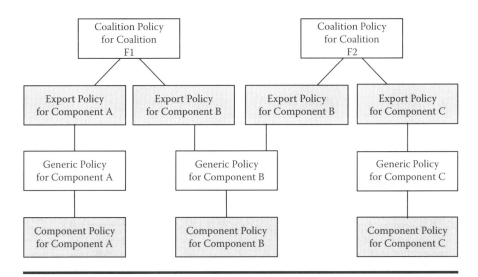

Figure 24.10   Security policy integration and transformation for coalitions.

It is important to maintain the privacy of patient data. However, it is also important that there are no unnecessary access controls so that information sharing is prohibited. One needs flexible policies so that during emergency situations it is critical that all of the data is shared in order for effective decisions to be made. During normal operations, it is important to maintain confidentiality and privacy. In addition, trust policies ensure that data is shared between trusted individuals. The standards efforts in this area include role-based access control (RBAC) [SAND96], as well as P3P (Platform for Privacy Preferences). Our partners at George Mason University are examining the use of models such as RBAC and UCON for AIS [SAND06].

There are two types of conflicting requirements: one is security versus data sharing. The goal of data sharing is for organizations to share as much data as possible so that the data is mined and nuggets are obtained. However, when security policies are enforced, then not all of the data is shared. The other type of conflict is between real-time processing and security. The soldier will need information at the right time. If it is even say 5 minutes late, the information may not be useful. This means that if various security checks are to be performed, then the information may not get to the soldier on time.

Web services play a major role in information sharing. For example, an organization, A, may invoke a Web service to obtain information from another organization, B. This Web service may invoke another Web service to determine what the incentives are for organization B to share the information. In the case of assured information sharing, organization B may also examine the security policies to determine whether the information can be shared. We are building an assured information sharing life cycle, and service-oriented architecture is central to our approach. Figure 24.11 illustrates aspects of Web services for assured information sharing.

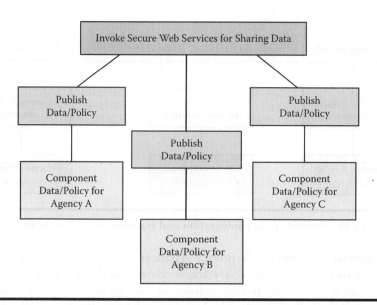

Figure 24.11 Aspects of Web services for assured information sharing.

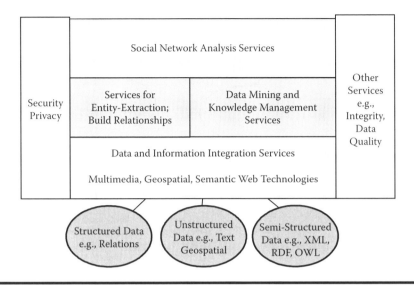

Figure 24.12   Aspects of Web services for secure social networks.

24.6 Secure Social Networking

Social networks have exploded in recent years. We now have Facebook, Friendster, and Twitter among others. Social networks are being mined to extract useful information so that better services can be provided to the members. In addition, the mined information can also be used to help counter-terrorism and law enforcement. At the same time it is important to protect the privacy of law-abiding citizens.

There has been much interest recently in securing social networks as well as developing privacy preserving techniques for social networks. For example, how can the members reveal the right amount of information so that their privacy is enforced? Should the system provide some feedback to the members that they are revealing too much information? Web services may be invoked to manage the social networks. For example, a member may invoke a Web service to post information on the network. These Web services have to ensure appropriate security and privacy policies. Aspects of Web services for social networks are illustrated in Figure 24.12.

24.7 Secure Supply Chain

Security for supply chain management and logistics is receiving a lot of attention. With respect to logistics, a major goal is the secure movement of the objects. When items have to be moved from location A to B, the items have to be secured both

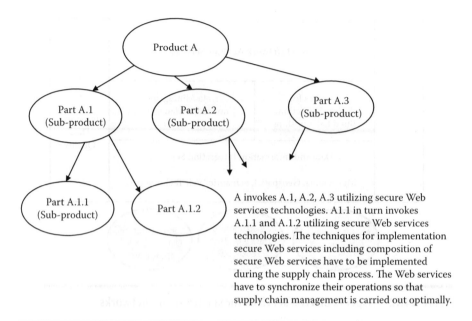

A invokes A.1, A.2, A.3 utilizing secure Web services technologies. A1.1 in turn invokes A.1.1 and A.1.2 utilizing secure Web services technologies. The techniques for implementation secure Web services including composition of secure Web services have to be implemented during the supply chain process. The Web services have to synchronize their operations so that supply chain management is carried out optimally.

Figure 24.13   Aspects of Web services for secure supply chains.

physically and digitally. RFID technologies are being used to track the objects for logistics and supply chain management. It is critical that the RFID technologies be secure.

With respect to supply chain there are also additional security considerations. For example, a product may be manufactured using several components. These components may come from different parts of the world and may be compromised. It is critical that the product be secure even if the components may be compromised. This is a very challenging problem. As discussed in Part I, Web services may be invoked to carry out supply chain management as well as logistics operations. These Web services have to be secure to ensure secure supply chain management. Figure 24.13 illustrates secure supply chain management.

24.8 Summary and Directions

In this chapter we have discussed Web services for secure activity management. In particular, we featured Web services for secure e-commerce, secure workflow, and secure information interoperability, secure supply chain, secure social networks, and assured information sharing.

The ideas discussed are preliminary. First, we need standards for Web services for the various activities. Then we need to examine the security impact. While standards are being developed for some of the activities such as e-business and workflow, we need standards for other services such as supply chain management and assured information sharing.

Exercises

1. Conduct a survey of secure Web services for e-business applications.
2. Describe how secure semantic Web service may be utilized for assured information sharing.
3. Conduct a survey of the standards for secure Web services for collaboration and workflow applications.

References

[BERT06] Bertino, E., L. Khan, R. Sandhu, and B. Thuraisingham, Secure knowledge management, *IEEE Transactions on Systems, Man and Cybernetics*, May 2006.

[BERT99] Bertino, E., E. Ferrari, and V. Atluri, The specification and enforcement of authorization constraints in workflow management systems, *ACM Transactions on Information and Systems Security*, 2, 1, 65–104, 1999.

[CHEN] Chen-Burger, Y.-H., K.-Y. Hui, A. D. Preece, P. M. D. Gray, and A. Tate, Supporting Collaboration through Semantic-based Workflow and Constraint Solving, http://www.csd.abdn.ac.uk/~apreece/research/download/ekaw2004.pdf

[DEMU93] Demurjian, S., B. Thuraisingham, and T. Ting, User role-based security for collaborative computer systems, *Multimedia Review: The Journal of Multimedia Computing*, Summer 1993.

[GHOS98] Ghosh, A., *E-Commerce Security: Weak Links, Best Defenses*, John Wiley, New York, 1998.

[HASS00] Hessler, V., *Security Fundamentals for E-Commerce*, Artech House, Boston, MA, 2000.

[HUAN98] Huang, W. and V. Atluri, Analyzing the safety of workflow authorization models, *DBSec*, 43–57, 1998.

[MARI02] Marinescu, D. C., *Internet Based Workflow Management: Towards a Semantic Web*, Wiley Interscience, New York, 2002.

[MARK03] Markle Report, Creating a Trusted Network for Homeland Security, New York, 2003.

[MORE01] Morey, D., M. Maybury, and B. Thuraisingham (Eds.), *Knowledge Management*, MIT Press, Cambridge, MA, 2001.

[RAY00] Ray, I. and I. Ray, An optimistic fair exchange e-commerce protocol with automated dispute resoloved, *EC-Web*, 84–47, 2000.

[SAND96] Sandhu, R. S., E. J. Coyne, H. L. Feinstein, and C. E. Youman, Role-based access control models, *IEEE Computer*, 29(2), 38–47, 1996.

[SAND06] Sandhu, R. S., K. Ranganathan, and X. Zhang, Secure information sharing enabled by trusted computing and PEI models, *ASIACCS*, 2–12, 2006.

[SHET90] Sheth, A. P. and J. A. Larson, Federated database systems for managing distributed, heterogeneous, and autonomous databases, *ACM Comput. Surv.* 22(3), 183–236, 1990.

[THUR90] Thuraisingham, B., Security for multimedia database systems, *Proceedings IFIP Data Security Conference*, 1990.

[THUR94] Thuraisingham, B., Security issues for federated database systems, *Computers and Security*, 13(6), 509–525, 1994.

[THUR05] Thuraisingham, B., *Database and Applications Security*, CRC Press, Boca Raton, FL, 2005.

[WARR06] Warren, P., Knowledge management and the Semantic Web: From scenario to technology, *IEEE Intelligent Systems*, 21, 1, 53–59, 2006.

[WFMC] http://xml.coverpages.org/wf-xml.html

Chapter 25

Secure Specialized Web Services

25.1 Overview

In the last three chapters, we have discussed Web services for secure data, information, and knowledge management (Chapter 22), for secure complex data management including secure geospatial data management (Chapter 23), and for secure activity management including secure e-business and secure information interoperability (Chapter 24). In each of these chapters we examined some of the concepts discussed in Chapter 5 and investigated security issues. In this chapter, we will continue along the same lines and explore Web services for secure domain services, as well as merging services such as secure cloud and secure data as services.

The organization of this chapter is as follows. In Section 25.2, we will examine domain Web services such as Web services for healthcare, finance, and defense, and also examine security issues, as well as the applications of Web services and the semantic Web. In Section 25.5, we will look at emerging Web services such as secure cloud services and review security issues. Note that many of the security technologies in emerging Web services are still new and therefore the discussion in this chapter is somewhat preliminary. Our goal is to provide direction in this area for future work. The chapter concludes with Section 25.6.

25.2 Secure Domain Web Services

We will examine the discussions in Chapter 5 for domain services and cover security issues.

Defense: As we have stated in Chapter 5, the U.S. Department of Defense is adopting services technologies and the global information grid based on the service-oriented architecture paradigm. Much of the development is influenced by XML and Ontologies. As we have stated, Web services also play a major role for applications in homeland security. For many of the domain applications, the focus has been on implementing attribute-based access control, based on XACML security standards. The goal is for the user to present his/her credentials and request resources. The system would then make a decision as to whether the user can access the resources based on the policies enforced and the credentials of the user. This is essentially the function of the Policy Decision Point. Then the Policy Enforcement Point will enforce the access request.

Healthcare and life cycles: As stated earlier, semantic Web technologies have played a major role in the development of healthcare information technologies. For example, ontologies have been developed for electronic healthcare records, as well as for several items in life sciences. The major security challenge for healthcare information systems involves privacy. The goal is to ensure the privacy of the patient records. Typically, patients would determine what information they want to protect and under what conditions. When an organization requests data about patients, the organization will specify what its policies are. If the policies are in agreement with what the patient has specified, then the information is released to the organization. W3C standards such as P3P may be utilized to enforce privacy. Furthermore, the entire operation could be implemented as Web services.

Finance: Since financial domain involves money, confidentiality is critical for financial data. While it is difficult to get healthcare data due to patient privacy, we are finding that it is almost impossible to obtain financial data such as credit card data to conduct research. Several groups are developing Web services and semantic Web technologies for financial domains. As we have stated, the group in Madrid has done some very good research on applying the semantic "ontology-based platform that provides (a) the integration of contents and semantics in a knowledge base that provides a conceptual view on low-level contents, (b) an adaptive hypermedia-based knowledge visualization and navigation system, and (c) semantic search facilities" [CAST04]. The challenge we have is to integrate the security and private policies to protect financial data as well as the customer information into these semantic Web technologies. Web services will then execute the financial operations.

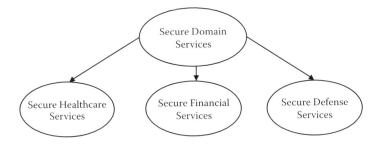

Figure 25.1   Secure domain Web services.

Other Domains: In Chapter 5 we discussed Web services for telecommunication applications among other domains. Security for such domains has been studied extensively. For example, Web services for mobile applications including cell phones and pads are being proposed. Furthermore, security efforts for the telecommunication and mobile computing domains are exploding. Secure Web services for such domains are also being investigated. Figure 25.1 illustrates Web services for various secure domain applications.

25.3 Security for X as a Service

As we have discussed in Chapter 5, the concept of X as a service where X may be data, software, or some other concept such as a platform, operating system, compiler, or infrastructure, is becoming very popular. In the services computing world, everything becomes a service including data as well as real-world services such as healthcare and finance.

Security for data as a service has been investigated in recent years. With the explosion of outsourcing of jobs, many data-oriented jobs are also being outsourced, therefore protecting the sensitive aspects of data is critical. Furthermore, when data is utilized as a service from service providers, it is important that the data be of high quality and not corrupted. With respect to software, it is important that the software that is being utilized as a service is error fee and is not infected with worms and viruses. Figure 25.2 illustrates the notion of providing security for X as a service.

25.4 Security for Amazon Web Services

As stated in Chapter 5, Amazon Web Services (AWS) has provided companies of all sizes with an infrastructure Web services platform in the cloud. With AWS one can

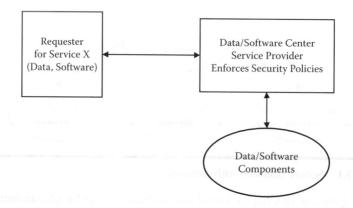

Figure 25.2 Security for X as a service.

requisition computing power, storage and other services. Also stated in Chapter 5, AWS provides database components called SimpleDB, which offers database functions such as querying. Amazon uses SOAP protocols for communication between the client and the service provider. Therefore, all of the security issues that pertain to SOAP are relevant. Furthermore, cloud computing security issues are also relevant to these discussions. In the case of cloud, the security concerns include enforcing appropriate access control policies, as well as the secure storage of the data at multiple locations. Recently, researchers are exploring the scrutiny issues related to virtualization in a cloud. More details of cloud computing security issues will be discussed in Section 25.5.

Our research is focusing on implementing access control and encryption for Amazon Web Services. The data that is being stored in the Amazon environment is encrypted for protection. On top of that we are also implementing role-based access control in this environment. We are also implementing XACML in the cloud environment and more details will be given in the next section. More details on this topic can be found in [PRAN09].

25.5 Secure Web Services for Cloud and Grid

There is a critical need to securely store, manage, share, and analyze massive amounts of complex (e.g., semi-structured and unstructured) data to determine patterns and trends in order to improve the quality of healthcare, better safeguard the nation, and explore alternative energy. The emerging cloud computing model attempts to address the growth of Web-connected devices and handle massive amounts of data. Google has now introduced the MapReduce framework for processing large amounts of data on commodity hardware.

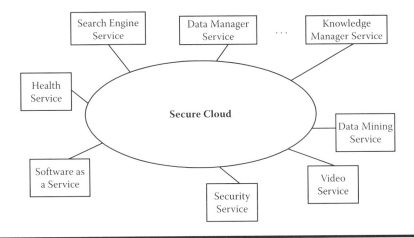

Figure 25.3 Secure cloud.

Apache's Hadoop distributed file system (HDFS) is emerging as a superior software component for cloud computing, combined with integrated parts such as MapReduce. The need to augment human reasoning, interpreting, and decision-making abilities have resulted in the emergence of the semantic Web, which is an initiative that attempts to transform the Web from its current, merely human-readable form, to a machine processable form. This in turn has resulted in numerous social networking sites with massive amounts of data to be shared and managed.

We are just beginning research in cloud computing. In particular, we are developing semantic query processing strategies for clouds. However, our clouds do not incorporate security. We are working on (1) XACML-based access control strategies for clouds and (2) a lab that will conduct security experiments in clouds that will be incorporated into our current network security courses, as well as future secure cloud computing courses. More details of our efforts are given in [HAML10]. Figure 25.3 illustrates a secure cloud based on Hadoop and MapReduce.

25.6 Summary and Directions

In this chapter we have described security for emerging Web services. In particular, we have discussed security for domain Web services as well as for Amazon.com Web services and clouds. We have also examined security for X as a service.

We believe that much of the future research on Web services as well as on secure Web services will be on the topics we have discussed in this chapter. Security for clouds is receiving a lot of attention. Therefore, Web services for secure clouds are becoming popular. We urgently need standards in these emerging secure Web services.

Exercises

1. Describe security issues for cloud computing.
2. Conduct a survey of cloud computing systems.

References

[CAST04] Castells, P., B. Foncillas, R. Lara, M. Rico, and J. L. Alonso, Semantic Web Technologies for Economic and Financial Information Management, Proceedings of the 1st European Semantic Web Symposium, Heraklion, Greece, 2004.

[HAML10] Hamlen, K. et al., Security Issues for Cloud Computing, Technical Report, the University of Texas at Dallas, January 2010.

[PRAN09] Pranav, P., Security for Amazon Web Services, MS Thesis, The University of Texas at Dallas, November 2009.

Chapter 26

Summary and Directions

26.1 About This Chapter

This chapter brings us to the close of *Secure Semantic Service-Oriented Systems*. We discussed several aspects including services technologies, secure services technologies, secure semantic Web technologies, and emerging secure Web services. In particular, we discussed secure service-oriented architectures, access control for Web devices, federated identity management, and secure XML standards. Applications of secure Web services for semantic interoperability, digital libraries, and e-business were also reviewed. This chapter provides a summary of the book as well as giving directions for trustworthy semantic Webs.

The organization of this chapter is as follows. In Section 26.2 we give a summary of each chapter. In Section 26.3, we discuss directions for secure semantic service-oriented information systems, and in Section 26.4, give suggestions as to where to go from here.

26.2 Summary of This Book

We summarize the contents of each chapter essentially taken from the summary and directions section of each chapter. Chapter 1 provided an introduction to the book. We first gave a brief overview of the supporting technologies for trustworthy semantic Web, which included information security, data, information, and knowledge management and semantic Web. Then we discussed various topics addressed in this book including the secure semantic Web, dependable semantic

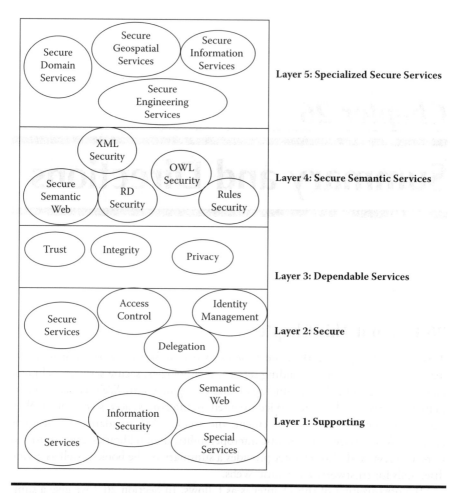

Figure 26.1   Components addressed in this book.

Web, applications of semantic Web and specialized semantic Web, such as the domain-specific semantic Web and geospatial semantic Web. Our framework is a five-layer framework, and each layer was addressed in one part of this book. This framework was illustrated in Figure 1.10. We replicate this framework in Figure 26.1.

The book is divided into five parts. Part I, which described services and security technologies, consisted of six chapters: 2, 3, 4, 5, 6, and 7. Chapter 2 provided an overview of service-oriented computing. We first discussed what is meant by services. Next, we discussed high level concepts in service-oriented computing. Realizing service-oriented information systems through service-oriented archive turns and Web services was discussed next. Semantic Web services were introduced next. Some specialized services such as services in healthcare and telecommunication industries were discussed next. Finally, we discussed how service-oriented information systems may be designed.

Chapter 3 discussed various aspects of SOA and Web services. We started with a review of the various relevant standards organizations and then provided an overview of both SOA and Web services. This was followed by a consideration of the WS protocol stack; as we have stressed, this protocol stack will continue to evolve. Then we analyzed an alternate way to implement service-oriented computing, and that is through the REST interface. Finally, we discussed a popular WS technology by Amazon. Chapter 4 described SOAD. In particular, we started with a discussion of modeling services and the top-down and bottom-up approaches to services modeling. We also viewed the service-oriented life cycle. Finally, we surveyed SOAD approaches.

Chapter 5 discussed various types of specialized Web services. First, we examined Web services for data management and complex data management. Then we covered Web services for information management and knowledge management. Next, we appraised Web services for activity management. This was followed by a discussion of domain Web services. Finally, we looked at some emerging Web services including the paradigm of "X as a service."

Chapter 6 provided an overview of semantic Web technologies and the notion of semantic Web services. In particular, we analyzed Tim Berners-Lee's technology stack as well as a functional architecture for the semantic Web. Then we discussed XML, RDF, and ontologies as well as Web rules for the semantic Web. Finally, we covered semantic Web services and how they can make use of semantic Web technologies.

Chapter 7 provided a brief overview of the developments in trustworthy systems. We first discussed secure systems including basic concepts in access control as well as discretionary and mandatory policies, types of secure systems such as secure operating systems, secure databases, secure networks, emerging technologies, the impact of the Web, and the steps to building secure systems. Next we talked about dependable systems including aspects on trust, rights, privacy, integrity, quality, and real-time processing. Then, we focused in more detail on the aspects of Web security, including threats to Web security and secure Web databases.

Part II, which described secure services, consisted of six chapters: 8, 9, 10, 11, 12, and 13. We provided an overview of the semantic Web and discussed security standards. Chapter 8 provided an overview of secure service-oriented computing. We first answered what is meant by secure services. Next, we discussed high-level concepts in secure service-oriented computing. Realizing service-oriented information systems through secure service-oriented archive turns and Web services was studied next. Then we observed how secure service-oriented information systems may be designed. Finally, aspects of federated identity management, delegation of Web services, and severity standards were outlined.

Chapter 9 provided an overview of secure Web services and discussed the applications of semantic Web technologies for secure Web services. Web services are the services that are invoked to carry out activities on the Web. A collection of Web services comprises the service-oriented architecture. We also discussed aspects of XACML and SAML. Chapter 10 provided a brief overview for secure SOAD. We started with an overview of secure OOAD. Then we observed the concept of secure service-oriented life cycles. This was followed by a discussion of secure SOAD and secure services modeling. Finally, approaches to secure SOAD were discussed.

Chapter 11 focused on various standards for access control and then discussed attribute-based access control. Also mentioned were some other features such as establishing trust in a Web environment as well as approaches for inference control based on access control.

Chapter 12 provided an overview of identity management systems. We discussed the notion of identity management and described single sign-on followed by a discussion of the identity metasystem and various example systems including Information Card and Open-ID and Shibboleth. Last, we talked about the contributions of the Liberty Alliance.

In Chapter 13, we discussed our research on secure Web services. Specifically, we focused on delegation models and information flow models.

Part III consisted of three chapters: 14, 15, and 16. Chapter 14 discussed trust management and its connection to Web services and semantic Web. We first discussed aspects of trust management including defining trust and also describing trust negotiations. Then we considered enforcing trust within the context of the semantic Web. Furthermore, we also discussed the use of semantic Web technologies for specifying trust policies. Next, we covered related concepts including risk-based trust management and reputation networks.

Chapter 15 observed the various notions of privacy and provided an overview of privacy management. Then we discussed the semantic Web technology applications for privacy management. Privacy for the Web was featured next. This was followed by a discussion of the standard Platform for Privacy Preferences. Chapter 16 provided an overview of data integrity, which includes data quality and data provenance. We considered the applications of semantic Web technologies for data integrity, as well as discussed integrity for semantic Web technologies. Finally, we provided an overview of the relationship between data quality and data provenance.

Part IV consisted of five chapters: 17, 18, 19, 20, and 21. Chapter 17 provided an overview of security issues for the semantic Web. Chapter 18 provided an overview of XML security. We first discussed issues on securing XML documents including security issues for XML elements, attributes, and schemas. Then we saw the use of XML for specifying security policies. We also discussed the secure publications of XML documents. Chapter 19 provided an overview of RDF security. We first reviewed securing the components of RDF including RDF statements and schemas. Next, we went through the use of RDF for specifying policies. We also discussed secure RDF databases. Chapter 20 surveyed ontologism and security. We argued that portions of the ontologies may need to be classified for different applications. We also showed how ontologies may be used to specify security policies. Chapter 21 provided an overview of Web rules and security. First, we discussed our system based on a logic we developed for secure databases called NTML, and then considered security issues for rules. Following that, we showed how rules may be used to specify policies. We also discussed the use of rules for handling the inference and privacy problems. Finally, we remarked on the application of rules for secure Web services.

Part V consisted of four chapters: 22, 23, 24, and 25. Chapter 22 showed how data, information, and knowledge management may be implemented as Web services. Chapter 23 provided an overview of Web services for secure geospatial data management. In particular, we focused on our research in building secure geospatial semantic Webs. We also discussed the work on GeoRSS. Chapter 24 commented on a number of Web services and security issues for activity management, including for e-business and assured information sharing. In Chapter 25 we discussed emerging secure Web services such as secure Amazon.com Web services.

As we have stressed, there are many developments in the field, and it is impossible for us to list all of them. We have provided a broad but fairly comprehensive overview of the field. The book is intended for technical managers as well as technologists who want to get a broad understanding of the field. It is also intended for students who wish to pursue research in data and applications security in general and secure services in particular.

26.3 Directions for Secure Semantic Service-Oriented Information Systems

There are many directions for database and applications security. We discuss some of them for each topic addressed in this book. Figure 26.2 illustrates the directions and challenges.

Secure Services: As we have discussed in Part II, Web services and service-oriented architectures are at the heart of the next-generation Web. We expect them to make use of semantic Web technologies to generate machine-understandable Web pages. This is one of the major developments in the late 1990s and early 2000s. While there are numerous developments in Web services, the application of semantic Web technologies and securing the Web services are major challenges. Furthermore, major initiatives such as the global information grid and the network centric enterprise services are based on Web services and service-oriented architectures. Therefore, securing these technologies as well as making Web services more intelligent by using the semantic Web will be critical for the next-generation Web.

Next, SOAD as well as secure SOAD are in their infancy. While initially there are various approaches for secure SOAD, we believe that eventually these approaches will be unified to develop a unified approach. In the same

Secure	Dependable Web
Novel access control policies, federated identity management, information flow models, delegation based services, service oriented analysis and design, standards	New models and techniques trust management negotiation, Privacy management, security, and management

Secure Semantic	Emerging
New models mechanisms securing XML, RDF, ontologies and reasoning	Novel secure service models for data, information and knowledge management; secure services for domains such as healthcare, finance and defense; services for cloud computing

Figure 26.2 Directions and challenges in secure semantic service-oriented information systems.

way, one can also expect secure SOAD approaches to be unified. However, first we need some approaches for securely modeling services, and research is just beginning in this area.

With respect to access control, a lot of work remains to be done. We need an appropriate security model for services. ABAC is one such model. We need to examine how ABAC can be integrated with UCON. We also need to examine the inference problem in more detail for services. Finally, we need to develop standards similar to SAML and XACML to include more sophisticated forms of fine-grained access control.

Finally, as Web services explode and we carry out more and more transactions on the Web, as well as get involved in social networks, it is critical that we protect the identity of individuals and ensure authorized access. Furthermore, a user may be involved in multiple social networks and multiple transactions. The user may have different identities in different systems. Therefore, we need an effective mechanism to manage the numerous identities of possibly billions of users. Research on identity management is just beginning. We need a lot more work in this area and also develop appropriate standards.

Dependable Systems: We have assumed that dependability includes trust, privacy, and integrity. We have also included multilevel security as part of dependability. We need trust management and negotiation techniques that take advantage of semantic Web technologies. We need to examine standards such as P3P and develop appropriate technologies to enforce the various privacy policies. When agents carry out activities on the Web, we need to ensure that the data is of high quality. We need a better annotation system to manage data provenance. With respect to multilevel security, we need to ensure that agents at multiple levels communicate with each other securely.

Secure Semantic Web: We need to develop tools and techniques to ensure the security of operation of the semantic Web. We need languages to express policies as well as agents to securely carryout various activities on the Web. In addition, we require techniques for securing semantic Web technologies such as XML, RDF, and OWL documents. We also should have a better handle on the inference problem using semantic Web technologies.

Specialized Secure Services: We have to develop specialized secure services for various types of data such as geospatial and sensor streams. We also must develop services to manage multimedia data. In addition, we have to have better domain-specific secure services for applications such as healthcare, finance, and defense, among others.

26.4 Where Do We Go from Here?

This book has discussed a great deal about secure semantic service-oriented information systems. We have stated many challenges in this field in Section 26.3. We need to continue with research and development efforts if we are to make progress in this very important area.

The question is where do we go from here? First of all, those who wish to work in this area must have a good knowledge of the supporting technologies including services, the semantic Web, information security and data, and information and knowledge management. For example, it is important to understand the technologies that comprise the Web services and how they are used. Furthermore, one also needs to understand the numerous standards that are being developed and be able to identify the standards that are most appropriate for their organizations.

Next, since the field is expanding rapidly and there are continually many developments, the reader has to keep up with these, including reading about new commercial products and prototypes. We also encourage the reader to work on the exercises we have given in this book. Finally, we advise experimentation with the products and also the development of security tools. This is the best way to get familiar with a particular field. That is, work on hands-on problems and provide solutions to have a better understanding. While we have not given any implementation exercises in this book, our design problems could be extended to include implementation. The Web will continue to have a major impact on securing these semantic Webs and services, as well as the secure integration of heterogeneous data sources. Ontologies will be critical for many of the developments. In addition, we believe that XML and RDF will continue to evolve for various domains. Therefore, it is important to keep up with all these developments.

We need research and development support from federal and local government funding agencies. Agencies such as the National Security Agency, the U.S. Army, Navy, Air Force, the Defense Advanced Research Projects Agency, the Intelligence Advanced Research Projects Activity, and the Department of Homeland Security are funding research in security. It is important to continue with this funding and also focus on interacting security with this semantic Web. The Cyber Trust and the more recent Trustworthy Computing Themes at the National Science Foundation are excellent initiatives to support some fundamental research on secure Web services. We also need commercial corporations to invest research and development funds so that progress can be made in industrial research and the transferring of research to commercial products. We also need to collaborate with the international research community to solve problems and promote standards that are not only of national interest but also of international interest. In summary, we need public, private, and academic partnerships to develop breakthrough technologies in the very important area of secure semantic service-oriented information systems.

Conclusion to Part V

In Part V we provided an overview of Web services applications in many areas, including secure data, information, and knowledge management, and secure geospatial information management and secure activity management. We also discussed secure Web services applications for domains such as healthcare, finance, and defense.

This brings us to the end of the technical contents of this book. First, we provided an overview of services and security technologies. This was followed by the core topic of this book, and that is secure services. Next we examined dependable services. This was followed by secure semantic services. Finally, we discussed several applications of secure Web services.

Appendix A: Data Management Systems: Developments and Trends

A.1 Overview

In this appendix, we provide an overview of the developments and trends in data management as discussed in our previous book *Data Management Systems Evolution and Interoperation* [THUR97]. Since database systems are an aspect of data management, and database security is an aspect of database systems, we need a good understanding of data management issues for Data and Applications Security.

As stated in Chapter 1, recent developments in information systems technologies have resulted in the computerization of many applications in various business areas. Data has become a critical resource in many organizations and, therefore, efficient access to data, sharing the data, extracting information from the data, and making use of the information have become urgent needs. As a result, there have been several efforts to integrate the various data sources scattered across several sites. These data sources may be databases managed by database management systems or they could simply be files. To provide the interoperability between the multiple data sources and systems, various tools are being developed. These tools enable users of one system to access other systems in an efficient and transparent manner.

We define data management systems to be systems that manage data, extract meaningful information from the data, and make use of the information extracted. Therefore, data management systems include database systems, data warehouses, and data mining systems. Data can be structured, such as that found in relational databases, or it can be unstructured, such as text, voice, imagery, and video. There have been numerous discussions in the past regarding distinguishing between data, information, and knowledge. We do not attempt to clarify these terms. For our purposes, data can be just bits and bytes or it can convey some meaningful information to the user. We will, however, distinguish between database systems and database management systems. A database management system is that component which manages the database containing persistent data. A database system consists of both the database and the database management system.

A key component to the evolution and interoperation of data management systems is the interoperability of heterogeneous database systems. Work on the interoperability between database systems has been reported since the late 1970s. However, it is only recently that we are seeing commercial developments in heterogeneous database systems. Major database system vendors are now providing interoperability between their products and other systems. Furthermore, many of the database system vendors are migrating toward an architecture called the client-server architecture, which facilitates distributed data management capabilities. In addition to work on the interoperability between different database systems and client-server environments, work is also directed toward handling autonomous and federated environments.

The organization of this appendix is as follows. Since database systems are a key component of data management systems, we first provide an overview of the developments in database systems. These developments are discussed in Section A.2. Then we provide a vision for data management systems in Section A.3. Our framework for data management systems is discussed in Section A.4. Note that data mining, warehousing, as well as Web data management are components of this framework. Building information systems from our framework with special instantiations is discussed in Section A.5. The relationship between the various texts that we have written (or are writing) for CRC Press is discussed in Section A.6. This appendix is summarized in Section A.7.

A.2 Developments in Database Systems

Figure A.1 provides an overview of the developments in database systems technology. While the early work in the 1960s focused on developing products based on the network and hierarchical data models, much of the developments in database systems took place after the seminal paper by Codd describing the relational model [CODD70] (see also [DATE90]). Research and development work on relational database systems was carried out during the early 1970s, and several prototypes were developed throughout the 1970s. Notable efforts include IBM's (International Business Machine Corporation's) System R and the University of California at Berkeley's INGRES. During the 1980s, many relational database system products were being marketed (notable among these products are those of Oracle Corporation, Sybase Inc., Informix Corporation, INGRES Corporation, IBM, Digital Equipment Corporation, and Hewlett-Packard Company). During the 1990s, products from other vendors emerged (e.g., Microsoft Corporation). In fact, to date, numerous

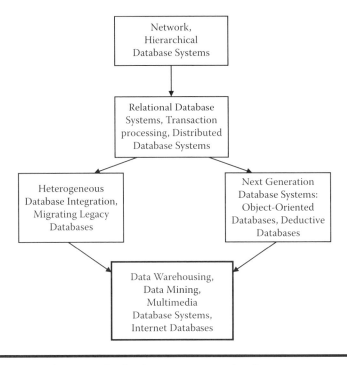

Figure A.1   Developments in database systems technology.

relational database system products have been marketed. However, Codd has stated that many of the systems that are being marketed as relational systems are not really relational (see, for example, the discussion in [DATE90]). He then discussed various criteria that a system must satisfy to be qualified as a relational database system. While the early work focused on issues such as data model, normalization theory, query processing and optimization strategies, query languages, and access strategies and indexes, later the focus shifted toward supporting a multiuser environment. In particular, concurrency control and recovery techniques were developed. Support for transaction processing was also provided.

Research on relational database systems as well as on transaction management was followed by research on distributed database systems around the mid-1970s. Several distributed database system prototype development efforts also began around the late 1970s. Notable among these efforts include IBM's System R*, DDTS (Distributed Database Testbed System) by Honeywell Inc., SDD-I and Multibase by CCA (Computer Corporation of America), and Mermaid by SDC (System Development Corporation). Further, many of these systems (e.g., DDTS, Multibase, Mermaid) function in a heterogeneous environment. During the early 1990s, several database system vendors (such as Oracle Corporation, Sybase, Inc., and Informix Corporation) provided data distribution capabilities for their systems. Most distributed relational database system products are based on client–server architectures. The idea is to have the client of vendor A communicate with the server database system of vendor B. In other words, the client–server computing paradigm facilitates a heterogeneous computing environment. Interoperability between relational and nonrelational commercial database systems is also possible. The database systems community is also involved in standardization efforts. Notable among the standardization efforts are the ANSI/SPARC 3-level schema architecture, the IRDS (Information Resource Dictionary System) standard for Data Dictionary Systems, the relational query language SQL (Structured Query Language), and the RDA (Remote Database Access) protocol for remote database access.

Another significant development in database technology is the advent of object-oriented database management systems. Active work on developing such systems began in the mid-1980s, and they are now commercially available (notable among them include the products of Object Design, Inc., Ontos, Inc., Gemstone Systems, Inc., and Versant Object Technology). It was felt that new-generation applications such as multimedia, office information systems, CAD/CAM, process control, and software engineering have different requirements. Such applications utilize complex data structures. Tighter integration between the programming language and the data model is also desired. Object-oriented database systems satisfy most of the requirements of these new-generation applications [CATT91].

According to the Lagunita report published as a result of a National Science Foundation (NSF) workshop in 1990 (see [NSF90] and [SIGM90]), relational database systems, transaction processing, and distributed (relational) database systems are mature technologies. Further, vendors are marketing object-oriented database systems and demonstrating interoperability between different database systems. The report goes on to state that as applications are getting increasingly complex, more sophisticated database systems are needed. Further, since many organizations now use database systems, in many cases of different types, the database systems need to be integrated. Although work has begun to address these issues and commercial products are available, several issues still needed to be resolved. Therefore, challenges faced by the database systems researchers in the early 1990s were in two areas. One was next-generation database systems and the other was heterogeneous database systems.

Next-generation database systems include object-oriented database systems, functional database systems, special parallel architectures to enhance the performance of database system functions, high-performance database systems, real-time database systems, scientific database systems, temporal database systems, database systems that handle incomplete and uncertain information, and intelligent database systems (also sometimes called logic or deductive database systems). Ideally, a database system should provide support for high-performance transaction processing, model complex applications, represent new kinds of data, and make intelligent deductions. While significant progress was made during the late 1980s and early 1990s, there was much to be done before such a database system could be developed.

Heterogeneous database systems attracted considerable attention in the 1990s [ACM90]. The major issues included handling different data models, different query processing strategies, different transaction processing algorithms, and different query languages. Should a uniform view be provided to the entire system or should users of individual systems maintain their own views of the entire system? These were questions that had yet to be answered satisfactorily. It was also envisaged that a complete solution to heterogeneous database management systems was a generation away. While research was directed toward finding such a solution, work was also carried out to handle limited forms of heterogeneity to satisfy customer needs. Another type of database system that received some attention lately is a federated database system. Note that some had used the terms *heterogeneous database system* and *federated database system* interchangeably. While heterogeneous database systems can be part of a federation, a federation also included homogeneous database systems.

The explosion of users on the Web as well as developments in interface technologies resulted in even more challenges for data management researchers. A second workshop was sponsored by NSF in 1995, and several emerging technologies were identified to be important for the 21st century [NSF95]. These included digital libraries, managing very large databases, data administration issues, multimedia databases, data warehousing, data mining, data management for collaborative computing environments, and security and privacy. Another significant development in the 1990s was the development of object-relational systems. Such systems combined the advantages of both object-oriented database systems and relational database systems. Also, many corporations began focusing on integrating their data management products with Web technologies. Finally, for many organizations there was an increasing need to migrate some of the legacy databases and applications to newer architectures and systems such as client-server architectures and relational database systems. We believe there is no end to developments in data management systems. As new technologies are developed, there are new opportunities for data management research and development.

A comprehensive view of all data management technologies is illustrated in Figure A.2. As shown, traditional technologies include database design, transaction processing, and benchmarking. Then there are database systems based on data models such as relational and object-oriented models. Database systems may depend on features they provide, such as security and real-time response. These database systems may be relational or object-oriented. There are also database systems based on multiple sites or processors such as distributed and heterogeneous database systems, parallel systems, and systems being migrated. Finally, there are the emerging technologies such as data warehousing and mining, collaboration, and the Web. Any comprehensive text on data management systems should address all of these technologies. We have selected some of the relevant technologies and put them in a framework. This framework is described in Section A.4.

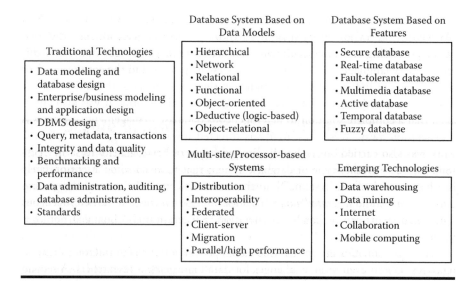

Figure A.2 **Comprehensive view of data management systems.**

A.3 Status, Vision, and Issues

Significant progress has been made on data management systems. However, many of the technologies are still stand-alone technologies, as illustrated in Figure A.3. For example, multimedia systems are yet to be successfully integrated with warehousing and mining technologies. The ultimate goal is to integrate multiple technologies so that accurate data, as well as information, are produced at the right time and distributed to the user in a timely manner. Our vision for data and information management is illustrated in Figure A.4.

The work discussed in [THUR97] addressed many of the challenges that have to be over come to accomplish this vision. In particular, integration of heterogeneous databases, as well as the use of distributed object technology for interoperability, was

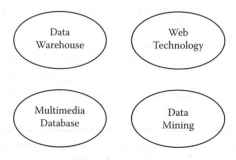

Figure A.3 **Stand-alone systems.**

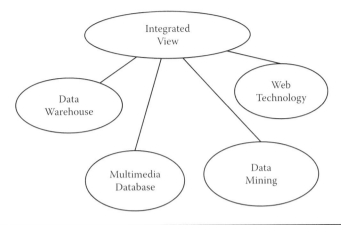

Figure A.4   Vision.

discussed. While much progress has been made on the system aspects of interoperability, semantic issues still remain a challenge. Different databases have different representations. Furthermore, the same data entity may be interpreted differently at different sites. Addressing these semantic differences and extracting useful information from the heterogeneous, and possibly multimedia, data sources are major challenges. This book has attempted to address some of the challenges through the use of data mining.

A.4 Data Management Systems Framework

For the successful development of evolvable interoperable data management systems, heterogeneous database systems integration is a major component. However, there are other technologies that have to be successfully integrated to develop techniques for efficient access and sharing of data as well as for the extraction of information from the data. To facilitate the development of data management systems to meet the requirements of various applications in fields such as medical, financial, manufacturing, and military, we have proposed a framework that can be regarded as a reference model for data management systems. Various components from this framework have to be integrated to develop data management systems to support the various applications.

Figure A.5 illustrates our framework, which can be regarded as a model for data management systems. This framework consists of three layers. One can think of component technologies, which we will also refer to as components, as belonging to a particular layer to be more or less built upon the technologies provided by the lower layer. Layer I is the Database Technology and Distribution Layer. This layer consists of database systems and distributed database systems technologies. Layer II is the Interoperability and Migration Layer. This layer consists of technologies such as heterogeneous database integration, client–server databases, multimedia

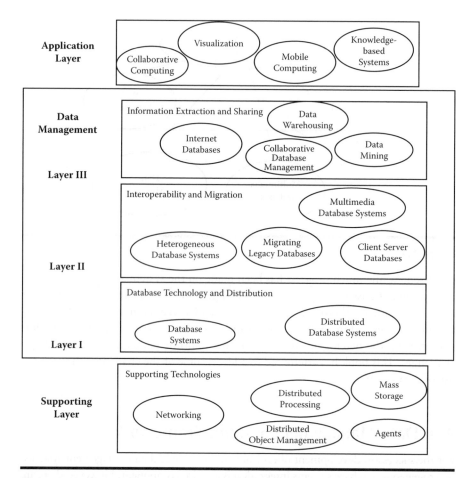

Figure A.5 Data management systems framework.

database systems to handle heterogeneous data types, and migrating legacy databases. Layer III is the Information Extraction and Sharing Layer. This layer essentially consists of technologies for some of the newer services supported by data management systems. These include data warehousing, data mining [THUR98], Web databases, and database support for collaborative applications. Data management systems may utilize lower-level technologies such as networking, distributed processing, and mass storage. We have grouped these technologies into a layer called the Supporting Technologies Layer. This supporting layer does not belong to the data management systems framework. This supporting layer also consists of some higher-level technologies such as distributed object management and agents. Also, shown in Figure A.5 is the Application Technologies Layer. Systems such as collaborative computing systems and knowledge-based systems, which belong to the Application Technologies Layer, may utilize data management systems. Note that

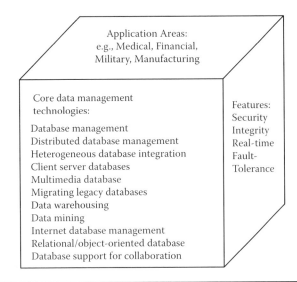

Figure A.6   A three-dimensional view of data management.

the Application Technologies Layer is also outside of the data management systems framework.

The technologies that constitute the data management systems framework can be regarded as some of the core technologies in data management. However, features such as security, integrity, real-time processing, fault tolerance, and high performance computing are needed for many applications utilizing data management technologies. Applications utilizing data management technologies may be medical, financial, or military, among others. We illustrate this in Figure A.6, where a three-dimensional view relating data management technologies with features and applications is given. For example, one could develop a secure distributed database management system for medical applications or a fault-tolerant multimedia database management system for financial applications.

Integrating the components belonging to the various layers is important to developing efficient data management systems. In addition, data management technologies have to be integrated with the application technologies to develop successful information systems. However, at present, there is limited integration between these various components. One of our previous books, *Data Management Systems Evolution and Interoperation*, focused mainly on the concepts, developments, and trends associated with each of the components shown in the framework. Another of our previous books on Web data management, *Web Data Management and Electronic Commerce*, focused on the Web database component of Layer III of the framework of Figure A.5.

Note that security cuts across all the layers. Security is needed for the supporting layers such as agents and distributed systems. Security is needed for all of the layers in the framework, including database security, distributed database security, warehousing security, Web database security and collaborative data management security. This is the topic of this book. That is, we have covered all aspects of data and applications security, including database security and information management security.

A.5 Building Information Systems from the Framework

Figure A.5 illustrated a framework for data management systems. As shown in that figure, the technologies for data management include database systems, distributed database systems, heterogeneous database systems, migrating legacy databases, multimedia database systems, data warehousing, data mining, Web databases, and database support for collaboration. Furthermore, data management systems take advantage of supporting technologies such as distributed processing and agents. Similarly, application technologies such as collaborative computing, visualization, expert systems, and mobile computing take advantage of data management systems.

Many of us have heard the term *information systems* on numerous occasions. These systems have sometimes been used interchangeably with data management systems. In our terminology, information systems are much broader than data management systems, but they do include data management systems. In fact, a framework for information systems will include not only the data management system layers, but also the supporting technologies layer as well as the application technologies layer. That is, information systems encompass all kinds of computing systems. They can be regarded as the finished product that can be used for various applications. That is, while hardware is at the lowest end of the spectrum, applications are at the highest end.

We can combine the technologies of Figure A.5 to put together information systems. For example, at the application technology level, one may need collaboration and visualization technologies so that analysts can collaboratively carry out some tasks. At the data management level, one may need both multimedia and distributed database technologies. At the supporting level, one may need mass storage as well as some distributed processing capability. This special framework is illustrated in Figure A.7. Another example is a special framework for interoperability. One may need some visualization technology to display the integrated information from the heterogeneous databases. At the data management level, we have heterogeneous database systems technology. At the supporting technology level, one may use distributed object management technology to encapsulate the heterogeneous databases. This special framework is illustrated in Figure A.8.

Finally, let us illustrate these concepts with a specific example. Suppose a group of physicians/surgeons want a system to help them collaborate and make decisions about various patients. This could be a medical video teleconferencing application. That is, at the highest level, the application is a medical application and,

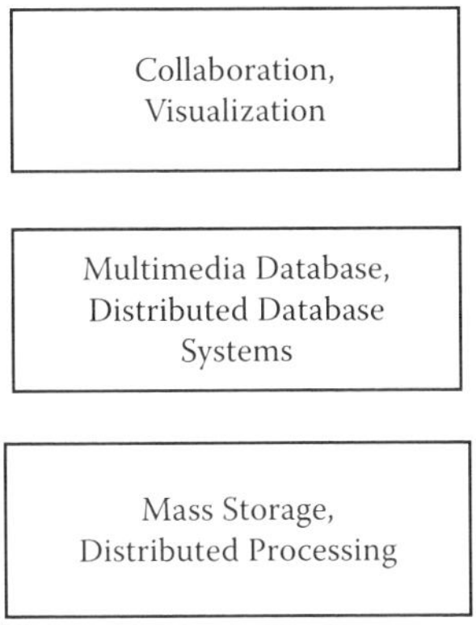

Figure A.7 Framework for multimedia data management for collaboration.

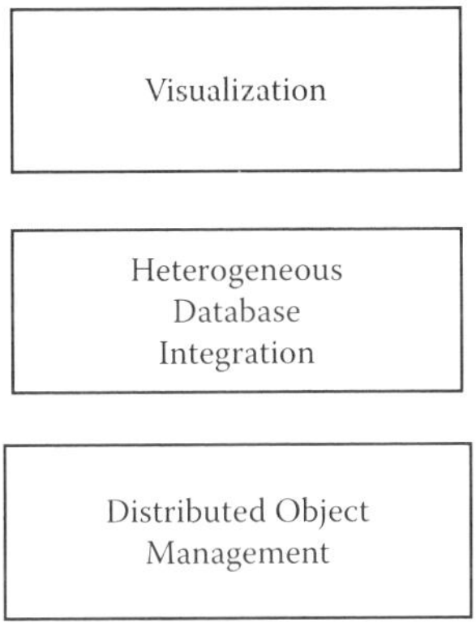

Figure A.8 Framework for heterogeneous database interoperability.

more specifically, a medical video teleconferencing application. At the application technology level, one needs a variety of technologies, including collaboration and teleconferencing. These application technologies will make use of data management technologies such as distributed database systems and multimedia database systems. That is, one may need to support multimedia data such as audio and video. The data management technologies in turn draw upon lower-level technologies such as distributed processing and networking. We illustrate this in Figure A.9.

In summary, information systems include data management systems as well as application-layer systems such as collaborative computing systems and supporting-layer systems such as distributed object management systems.

While application technologies make use of data management technologies and data management technologies make use of supporting technologies, the ultimate user of the information system is the application itself. Today, numerous

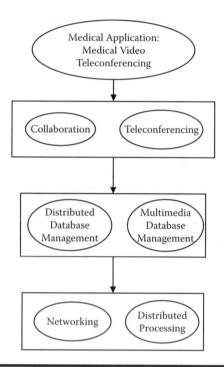

Figure A.9 Specific example.

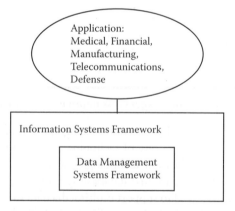

Figure A.10 Application-framework relationship.

applications make use of information systems. These applications are from multiple domains such as medical, financial, manufacturing, telecommunications, and defense. Specific applications include signal processing, electronic commerce, patient monitoring, and situation assessment. Figure A.10 illustrates the relationship between the application and the information system.

A.6 Relationships among the Texts

We have published eight books on data management and mining. These books are *Data Management Systems Evolution and Interoperation* [THUR97]; *Data Mining Technologies, Techniques, Tools, and Trends* [THUR98]; *Web Data Management and Electronic Commerce* [THUR00]; *Managing and Mining Multimedia Databases for the Electronic Enterprise* [THUR01]; *XML, Databases, and The Semantic Web* [THUR02]; *Web Data Mining and Applications in Business Intelligence and Counter-Terrorism* [THUR03]; and *Database and Applications Security: Integrating Information Security and Data Management* [THUR05]. Our last book [THUR07] evolved from Chapter 25 of [THUR05]. All of these books have evolved from the framework that we illustrate in this appendix and address different parts of the framework. The connection between these texts is illustrated in Figure A.11. Our current book [THUR10] is the ninth in the first series and has evolved from Chapter 16 of [THUR07]. As illustrated in Figure A.11, our second series began with the design and implementation of data mining tools published in 2009 [AWAD09]. This is illustrated in Figure A.12.

Note that security was addressed in all of our previous books. For example, we discussed security for multimedia systems in [THUR01]. Security and data mining was discussed in [THUR98]. Secure data interoperability was discussed in [THUR97]. This book integrates all of the concepts in security discussed in our previous books. In addition, we have also addressed many more topics in *Database and Applications Security*.

A.7 Summary and Directions

In this appendix, we have provided an overview of data management. We first discussed the developments in data management and then provided a vision for data management. Then we illustrated a framework for data management. This framework consists of three layers: the database systems layer, interoperability layer, and information extraction layer. Web data management belongs to Layer III. Finally, we showed how information systems could be built from the technologies of the framework.

Let us repeat what we mentioned in Chapter 1 now that we have described the data management framework we introduced in [THUR97]. The chapters in this book discuss security, which cuts across all the layers. Many of the technologies discussed in the framework of Figure A.5 need security. These include database systems, distributed database systems, data warehousing, and data mining.

We believe that data management is essential to many information technologies, including data mining, multimedia information processing, interoperability, and collaboration and knowledge management. This appendix focuses on data management. Security is critical for all data management technologies.

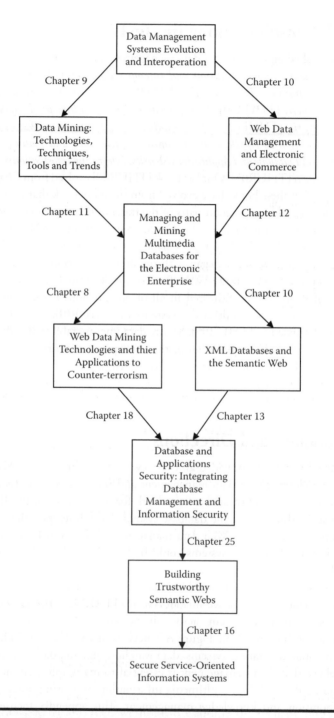

Figure A.11 Relationship between texts—series I.

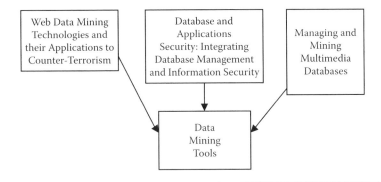

Figure A.12 Relationship between texts—series II.

References

[ACM90] Special Issue on Heterogeneous Database Systems, *ACM Computing Surveys*, September 1990.

[AWAD09] Awad, M., L. Khan, and L. Wang, *Design and Implementation of Data Mining Tools*, CRC Press, Boca Raton, FL, 2009.

[CATT91] Cattell, R., *Object Data Management Systems*, Addison-Wesley, Reading, MA, 1991.

[CODD70] Codd, E. F., A relational model of data for large shared data banks, *Communications of the ACM*, 13, 6, June 1970.

[DATE90] Date, C. J., *An Introduction to Database Management Systems*, Addison-Wesley, Reading, MA, 1990 (6th edition published in 1995 by Addison-Wesley).

[NSF90] *Proceedings of the Database Systems Workshop*, Report published by the National Science Foundation, 1990 (also in ACM SIGMOD Record, December 1990).

[NSF95] *Proceedings of the Database Systems Workshop*, Report published by the National Science Foundation, 1995 (also in ACM SIGMOD Record, March 1996).

[SIGM90] Next Generation Database Systems, *ACM SIGMOD Record*, December 1990.

[THUR97] Thuraisingham, B., *Data Management Systems Evolution and Interoperation*, CRC Press, Boca Raton, FL, 1997.

[THUR98] Thuraisingham, B., *Data Mining: Technologies, Techniques, Tools and Trends*, CRC Press, Boca Raton, FL, 1998.

[THUR00] Thuraisingham, B., *Web Data Management and Electronic Commerce*, CRC Press, Boca Raton, FL, 2000.

[THUR01] Thuraisingham, B., *Managing and Mining Multimedia Databases for the Electronic Enterprise*, CRC Press, Boca Raton, FL, 2001.

[THUR02] Thuraisingham, B., *XML, Databases and the Semantic Web*, CRC Press, Boca Raton, FL, 2002.

[THUR03] Thuraisingham, B., *Web Data Mining and Applications in Business Intelligence and Counter-Terrorism*, CRC Press, Boca Raton, FL, 2003.

[THUR05] Thuraisingham, B., *Database and Applications Security: Integrating Information Security and Data Management*, CRC Press, Boca Raton, FL, 2005.

[THUR07] Thuraisingham, B., *Building Trustworthy Semantic Webs*, CRC Press, Boca Raton, FL, 2007.

[THUR10] Thuraisingham, B., *Security for Service Oriented Information Systems*, CRC Press, Boca Raton, FL, 2010.

Figure 4.12 Relationship between ...

References

Appendix B: Database Management

B.1 Overview

Database management is fundamental to many information management technologies. Therefore, we give a brief introduction to database management in this appendix. Database systems technology has advanced a great deal during the past four decades from the legacy systems based on network and hierarchical models to relational and object-oriented database systems based on client–server architectures. We consider a database system to include both the database management system (DBMS) and the database (see also the discussion in [DATE90]). The DBMS component of the database system manages the database. The database contains persistent data. That is, the data are permanent, independent of the application programs.

The organization of this appendix is as follows. In Section B.2, relational data models, as well as entity relationship models, are discussed. In Section B.3, various types of architectures for database systems are described. These include architecture for a centralized database system, schema architecture, as well as functional architecture. Database design issues are discussed in Section B.4. Database administration issues are discussed in Section B.5. Database system functions are discussed in Section B.6. These functions include query processing, transaction management, metadata management, storage management, maintaining integrity and security, and fault tolerance. Distributed database systems are the subject of Section B.7. Heterogeneous database integration aspects are summarized in Section B.8. Managing federated databases is the subject of Section B.9. Client–server database management is the subject of Section B.10. Migrating legacy databases is discussed in Section B.11. Data warehousing will be discussed in Section B.12, while data mining will be the subject of Section B.13. The impact of the Web will be discussed in Section B.14. A brief overview of object technologies will be discussed in Section B.15. Some other database systems will be discussed in Section B.16. The appendix is summarized in Section B.17. More details can be found in [THUR97].

B.2 Relational and Entity-Relationship Data Models

B.2.1 Overview

In general, the purpose of a data model is to capture the universe that it is representing as accurately, completely, and naturally as possible [TSIC82]. In this section we discuss the essential points of the relational data model, as it is the most widely used model today. In addition we also discuss entity-relationship data models, as some of the ideas have been used in object models and, furthermore, entity-relationship models are being used extensively in database design.

Many other models exist, such as logic-based models, hypersemantic models and functional models. Discussion of all of these models is beyond the scope of this book. We do provide an overview of an object model in Section B.15, as object technology is useful for data modeling as well as for database integration.

B.2.2 Relational Data Model

With the relational model [CODD70], the database is viewed as a collection of relations. Each relation has attributes and rows. For example, Figure B.1 illustrates a database with two relations, EMP and DEPT. EMP has four attributes: SS#, Ename, Salary, and D#. DEPT has three attributes: D#, Dname, and Mgr. EMP has three rows, also called tuples, and DEPT has two rows. Each row is uniquely identified by its primary key. For example, SS# could be the primary key for EMP and D# for DEPT. Another key feature of the relational model is that each element in the relation is an atomic value, such as an integer or a string. That is, complex values such as lists are not supported.

Various operations are performed on relations. The SELECT operation selects a subset of rows satisfying certain conditions. For example, in the relation EMP, one may select tuples where the salary is more than $20K. The PROJECT operation

EMP

SS#	Ename	Salary	D#
1	John	20K	10
2	Paul	30K	20
3	Mary	40K	20

DEPT

D#	Dname	Mgr
10	Math	Smith
20	Physics	Jones

Figure B.1 Relational databases.

projects the relation onto some attributes. For example, in the relation EMP one may project onto the attributes Ename and Salary. The JOIN operation joins two relations over some common attributes. A detailed discussion of these operations is given in [DATE90] and [ULLM88].

Various languages to manipulate the relations have been proposed. Notable among these languages is the ANSI Standard SQL (Structured Query Language). This language is used to access and manipulate data in relational databases [SQL3]. There is wide acceptance of this standard among database management system vendors and users. It supports schema definition, retrieval, data manipulation, schema manipulation, transaction management, integrity, and security. Other languages include the relational calculus, first proposed in the INGRES project at the University of California at Berkeley [DATE90]. Another important concept in relational databases is the notion of a view. A view is essentially a virtual relation and is formed from the relations in the database.

B.2.3 Entity-Relationship Data Model

One of the major drawbacks of the relational data model is its lack of support for capturing the semantics of an application. This resulted in the development of semantic data models. The entity-relationship (ER) data model developed by Chen [CHEN76] can be regarded as the earliest semantic data model. In this model, the world is viewed as a collection of entities and relationships between entities. Figure B.2 illustrates two entities, EMP and DEPT. The relationship between them is WORKS.

Relationships can be one–one, many–one, or many–many. If it is assumed that each employee works in one department and each department has one employee, then WORKS is a one–one relationship. If it is assumed that an employee works in one department and each department can have many employees, then WORKS is a many–one relationship. If it is assumed that an employee works in many departments and each department has many employees, then WORKS is a many–many relationship.

Several extensions to the entity-relationship model have been proposed. One is the entity-relationship attribute model, where attributes are associated with entities as well as relationships, and another has introduced the notion of categories into the model (see, for example, the discussion in [ELMA85]). It should be noted that ER models are used mainly to design databases. That is, many database CASE (Computer Aided Software Engineering) tools are based on the ER model, where the application is represented using such a model and subsequently the database

Figure B.2   Entity-relationship representation.

(possibly relational) is generated. Current database management systems are not based on the ER model. That is, unlike the relational model, ER models did not take off in the development of database management systems.

B.3 Architectural Issues

This section describes various types of architectures for a database system. First, we illustrate a centralized architecture for a database system. Then we describe a functional architecture for a database system. In particular, the functions of the DBMS component of the database system are illustrated in this architecture. Then we discuss ANSI/SPARC's (American National Standard Institute) three-schema architecture, which has been more or less accepted by the database community [DATE90]. Finally, we describe extensible architectures.

Figure B.3 is an example of a centralized architecture. Here, the DBMS is a monolithic entity and manages a database, which is centralized. Functional architecture illustrates the functional modules of a DBMS. The major modules of a DBMS include the query processor, transaction manager, metadata manager, storage manager, integrity manager, and security manager. The functional architecture of the DBMS component of the centralized database system architecture (of Figure B.3) is illustrated in Figure B.4.

Schema describes the data in the database. It has also been referred to as the data dictionary or contents of the metadatabase. The three-schema architecture was proposed for a centralized database system in the 1960s. This is illustrated in Figure B.5. The levels are the external schema, which provides an external view; the conceptual schema, which provides a conceptual view; and the internal schema, which provides an internal view. Mappings between the different schemas must be provided to transform one representation into another. For example, at the external level, one could use ER representation. At the logical or conceptual level, one could use relational representation. At the physical level, one could use a representation based on B-trees.

There is also another aspect to architectures, and that is extensible database architectures. For example, for many applications, a DBMS may have to be

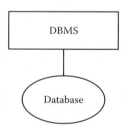

Figure B.3   Centralized architecture.

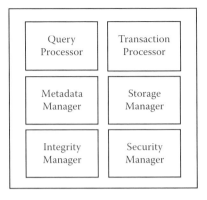

Figure B.4   Functional architecture for a DBMS.

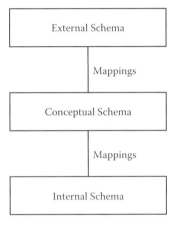

Figure B.5   Three-schema architecture.

extended with a layer to support objects or to process rules or to handle multimedia data types or even to do mining. Such an extensible architecture is illustrated in Figure B.6.

B.4 Database Design

Designing a database is a complex process. Much of the work has been on designing relational databases. There are three steps, which are illustrated in Figure B.7. The first step is to capture the entities of the application and the relationships between the entities. One could use a model such as the entity-relationship model for this purpose. More recently, object-oriented data models, which are part of object-oriented analysis and design methodologies, are becoming popular to represent the application.

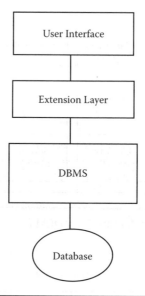

Figure B.6   Extensible DBMS.

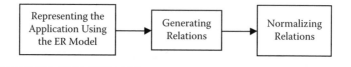

Figure B.7   Database design process.

The second step is to generate the relations from the representations. For example, from the entity-relationship diagram of Figure B.2, one could generate the relations EMP, DEPT, and WORKS. The relation WORKS will capture the relationship between employees and departments.

The third step is to design good relations. This is the normalization process. Various normal forms have been defined in the literature (see, for example, [MAIE83] and [DATE90]). For many applications, relations in third normal form would suffice. With this normal form, redundancies, complex values, and other situations that could cause potential anomalies are eliminated.

B.5 Database Administration

A database has a database administrator (DBA). It is the responsibility of the DBA to define the various schemas and mappings. In addition, the functions of the

Figure B.8   Some database administration issues.

administrator include auditing the database as well as implementing appropriate backup and recovery procedures.

The DBA could also be responsible for maintaining the security of the system. In some cases, the system security officer (SSO) maintains security. The administrator should determine the granularity of the data for auditing. For example, in some cases there is tuple-level (or row-level) auditing, while in other cases there is table-level (or relation-level) auditing. It is also the administrator's responsibility to analyze the audit data.

Note that there is a difference between database administration and data administration. Database administration assumes there is an installed database system. The DBA manages this system. Data administration functions include conducting data analysis, determining how a corporation handles its data, and enforcing appropriate policies and procedures for managing the data of a corporation. Data administration functions are carried out by the data administrator. For a discussion of data administration, we refer the reader to [DMH97]. Figure B.8 illustrates various database administration issues.

B.6 Database Management System Functions

B.6.1 Overview

The functional architecture of a DBMS was illustrated in Figure B.4 (see also [ULLM88]). The functions of a DBMS carry out its operations. A DBMS essentially manages a database, and it provides support to the user by enabling him to query and update the database. Therefore, the basic functions of a DBMS are query processing and update processing. In some applications such as banking, queries and updates are issued as part of transactions. Therefore, transaction management is also another function of a DBMS. To carry out these functions, information about the data in the database has to be maintained. This information is called the metadata. The function that is associated with managing the metadata is metadata management. Special techniques are needed to manage the data stores that actually store the data. The function that is associated with managing these techniques is storage management. To ensure that the foregoing functions are carried out properly and that the user gets accurate data, there are some additional functions. These include security management, integrity management, and fault management (i.e., fault tolerance).

This section focuses on some of the key functions of a DBMS. These are query processing, transaction management, metadata management, storage management, maintaining integrity, and fault tolerance. We discuss each of these functions in Sections B.6.2 to B.6.7. In Section B.6.8, we discuss some other functions.

B.6.2 Query Processing

Query operation is the most commonly used function in a DBMS. It should be possible for users to query the database and obtain answers to their queries. There are several aspects to query processing. First of all, a good query language is needed. Languages such as SQL are popular for relational databases. Such languages are being extended for other types of databases. The second aspect is techniques for query processing. Numerous algorithms have been proposed for query processing in general and for the JOIN operation in particular. Also, different strategies can be used to execute a particular query. The costs for the various strategies are computed, and the one with the least cost is usually selected for processing. This process is called *query optimization*. Cost is generally determined by the disk access. The goal is to minimize disk access in processing a query.

Users pose a query using a language. The constructs of the language have to be transformed into constructs understood by the database system. This process is called *query transformation*. Query transformation is carried out in stages based on the various schemas. For example, a query based on the external schema is transformed into a query on the conceptual schema. This is then transformed into a query on the physical schema. In general, rules used in the transformation process include the factoring of common subexpressions and pushing selections and projections down in the query tree as much as possible. If selections and projections are performed before the joins, then the cost of the joins can be reduced by a considerable amount.

Figure B.9 illustrates the modules in query processing. The user interface manager accepts queries, parses the queries, and then gives them to the query transformer. The query transformer and query optimizer communicate with each other to produce an execution strategy. The database is accessed through the storage manager. The response manager gives responses to the user.

B.6.3 Transaction Management

A transaction is a program unit that must be executed in its entirety or not executed at all. If transactions are executed serially, then there is a performance bottleneck. Therefore, transactions are executed concurrently. Appropriate techniques must ensure that the database is consistent when multiple transactions update the

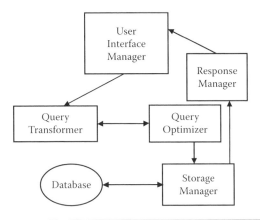

Figure B.9   Query processor.

database. That is, transactions must satisfy the ACID (atomicity, consistency, iso-lation, and durability) properties. Major aspects of transaction management are serializability, concurrency control, and recovery. We discuss them briefly in this section. For a detailed discussion of transaction management, we refer the reader to [KORT86] and [BERN87].

Serializability: A schedule is a sequence of operations performed by multiple transactions. Two schedules are equivalent if their outcomes are the same. A serial schedule is a schedule where no two transactions execute concurrently. An objective in transaction management is to ensure that any schedule is equivalent to a serial schedule. Such a schedule is called a serializable sched-ule. Various conditions for testing the serializability of a schedule have been formulated for a DBMS.

Concurrency Control: Concurrency control techniques ensure that the data-base is in a consistent state when multiple transactions update the database. Three popular concurrency control techniques that ensure the serializability of schedules are locking, time stamping, and validation (which is also called *optimistic concurrency control*).

Recovery: If a transaction aborts due to some failure, then the database must be brought to a consistent state. This is transaction recovery. One solution to han-dling transaction failure is to maintain log files. The transaction's actions are recorded in the log file. So, if a transaction aborts, then the database is brought back to a consistent state by undoing the actions of the transaction. The infor-mation for the undo operation is found in the log file. Another solution is to record the actions of a transaction but not make any changes to the database. Only if a transaction commits should the database be updated. This means that log files have to be kept in stable storage. Various modifications to the foregoing techniques have been proposed to handle the different situations.

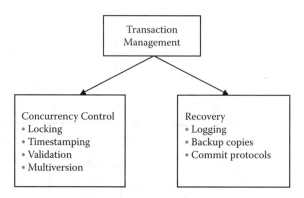

Figure B.10   Some aspects of transaction management.

When transactions are executed at multiple data sources, then a protocol called two-phase commit is used to ensure that the multiple data sources are consistent. Figure B.10 illustrates the various aspects of transaction management.

B.6.4 Storage Management

The storage manager is responsible for accessing the database. To improve the efficiency of query and update algorithms, appropriate access methods and index strategies have to be enforced. That is, in generating strategies for executing query and update requests, the access methods and index strategies that are used need to be taken into consideration. The access methods used to access the database would depend on the indexing methods. Therefore, creating and maintaining appropriate index files is a major issue in database management systems. By using an appropriate indexing mechanism, the query processing algorithms may not have to search the entire database. Instead, the data to be retrieved could be accessed directly. Consequently, the retrieval algorithms are more efficient. Figure B.11 illustrates an example of an indexing strategy where the database is indexed by projects.

Much research has been carried out on developing appropriate access methods and index strategies for relational database systems. Some examples of index strategies are B-trees and hashing [DATE90]. Current research is focusing on developing such mechanisms for object-oriented database systems with support for multimedia data as well as for Web database systems, among others.

B.6.5 Metadata Management

Metadata describes the data in the database. For example, in the case of the relational database illustrated in Figure B.1, metadata would include the following information: the database has two relations, EMP and DEPT; EMP has four attributes and DEPT has three attributes, etc. One of the main issues is developing

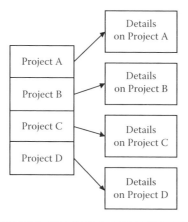

Figure B.11   An example index on projects.

Relation REL

Relation	Attribute
EMP	SS#
EMP	Ename
EMP	Salary
EMP	D#
DEPT	D#
DEPT	Dname
DEPT	Mgr

Figure B.12   Metadata relation.

a data model for metadata. In our example, one could use a relational model to model the metadata also. The metadata relation REL shown in Figure B.12 consists of information about relations and attributes.

In addition to information about the data in the database, metadata also includes information on access methods, index strategies, security constraints, and integrity constraints. One could also include policies and procedures as part of the metadata. In other words, there is no standard definition for metadata. There are, however, efforts to standardize metadata (see, for example, the IEEE Mass Storage Committee efforts as well as IEEE Conferences on Metadata [MASS]. Metadata continues to evolve as database systems evolve into multimedia database systems and Web database systems.

Once the metadata is defined, the issues include managing the metadata. What are the techniques for querying and updating the metadata? Since all of the other DBMS components need to access the metadata for processing, what are the interfaces between the metadata manager and the other components? Metadata management is fairly well understood for relational database systems. The current challenge is in managing the metadata for more complex systems such as digital libraries and Web database systems.

B.6.6 Database Integrity

Concurrency control and recovery techniques maintain the integrity of the database. In addition, there is another type of database integrity, and that is enforcing integrity constraints. There are two types of integrity constraints enforced in database systems. These are application-independent integrity constraints and application-specific integrity constraints. Integrity mechanisms also include techniques for determining the quality of the data. For example, what is the accuracy of the data and that of the source? What are the mechanisms for maintaining the quality of the data? How accurate is the data on output? For a discussion of integrity based on data quality, we refer the reader to [DQ]. Note that data quality is very important for mining and warehousing. If the data that is mined is not good, then one cannot rely on the results.

Application-independent integrity constraints include the primary key constraint, the entity integrity rule, referential integrity constraint, and the various functional dependencies involved in the normalization process (see the discussion in [DATE90]). Application-specific integrity constraints are those constraints that are specific to an application. Examples include "an employee's salary cannot decrease" and "no manager can manage more than two departments." Various techniques have been proposed to enforce application-specific integrity constraints. For example, when the database is updated, these constraints are checked, and the data are validated. Aspects of database integrity are illustrated in Figure B.13.

B.6.7 Fault Tolerance

The previous two sections discussed database integrity and security. A closely related feature is fault tolerance. It is almost impossible to guarantee that the database will

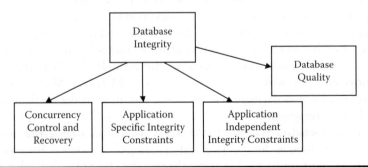

Figure B.13 Some aspects of database integrity.

```
Checkpoint A
Start Processing
*

*

Acceptance Test
If OK, the go to Checkpoint B
Else Roll Back to Checkpoint A

Checkpoint B
Start Processing
*

*
```

Figure B.14   Some aspects of fault tolerance.

function as planned. In reality, various faults could occur. These could be hardware faults or software faults. As mentioned earlier, one of the major issues in transaction management is to ensure that the database is brought back to a consistent state in the presence of faults. The solutions proposed include maintaining appropriate log files to record the actions of a transaction in case its actions have to be retraced.

Another approach to handling faults is checkpointing. Various checkpoints are placed during the course of database processing. At each checkpoint, it is ensured that the database is in a consistent state. Therefore, if a fault occurs during processing, then the database must be brought back to the last checkpoint. In this way, it can be guaranteed that the database is consistent. Closely associated with checkpointing are acceptance tests. After various processing steps, the acceptance tests are checked. If the techniques pass the tests, then they can proceed further. Some aspects of fault tolerance are illustrated in Figure B.14.

B.6.8 Other Functions

In this section, we will briefly discuss some of the other functions of a database system. They are security, real-time processing, managing heterogeneous data types, auditing, view management, and backup and recovery.

Security: Data has to be protected from unauthorized access and modification.
Real-time processing: In some situations, the database system may have to meet real-time constraints. That is, the transactions will have to meet deadlines.
Heterogeneous data types: The database system may have to manage multimedia data types such as voice, video, text, and images.
Auditing: The databases may have to be audited so that unauthorized access can be monitored.

View management: As stated earlier, views are virtual relations created from base relations. There are many challenges related to view management.

Backup and recovery: The DBA has to backup the databases and ensure that the database is not corrupted. Some aspects were discussed under fault tolerance. More details are given in [DATE90].

B.7 Distributed Databases

Although many definitions of a distributed database system have been given, there is no standard definition. Our discussion of distributed database system concepts and issues has been influenced by the discussion in [CERI84]. A distributed database system includes a distributed database management system (DDBMS), a distributed database, and a network for interconnection. The DDBMS manages the distributed database. A distributed database is data that is distributed across multiple databases. Our choice architecture for a distributed database system is a multidatabase architecture, which is tightly coupled. This architecture is illustrated in Figure B.15. We have chosen such an architecture, as we can explain the concepts for both homogeneous and heterogeneous systems based on this approach. In this architecture, the nodes are connected via a communication subsystem, and local applications are handled by the local DBMS. In addition, each node is also involved in at least one global application, so there is no centralized control in this architecture. The DBMSs are connected through a component called the Distributed Processor (DP). In a homogeneous environment, the local DBMSs are homogeneous, while in a heterogeneous environment, the local DBMSs may be heterogeneous.

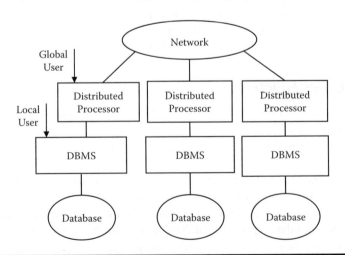

Figure B.15   An architecture for a DDBMS.

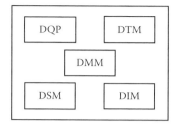

Figure B.16   Modules of the DP.

Distributed database system functions include distributed query processing, distributed transaction management, distributed metadata management, and enforcing security and integrity across the multiple nodes. The DP is an essential component of the DDBMS. It is this module that connects the different local DBMSs. That is, each local DBMS is augmented by a DP. The modules of the DP are illustrated in Figure B.16. The components are the Distributed Metadata Manager (DMM), the Distributed Query Processor (DQP), the Distributed Transaction Manager (DTM), the Distributed Security Manager (DSM), and the Distributed Integrity Manager (DIM). DMM manages the global metadata. The global metadata includes information on the schemas, which describe the relations in the distributed database, the way the relations are fragmented, the locations of the fragments, and the constraints enforced. DQP is responsible for distributed query processing; DTM is responsible for distributed transaction management; DSM is responsible for enforcing global security constraints; and DIM is responsible for maintaining integrity at the global level. Note that the modules of DP communicate with their peers at the remote nodes. For example, the DQP at node 1 communicates with the DQP at node 2 for handling distributed queries.

B.8 Heterogeneous Database Integration

Figure B.17 illustrates an example of interoperability between heterogeneous database systems. The goal is to provide transparent access, both for users and application programs, for querying and executing transactions (see, for example, [IEEE91] and [WIED92]). Note that in a heterogeneous environment, the local DBMSs may be heterogeneous. Furthermore, the modules of the DP have both local DBMS–specific processing as well as local DBMS–independent processing. We call such a DP a heterogeneous distributed processor (HDP).

There are several technical issues that need to be resolved for the successful interoperation between these diverse database systems. Note that heterogeneity could exist with respect to different data models, schemas, query processing techniques, query languages, transaction management techniques, semantics, integrity,

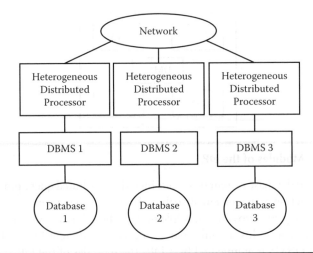

Figure B.17 **Interoperability of heterogeneous database systems.**

and security. There are two approaches to interoperability. One is the federated database management approach, in which a collection of cooperating, autonomous, and possibly heterogeneous component database systems, each belonging to one or more federations, communicates with each other. The other is the client–server approach, where the goal is for multiple clients to communicate with multiple servers in a transparent manner. We discuss both federated and client–server approaches in Sections B.9 and B.10.

B.9 Federated Databases

As stated by Sheth and Larson [SHET90], a federated database system is a collection of cooperating but autonomous database systems belonging to a federation. That is, the goal is for the database management systems, which belong to a federation, to cooperate with one another and yet maintain some degree of autonomy. Note that to be consistent with the terminology, we distinguish between a federated database management system and a federated database system. A federated database system includes a federated database management system, the local DBMSs, and the databases. The federated database management system is that component which manages the different databases in a federated environment.

Figures B.18 illustrates a federated database system. Database systems A and B belong to federation F1, while database systems B and C belong to federation F2. We can use the architecture illustrated in Figure B.18 for a federated database system. In addition to handling heterogeneity, the HDP also has to handle the federated environment. That is, techniques have to be adapted to handle cooperation

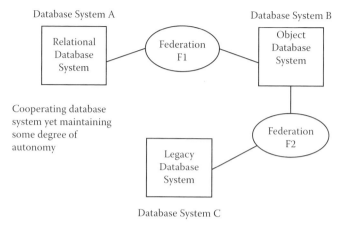

Figure B.18   Federated database management.

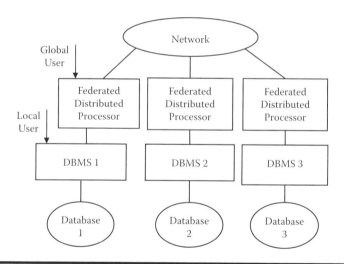

Figure B.19   Architecture for a federated database system.

and autonomy. We have called such an HDP an FDP (Federated Distributed Processor). An architecture for an FDS is illustrated in Figure B.19.

Figure B.20 illustrates an example of an autonomous environment. There is communication between components A and B and between B and C. Due to autonomy, it is assumed that components A and C do not wish to communicate with each other. Now, component A may get requests from its own user or from component B. In this case, it has to decide which request to honor first. Also, there is a possibility for component C to get information from component A through

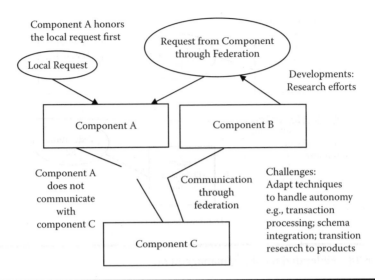

Figure B.20 Autonomy.

component B. In such a situation, component A may have to negotiate with component B before it gives a reply to component B. The developments to deal with autonomy are still in the research stages. The challenge is to handle transactions in an autonomous environment. Transitioning the research into commercial products is also a challenge.

B.10 Client–Server Databases

Earlier sections described interoperability between heterogeneous database systems and focused on the federated database systems approach. In this approach, different database systems cooperatively interoperate with each other. This section describes another aspect of interoperability, which is based on the client–server paradigm. Major database system vendors have migrated to an architecture called the client–server architecture. With this approach, multiple clients access the various database servers through some network. A high-level view of client–server communication is illustrated in Figure B.21. The ultimate goal is for multivendor clients to communicate with multivendor servers in a transparent manner, as illustrated in Figure B.22.

One of the major challenges in client–server technology is to determine the modules of the distributed database system that need to be placed at the client and server sides. In one approach, all the modules of the distributed processor may be placed at the client side, while the modules of the local DBMS are placed at the server side. Note that with this approach, the client does a lot of processing, and this is called the "fat client" approach. There are other options also. For example,

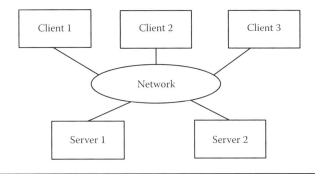

Figure B.21   Client-server-architecture-based interoperability.

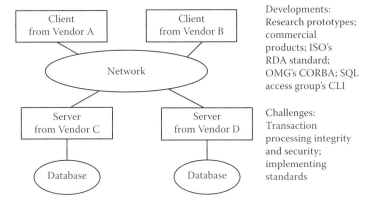

Figure B.22   Multivendor client–server interoperability.

some of the modules of the distributed processor could be part of the server, in which case the client would be "thinner."

In order to facilitate the communication between multiple clients and servers, various standards are being proposed. One example is the International Standards Organization's (ISO) Remote Database Access (RDA) standard. This standard provides a generic interface for communication between a client and a server. Microsoft Corporation's Open Database Connectivity (ODBC) is also becoming increasingly popular for clients to communicate with the servers. OMG's Common Object Request Architecture (CORBA) provides specifications for client–server communication based on object technology (see [OMG95]). Here, one possibility is to encapsulate the database servers as objects and for the clients to issue appropriate requests and access the servers through an object request broker. Other standards include IBM's DRDA (Distributed Relational Database Access) and the SQL Access Group's Call Level Interface (CLI).

In one of our previous books [THUR97], we described various aspects of client–server interoperability. In particular, technical issues for client–server interoperability, architectural approaches, and the standards proposed for communication between clients and servers were discussed. A useful reference on client–server data management is [ORFA94]. It should be noted that client–server data management technology is advancing rapidly, and for up-to-date information we encourage the reader to keep up with the developments from the Web.

B.11 Migrating Legacy Databases and Applications

Many database systems developed some 20 to 30 years ago are becoming obsolete. These systems use older hardware and software. Between now and the next few decades, many of today's information systems and applications may become obsolete. Due to resource and, in certain cases, budgetary constraints, new developments of next-generation systems may not be possible in many areas. Therefore, current systems need to become easier, faster, less costly to upgrade, and less difficult to support. Legacy database system and application migration is a complex problem, and many of the efforts under way are still not mature. While a good book has been published on this subject [BROD95], there is no uniform approach to migration. Since migrating legacy databases and applications is becoming a necessity for most organizations, both government and commercial, one could expect a considerable amount of resources to be expended in this area in the near future. The research issues are also not well understood.

Migrating legacy applications and databases also have an impact on heterogeneous database integration. Typically, a heterogeneous database environment may include legacy databases as well as some next-generation databases. In many cases, an organization may want to migrate the legacy database system to an architecture such as the client–server architecture and still want the migrated system to be part of the heterogeneous environment. This means that the functions of the heterogeneous database system may be impacted due to this migration process.

Two candidate approaches have been proposed for migrating legacy systems. One is to complete all of the migration at once. The other is incremental migration. That is, as the legacy system gets migrated, the new parts have to interoperate with the old parts. Various issues and challenges to migration are discussed in [THUR97]. Figure B.23 illustrates an incremental approach to migrating legacy databases through the use of object request brokers.

B.12 Data Warehousing

Data warehousing is one of the key data management technologies to support data mining and data analysis. Several organizations are building their own warehouses. Commercial database system vendors are marketing warehousing products. What then is a data warehouse? The idea behind this is that it is often cumbersome to

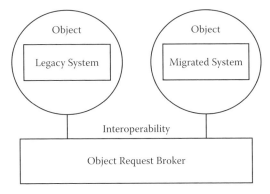

Figure B.23   Migrating legacy databases.

access data from heterogeneous databases. Several processing modules need to cooperate with one another to process a query in a heterogeneous environment. Therefore, a data warehouse will bring together the essential data from heterogeneous databases. In this way, the users need to query only the warehouse.

As stated by Inmon [INMO93], data warehouses are subject oriented. Their design depends to a great extent on the application utilizing them. They integrate diverse and possibly heterogeneous data sources. They are persistent. That is, the warehouses are very much like databases. They vary with time. This is because as the data sources from which the warehouse is built get updated, the changes have to be reflected in the warehouse. Essentially, data warehouses provide support for decision support functions of an enterprise or an organization. For example, while the data sources may have the raw data, the data warehouse may have correlated data, summary reports, and aggregate functions applied to the raw data.

Figure B.24 illustrates a data warehouse. The data sources are managed by database systems A, B, and C. The information in these databases is merged and put into a warehouse. The question is, how do you merge the data sources and build the warehouse? One way is to determine the types of queries that users would pose, then analyze the data, and store only the data that is required by the user. This is called online analytical processing (OLAP) as opposed to online transaction processing (OLTP).

Note that it is not always the case that the warehouse has all the information for a query. In this case, the warehouse may have to get the data from the heterogeneous data sources to complete the execution of the query. Another challenge is, what happens to the warehouse when the individual databases are updated? How are the updates propagated to the warehouse? How can security be maintained? These are some of the issues that are being investigated.

With a data warehouse, data may often be viewed differently by different applications. That is, the data is multidimensional. For example, the payroll department may want data to be in a certain format, while the project department may want

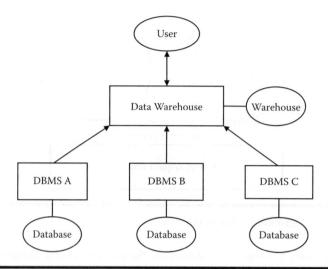

Figure B.24 Data warehouse example.

data to be in a different format. The warehouse must provide support for such multidimensional data.

B.13 Data Mining

Data mining is the process of posing various queries and extracting useful information, patterns, and trends often previously unknown from large quantities of data possibly stored in databases. For many organizations, the goals of data mining include improving marketing capabilities, detecting abnormal patterns, and predicting the future based on past experiences and current trends. There is clearly a need for this technology. There are large amounts of current and historical data being stored. Therefore, as databases become larger, it becomes increasingly difficult to support decision making. In addition, the data could be from multiple sources and multiple domains. There is a clear need to analyze the data to support planning and other functions of an enterprise.

Various terms have been used to refer to data mining. These include knowledge/data/information discovery and knowledge/data/information extraction. Note that some define data mining to be the process of extracting previously unknown information, while knowledge discovery is defined as the process of making sense out of the extracted information.

Some data mining techniques include those based on statistical reasoning techniques, inductive logic programming, machine learning, fuzzy sets, and neural networks, among others. The data mining outcomes include classification (finding rules to partition data into groups), association (finding rules to make associations between data), and sequencing (finding rules to order data). Essentially, one arrives at some hypothesis, which is the information extracted, from examples and patterns observed. These patterns are observed by posing a series of queries; each query may depend on the responses obtained to the previous queries posed. There have been several developments in data mining. A discussion of the various tools is given in [KDN]. A good discussion of the outcomes and techniques are given in [AGRA93] and [BERR97].

Data mining is an integration of multiple technologies. These include data management such as database management, data warehousing, statistics, machine learning, decision support, and others such as visualization and parallel computing. There is a series of steps involved in data mining. These include getting the data organized for mining, determining the desired outcomes, selecting tools, carrying out the mining, pruning the results so that only the useful ones are considered further, taking actions from the mining, and evaluating the actions to determine benefits.

While several developments have been made, there are also many challenges. For example, due to the large volumes of data, how can the algorithms determine which technique to select and what type of data mining to do? Furthermore, the data may be incomplete or inaccurate. At times there may be redundant information, and at times there may not be sufficient information. It is also desirable to have data mining tools that can switch to multiple techniques and support multiple outcomes. Some of the current trends in data mining include mining Web data, mining distributed and heterogeneous databases, and privacy-preserving data mining where one ensures that one can get useful results from mining and at the same time maintain the privacy of the individuals. We have discussed many of these trends in [THUR98], [THUR01], and [THUR03]. Figure B.25 illustrates the various aspects of data mining.

B.14 Impact of the Web

The explosion of users on the Internet and the increasing number of World Wide Web servers with large quantities of data are rapidly advancing database management on the Web. For example, the heterogeneous information sources have to be integrated so that users access the servers in a transparent and timely manner. Security and privacy are becoming major concerns. So are other issues such as copyright protection and ownership of the data. Policies and procedures have to be set up to address these issues.

Database management functions for the Web include query processing, metadata management, storage management, transaction management, security, and integrity. In [THUR00], we have examined various database management system functions and discussed the impact of Internet database access on these functions. Figure B.26 illustrates applications accessing various database systems on the Web.

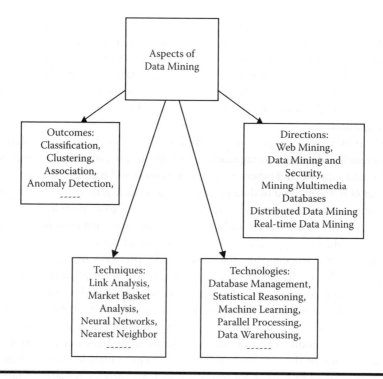

Figure B.25   Aspects of data mining.

For more details on Web data management, we refer the reader to [THUR00] and [THUR02]. We provide an overview in Appendix D.

B.15 Object Technology

B.15.1 Overview

Object technology, also referred to as OT or OOT (object-oriented technology), encompasses different technologies. These include object-oriented programming languages, object database management systems, object-oriented analysis and design, distributed object management, and components and frameworks. The underlying theme for all these types of object technologies is the object model. That is, the object model is the very essence of object technology. Any object system is based on some object model, whether it is a programming language or a database system. The interesting aspect of an object model is that everything in the real world can be modeled as an object.

The organization of this section is as follows. In Section B.15.2, we describe the essential properties of object models (OODM). All of the other object technologies

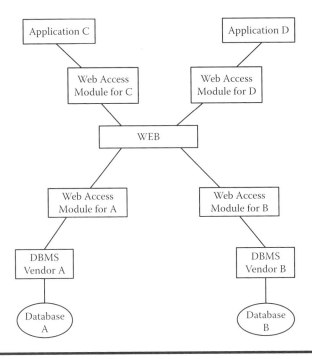

Figure B.26   Database access through the Web.

will be summarized in Section B.15.3. These include object-oriented programming languages (OOPL), object-oriented database systems (OODB), object-oriented analysis and design (OOAD), distributed object management (DOM), and components and frameworks (C&F). An overview of the various object technologies is illustrated in Figure B.27.

B.15.2 Object Data Model

Several object data models were proposed in the 1980s. Initially, these models were to support programming languages such as Smalltalk. Later, these models were enhanced to support database systems as well as other complex systems. This section provides an overview of the essential features of object models. While there are no standard object models, the Unified Modeling Language (UML) proposed by the prominent object technologists [BOOC98] has gained increasing popularity and has almost become the standard object model in recent years. Our discussion of the object model has been influenced by much of our work in object database systems as well as the one proposed by Won Kim et al. [BANE87]. We call it an object-oriented data model.

The key points in an object-oriented model are encapsulation, inheritance, and polymorphism. With an object-oriented data model, the database is viewed

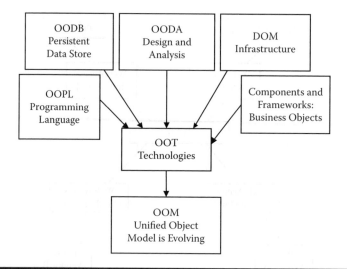

Figure B.27   Object technologies.

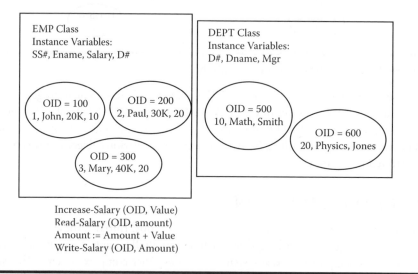

Figure B.28   Objects and classes.

as a collection of objects [BANE87]. Each object has a unique identifier called the object-ID. Objects with similar properties are grouped into a class. For example, employee objects are grouped into EMP class, while department objects are grouped into DEPT class as shown in Figure B.28. A class has instance variables describing the properties. Instance variables of EMP are SS#, Ename, Salary, and D#, while the instance variables of DEPT are D#, Dname, and Mgr. The objects in

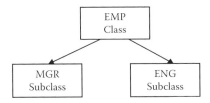

Figure B.29 Class–subclass hierarchy.

a class are its instances. As illustrated in the figure, EMP has three instances, and DEPT has two instances.

A key concept in object-oriented data modeling is encapsulation. That is, an object has well-defined interfaces. The state of an object can only be accessed through interface procedures called methods. For example, EMP may have a method called Increase-Salary. The code for Increase-Salary is illustrated in Figure B.29. A message, say Increase-Salary (1, 10K), may be sent to the object with object ID of 1. The object's current salary is read and updated by 10K.

A second key concept in an object model is inheritance, where a subclass inherits properties from its parent class. This feature is illustrated in Figure B.29, where the EMP class has MGR (manager) and ENG (engineer) as its subclasses. Other key concepts in an object model include polymorphism and aggregation. These features are discussed in [BANE87]. Note that a second type of inheritance is when the instances of a class inherit the properties of the class.

A third concept is polymorphism. This is the situation where one can pass different types of arguments for the same function. For example, to calculate the area, one can pass a sphere or a cylinder object. Operators can be overloaded also. That is, the add operation can be used to add two integers or real numbers.

Another concept is the aggregate hierarchy also called the composite object or the is-part-of hierarchy. In this case, an object has component objects. For example, a book object has component section objects. A section object has component paragraph objects. Aggregate hierarchy is illustrated in Figure B.30.

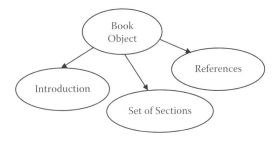

Figure B.30 Aggregate object.

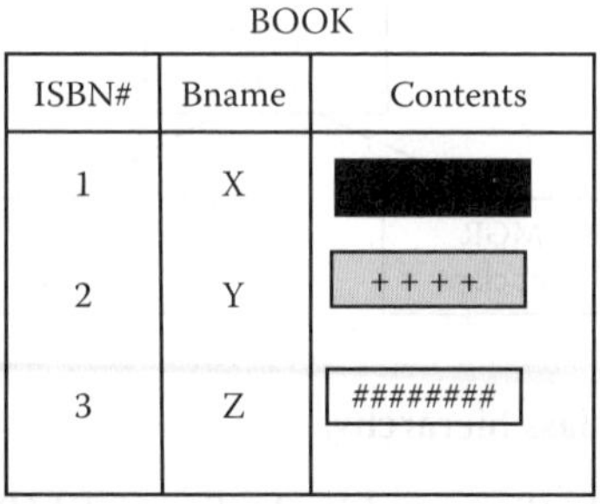

BOOK

ISBN#	Bname	Contents
1	X	████████
2	Y	+ + + +
3	Z	########

Figure B.31   Object-relational data model.

Objects also have relationships among themselves. For example, an employee object has an association with the department object, which is the department he is working in. Also, the instance variables of an object could take integers, lists, arrays, or even other objects as values. Many of these concepts are discussed in the book by Cattell [CATT91]. The Object Data Management Group has also proposed standards for object data models [ODMG93].

Relational database vendors are extending their system with support for objects. In one approach, the relational model is extended with an object layer. The object layer manages objects, while the relational database system manages the relations. Such systems are called *extended relational database systems.* In another approach, the relational model has objects as its elements. Such a model is called an *object-relational data model* and is illustrated in Figure B.31. A system based on the object-relational data model is called an *object-relational database system.*

B.15.3 *Other Object Technologies*

Programming languages: Object-oriented programming languages (OOPLs) date back to Simula in the 1960s. However, it really became popular with the advent of Smalltalk by Xerox Palo Alto Research Center in the late 1970s. Smalltalk is a pure object-oriented programming language where everything is considered to be an object. Around the mid-1980s, languages such as LISP and C were being made object-oriented by extending them to support objects. One such popular extension is the language C++. Around the 1990s, Sun Microsystems wanted to develop a language for its embedded computing and appliance business that would not have all of the problems associated with C++, such as pointers. The resulting language was the popular language Java.

Database systems: We have discussed three types of object database systems: object-oriented database systems, which make object-oriented programming languages persistent; extended-relational systems, which extend relational database systems with object layers; and object-relational database systems, where objects are nested within relations.

Design and analysis: In the 1980s, there was a lot of interest in using object technology to design and analyze applications. Various design and analysis methodologies were proposed. Notable among them were the method of Booch [BOOC93], Use cases by Jacobson [JACO92], and OMT (Object Modeling Technique) by Rumbaugh et al. [RUMB90]. Then the various groups merged and produced a unified methodology called UML (Unified Modeling Language) [FOWL97]. UML has essential features from the three approaches and is now more or less a standard for object modeling and analysis.

Distributed object management: Distributed object management (DOM) technology is used to interconnect heterogeneous databases, systems, and applications. With this approach, the various systems and applications are encapsulated as objects, and the objects communicate with each other by exchanging messages. An example of a distributed object management (DOM) system that is being used as a middleware to connect heterogeneous database systems is a system based on OMG's CORBA. CORBA is a specification that enables heterogeneous applications, systems, and databases to interoperate with each other (see [OMG95]).

Components and frameworks: This is one of the more recent object technologies and has really taken off since the mid-1990s. A framework can be considered to be a skeleton with classes and interconnections. One then instantiates this skeleton for various applications. Frameworks are being developed for different application domains, including financial and medical. Components, on the other hand, are classes, objects, and relationships between them that can be reused. Components can be built for different applications. A survey of the field was provided in *Communications of the ACM* in October 1997 by Fayad and Schmidt [ACM97].

B.16 Other Database Systems

This section briefly discusses various other database systems, as illustrated in Figure B.32.

Real-time database systems: These are systems where the queries and transactions will have to meet timing constraints. Details are given in [RAMA93].

Deductive database systems: These are systems that use logic as a data model. These are logic programming systems that manage data. More details can be found in [FROS86] and [LLOY87].

Multimedia database systems: These are database systems that manage multimedia data such as text, audio, video, and images. Details can be found in [PRAB97].

```
Types of Database Systems:
Network and Hierarchical Databases;
Relational Databases;
Object and Object Relational Databases;
Distributed and Heterogeneous Databases
Functional Databases;
Real-time and Fault Tolerant Databases
Multimedia Databases;
Spatio-Temporal and Scientific Databases;
High Performance and Parallel Databases;
---------
```

Figure B.32 Types of database systems.

Functional database systems: These systems were developed in the early 1980s. The database is viewed as a collection of functions, and query evaluation amounts to function execution. Details can be found in [BUNE82].

Parallel database systems: These systems use parallel processing techniques for executing queries and transactions so that the speed can be improved. More details can be found in [DEWI90].

Spatio-temporal database systems: For applications such as geospatial information systems and motion data management, one needs to model objects with spatial and temporal properties. Therefore, managing spatio-temporal data structures is important for such applications.

Other systems: Many other systems such as scientific database systems and engineering information systems have been developed. An overview of some of these systems is given in [ACM90].

B.17 Summary and Directions

This appendix has discussed various aspects of database systems and provided some background information to understand the various chapters in this book. We began with a discussion of various data models. We chose relational and entity-relationship models as they are more relevant to what we have addressed in this book. Then we provided an overview of various types of architectures for database systems. These include functional and schema architectures. Next, we discussed database design aspects and database administration issues. We also provided an overview of the various functions of database systems. These include query processing, transaction management, storage management, metadata management, integrity, and fault tolerance. Next, we briefly discussed distributed databases and interoperability. This was followed by a discussion of data warehousing, data mining, and the impact of the Web. We also provided a brief overview of object technology, and discussed various other database systems.

Various texts and articles have been published on database systems, and we have referenced them throughout the book. There are also some major conferences on database systems, including ACM SIGMOD Conference series [SIGM], Very Large Database Conference series [VLDB], IEEE Data Engineering Conference series [DE], and the European Extended Database Technology Conference series [EDBT].

References

[ACM90] Special Issue on Heterogeneous Database Systems, *ACM Computing Surveys*, 22, 3, 183–293, 1990.

[ACM97] Special Issue on Components and Frameworks, *Communications of the ACM*, Volume, 10, 1997.

[AGRA93] Agrawal, A., T. Imielinski, and A. Swani, Database mining a performance perspective, *IEEE Transactions on Knowledge and Data Engineering*, 5, 6, 1993.

[BANE87] Banerjee, J., H. Chou, J. Garza, W. Kim, D. Woelk, N. Ballou, and H. Kim, A data model for object-oriented applications, *ACM Transactions on Office Information Systems*, 5, 1, 1987.

[BERN87] Bernstein, P., V. Hadzilacos, and N. Goodman, *Concurrency Control and Recovery in Database Systems*, Addison-Wesley, Reading, MA, 1987.

[BERR97] Berry, M. and G. Linoff, *Data Mining Techniques for Marketing, Sales, and Customer Support*, John Wiley & Sons, New York, 1997.

[BOOC93] Booch, G., *Object-Oriented Analysis and Design with Applications*, Second Edition, Addison-Wesley, Menlo Park CA, 1993.

[BOOC98] Booch, G., J. Rumbaugh, and I. Jacobson, *The Unified Modeling Language User Guide*, Addison-Wesley, Reading, MA, 1998.

[BROD95] Brodie, M. and M. Stonebraker, *Migrating Legacy Databases*, Morgan Kaufmann, San Mateo, CA, 1995.

[BUNE82] Buneman, P., R. Frankel, and R. Nikhil, An implementation technique for database query languages, *ACM Transactions on Database Systems*, 7, 2, 1982.

[CATT91] Cattel, R., *Object Data Management Systems*, Addison-Wesley, Reading, MA, 1991.

[CERI84] Ceri, S. and G. Pelagatti, *Distributed Databases, Principles and Systems*, McGraw-Hill, New York, 1984.

[CHEN76] Chen, P., The entity relationship model—Toward a unified view of data, *ACM Transactions on Database Systems*, 1, 1, 36, 1976.

[CODD70] Codd, E. F., A relational model of data for large shared data banks, *Communications of the ACM*, 13, 6, 1970.

[DATE90] Date, C., *An Introduction to Database Systems*, Addison-Wesley, Reading, MA, 1990.

[DEWI90] Dewitt, D. J., S. Ghandeharizadeh, D. Schneider, A. Bricker, H. Hisao, and R. Rasmussen, The Gamma Database Machine Project, *IEEE Transactions on Knowledge and Data Engineering*, March 1990.

[DE] *Proceedings of the IEEE Data Engineering Conference Series*, IEEE Computer Society Press, CA.

[DMH96] *Data Management Handbook Supplement*, Ed. B. Thuraisingham, Auerbach Publications, New York, 1996.

[DMH97] *Data Management Handbook*, Ed. B. Thuraisingham, Auerbach Publications, New York, 1997.

[DQ] MIT Total Data Quality Management Program, http://web.mit.edu/tdqm/www/index.shtml

[EDBT] *Proceedings of the Extended Database Technology Conference Series*, Springer Verlag, Heidelberg, Germany.

[ELMA85] Elmasri, R., J. Weeldreyer, and A. Hevner, The category concept: An extension to the entity relationship model, *Data and Knowledge Engineering Journal*, 1(2), 75–116, 1985.

[FOWL97] Fowler, M., ed., with Scott, K., *UML Distilled: Applying the Standard Object Modeling Language*, Addison Wesley, Reading, MA, 1997.

[FROS86] Frost, R., *On Knowledge Base Management Systems*, Collins Publishers, U.K., 1986.

[IEEE91] *IEEE Data Engineering Bulletin*, 21(2), 1991.

[INMO93] Inmon, W., *Building the Data Warehouse*, John Wiley & Sons, New York, 1993.

[JACO92] Jacobson, I., *Object Oriented Software Engineering: A Use Case Driven Approach*, Addison Wesley, Reading, MA, 1992.

[KDN] Kdnuggets, www.kdn.com

[KORT86] Korth, H. and A. Silberschatz, *Database System Concepts*, McGraw Hill, New York, 1986.

[LLOY87] Lloyd, J., *Foundations of Logic Programming*, Springer Verlag, Heidelberg, Germany, 1987.

[MAIE83] Maier, D., *Theory of Relational Databases*, Computer Science Press, MD, 1983.

[MASS] IEEE Mass Storage Systems Technical Committee, http://www.msstc.org/

[ODMG93] *Object Database Standard: ODMB 93*, Object Database Management Group, Morgan Kaufmann, CA, 1993.

[OMG95] *Common Object Request Broker Architecture and Specification*, OMG Publications, John Wiley & Sons, New York, 1995.

[ORFA94] Orfali, R., D. Harkey, and J. Edwards, *Essential Client Server Survival Guide*, John Wiley & Sons, New York, 1994.

[PRAB97] Prabhakaran, B., *Multimedia Database Systems*, Kluwer Publications, MA, 1997.

[RAMA93] Ramaritham, K., Real-time databases, *Journal of Distributed and Parallel Systems*, 1, 2, 1993.

[RUMB91] Rumbaugh, J., M. Blaha, W. Premerlani, F. Eddy, and W. William Lorensen, (1990). *Object-Oriented Modeling and Design*. Prentice Hall, Englewood Cliffs, NJ

[SHET90] Sheth, A. and J. Larson, Federated database systems, *ACM Computing Surveys*, 22, 3 1990.

[SIGM] *Proceedings of the ACM Special Interest Group on Management of Data Conference Series*, ACM Press, New York.

[SQL3] SQL3, American National Standards Institute, Draft, 1999.

[THUR97] Thuraisingham, B., *Data Management Systems Evolution and Interoperation*, CRC Press, Boca Raton, FL, 1997.

[THUR98] Thuraisingham, B., *Data Mining: Technologies, Techniques, Tools and Trends*, CRC Press, Boca Raton, FL, 1998.

[THUR00] Thuraisingham, B., *Web Data Management and Electronic Commerce*, CRC Press, Boca Raton, FL, 2000.

[THUR01] Thuraisingham, B., *Managing and Mining Multimedia Databases for the Electronic Enterprise*, CRC Press, Boca Raton, FL, 2001.

[THUR02] Thuraisingham, B., *XML, Databases and the Semantic Web*, CRC Press, Boca Raton, FL, 2002.

[THUR03] Thuraisingham, B., *Web Data Mining Technologies and Their Applications in Business Intelligence and Counter-Terrorism*, CRC Press, Boca Raton, FL, 2003.

[TSIC82] Tsichritzis, D. and F. Lochovsky, *Data Models*, Prentice Hall, Englewood Cliffs, NJ, 1982.

[ULLM88] Ullman, J. D., *Principles of Database and Knowledge Base Management Systems*, Volumes I and II, Computer Science Press, New York, 1988.

[VLDB] *Proceedings of the Very Large Database Conference Series*, Morgan Kaufman, San Francisco, CA.

[WIED92] Wiederhold, G., Mediators in the architecture of future information systems, *IEEE Computer*, March 1992.

Appendix C:
Secure Objects

C.1 Overview

Parts II–V discussed discretionary and mandatory security for databases and distributed databases mainly based on the relational data model. In particular, we discussed discretionary security mechanisms, mandatory security mechanisms, designs of MLS/DBMSs, secure data models, the inference problem, and secure distributed database management with the relational model in mind. However, many of the discussions and arguments can be extended for nonrelational database systems. Most popular among the nonrelational database systems are object-oriented database systems. At one time, it was thought that object databases would supersede relational databases. While that has not happened, relational databases have become more powerful by incorporating support for objects. Such databases are called object-relational databases.

Whether we are dealing with object databases or object-relational databases, we need to examine security for object models. Further, secure object models can also be used for secure distributed object systems as well as to design secure applications. In this chapter, we will discuss both discretionary security as well as mandatory security for object data models. We will also give examples of secure object database systems. In addition, we will explore aspects of objects and security (see Figure C.1). In particular, we will explore secure object request brokers and the use of object modeling for secure applications. Note that some argue that database systems have to be integrated with middleware to produce middleware data management systems (see, for example, the panel discussion at the 2002 IEEE Data Engineering Conference). Further, object models such as OMT and UML (see [RUMB91] and [FOWL97]) are being examined to design secure database applications. Therefore,

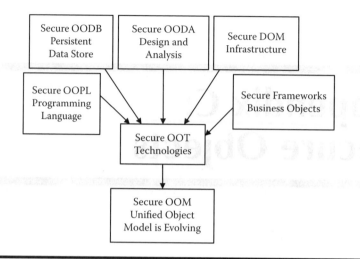

Figure C.1 Objects and security.

distributed object systems as well as object modeling have close connections with data management.

There are also other object technologies that have been integrated with security, and these include object programming languages as well as components and frameworks. A discussion of secure programming languages such as Secure Java is beyond the scope of this book. Various articles and books have appeared on this topic (see [GOSL96], [JAVA]). The organization of this chapter is as follows. In Section C.2, we will discuss discretionary security for object database systems. In Section C.3, we will discuss multilevel security. Securing object models as well as designs of systems will be described. In Section C.4, we will discuss secure object request brokers, and in Section C.5 we will provide an overview of object models for secure applications. The chapter will be summarized in Section C.6. Aspects of objects and security are illustrated in Figure C.1.

C.2 Discretionary Security

C.2.1 Overview

Discretionary security mechanisms for object databases include access control and authorization for objects as well as controls for method execution. One can also enforce access control at the level of object classes, instance variables, instances, composite objects, and class hierarchies. One of the comprehensive models for discretionary security for object systems is the ORION model proposed by

Rabbitti, Kim, Bertino et al. (see [RABB91]). This model has had a major impact on commercial products. In this section, we will discus some of the key issues.

The organization of this section is as follows. Discretionary security policies will be discussed in Section C.2.2. Policy enforcement issues will be discussed in Section C.2.3. Example systems, including a discussion of ORION, will be given in Section C.2.4.

C.2.2 Policy Issues

A discretionary security policy for object database systems includes access control for objects, classes, instances, instance variables, class hierarchy, and component hierarchy as well as access control for method execution. For example, some access control rules would include "User Group A has read access to Object Class EMP and write access to Object Class DEPT." This could mean that A can access everything in class EMP for reading and everything in class DEPT for writing. We can also have finer granularity and grant access to instances and instance variables. That is, unless a positive authorization is explicitly specified, we may not assume that A has read access to everything in EMP. As an example, A has read access to instance variables Name and Department # and does not have read access to salary in EMP. Another example is for A to have read access to the instance with ID = 10 and write access to the instance with ID = 20.

One can also enforce access control on method execution. For example, the method update-salary could be executed only by processes acting on behalf of user group B, while the method update-age could be executed by both user groups A and B. Figure C.2 illustrates access control on objects and methods.

We can also enforce access control on the class hierarchy. For example, we can have a rule that states that while John has read access to class EMP, he does not have read access to all subclasses of EMP. This is illustrated in Figure C.2. We can enforce access control on component hierarchy, as illustrated in Figure C.3. Here, John has read access to Sections 1 and 3, and he does not have read access to Sections 2 and 4. In the next section, we will discuss policy enforcement issues.

In the case of object-relational models, we need to integrate security both for object models as well as for the relational models. For example, one may grant or revoke access to the object, object instances, etc., as well as to the relationships. This is illustrated in Figure C.4.

C.2.3 Policy Enforcement

The security policy enforcement mechanism includes query modification. While SQL has been developed for relational database systems, variations of SQL, such as Object SQL, have been developed for object systems. Queries may be expressed

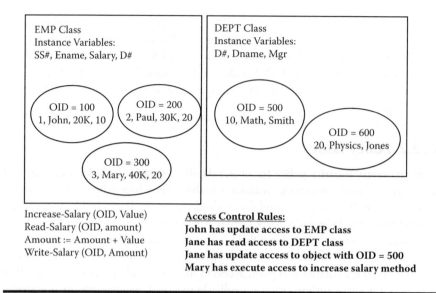

Increase-Salary (OID, Value)
Read-Salary (OID, amount)
Amount := Amount + Value
Write-Salary (OID, Amount)

Access Control Rules:
John has update access to EMP class
Jane has read access to DEPT class
Jane has update access to object with OID = 500
Mary has execute access to increase salary method

Figure C.2   Access control on objects and methods.

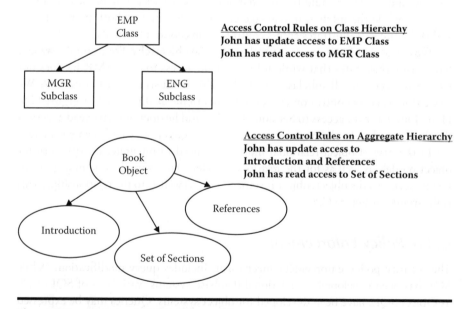

Access Control Rules on Class Hierarchy
John has update access to EMP Class
John has read access to MGR Class

Access Control Rules on Aggregate Hierarchy
John has update access to
Introduction and References
John has read access to Set of Sections

Figure C.3   Access control on hierarchies.

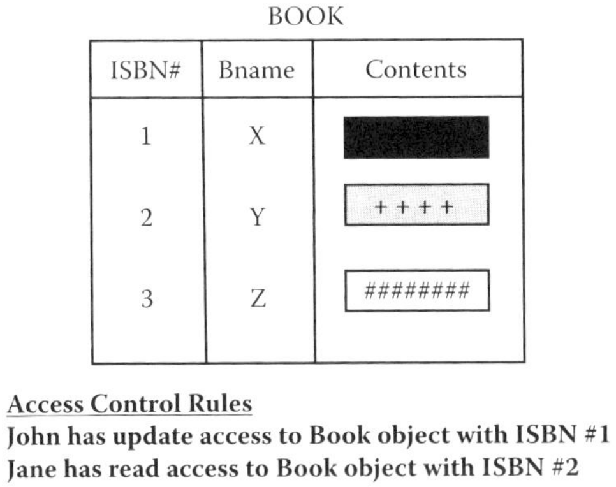

BOOK

ISBN#	Bname	Contents
1	X	███████
2	Y	+ + + +
3	Z	########

Access Control Rules
John has update access to Book object with ISBN #1
Jane has read access to Book object with ISBN #2

Figure C.4   Secure object relational model.

in Object SQL and modified according to the access control rules. For example, consider a rule where John does not have access to employee instances with ID= 20 and he cannot read any salary values of employees. Suppose the employee instance variables are ID, Name, Salary, and Age. If John queries

> "Retrieve information about all employees from the EMP class," then the query is modified to "Retrieve all information from EMP.ID, EMP. Name, EMP.Age where EMP.ID <> 20."

As mentioned in Section C.2.2, access control rules may be enforced on method execution. Further, credentials may be passed from one method to another during method calls. For example, suppose John has some credentials. The process acting on his behalf could call method A with his credentials. If A calls method B during execution, then B can get the credentials with which A executes. One could also place some restrictions on what credentials can be passed.

Other policy enforcement mechanisms include those discussed for relational databases. These include visualization of security policies. Object models, with their power to represent complex data types, are richer than relational models. Therefore, policies expressed on the object models may be more complex, especially when policies are enforced on class and component hierarchies. For example, do the rules propagate down the hierarchies? Visualization techniques may help one understand the policies enforced. Figure C.5 illustrates the policy enforcement mechanisms, including extensions to Object SQL to specify policies, query modification, and visualization. Further, security policies may be integrated for different objects. Object models have been explored to specify role-based access controls (see, for example, the work reported in the Proceedings of the IFIP Database Security Conference Series). Policy integration is another issue that must be investigated for object systems.

Policy Enforcement Mechanisms:

Query Modification Algorithm on objects and instance variables.

Rule processing integrated with method execution for enforcing access control.

Visualizing access control policies

Figure C.5 Policy enforcement.

C.2.4 Example Systems

C.2.4.1 Overview

Since the late 1980s, we have seen at least a dozen commercial object databases emerge. Many of the designs have been influenced by research systems, including MCC's ORION system and HP's IRIS system. These systems have been developed mainly for CAD/CAM (Computer-Aided Design/Computer-Aided Manufacturing) and similar applications, which require representation of complex data structures. Further, relational systems such as System R have been extended to support rules. These systems are called active database systems.

In this section, we provide a brief overview of some of these systems. These include research systems such as ORION and IRIS as well as Commercial systems such as GemStone. We will also provide an overview of the Starburst authorization model, and this system is really an extended relational database system, which extends a relational system with support for rules. Such systems are called *active database systems*. The various systems are illustrated in Figure C.6. Note that we will discuss only some of the systems shown in this figure. There have been many other research efforts on discretionary security, including those by Demurjian et al. at the University of Connecticut, Olivier et al. at Raand Afrikaans University, and Osborn et al. at the University of Western Ontario. These efforts have been reported at the IFIP Database Security Conference Proceedings (see for example, [OSBO00] and [DEMU00]).

C.2.4.2 ORION

The ORION system was one of the first to explore security. The ORION authorization model supports both positive and negative authorizations as well as weak and strong authorizations [RABB91]. Strong authorization always has higher priority than weak authorization. Authorizations are granted to roles instead of to single users, and a user is authorized to exercise a privilege on an object if the user has a

```
Example Systems:

Security for
• GemStone (originally Servio Logic)
• Objectstore (originally Object Design)
• Ontos (originally Ontos Inc)
• Starburst (IBM Almaden)
• O2 (Altair Group)
• ORION (MCC)
• IRIS (HP Labs)
```

Figure C.6   Example systems.

role that is authorized to access the object. Roles, objects, and privileges are organized into hierarchies. Rules apply to the propagation of the authorization policies as follows:

- ■ If a role has an authorization to access an object, all the roles that precede it in the role hierarchy have the same authorization.
- ■ If a role has a negative authorization to access an object, then all the roles that follow it in the role hierarchy have the same negative authorization.

Similar propagation rules are defined for privileges. Finally propagation rules on objects allow authorization on an object to be derived from the authorizations on objects semantically related to it. For example, the authorization to read a class implies the authorization to read all its instances. ORION also specifies conflict rules so that the authorization rules are consistent. Extensions to the original ORION model have been proposed (see [BERT98]).

C.2.4.3 IRIS

The IRIS model developed at HP supports attributes and methods represented as functions. Essentially, it combines both concepts in object models and functional models. The only privilege supported by the model is the "Call" privilege. A subject who owns the privileges to a function can call that function. The owner of the function automatically gets the privilege. The owner can grant the privilege to other subjects. Privileges can be granted or revoked on a user or group basis. A user can belong to multiple groups, and groups can be nested. The model also protects derived functions, which are functions derived from other functions. In what is called static authorization, a subject requesting the execution of the derived function must have the call privilege on the function. In the dynamic authorization approach, the subject must have privileges on the derived function as well as on all the functions executed by the derived function. When a function is created, the creator must specify which of the two authorizations must be used to check the execution request of the function.

The IRIS model also supports guard and proxy functions to control access. The guard function expresses preconditions on the call of a function. The function to which the guard function refers is the target function. A target function is executed only if the preconditions associated with the guard function are satisfied. Proxy functions provide different implementations of specific functions for different subjects. When a function is invoked, the appropriate proxy function is executed instead of the original one. More details on this model can be found in [FERR00].

C.2.4.4 STARBURST

We discuss the STARBURST authorization model even though it is not strictly an object database system and is considered to be an extended relational system. Starburst is a prototype developed by IBM and is characterized by a rule language fully integrated with the system. The authorization model for STARBURST provides a hierarchy of privileges that can be exercised on the database objects where higher types subsume lower types. Examples of privileges include control, which subsumes all other privileges, and write, alter, and attach. When a table is created, the owner receives control privilege on the table. The owner can grant or revoke all other privileges.

The creation and modification of rules are governed by various criteria, including the following. A creator of a rule on a table must have both attach and read privileges on the table. Subjects requesting the activation/deactivation of a rule must have the activation/deactivation privilege on the rule. Various other criteria have been defined and can be found in [WIDO91].

C.2.4.5 GemStone

GemStone was one of the first commercial systems to be developed. It provides a simple authorization model. Authorization can be granted to users or groups. The only type of authorization provided is the segment. A segment groups together a set of objects with the same level of protection. This implies that if a subject has the authorization to read a segment, then it can read all the objects within the segment. Each segment has one owner who can grant or revoke access to the segment.

Privileges that can be granted on a segment are of two distinct types: the read privilege and the write privilege. The read privilege allows a subject to read all the objects in a segment, while the write privilege allows a subject to modify all the objects in a segment. In some ways, the GemStone authorization model resembles the Hinke–Schafer approach, where access is granted to segments and each segment is stored at a security level. However, the Hinke–Schafer approach is for multilevel security, while GEMSTONE provides only discretionary security.

C.3 Multilevel Security

C.3.1 Overview

While Section C.2 focused on discretionary security, in this section we discuss multilevel security. Several studies on multilevel security for object systems were reported in the late 1980s and early 1990s. The earliest attempt was the SOAD model of Keefe, Tsai, and Thuraisingham [KEEF89]. Later, Thuraisingham extended ORION and O2 models for security [THUR89a], [THUR89b]. These models were called SORION and SO2. In the early 1990s, Jajodia and Kogan developed a system based on message passing [JAJO90]. Thuraisingham and Chase also explored the message passing approach [THUR89c]. Around the same time, Millen and Lunt developed a model similar to the one proposed by SORION (see [MILL92]). Around 1993, MITRE began work aimed at securing object databases and developed the UFOS model (see [ROSE94]). Almost all of these models featured security properties for objects. Thuraisingham went further and described designs of secure object systems (see [THUR90a], [THUR91], [THUR95]).

In this section, we will discuss multilevel security. The organization of this section is as follows. Policy issues will be discussed in Section C.3.2. System design issues will be discussed in Section C.3.3. Example systems, including a discussion of systems such as SORION and SO2, will be discussed in Section C.3.4.

C.3.2 Policy Issues

Mandatory security policies for object systems are essentially variations of the Bell and LaPadula policy enforced for relational systems. This policy is essentially Read at or below your level and Write at your level policies. Much of the work has focused on developing security properties between the levels of the various object constructs. The investigations have also focused on classifying metadata for objects as well as assigning levels for the methods themselves.

Some examples are the following:

Property 1: The security level of a class must be dominated by the security levels of the instances and the instance variables.
Property 2: The security level of a subclass must dominate the security level of the superclass.
Property 3: The security level of the components of an object must dominate the security level of the object.

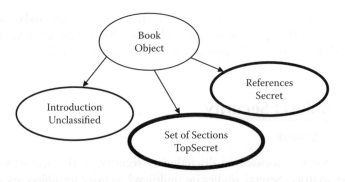

Figure C.7   Multilevel security for objects.

Property 4: A variation of Bell and La Padula policy, which is Read at or above your level and Write at your level policy, is enforced for method execution.
Property 5: The security level of the method is dominated by the level at which it executes.

Note that these properties are just some examples discussed in the SORION model. Variations of these properties have been examined by the different researchers. For example, the UFOS model does not classify the instance variables. It classifies the association between the instance variables and the values. Delegation-based models have also been explored. We will discuss the examples further in Section C.3.4. Figure C.7 illustrates mandatory security for object systems. Note that security has to be enforced for object relational systems also. Here we need to integrate concepts from relational systems as well as object systems. That is, in addition to securing the various components for objects, we may also assign, say, tuple-level classifications for the relations. An example is given in Figure C.8.

BOOK

ISBN#	Bname	Contents	Level
1	X	██████	TopSecret
2	Y	+ + + +	Secret
3	Z	########	Unclassified

Figure C.8   Multilevel security for object-relational model.

C.3.3 System Design Issues

In [THUR95], designs of multilevel object databases were explored. For example, can we apply the architectures developed for relational systems? That is, can approaches such as operating systems providing access control, trusted subject, integrity lock, extended kernel, and distributed architectures discussed in [THUR05] be used to design secure object systems? We will discuss some of the issues.

If the operating system is providing access control, it is assumed that the object database is untrusted. The challenge here is to store the multilevel objects as single-level files. In the trusted subject approach, the database is trusted with respect to mandatory access control. The challenge here is to determine which portions of the database are trusted. In the integrity lock approach, the trusted front-end computes checksums. The challenge here is to compute checksums for classes, instances, instance variables, class hierarchies, and component hierarchies. In the extended kernel approach, additional constraints are enforced on objects. The challenge is to develop algorithms to enforce the constraints on objects. Finally, in the distributed approach, the challenge is to partition the objects according to the security levels. Here again, the multilevel objects have to be decomposed into single-level objects. In the case of the replicated distributed approach, one would have to simply replicate the lower-level objects at the higher levels.

Some work has been reported on designing secure object systems (see [THUR95]). There is still much to be done. For example, we need to carry out an investigation as to which approach is suitable for secure object systems. Figure C.9 illustrates the various approaches.

Design Approaches:

SORION (Thuraisingham, MITRE)

SO2 (Thuraisingham, MITRE)

Millen-Lunt (Millen and Lunt, SRI)

SOAD (Keef et al., U. of MN)

Morgenstern (Morgenstern, SRI)

UFOS (Rosenthal et al., MITRE)

Message Passing (Jajodia and Kogan, GMU)

Figure C.9   Design approaches.

C.3.4 Example Systems

C.3.4.1 Overview

The first MLS/DBMS based on the object model was designed by Keefe, Tsai, and Thuraisingham, and it was called the SOAD model (see [KEEF88] and KEEF89]). Since then, several attempts have been reported. The most popular effort is Thuraisingham's effort to secure the ORION model, and she called it the SORION model (Secure ORION). This work was published in the ACM OOPSLA Conference proceedings in 1989, and received a lot of attention and influenced many of the other efforts. Thuraisingham also examined security for the O2 model, and this model was called SO2. Later, other efforts were reported, including the approach by Millen and Lunt, Jajodia and Kogan, and Morgenstern and Rosenthal et al. We describe each of these models in this section.

Note that in the early 1990s, Ontos Corporation developed a MLS/DBMS funded by Rome Laboratory, and very little has been reported on this. Therefore, we will not discuss any commercial efforts. While MLS/DBMSs based on the object model have had limited success, many of the ideas have been applied to designing secure applications as well as secure distributed object systems.

C.3.4.2 SOAD System

Keefe, Tsai, and Thuraisingham were the first to incorporate multilevel security in object-oriented database systems. The system they subsequently developed, called SOAD (service-oriented analysis and design), has a number of unique properties, both in its security model and in its data model (see [KEEF88], [KEEF89]).

The rules that govern operations within SOAD are designed to enforce the Bell and La Padula properties, and are conceptually quite simple. First, any method activation can read a value within a labeled object or a labeled instance variable provided the classification of the object is dominated by the clearance level of the method. However, if the classification of the object dominates the current classification of the method, the method's classification is raised to the level of the object being read. Second, a method activation may modify or create a new object of a particular classification if the method's current classification equals that of the object in question, the method's current classification is dominated by the upper bound of the classification range (as specified by the constraint) and the lower bound of the classification range (as specified by the constraint) is dominated by the subject's clearance. If these rules are not satisfied then a write/create operation fails. Because method activations in SOAD can have their classifications dynamically upgraded, the trusted computing base (TCB) must be involved to perform the level change. If the nature of methods can be determined in advance, then a level change operation could be restricted to the message-passing mechanism. However, this situation is not generally the case, and the TCB must be invoked when method activation attempts to read an object whose classification dominates the method's current classification. The TCB must then restart the method activation at the point where it invoked the TCB.

C.3.4.3 SORION Model

Thuraisingham investigated security issues for the ORION object-oriented data model (see [THUR89a]). The secure data model was called SORION. It extends MCC's ORION model with multilevel security properties. In SORION's security policy, subjects and objects are assigned security levels. The following rules constitute the policy:

1. A subject has read access to an object if the subject's security level dominates that of the object.
2. A subject has write access to an object if the subject's security level is equal to that of the object.
3. A subject can execute a method if the subject's security level dominates the security level of the method and that of the class with which the method is associated.
4. A method executes at the level of the subject who initiated the execution.
5. During the execution of a method m1, if another method m2 has to be executed, m2 can execute only if the execution level of m1 dominates the levels of m2 and of the class with which m2 is associated.
6. Reading and writing of object during method execution are governed by rules 1 and 2.

Different architectures for implementing a system based on the SORION model have been examined, and an approach in which the TCB enforces all MAC has been general purpose. Basically, the system runs as an untrusted application on a general-purpose TCB. The TCB controls all access to read, write, and method executions.

C.3.4.4 SO2 Model

Thuraisingham also developed the SO2 model [THUR89b]. This model extends Altair Group's O2 model with multilevel security properties. The O2 model is based on theoretical foundations and type theory. Thuraisingham subsequently developed a multilevel type theory (see also [THUR90b]).

The SO2 model specifies properties for read, write, and method execution. In addition, the interpretation of the model specifies the versions that users can read at different security levels. Thuraisingham also explores the algebra- and calculus-based approaches to multilevel secure object models.

C.3.4.5 Millen–Lunt Model

Millen and Lunt have proposed a secure object model for knowledge-based applications based on a layered architecture (see [MILL92]). At the lowest layer is the security kernel, which provides MAC. At the next layer is the object system, which implements object-oriented services, providing the abstraction of objects, methods, and messages. The object system layer is assumed to be layered with respect to mandatory security. Here are the security properties of the model:

- The hierarchy property states that the level of an object dominates that of its class.
- The subject-level property states that the level of a subject created to handle a message dominates the level of the subject that originated the message and the level of the object receiving the message.
- The object locality property states that a subject can execute a method or read variables only in the object where it is located or any superclass of that object. It can write variables only in that object.
- The *-property states that a subject may write into an object only if its security level is equal to that of the object.
- The return value property states that an invoking subject can receive a return value from a message only if the message handler subject is at the same security level as the invoking subject.
- The object-creation property states that the security level of a newly created object must dominate the level of the subject that requested its creation.

C.3.4.6 Jajodia–Kogan Model

Jajodia and Kogan describe a secure object model that is unique in that it relies almost on the message-passing mechanism for enforcing security [JAJO90]. Some preliminary work was carried out on the law-governed approach to secure object systems proposed by Thuraisingham and Chase [THUR89c]. However, Jajodia and Kogan have described a comprehensive model.

Two concepts are key to this model. One is that the methods must have two states: they are either restricted or unrestricted. If restricted, the method is prevented from modifying attributes or creating new objects. If unrestricted, the method can modify object attributes and create new objects. Under certain circumstances, method activation can attain a restricted status, and once attained, any further method invocations will also be restricted. The second concept is an assumption that is made in the model with respect to the nature of the methods of the following four types.

- Read: a method that reads the value of an attribute
- Write: a method that modifies the value of an attribute

- Invoke: a method that invokes another method via sending of a message
- Create: a method that creates a new object

The rules enforced by the message-filtering algorithms are separated into two sets. The first set restricts messages sent from one object to another. The second restricts messages sent from an object to itself. Because the message-passing mechanism contains the filtering algorithm and all information flows are determined at the time the message is set, the TCB of this model could include the message passer and nothing more.

C.3.4.7 Morgenstern's Model

Morgenstern has proposed an object security model for multilevel objects with bidirectional relationships [MORG90]. He argues that the use of multilevel attributes in the relational model suggests the need for multilevel objects in the object model. The model also distinguishes between the security levels of binary and n-ary relationships. Security constraints are used to specify the types of operations to be executed. Some of the constraints are listed here.

- The method invocation constraint states that the level of a method invocation is the least upper bound of (1) the minimum level among the range of levels associated with the method; (2) the level of the subject who requested the invocation; and (3) the levels of the arguments provided for that invocation.
- The method output constraint states that the level of any output or insertion produced by the method execution must dominate the level of the method invocation.
- The property update constraint states that the modification of a property must not change its level.

Morgenstern's model does not address issues on TCB enforcement. Because multilevel objects are decomposed by access classes, one could envision that the operating system provides the MAC to the decomposed objects. However, the module that enforces the security constraints must be trusted.

C.3.4.8 UFOS Model

Rosenthal, Thuraisingham et al. developed a model called the UFOS model (Uniform Fine-grained Object Security), and this work is reported in [ROSE94]. This is, in fact, the last of the major models described in the literature. The team examined the various models such as SORION and found that there was a need for a model to be consistent with industry trends and be flexible. The team also felt that element-level access control was needed in addition to supporting collections of data. The key idea behind UFOS is to classify the associations between an instance variable and its value. For example, consider a ship on a mission called JANE. Now, mission as well as JANE may be Unclassified, but the fact that JANE is the mission may be Secret.

The UFOS model also supports polyinstantiation. That is, the association between mission and its name could be different at different levels. For example, at the Secret level, it could be JANE and at the TopSecret level it could be FLOWER. The security policy enforced by UFOS is read at or below your level and write at your level policy. UFOS focuses mainly on the model. Details of the TCB and the design are not discussed in [ROSE94].

C.4 Security for Object Request Brokers

C.4.1 Overview

Work on security for object request brokers started around 1993. It was during that time that we had a workshop on secure objects at OOPSLA and also had a panel on this topic at the OOPSLA conference (see [THUR93], [THUR94]). During that time there was much interest in exploring all aspects of secure objects, including object databases, programming languages, and applications. Around the time of the workshop, the Object Management Group started the Security Special Interest Group (SIG). The SIG later evolved into a Task Force, which focused on security for distributed objects. In this section, we discuss some of the developments on this topic.

Figure C.10 provides a high-level illustration of secure object request brokers. The idea is for clients and servers to communicate with each other securely. That is, we have secure clients, secure servers, and secure ORBs. All of the secure object modeling properties and secure method execution issues we discussed in Chapter 18 are applicable for secure object brokers. The question is, what are the additional challenges in securing the ORBs? In Section C.4.2, we will discuss some of the developments with OMG as given in [OMG]. In Section C.4.3, we will discuss some other aspects of secure objects such as secure components and frameworks.

C.4.2 OMG Security Services

Since 1994, OMG has developed various specifications for security. We discuss some of the recent developments, including OMG security services as given in [OMG]. OMG has specifications both for secure infrastructure and security functionality at the API (application programming interface) level. The infrastructure security services are CSlv2 (Common Secure Interoperability, Version 2) and CORBA security service. The API-level security specifications are ATLAS (Authorization Token Layer Acquisition Service) and RAD (Resource Access Decision Facility). We briefly discuss each of the specifications as given in [OMG].

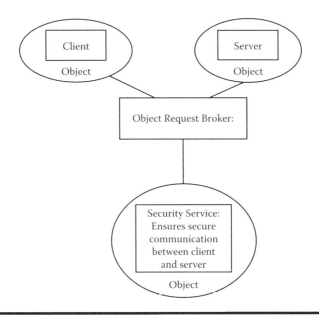

Figure C.10 Secure object request brokers.

ATLAS is a service that is needed to get authorization tokens to access a target system. The target system is accessed using the CSlv2 protocol. The client gets an authorization token with this service and uses CSlv2 to access a CORBA invocation on the target. With this service, the client gets privileges that the target will understand.

CSlv2 is a Security Attribute Service (SAS) that supports interoperation, authentication, delegation, and privileges. Essentially, SAS is a protocol that ensures secure interoperability and uses the transport layer security mechanism. The transport layer protects messages and also ensures client/target authentication. If the transport layer does not provide the protection service, the SAS will provide a message protection and authentication service on top of the transport service. SAS also provides security contexts for the duration of single request and reply combination. These security contexts may be reused according to certain rules specified by SAS.

Applications such as healthcare, finance, and telecommunications require access control at finer granularity. An infrastructure security service such as the CORBA security service supports coarser granularity. For example, access may be granted to entire objects. In order to provide access to the components of an object, OMG's RAD was developed. RAD is a specification that supports an enterprise security policy. This policy can be used by various software components of an enterprise. RAD provides support for credentials supplied by various sources including Public or Private Key Infrastructure. RAD also supports flexible policies and access control rules. Vendors who provide security solutions can also deliver RAD.

Finally, the CORBA security service provides basic security for the infrastructure. It provides a security architecture that can support various security policies. The

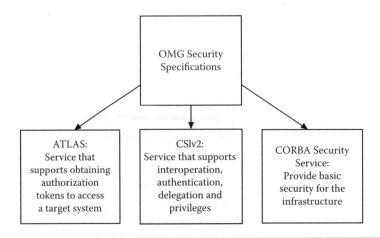

Figure C.11 OMG security specifications.

functionality provided by this service includes identification and authentication, authorization and access control, auditing, secure communication between objects, and non-repudiation. The security model developed by OMG is neutral to any particular technology. This way, if the policies change, the security model can still be used. Further, the approach can also accommodate products from different vendors as long the products conform to the interface specifications specified by OMG. The CORBA security service can also be ported to different environments. However, if an object requires application-level security, some additional mechanisms are needed. These mechanisms are discussed in [OMG]. Figure C.11 illustrates CORBA security features. Note that as progress is made with the standards, the features also evolve.

C.4.3 Secure Components and Frameworks

As stated in Chapter 2, the purpose of object components is to be able to reuse software. That is, a vendor could supply components that can be used for multiple applications. The components are put together to form frameworks. There has been work on security for components and frameworks. For example, enterprise security with components such as Sun Microsystem's EJB (Enterprise JavaBeans) has been studied (see, for example, [EJB]). Security architecture as well as role-based access control policies has been developed for EJB.

Now, when components are put together to form a framework that can be used for various applicators, it is critical that the composition of the components be secure. Note that each component may enforce its own security policies. The composition as well as the interfaces between the various components has to be secure. Furthermore, even within a component, integration of the secure objects that form the component has to enforce security.

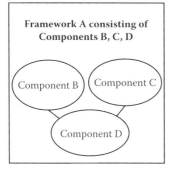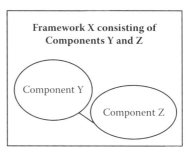

Access Control on Components and Frameworks:
John has update access to components B, C, and Y
Jane has update access to Framework A and
read access to Framework X

Figure C.12   Secure component objects.

EJB relies on the container to invoke external objects. Therefore, it relies on the container to provide security when creating EJB instances as well as to invoke methods and connect to an EJB. The vendors of the EJB container and server must provide various security features, including authentication, identity delegation, identity propagation, and secure communication. A tutorial on EJB security is given in [EJB]. Figure C.12 illustrates the composition of secure objects to form a secure framework.

C.5 Object Modeling for Secure Applications

C.5.1 Overview

Structures such as semantic nets have reasoning power and, therefore, they can represent and reason about applications and detect security violations via inference. While semantic nets are very useful, many real-world applications have been modeled using the entity-relationship models and, more recently, object models.

In the early 1990s, we explored the use of object models for secure database applications. In fact, Sell and Thuraisingham were one of the first to model secure applications using object models (see [SELL93]). They extended the Object Modeling Technique of Rumbaugh et al. (see [RUMB91]) and called the resulting model Multilevel OMT or MOMT (see also [MARK96]). Since then, the Unified Modeling Language (UML) was conceived and extensions have been proposed to model secure applications (see [RAY03]). In this section, we will first explore the use of OMT and then discuss how UML may be used for modeling secure applications. MOMT will be discussed in Section C.5.2. Secure UML will be discussed in Section C.5.3. Figure C.13 illustrates the use of object models for designing secure applications.

**Object Modeling Technique for
Secure Database Applications:**

Object Model: Models the static aspects
of the application and security properties
using objects

Dynamic Model: Models the activities
and the security properties of the activities

Functional Model: Generates the data flow
diagrams and the security levels of the methods

Figure C.13   Object models for secure applications.

C.5.2 Multilevel OMT

OMT was developed by Rumbaugh et al. back in the late 1980s [RUMB91]. We have extended OMT to MOMT (Multilevel OMT) and used it to model secure applications (see [SELL93] and [MARK96]). MOMT consists of three phases: the Object Model, Dynamic Model, and Functional Model. We discuss each of the phases.

The object modeling phase consists of developing a secure data model to represent the entities of the applications. We have defined security properties for objects, classes, methods, links, associations, and inheritance. We essentially follow the model developed in the SORION project with some minor variations given in [MARK96]. Figure C.14 illustrates the security model for object attributes and instances of class SHIP.

The dynamic modeling stage generates event diagrams. For example, Figure C.15 illustrates an example where a ship's captain requests a mission to be carried out. Here we have four classes: Captain, Ship, Mission-Plan, and Mission. Figure C.15 illustrates the communication between the different entities. There is a problem when communication flows from, say, Secret to the Unclassified level. The purpose of this phase is to eliminate activities that cause security violations.

The third phase is the function modeling phase. During this phase, methods for the classes are generated. These methods are based on the activity diagrams that are generated during the dynamic modeling phase. The methods are generated by carrying out a data flow analysis. For example, suppose a captain operating at the confidential level reserves an unclassified ship to carry out a mission operating at the Secret level. The object and dynamic models would have generated the classes, instances, attributes, and activity/event diagrams. The functional model would generate the data flow diagram illustrated in Figure C.16. The methods are generated from the functional diagrams.

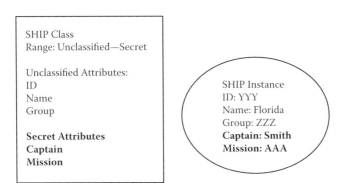

Figure C.14   Object attributes and instances.

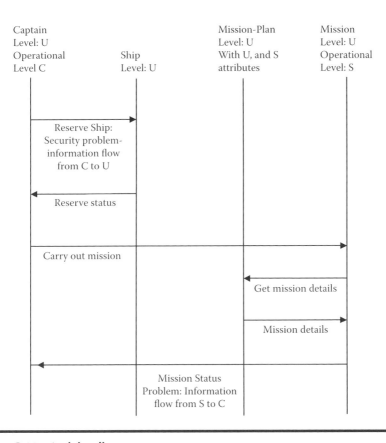

Figure C.15   Activity diagram.

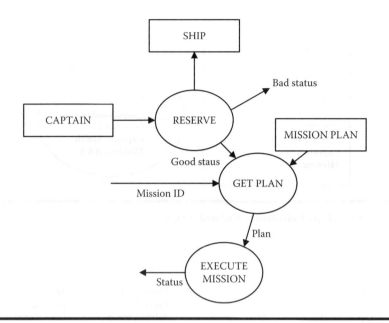

Figure C.16   Data flow diagram.

The foregoing discussion highlighted some of the chief features of MOMT. It has the representational power of OMT and incorporates security properties for objects and activities. For further details on the MOMT, we refer the reader to [SELL93] and [MARK96]. As we stated in Chapter 2, the various design and analysis methodologies have now merged, and a language called UML has been developed. We examine UML and security in the next section.

C.5.3 UML and Security

Various efforts have been reported recently on using UML for designing secure applications. Let us call such a language SUML (Secure UML). An example of an effort is given by Wijesekera in a set of lecture notes (see [WIJE]). The author uses UML to specify role-based access control rules. As we stated in Chapter 5, with role-based access control, a user is given access to resources depending on his role. In [WIJE], the UML model is examined and the role-based access control rules are incorporated into the model. Further, application-specific RBAC constraints are specified in OCL (Object Constraints Language) and the object constraints language specified by UML. Figure C.17 shows an example of specifying RBAC in UML.

Other efforts on using UML for security include the work by Ray [RAY03]. Here, the author argues that there is a need to merge policies that are different. Examples of policies are RBAC and MAC. She goes on to argue that when the

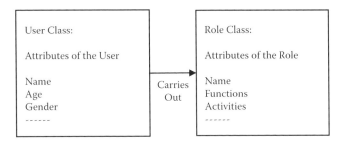

Figure C.17 RABC policy in UML-like specification.

policies are merged, security should still be maintained. She then shows how UML could be used to merge the policies specified in RBAC and MAC. Figure C.18 illustrates policy merging.

MOMT is the first step toward using object technology for modeling secure applications. Since UML is the standard object language for modeling applications, an SUML-like language is also becoming the preferred approach to modeling security policies. We have discussed a few efforts. Various other efforts have been reported in the IFIP Database Security Conference Series.

C.6 Summary and Directions

We have provided an overview of discretionary security and mandatory security for object database systems. We started with a discussion of discretionary security policies and also provided an overview of prototypes and products, including a discussion of ORION and GEMSTONE systems. Then we discussed mandatory security policy as well as system design issues. This was followed by a discussion of the various efforts to develop multilevel secure object database systems. We also discussed the various aspects of objects and security. We note that security could be incorporated into object databases, object languages such as Java, and object-based middleware such as object request brokers. We also noted that object models could be used to represent and reason about secure applications. We first discussed security for object request brokers and described various standards being developed by OMG. Then we discussed the use of object models for designing secure applications and described in particular the use of OMT and UML.

While not much has been done since on secure object databases, the work reported in this chapter has had a major impact on many of the developments on secure object systems, including secure distributed object systems as well as the use of object modeling for secure applications. This has also impacted the work on secure Web services,

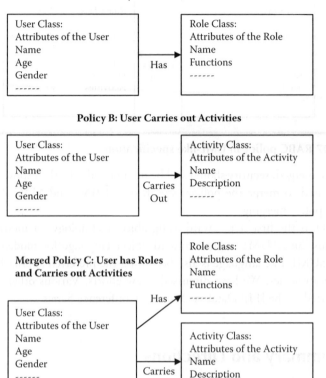

Figure C.18   Merging security policies with UML-like specifications.

References

[BERT98] Bertino, E. and G. Guerrini, Extending the ODMG object model with composite objects, *Proceedings of the ACM OOPSLA Conference*, Vancouver, BC, 1998.

[DEMU00] Demurjian, S., T. Ting, R. H. Balthazaar, C. Phillips, and P. Barr, Role-Based Securing in a Distributed Resource Environment, Preceedings of IFIP WG11.3 Working Conference on Database Security, 259–270, 2000.

[EJB] http://www.samspublishing.com/articles/article.asp?p=21643

[FERR00] Ferrari E. and B. Thuraisingham, Secure Database Systems, in *Advances in Database Management*, M. Piatini and O. Diaz (Eds.), Artech House, London, U.K., 2000.

[FOWL97] Fowler, M. with Scott, K., *UML Distilled: Applying the Standard Object Modeling Language*, Addison Wesley, Reading, MA, 1997.

[GOSL96] Gosling, J., B. Jay, and G. Steele, *The Java™ Language Specification*, Addison-Wesley, Reading, MA 1996.

[JAJO90] Jajodia, S. and B. Kogan, Integrating an Object-Oriented Data Model with Multilevel Security. *IEEE Symposium on Security and Privacy*, Oakland, CA, May 1990.

[JAVA] Java Security, http://java.sun.com/security/

[KEEF88] Keefe, T., W. Tsai, and B. Thuraisingham, A multilevel security policy for object-oriented systems, *Proceedings of the 11th National Computer Security Conference*, Baltimore, MD, 1988.

[KEEF89] Keefe, T. et al., SOAD—A secure object-oriented database system, *Computers and Security Journal*, Volume 9, #5, 1989.

[MARK96] Marks, D., P. Sell, and B. Thuraisingham, MOMT: A multilevel object modeling technique for designing secure database applications, *Journal of Object-Oriented Programming*, 8, 3, 1996.

[MILL92] Millen, J. and T. Lunt, Security for object-oriented database systems, *Proceedings of the IEEE Symposium on Security and Privacy*, Oakland, CA, May 1992.

[MORG90] Morgenstern, M., A security model for multilevel objects with bi-directional relationships, *Proceedings of the IFIP Database Security Conference*, Halifax, UK, 1990, North Holland, 1991.

[OMG] http://www.omg.org/technology/documents/formal/omg_security.htm

[OSBO00] Osborne, S., Database Security Integration Using Role-Based Access Control, Proceeding of IFIP WG11.3 Working Conference on Database Security, 245–258, 2000.

[RABB91] Rabitti, F., E. Bertino, W. Kim, and D. Weelk, A model of authorization for next-generation database systems, *ACM Transactions on Database Systems*, 16, 1, 1991.

[RAY03] Ray, I., N. Li, D. Kim, and R. France, Using parameterized UML to specify and compose success control models, *Proceedings of the IFIP Integrity and Control Conference*, Lausanne, Switzerland, November 2003. Kluwer, 2003.

[ROSE94] Rosenthal, A., W. Herndon, R. Graubert, and B. Thuraisingham, Security for object-oriented systems, *Proceedings of the Database Security Conference*, Hildesheim, Germany, 1994. North Holland, 1995.

[RUMB90] Rumbaugh, J., M. Blaha, W. Lorenson, Eddy, and Premerlani, W., *Object-Oriented Modeling and Design*, Prentice Hall, Upper Saddle River, NJ, 1991.

[SELL93] Sell, P. and B. Thuraisingham, Applying OMT for Designing Multilevel Database Applications, *Proceedings of the IFIP Database Security Conference*, Huntsville, Alabama, September 1993. North Holland, 1994.

[THUR89a] Thuraisingham, B., Mandatory security in object-oriented database systems, October 1989, *Proceedings of the ACM Conference on Object-Oriented Programming, Systems, Languages and Applications (ACM OOPSLA) Conference*, New Orleans, LA, October 1989.

[THUR89b] Thuraisingham, B., Multilevel security in object-oriented database systems, October 1989, *Proceedings of the 12th National Computer Security Conference*, Baltimore, MD, October 1989.

[THUR89c] Thuraisingham, B. and F. Chase, An object-oriented approach for designing secure systems, *IEEE CIPHER*, 1989.

[THUR90a] Thuraisingham, B., Security in object-oriented database systems, *Journal of Object-Oriented Programming*, 3, 2, 1990.

[THUR90b] Thuraisingham, B., Mathematical Formalisms for Multilevel Object-Oriented Systems, June 1990, Technical Report, MTP-291 (also presented at the Object Systems Security Workshop, Karlsruhe, Germany, April 1990).

[THUR91] Thuraisingham, B., Multilevel secure object-oriented data model—issues on noncomposite objects, composite objects, and versioning, *Journal of Object-Oriented Programming*, 4, 6 1991.

[THUR95] Thuraisingham, B., Towards the design of a multilevel secure object-oriented database management system, *Journal of Object-Oriented Programming*, 8, 3 1995.

[THUR05] Thuraisingham, B., *Database and Applications Security: Integrating Data Management and Information Security*, CRC Press, Boca Raton, FL, 2005.

[WIDO91] Widom, J., R. Cochrane, and B. Lindsay, Implementing set-oriented production rules as an extension to Starburst, *Proceedings Very Large Database Conference*, Barcelona, Spain, August 1991.

[WIJE] Wijesekera, D., http://www.isse.gmu.edu/ duminda classes/spring02/umlSecurity3. ppt

Appendix D: Developments with Standards, Products, and Tools

D.1 Overview

This book has discussed various concepts, directions, and challenges in secure service-oriented information systems. As we have stated throughout this book, while the developments with Web services have progressed a great deal, security has not received much attention. However, in order to provide security, we need to make progress with the technologies. Therefore, in this appendix, we will describe the various standards, products, and tools that are emerging for Web services and the semantic Web.

As we have discussed, the semantic Web itself is a standard produced by W3C. Portions of semantic Web technologies such as XML are being standardized by various organizations. OASIS is specifying security standards such as XACML and SAML. Furthermore, organizations such as OGC are developing standards for geospatial data.

The organization of this appendix is as follows. Section D.2 describes the various standards organizations working on topics related to services. Section D.3 describes Web services products. Section D.4 describes W3C standards. Section D.5 describes the various semantic Web tools. The appendix concludes with Section D.6. It should be noted that numerous SOA-related products have emerged and for brevity we have not included several excellent products. We have only mentioned the products that we are familiar with. It should also be noted that many of the products are trademarks of the associated corporations.

D.2 Oasis Service Standards

In this section, we will discuss some of the relevant standards by OASIS. The information in this section has been obtained from [OASIS].

- **Application Vulnerability Description Language (AVDL):** "The goal of AVDL is to create a uniform format for describing application security vulnerabilities."
- **Common Alerting Protocol:** "The Common Alerting Protocol (CAP) provides an open, nonproprietary digital message format for all types of alerts and notifications."
- **Digital Signature Service (DSS):** Two XML-based request/response protocols are developed. The client and server communicate through these protocols. One is a signing protocol, and the other is a verifying protocol. As stated in the documentation, "through these protocols a client can send documents (or document hashes) to a server and receive back a signature on the documents; or send documents (or document hashes) and a signature to a server, and receive back an answer on whether the signature verifies the documents."
- **The Directory Services Markup Language (DSML):** It "provides a means for representing directory structural information as an XML document."
- **Electronic Business using eXtensible Markup Language (ebXML):** It is a collection of XML-based standards that enable organizations to interoperate with each other and carry out e-business activities.
- **Extensible Access Control Markup Language (XACML):** As stated in the documentation, "the XACML is a collection of core XML schema for representing authorization and entitlement policies."
- **Reference Model for Service-Oriented Architectures (SO):** "The goal of this reference model is to define the essence of service-oriented architecture, and emerge with a vocabulary and a common understanding of SOA."
- **Security Assertion Markup Language (SAML):** It is an XML-based framework for communicating user authentication, entitlement, and attribute information.
- **Universal Description, Discovery and Integration (UDDI):** It is a platform-independent, XML-based registry used by everyone to register themselves on the Web.
- **Web Service Resource specification (WS-Resource):** It is a specification that describes the relationship between a Web service and a resource in the WS-Resource Framework.

- **Web Services Resource Framework:** It specifies a generic and open framework for modeling and accessing stateful resources using Web services.
- **Web Services Security (WSS):** As stated in the documentation, WSS specification proposes a standard set of SOAP extensions that can be used when building secure Web services to implement message content integrity and confidentiality.

D.3 Web Services Products

We divide the products into two groups: one is the Enterprise Service Bus (ESB)-related products, and the other is Web Services Suites. Details can be found in [PROD1].

D.3.1 Enterprise Service Bus-Related Products

As stated in [ESB], in **computing**, an enterprise service bus (ESB) consists of a software architecture construct that provides fundamental services for complex architectures via an event-driven and standards-based messaging engine (the bus). Developers typically implement an ESB using technologies found in a category of middleware infrastructure products, usually based on recognized standards. We will discuss some ESB products.

BEA Systems (BEA AquaLogic Service Bus) Acquired by Oracle
As stated by BEA, this is an intermediary for use as a core element of distributed services networks. It enables service-oriented architecture (SOA), allowing accelerated service reuse and deployment.

IBM Corporation (WebSphere Enterprise Service Bus)
As stated by IBM, WebSphere is for SOA environments that enable dynamic, interconnected business processes, and deliver highly effective application infrastructures for business situations.

IONA Technologies (Artix ESB)—Acquired by Progress
As stated by Progress Software, this product comprises technology-neutral SOA infrastructure products that work together or independently to provide flexibility in SOA adoption.

Oracle Corporation (Oracle Enterprise Service Bus)
As stated by Oracle, this product is a fundamental component of Oracle's services-oriented architecture that provides a loosely coupled framework for inter-application messaging. Oracle also states that Oracle Enterprise Service Bus (ESB) is not Oracle Service Bus (OSB). ESB was developed by Oracle. OSB, formally known as Aqualogic Service Bus, was acquired when Oracle bought BEA. The two products are related but not interchangeable.

Progress Software Corporation (Sonic ESB)
As stated by Progress, this is a messaging-based enterprise service bus that simplifies the integration and flexible reuse of business applications within a service-oriented architecture (SOA).

WSO2 (WSO2 ESB)
WSO2 is an open source SOA company. As stated by WSO2, this product offers an approach to creating an SOA by adding monitoring, management, and virtualization to existing service interactions.

D.3.2 Web Services Suites

The Web Services suites provide a framework for developing services and managing service-oriented architectures. A list of some of the products follows.

BEA Systems, Inc. (BEA AquaLogic)—Acquired by Oracle
As stated by BEA, AquaLogic consists of a software suite developed by BEA Systems for managing SOA. Following the acquisition of BEA by Oracle Corp., most of the software has been renamed and the term AquaLogic is not used in any new Oracle product.

iWay Software (iWay Data Integration Solutions)
As stated by IWay Software, iWay Software data integration solutions allow for direct access to all the data, so an organization can design its architecture to address the unique information needs of its users.

Magic Software Enterprises (iBOLT Integration Suite)
As stated by Magic Software, iBOLT integrates enterprise software applications including SAP, Salesforce.com, Oracle JD Edwards, Lotus Notes, Microsoft Office, IBM i (AS/400), HL7, and Google Apps, among others.

Novell (Novell exteNd Composer)
As stated by Novell, the exteNd platform provides a visual environment that simplifies the development and deployment of business solutions that exploit existing systems.

Software AG (webMethods Product Suite)
As stated by Software AG, the webMethods product suite delivers business infrastructure that helps an organization to integrate its applications and automate its business processes.

D.4 Semantic Web Standards

In this section, we will specify some of the key standards of W3C that are relevant to the semantic Web and the secure semantic Web. Note that in many ways all of the standards are relevant as they are interrelated. We strongly urge the reader to keep up with these developments. Much of the information in this section has been obtained from [W3C].

The Document Object Model is a "platform and language-neutral interface that will allow programs and scripts to dynamically access and update the content, structure and style of documents."

HTML is language for publishing hypertext on the Web. It uses tags to structure text into headings, paragraphs, and lists, among others.

XML (eXtensible Markup Language) is a text format derived from SGML (Generalized Markup Language, an ISO standard). It is crucial for document exchange on the Web.

SOAP is a stateless, one-way message exchange paradigm and uses XML for its messages.

The Resource Description Framework (RDF) uses XML as an interchange syntax and integrates a variety of applications.

OWL is a *Web* Ontology language. OWL is used to specify ontologies and builds on RDF.

Rules: The RIF (Rules Interchange Format) Working Group is developing a "core rule language plus extensions which together allow rules to be translated between rule languages and thus transferred between rule systems."

The Semantic Web "provides a common framework that allows data to be shared and reused across application, enterprise, and community boundaries." It is based on RDF.

The Synchronized Multimedia Integration Language (SMIL, pronounced "smile") enables simple authoring of interactive audiovisual presentations.

MathML is a low-level specification for describing mathematics as a basis for machine-to-machine communication.

The Platform for Privacy Preferences Project (P3P) "enables Web sites to express their privacy practices in a standard format that can be retrieved automatically and interpreted easily by user agents."

The XML Encryption working group has developed a process for encrypting/decrypting digital content that includes XML documents. This group does not address XML security issues.

XML Key Management working group has developed a protocol for a client to obtain key information (e.g., value, certificates) from a Web service. This group also does not address the security issues.

The XML Signature working group has developed "an XML-compliant syntax used for representing the signature of Web resources and portions of protocol messages (anything referenceable by a URI) and procedures for computing and verifying such signatures." As with the first two groups, this group also does not address XML security issues.

D.4.1 Products

We have mentioned in this book that we cannot purchase a semantic Web. What we can do is purchase a collection of products from different vendors and assemble them to put together a semantic Web. In this section, we will discuss the various products that have been developed for the semantic Web. Much of the information has been obtained from [PROD2]. The products Web page is maintained by the W3C semantic Web staff and the semantic Web community.

Aduna's Metadata Server: This product automatically extracts metadata from information sources.
http://aduna.biz/products/metadataserver/index.html

Altova's SemanticWorks: Altova SemanticWorks™ 2006 is a visual RDF/OWL editor. http://www.altova.com/products_semanticworks.html

Franz Inc.'s Allegrograph: As stated in the product documentation, "SPARQL, the W3C standard RDF query language, gives native object, RDF, and XML responses to queries. Query over sockets, HTTP, Lisp or a Java API. Also supports OWL DL, RDF Prolog, SWRL and simple inferencing." http://www.franz.com/products/allegrograph/

IBM's IODT: This is a toolkit for ontology-driven development. http://www.alphaworks.ibm.com/tech/semanticstk

Intellidimension's RDF Gateway, InferEd: "RDF Gateway is a platform for the development and deployment of semantic Web applications."
"InferEd is a powerful authoring environment that gives you the ability to navigate and edit RDF (Resource Description Framework) documents." http://www.intellidimension.com/

Ontotext's OWLIM: This is a "high-performance semantic repository, packaged as a Storage and Inference Layer (SAIL) for the Sesame RDF database." http://www.ontotext.com/owlim/

OpenLink's Semantic Web Data Spaces Platform: This is a distributed platform that creates "semantic web presence from Wewbv 2.0 application profiles" such as Weblogs and wikis, and uses an RDF-based metadata model with shared ontologies (such as FOAF).
Open Source Project Page: http://virtuoso.openlinksw.com/wiki/main/Main/OdsIndex/

OpenLink's Virtuoso Object-Relational Database: This is an Object-Relational Database Management System (ORDBMS) that includes SQL, XML, and RDF, together with Web content management.
Main Product Site: http://virtuoso.openlinksw.com
Open Source Project Page: http://virtuoso.openlinksw.com/wiki/main/

Oracle's 10.2 Database: As stated in the documentation, "Oracle Spatial 10g introduces the industry's first open, scalable, secure and reliable RDF management platform. Based on a graph data model, RDF triples are persisted, indexed, and queried, similar to other object-relational data types. The Oracle 10g RDF database ensures that application developers benefit from the scalability of Oracle 10g to deploy scalable and secure semantic applications." http://www.oracle.com/technology/tech/semantic_technologies/index.html

Thetus Publisher: This product provides knowledge discovery capabilities so that organizations can describe, search, and structure the information. It provides machine-readable metadata (RF/OWL) for semantic interoperability. http://www.thetus.com/

D.5 Semantic Web Products

This section describes tools as provided in [TOOL]. The tools Web page is maintained by the semantic Web community. They are essentially for programming and development and are RDF- and OWL-based tools. The Web page groups these tools depending on their category (e.g., Java developers, C developers, Perl developers, etc.).

Amilcare: University of Sheffield's Amilcare is an adaptive Information Extraction tool designed to support document annotation for the semantic Web.

DERI Ontology Management Environment (DOME): This comprises tool support for editing and browsing, versioning and evolution, as well as mapping and merging.

Graphl: A tool for collaborative editing and visualization of RDF graphs.

GrOWL: A graphical browser and an editor of OWL ontologies that can be used stand-alone or embedded in a Web browser.

IBM's Web Ontology Manager: A Web-based tool for managing ontologies expressed in Web Ontology Language (OWL).

IBM Semantic Layered Research Platform (SLRP): A family of open source semantic Web software components, including an enterprise RDF store, query engine, Web application framework, RCP development libraries, and more.

OWL verbalizer: An online tool that verbalizes OWL ontologies in (controlled) English.

Stanford's Protégé: Stanford University's general Protégé 2000 ontology editor tool has a plug-in architecture that enables the development of a number of semantic-Web-related tools.

SWOOP: University of Maryland's Hypermedia-based Ontology Editor.

Boca enterprise RDF store: "Java-based store and client libraries which feature named-graph-based RDF storage, access controls, versioning, replication and local persistence for offline access, and notifications to distributed clients." It is part of the IBM Semantic Layered Research Platform (SLRP).

D2RQ and D2R Server: D2RQ is a Java library that provides access to the content of relational databases through SPARQL, the Jena API, and the Sesame API. D2R Server is a SPARQL and RDF server based on D2RQ.

RDFStore: An RDF storage with Perl and C API-s and SPARQL facilities.

SemWeb for .NET: Supports persistent storage in MySQL, Postgres, and Sqlite; has been tested with 10–50 million triples; supports SPARQL.

Euler: An inference engine supporting logic-based proofs. It is a backward-chaining reasoner enhanced with Euler path detection.

Jena Java RDF API and toolkit: A Java framework to construct semantic Web Applications. It provides a programmatic environment for RDF, RDFS and OWL, and SPARQL, and includes a rule-based inference engine.

OWLJessKB: A description logic reasoner for OWL. The semantics of the language is implemented using Jess, the Java Expert System Shell.

Sesame: An open source RDF database with support for RDF Schema inferencing and querying.

Closed World Machine (CWM): A data manipulator, rules processor, and query system mostly using the Notation 3 textual RDF syntax.

KAON2: An infrastructure for managing OWL-DL, SWRL, and F-Logic ontologies.

Pellet: An open-source Java-based OWL DL reasoner. It can be used in conjunction with both Jena and OWL API libraries.

Disco: A primarily server-side semantic Web browser developed at the Free University of Berlin, Germany.

D.6 Summary and Directions

In this appendix, we have provided an overview of the various standards and products relevant to Web services and the semantic Web. Note that numerous products and tools as well as standards are emerging for secure Web services. We urge the reader to review the various Web pages that we have listed in this chapter for more information. Several links can also be found in W3C's main Web page as well as the OASIS and OGC Web sites.

We have utilized some tools, including the Oracle product, Jena, as well as the Pellet reasoner, in our research on the secure semantic Web and Web services. We strongly encourage the reader to experiment with these tools as well as build on the ontologies that are out there. It should be noted that security has received only some attention. We need to develop Web services tools for handling the inference problem and managing policies, as well as reasoning about the policies. We have discussed various aspects of secure Web services. We now need to design and develop the tools to build these secure Web services.

References

[ESB] http://en.wikipedia.org/wiki/Enterprise_service_bus

[OASIS] Organization for the Advancement of Structured Information Standards, http://www.oasis-open.org/home/index.php

[PROD1] Commercial products for Web Services, http://www.service-architecture.com/products/web_services.html

[PROD2] Commercial Products for the Semantic Web, http://esw.w3.org/topic/CommercialProducts

[W3C] World Wide Web Consortium, www.w3c.org

Index